The Politics of Drug Violence

The Politics of Drug Violence

Criminals, Cops, and Politicians in Colombia and Mexico

ANGÉLICA DURÁN-MARTÍNEZ

OXFORD
UNIVERSITY PRESS

OXFORD
UNIVERSITY PRESS

Oxford University Press is a department of the University of Oxford. It furthers
the University's objective of excellence in research, scholarship, and education
by publishing worldwide. Oxford is a registered trade mark of Oxford University
Press in the UK and certain other countries.

Published in the United States of America by Oxford University Press
198 Madison Avenue, New York, NY 10016, United States of America.

Library of Congress Cataloging-in-Publication Data
Names: Durán-Martínez, Angélica, 1979– author.
Title: The politics of drug violence : criminals, cops, and politicians in
Colombia and Mexico / by Angélica Durán-Martínez.
Description: New York : Oxford University Press, [2018] |
Includes bibliographical references and index.
Identifiers: LCCN 2017029902 | ISBN 9780190695958 (hbk : alk. paper) |
ISBN 9780190695965 (pbk : alk. paper) | ISBN 9780190695972 (updf) |
ISBN 9780190695989 (epub)
Subjects: LCSH: Drug traffic—Colombia. | Drug traffic—Mexico. |
Violent crimes—Colombia. | Violent crimes—Mexico. | Colombia—
Politics and government. | Mexico—Politics and government.
Classification: LCC HV8079.N3 D87 2018 | DDC 364.1/336509861—dc23
LC record available at https://lccn.loc.gov/2017029902

CONTENTS

LIST OF FIGURES, TABLES, AND MAPS

Figures

Tables

Maps

ACKNOWLEDGMENTS

In 1988, when I was nine years old, I was walking with my mom two blocks away from our home in Bogotá, and a bomb went off at a nearby auto repair shop. It was the time when Pablo Escobar and the Medellín drug cartel had declared a war against the extradition of Colombian nationals to the United States that unleashed a period of violence in Colombian history often referred to as "narcoterrorism." Only a few seconds saved us from being victims of that bomb. As people rushed to the scene, my mom ran away in the opposite direction—confused, scared, and thankful that we had escaped. That was my closest experience to violence. While growing up in Bogotá, I was relatively protected from the armed conflict that besieged many rural areas, but during the period of narcoterrorism, violence also overwhelmed Colombia's major cities in attacks like the one I escaped. Over the years, I have come to believe that such experience sparked my interest in studying violence, drug trafficking, and crime. However, such interest would have never materialized without years of discussion, mentoring, support, and valuable teachings—both at the core of family discussions and during my years studying political science at the Universidad Nacional de Colombia. It would be impossible for me to thank appropriately all the people who have shaped my intellectual journey and thus essential for the successful completion of this project.

I owe the publication of this book to Dave McBride, who believed in the manuscript and has been an outstanding editor at Oxford University Press. The book started as my doctoral dissertation at Brown University. Before the project took shape I had carried out short trips to Cali, Medellín, and Mexico City in 2008 and 2009, and then between 2010 and 2011, I spent fifteen months doing fieldwork in Colombia and Mexico. This fieldwork was possible thanks to generous funding from the United States Institute of Peace (USIP); the Social Science Research Council (SSRC); the Drugs, Security, and Democracy (DSD) fellowship jointly supported by SSRC, Open Society, the International

Development Research Centre, the Universidad de los Andes, and the Centro de Investigación y Docencia Económicas (CIDE); and travel grants from the Graduate Development Program, the Center for Latin American and Caribbean Studies, and the Watson Institute for International Studies at Brown University. Since I started a PhD at Brown, the intellectual guidance and personal support of Richard Snyder, Pauline Jones-Luong, and Peter Andreas were crucial in helping to craft my research proposal, in producing the dissertation, and in turning it into a book. As the chair of my dissertation committee, Richard always combined encouragement and acute criticism to push me in new directions and force me out of my comfort zone. He also created unique opportunities for me to advance and present my research. Peter posed sharp questions that revealed any holes in my thinking and thus encouraged me to sharpen ideas, to be careful with words, and to think broadly. He also gave me essential advice for this book's publication. His precise recommendations have always been timely. Pauline's insightful comments forced me to reflect on critical methodological questions, on broader theoretical debates, and on key conceptual dilemmas. Barbara Stallings has provided feedback over the years and supported my career. Special thanks also go to Melani Cammett, Matthew Guttman, Kay Warren, and the entire faculty at Brown who at different points encouraged me and made recommendations on my dissertation proposal. My colleagues and friends at Brown were crucial and my special thanks go to Sinem Adar, Erin Beck, Jennifer Costanza, Susan Ellison, Andrea Maldonado Eduardo Moncada, Heather Silber, and Dikshya Thapa, who read dissertation chapter drafts and made great comments on them. Susan Hirsch and Suzanne Borough always provided essential administrative support throughout my years at Brown.

This research would have not been possible without the generosity of those who shared their time, thoughts, and experiences with me. To protect their confidentiality I cannot share all their names, but every person who shared life experiences and opinions with me made this book possible. Many of those who graciously shared their knowledge dedicate their lives to document and resist corruption and violence. One of my most generous interviewees, journalist Javier Valdez, was murdered in Culiacán, Sinaloa, in May 2017, as I was preparing the book for publication. It is with great sadness that I dedicate this book to him and to those who devote and risk their lives working for human rights, justice, and peace.

I am forever indebted to those who generously opened the doors of their houses and their hearts for me and who became a family in each of my research locations, making me feel safe and welcomed: María Eugenia and Lucila in Medellín; Mireya and Blanca in Cali; Luz María, Pedro, and Pedro Pablo in Culiacán; Alan and Laura in Ciudad Juárez. The research assistance of Mundo Ramírez, Rocio Durán, and Luis Cañas was invaluable—thanks to them for their hard work, insights, and patience to go through hundreds of newspapers, in most cases dusty records, to create the data set on drug violence. Luis Astorga, both an intellectual guide and a friend, graciously introduced me to his family and provided key contacts and insights, and Simón Vargas opened crucial doors for me in Mexico. Angelika Rettberg at the Universidad de los Andes in Bogotá, Arturo Alvarado at the Colegio de México in Mexico City, Alberto Hernandez at the Colegio de la Frontera Norte in Tijuana, Mauricio Romero at the Universidad Javeriana in Bogotá, and Roddy Brett at the Universidad del Rosario, provided key institutional support and space for me to share preliminary findings while in the field. David Shirk at the University of San Diego has been extremely generous with intellectual and logistical support for my research at different points. Joel Wallman, from the Harry Frank Guggenheim Foundation, has been a supportive mentor. Joel and David's invitation to participate in a special issue of the *Journal of Conflict Resolution* on drug violence in Mexico gave me an incomparable outlet to publish some key findings of the project and to receive great feedback and insights from reviewers and from the other authors in the issue. I also thank Gema Santamaría, who has encouraged me and opened space for me to present some of this book's findings in panels she has organized and who invited me to be part of an edited volume she coordinated. Hillel Soifer has given me great insights for the book's overall argument. The book benefited from feedback during presentations at locations including Harvard University; Instituto Tecnológico Autónomo de México; and the American Political Science Association, Midwest Political Science Association, and Latin American Studies Association conferences. Justin Pickering did a fantastic job copyediting the manuscript before it underwent the Oxford University Press review process. Two anonymous reviewers provided insightful comments that greatly improved the manuscript.

This book reflects the knowledge that all my interviewees shared, as well as many discussions with friends and colleagues. The usual disclaimer is necessary: that any omissions are my sole responsibility. Colleagues at fellowship workshops with USIP, SSRC, and the DSD program, provided insights, criticisms, and encouragement at different stages of the project. The intellectual community of the DSD program was essential in the latter part of fieldwork and has remained a highly motivating network for research on topics of security, criminality, and violence in Latin America. Special thanks go to Desmond Arias, Ana Arjona, Susan Brewer, José Miguel Cruz, Yanilda González, Paul Gootenberg, Benjamin Lessing, Javier Osorio, Reynaldo Rojo, and Ana Villarreal for their feedback at different stages of the research and the writing process.

Brown University was my intellectual home as I embarked in the PhD adventure, and the friends I made over the years became my family away from home: to all of them my special thanks because their trust and friendship made my journey special and unforgettable. I also thank my longtime friends from Universidad Nacional and New York University because they have always accompanied me, despite distance and time.

The process of turning a dissertation into a book is long and full of uncertainty, and I could not think of a better place for me to have gone through such process than the University of Massachusetts at Lowell. My colleagues have not only given me great feedback on the project, but more importantly, they have given me a collegial and stimulating atmosphere at which to work. The university administration provided the material and logistical conditions that I needed to complete this book successfully, and I particularly thank Ardeth Thawnghmung, who as chair of the Department of Political Science has gone out of her way to support me and has also been a great friend. Parts of chapters 1 and 2 were originally published in the *Journal of Conflict Resolution* and in the book *Violence and Crime in Latin America: Representations and Politics* (University of Oklahoma Press, 2017), I thank them for granting me permission to republish.

None of my work could have been possible without the unconditional support of my family. To them I dedicate this book. To my mom, whose endless love and trust in me keep me going in moments of doubt, and whose love for knowledge, sacrifices, and example make me who I am. She is truly a precious human being. To Nancy and Rocio, my loving sisters, who never stop encouraging me, motivating me to go further, and teaching me about life and who have felt the most my work-related absence. They have also helped me in different parts of this project, Rocio with data collection and Nancy preparing some of the book's illustrations. To my loving husband, Jack, who came to my life when this project was just starting and has supported me through every single step of it, enduring moments of physical separation, sharing and even taking the burden of child care, editing chapters, inspiring me through long political conversations, and reminding me not only about the value of my work but also about the importance of keeping things in perspective. Jack, you have been a light in my life and I can never express in words how grateful I am to have you as my partner, friend, and husband. My daughter, Lily, was born as I started the process of transforming my dissertation into a book. There are no words to express the joy she has brought to my existence. She shows me the innocence and happiness that makes this world a better place. The most special dedication goes to my dad, my hero, who endured a very difficult life full of material limitations and who left too early to see me even graduating from college. All his sacrifices paid off, and I am sure he still looks out for me from heaven.

LIST OF ABBREVIATIONS

AFI	Federal Investigation Agency, Mexico
AFO	Arellano Félix organization, Mexico
AUC	United Self-Defense Forces of Colombia
BACRIM	Criminal gangs, Colombia
CENDRO	Center for Drug Control Planning, Mexico
CERAC	Conflict Analysis Resource Center, Colombia
CISEN	Intelligence and National Security Center, Mexico
CTI	Technical Investigation Body Attorney General's Office, Colombia
DANE	National Statistics Department, Colombia
DAS	Security Administration Department, Colombia
DEA	Drug Enforcement Administration (US)
DFS	Federal Security Directorate, Mexico
DIJIN	Directorate of Criminal Investigation and Interpol, Colombia
DNP	National Planning Department, Colombia
DTO	Drug-trafficking organization
ELN	National Liberation Army, Colombia
ENA	National Addiction Survey, Mexico
EPL	Popular Liberation Army, Colombia
ERPAC	Popular Revolutionary Anti-Insurgent Army of Colombia
EZLN	National Liberation Zapatista Army, Mexico
FARC	Revolutionary Armed Forces of Colombia
FEADS	Special Attorney for Crimes against Health, Mexico
GAFES	Airborne Special Forces Group, Mexico
GANFES	Amphibian Special Forces Group, Mexico
IACHR	Inter American Commission on Human Rights
IFE	Federal Electoral Institute, Mexico
INCD	National Institute for Combating Drugs, Mexico

INEGI	National Statistics and Geography Institute, Mexico
LACDD	Latin American Commission on Drugs and Democracy
M-19	19th of April Movement, Colombia
MAS	Death to Kidnappers, Colombia
MIO	Movement for Inclusion and Opportunities, Colombia
MOE	Electoral Observation Mission, Colombia
NAFTA	North American Free Trade Agreement
NDIC	National Drug Intelligence Center (U.S.)
NGO	Nongovernmental organization
PAN	National Action Party, Mexico
Pepes	Persecuted by Pablo Escobar, Colombia
PF	Federal Police, Mexico
PFP	Federal Preventive Police, Mexico
PGR	Attorney General's Office, Mexico
PIN	Party of National Integration, Colombia
PJF	Federal Judicial Police, Mexico
PRD	Democratic Revolution Party, Mexico
PRI	Institutional Revolutionary Party, Mexico
SEDENA	National Defense Secretariat, Mexico
SEGOB	Secretariat of Governance, Mexico
SEMAR	Marine Secretariat, Mexico
SINAIS	National System of Health Information, Mexico
SNSP	National System of Public Security, Mexico
SSP	Secretariat of Public Security, Mexico
UEDO	Specialized Unit for Organized Crime, Mexico
UNODC	United Nations Office for Drugs and Crime
UPP	Pacification Police Units, Brazil

The Politics of Drug Violence

States, Trafficking, and Violence

After April 30, 2008, a collective psychosis started. On May 5th, five federal police were killed. We went from deaf violence to high-impact violence, in which there were shootouts downtown.
                                        —Local journalist, Culiacán, March 2011

The situation today is not as bad because [in the 1990s] *the mafiosi changed their profile. One does not feel scared of going to Seventieth Street as before. The problem of the narco can even be worse now, but the fact is that the bombs made it a more aggressive period* [in the 1980s].
                                        —Medellín councilwoman, October 2010

When I arrived in Ciudad Juárez in 1988, there was coordination in every-thing; there was only one [trafficking] *group. There were executions, but the bodies disappeared; they were not thrown out in the streets.*
                                        —Former police officer, Mexico City, June 2011

The statements above exemplify responses I received while asking people to describe drug violence in their cities. Surprisingly, many interviewees not only identified an increase or a decrease in violence but also, and most importantly, changes in criminals' willingness to expose attacks. In Culiacán, a city long besieged by drug-trafficking violence, people identified 2008 as the crucial year when a war started and the "honor codes" of violence crumbled. By contrast, in Medellín, people talked about the hidden character of criminal violence since the mid-2000s. While reflecting on many similar statements I came across while conducting fieldwork, and on the complex stories of violence I found, I realized that our common understanding of drug violence is not only driven by stereo-types but also by attention to extreme situations. This book sets out to explain the enormous variation in the amount of violence existing within countries afflicted by drug trafficking and examine the puzzle of why criminals sometimes seek to publicize violence even though it can be detrimental for them in the long run. But it also pays equal attention to understanding why, at other times, crimi-nals prefer to conceal their actions without abandoning violence altogether.

The relationship between illegal markets and violence has been crucial both in the study of criminal organizations and in the study of civil wars. Illegal markets such as drug trafficking are expected to fuel violence, either as a result of greed in civil wars or as a result of the increasing power and extension of organized crime in other circumstances. This expectation limits our understanding of the conditions driving dramatic changes in violence that countries experience over time, such as the upsurge of drug violence in Mexico, a country that has been home to trafficking organizations since the mid-twentieth century, or the decrease of violence in Colombia despite the persistence of trafficking. Furthermore, we lack the analytical tools to capture the variation *within* countries with similar drug-trafficking problems. For example, during the 1980s, a highly violent period in Colombia, the city of Medellín was significantly more violent than Cali. Certainly one does not expect identical trends among cities, yet the magnitude of variation remains puzzling.

This book analyzes such complex patterns of drug violence. Large-scale violence associated with organized crime, and more specifically with the drug trade, is not new, yet it has grown to be more prevalent and noticeable. In Latin America, democratization processes since the 1990s have been coupled, in some areas, with an increase in organized crime and drug violence. This has led to growing scholarly and policy debates. These debates center not only on the causes of violence but also on the consequences of democratization and on the appropriateness of international drug regulations and local crime-control strategies. To advance such debates beyond simplistic connections between drugs and violence, this book makes two novel contributions. First, it introduces the notion of visibility—a crucial dimension of violence. Visibility refers to instances where traffickers publicly expose violence or claim responsibility for attacks. Second, it advances a political economy framework that treats drug violence not as a phenomenon that emerges in the margins of the state but rather as one shaped through interactions between the state and criminal actors. Specifically, I argue that the interaction between two critical factors—the cohesion of the state security apparatus and the amount of competition in illegal drug markets—determines the incentives and opportunities for drug traffickers to employ violence. The book draws on the systematic comparison of five cities that have experienced contrasting patterns of drug violence across the period 1984–2011: Cali and Medellín in Colombia, and Ciudad Juárez, Culiacán, and Tijuana in Mexico (see Maps 1.1 and 1.2).

The disaggregation of violence—that is, looking not only at the frequency of violence but also at its visibility—provides the tools to analyze not only extreme violence, which tends to garner most academic and media attention, but also the hidden and less visible forms of violence. The case studies show how the *frequency* of violence increases as the illegal market becomes more competitive, and the

Map 1.1 Map of Colombia, with Cali and Medellín located. Source: "Colombia Capital Map," www.mapsopensource.coml, used under CC BY license. Some cities added.

visibility of violence increases as the state security apparatus shifts from cohesive to fragmented. This takes place because cohesive states are more likely to credibly commit to protect or, alternatively, to prosecute criminals. Criminal actors may refrain from using visible violence that can trigger state reactions when they receive credible state protection and fear losing it, or when they believe that the state can dismantle them. This argument puts the state and law enforcement at the center of understanding criminality and violence, by unpacking power relations within the state security apparatus and their impact on state-criminal relations.

This book also explores an often-overlooked aspect of organization in criminal markets that has crucial implications for violence: the type of armed coercion

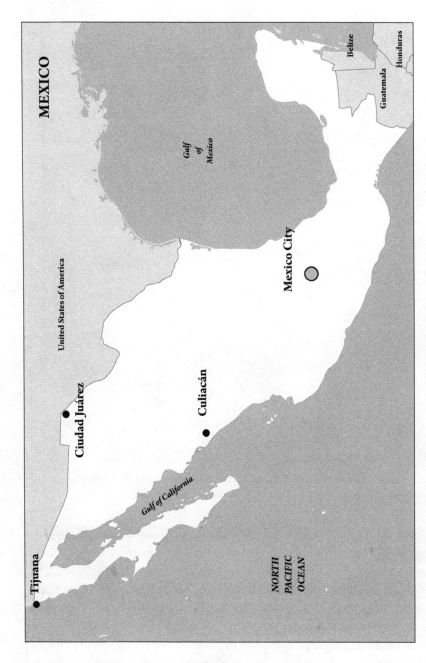

Map 1.2 Map of Mexico, with Ciudad Juárez, Culiacán, and Tijuana located. Source: "Mexico Capital Map," www.mapsopensource. coml, used under CC BY license. Some cities added.

criminals employ, and more specifically whether violence is "insourced" (that is, vertically integrated into the organization) or "outsourced" (that is, contracted out to youth gangs). When criminals outsource violence, they lose the ability or willingness to discipline their armed forces. This explains why some competitive illicit markets experience extreme spikes in drug violence. By introducing this variable, the argument also shows how organized criminals and street gangs can interact in varied ways, with crucial implications for security.

The Multiple Dimensions of Drug Violence

Lethal drug violence can affect civilians, state officials, and criminals alike, and as the journalist Dawn Paley[1] argues, the poorest and most marginalized sectors of society are often the most affected by it. It threatens governance and citizen security in places as diverse as Afghanistan, Bolivia, Brazil, El Salvador, Guatemala, Guinea Bissau, Honduras, India, Iran, Italy, Myanmar, Pakistan, Peru, and Russia. Colombia and Mexico represent paradigmatic examples of drug violence, as they have been at the frontline of the war on drugs and suffer the deleterious consequences of violence. In Mexico, drug violence caused at least 86,000 deaths between 2006 and 2015,[2] and in Colombia drug trafficking continues to complicate one of the world's longest-standing armed conflicts.

These prominent examples suggest that we might expect violence to be frequent, because in illegal markets that lack state regulation violence is deployed strategically to gain market share, solve contractual problems, and address disciplinary and succession issues.[3] Conversely, we might expect violence to be a rare strategy because it can attract enforcement attention, and criminals might therefore prefer to limit its use.[4] To understand variation in violence, we thus need to evaluate its frequency—that is, the rate at which violent events occur. However, as the excerpts opening this chapter suggests, the full "repertoire" of violence includes another dimension—its visibility.

As the reader will notice throughout the book, visible events do not take exactly the same form in each of the cities analyzed or throughout the multiple examples seen around the world—they can take the shape of banners on crime scenes, car bombs, beheadings, bus burnings, or public massacres, among others. Yet, there are causal regularities explaining why criminals perform violence in a very public manner. To capture these regularities, visibility is analyzed here considering the methods employed by killers, the number of victims per attack, the type of victims, and whether criminals claim responsibility, as explained in detail in chapter 2.[5] Such operationalization recognizes, as long established by the sociologist Charles Tilly, that culture and history shape context-specific repertoires of collective violence and contentious politics, yet such repertoires also display causal and performative regularities. Changes in the visibility of violence are not aimless or random, as an intelligence official I interviewed acknowledged while describing the violence deployed by current trafficking organizations in Colombia: "the BACRIM [*bandas criminales*, or criminal gangs][6] dismember bodies with machetes; of course, they are not as sophisticated as before when they used chain saws . . . . Now we see another type of violence, a new profile of the killer—there is more interest in hiding, but the new structures are absolutely violent."[7] Other intelligence officers echoed this idea, observing that as a response to enforcement actions, traffickers now prefer to be "traffickers in silence."[8]

The five cities analyzed in this book have experienced contrasting changes in both the frequency and visibility of drug violence. In Colombia, between 1984 and 1993, during a period of intense drug-related violence often referred to as "narcoterrorism," Medellín was more violent than Cali. Over time, frequency in Medellín decreased, whereas it remained stable in Cali[9] even though the large drug-trafficking organizations (DTOs) of the 1980s had been dismantled in both cities. Likewise, after 2006 violence in Ciudad Juárez became more visible as criminals claimed responsibility for beheadings, threatened and killed public officials, and carried out massacres in a pattern that contrasted with the silent disappearance of people prevailing in the early 1990s. Figure 1.1 illustrates the configurations that emerge from combining the two dimensions of violence and the intriguing variation that is uncovered not only across cities but also within the same city over time.

Examining drug violence in cities is crucial because since the 1990s cities across the developing world have become nodes for criminal violence.[10] Cities concentrate economic and human resources that make them attractive for criminal actors who can connect a wide range of illegal activities (from informal economies to local drug markets and extortion) and exploit opportunities for

	Low Frequency (LF)	High Frequency (HF)
Low Visibility (LV)	Cali 1984–88 Cd Juárez 1984–94, Tijuana 1984–87/2010–11 Medellín 2003–07	Cali 1989–2011, Cd Juárez 1995–05/2007, Tijuana 1988–96/1998–07 Culiacán 1984–2007 Medellín 1994–2002/2008–11
High Visibility (HV)	Cd Juárez 2006 Tijuana 1996–97	Cd Juárez 2008–11 Tijuana 2008–09 Culiacán 2008–11 Medellín 1984–93

Figure 1.1 Types of Drug-Related Violence and Location of Cases. Source: Author's elaboration.

money laundering in formal economies not readily available in the countryside. Urbanization and developmental processes make cities more prone to hosting large impoverished populations that *might* be employed by criminals. Cities also strategically connect drug production areas, trafficking routes, and consumer markets. Of course, criminal violence also exists in rural areas and is affected by national policies and contexts and by the enforcement of the international drug-prohibition regime. However, as Trejo and Ley argue, the multilevel character of drug trafficking demands policies that cut across different levels of author-ity.[11] Local authorities have become pivotal in security policies,[12] and therefore a focus on national or international trends cannot fully explain local dynamics of violence or the responses to it. More generally, as the 2014 UN World Homicide Report shows, violence trends are unevenly distributed not only between regions and countries but also within countries, which suggests that a strong theory to explain drug violence should carefully explore local dynamics.

The Aims of the Study

Existing research about the drug trade may overlook the variation described earlier because it expects violence to be a natural byproduct of drug traffick-ing. Analyses that emphasize the increasing threat of transnational organized crime—such as Moisés Naím's work[13]—and studies that link the existence of lootable goods (like drugs) to the duration of civil wars[14] or that follow insights about illegal flows as a distinctive component of new wars (as in the work of Mary Kaldor[15]) tend to create a direct connection between illegal markets (like drug trafficking) and violence that obscures important variation.[16] However, there has been an increase in studies unpacking the connection between illegal-ity and violence—and partially in response to violence in Mexico, prominent analyses have attempted to explain why drug violence explodes.[17] This book contributes to this growing research and builds on seminal studies like those of Peter Reuter or Thomas Schelling[18] to provide a unified framework for the study of violence in drug markets. The analysis of multiple violence patterns, from extreme violence to relative peace, avoids the selection bias that can emerge when inferring causes looking only at extremely high violence—that is, truncat-ing variation in the dependent variable.

The analysis across five cities over almost four decades (1984–2011) unpacks enormous variation by way of focusing not only on the frequency but also on the visibility of violence. The theory puts politics, state power, and law enforcement at the center of studying drug markets, thus challenging ideas of drug violence as an automatic result of illegality or as solely dependent on economic aspects of the trade.

The remainder of this chapter considers existing explanations for drug violence and their limitations as well as presents the building blocks of the political
economy approach I propose. It also provides conceptual clarifications to define
the illegal market and state security apparatus, and it describes the configurations of violence produced by the interaction between state cohesion, the criminal market, and type of criminal armed coercion. It also explains the research
design and methods and presents a road map of the book.

Drug Violence Beyond Profits and Prohibition

Books dealing with drug trafficking are numerous, and many of them provide
clues to understand violence in drug trafficking. There are three discernible arguments among those who seek to explain violence from which I take distance,
although such arguments are certainly important for understanding aspects of
the variation in the frequency—though not the visibility—of violence.

Some of the most popular explanations for variation in violence are *economic
approaches* contending that certain aspects of the drug trade chain (e.g., distribution), certain goods (e.g., cocaine), and higher volumes of trade generate more
revenue and, in turn, more violence.[19] Their rationale is that profitable markets
create incentives for criminals to protect their turf violently—for instance, as
occurs in cocaine markets, which tend to be more profitable and violent than
marijuana markets.[20] In other explanations based on economics, the rationale is
the opposite: that lower profits spur conflict because in order to maintain high
revenues, criminals need to eliminate rivals.[21]

Economic explanations account for associations such as the increasing incidence of cocaine trafficking in Mexico and increasing violence, but they are limited in explaining why violence can be associated with both high and low market
prices and with both shortages and ample supplies of drugs. For example, cities
simultaneously dealing with the presence of cocaine distribution organizations
(such as drug distribution hubs in the United States) and countries engaging in
coca production (such as Bolivia and Colombia) experience strikingly different
security environments.

Another variant of the economic explanation contends that the diversification of markets and business portfolios (e.g., trafficking organizations getting
involved in extortion, kidnapping, or local drug dealing) can increase violence.
The logic is that highly localized markets force organizations to fight more
fiercely for territorial control, as occurs when mafia organizations establish local
protection rackets.[22] The problem is that diversification can be a byproduct
as much as a cause of violence. Drug traffickers may turn to other illegal markets such as extortion, human smuggling, or kidnapping when they need extra

income to fight wars with rivals or when such wars or state enforcement have undermined their ability to monopolize drug profits. In Mexico, for instance, an unprecedented increase in extortion occurred after, not before, violence exploded.[23] There are also cases of diversified crime portfolios with low violence, as the twenty-first-century evolution of Medellín illustrates.

To understand drug violence one cannot overlook the role of the global prohibition regime in which drug trafficking flourishes. Explanations focused on *international policy* argue that violence in drug markets is the result of the global drug-prohibition regime and the US-led war on drugs, which emerged during the early prohibitions of 1914 and was consolidated during the 1961 UN Single Convention on Narcotic Drugs and the 1969 declaration of the War on Drugs by US president Richard Nixon. International prohibition has constrained the options available for countries—especially developing countries—to confront drug use, production, and trafficking, privileging militarized responses to drug trafficking and increasing the vulnerability to corruption of the very institutions aimed to confront the problem.[24] Important analyses thus argue that as enforcement associated with prohibition increases, the monetary stakes, competition, and, consequently, violence associated with drug markets increase as well[25]—as when relatively lenient US narcotics policy toward Mexico shifted in the mid-2000s, triggering militarized responses toward traffickers.[26] The global prohibition regime has indeed expanded black markets, legitimized human rights violations, and increased insecurity and violence. These problems and the arguments showing how prohibition constitutes a necessary condition for the overall criminalization and violence in drug markets have become more public and widespread, especially after 2009 when former Latin American presidents became champions of drug-policy reform.[27]

Undoubtedly, international and national prohibitionist policies shape trends in drug trafficking that enable traffickers to become more violent. For example, smuggling routes and production sites often relocate after criminal groups are dismantled, thus opening up possibilities for violence to flourish in new locations, something known in drug-policy discussions as balloon effect. Similarly, militarized drug enforcement may encourage traffickers to retaliate or may break organizations up, thus increasing possibilities for violence. Indeed, one widely recognized negative effect of prohibition is that by privileging the elimination of leaders, it encourages criminal fragmentation and competition, one key variable of the theory I develop in this volume. However, the international regime cannot fully account for variation in visibility or for the fine-grained differential effects of prohibition-inspired policies across and within countries. Furthermore, since more scholarly attention has been paid to the international and national rather than local dynamics of drug trade and drug policy, this book's contribution is to look at subnational determinants of drug violence, without ignoring that prohibition and repressive antinarcotics policies foster the problems repeated throughout the book: corruption, violence, and militarized law enforcement.

One last crucial line of explanation for the rise of drug violence focuses on *socioeconomic change,* linking processes like globalization, rapid urbanization, and economic transformation to criminal violence. These transformations are essential to understand the inequalities and marginalization that have contributed to the upsurge of urban violence in Latin America since the 1990s[28] and the neoliberal reforms that have contributed to the fragmentation of public security.[29] Yet these explanations overlook relatively nonviolent illegal markets as well as variation among cities undergoing similar socioeconomic transformations. In a fascinating book titled *Drug War Capitalism,* Dawn Paley[30] argues that drug violence rises to benefit transnational economic corporations, especially those engaged in natural resource exploitation projects, by displacing populations that own land or that can oppose such projects. While this provocative argument unveils critical factors largely absent from discussions on this topic, it does not systematically consider largely violent markets where those projects have not occurred, nor does it consider relatively peaceful markets that have also benefited transnational interests. In general, while broad socioeconomic transformations foster conditions—such as poverty, inequality, and social alienation—that enable crime (a point to which I return in the book's conclusion), they cannot account for rapid changes in violence[31]—for example, the increase in homicide rates of over 700 percent that besieged Ciudad Juárez between 2007 and 2008.

Overall, these explanations provide crucial insights, yet they do not provide unified frameworks to explain variation across time and space. Most importantly, no existing analysis of drug violence systematically employs the visibility dimension, even though its importance is evident while perusing the myriad of journalistic and academic accounts of drug trafficking, which often talk about visible violence but without analytical rigor.

A Political Economy Framework for Drug Violence

The political economy approach I propose understands drug violence as resulting from interactions between states and illegal markets, and it goes beyond purely economic explanations that link profits in illegal markets to violence or that assume violence to result from market illegality alone.[32] It also builds on, and contributes to, literature on civil wars and literature on drug trafficking and illicit markets.

Research on civil wars analyzing how changes in the local balance of power between states and insurgencies shape violence strategies,[33] provides crucial insights for this argument. This work is seldom concerned with criminals because criminals do not aim to control the state, yet a focus on local struggles for power can also explain the violent behavior of criminal organizations, which may challenge state sovereignty as much as insurgencies. By analyzing diverse interactions between states and criminals, which can range from confrontation to collaboration,[34] my analysis contributes to understanding violence when the state tolerates, promotes, or bargains with nonstate violent actors. The dynamic role of the state and political institutions in shaping violence has been overlooked in the civil war literature,[35] partially because the state is often conceptualized as unitary and because, as Lessing argues,[36] insurgents seek to topple the state while criminals seek to constrain it. Yet disaggregating state power is crucial in the study of both criminal and civil wars because power relationships *within* the state affect its ability to fight or to ally with, and protect, nonstate armed actors.

The literature on illicit markets illuminates how enforcement actions aimed at dismantling criminal organizations can shape illegal markets.[37] Enforcement actions may dislodge organizations by killing or capturing leaders, thus creating possibly violent internal power struggles.[38] Heightened enforcement may also increase the price of corruption, thus making violence more cost-effective,[39] and may attract competitors while weakening organizations.[40] A possible result could be a generation of violence that may vary depending on whether interventions against crime are conditional or whether they are aimed at "decapitating" criminal leadership.[41] This book expands the focus of this literature on individual enforcement actions by looking at how the distribution of state power that underlies these actions can determine whether enforcement unleashes visible or hidden violence.

The Logic of the Argument

In illegal markets, criminals may use violence to solve disputes given the absence of legal mediation. Violence can also signal toughness: the more violent an organization, the less likely that competitors will try to overpower it or that members of the organization will cheat or defraud it. The more visible violence is, the more likely that the toughness and power of the organization will be communicated to the public, which is to the criminals' advantage. At the same time, as Diego Gambetta argues, violence also has drawbacks, such as scaring away "nonviolent" partners but, especially, attracting police attention.[42]

If criminals believe the state can efficiently attack them, they may prefer to hide violence to minimize the risk of being targeted and prosecuted by police action.[43] Hiding violence can thus become a tactical adaptation to avoid state attention. Criminals may also prefer less visible violence if they receive state-sponsored protection that is dependent on their "peaceful" behavior.[44] True, state-sponsored protection can also guarantee impunity when criminals commit violent acts, but even a weak corrupt state may be forced to react to visible violence. Therefore, if criminals believe that the state can protect them effectively, they lose incentives to expose violence that can undermine protection by obliging enforcers to respond to the potential public outrage generated by criminal attacks.

By contrast, if criminals do not have credible protection, or do not fear the efficiency of state action, they lose incentives to hide and gain incentives to signal their power, and they pressure the state and rivals through visible violence. In the absence of predictable protection, lowering the profile of violence does not guarantee that criminals will be protected against enforcement. They may decide to display violence, or they can simply abandon the extra steps necessary to hide it.[45]

The state security apparatus determines the government's ability to credibly enforce the law or, alternatively, to protect criminal actors. I use this concept because it reflects the constant interaction between politics and enforcement and captures, at its core, relations between nodes of state power. Therefore, it refers to the elected authorities and enforcement agencies (police, army, and intelligence agencies)[46] that determine security and antinarcotics policies in a given location—although this book's unit of analysis is the city—and it can be cohesive or fragmented. Enforcement efficiency depends on the ability to coordinate state actions against crime, and thus it should increase as power within the security apparatus becomes more cohesive. Enforcement actions in a cohesive state can be efficient because they maximize resources by reducing the need for operational and logistic coordination, although this does not necessarily imply more professional or democratic enforcement. Likewise, the provision of reliable protection to criminals depends on the ability of state actors to guarantee that no other state authority will enforce the law against criminals. This is much more likely within a cohesive state. Conversely, as the security apparatus becomes fragmented, coordination becomes more difficult and protection becomes less reliable. Fragmentation can make enforcement less efficient[47] because it complicates coordination (political and operational) even when anticrime operations proliferate. By the same token, criminals may gain opportunities to bribe public officials, but they also face more possibilities of prosecution and corrupt deals become more costly, as they require the acquiescence of more people.

The *visibility* of violence thus depends primarily on the state security apparatus. A cohesive security apparatus is likely to *reduce* visibility, because it makes state protection more reliable or enforcement more efficient. By contrast, a fragmented security apparatus is likely to *increase* violence visibility, because it makes protection less predictable or enforcement less effective.

If state cohesion determines visibility, the *frequency* of violence depends on the number of organizations competing over drug trafficking or territorial control in a given city.[48] Research on civil wars has found that multiparty conflicts last longer and have higher fatality rates than two-party conflicts.[49] Similarly, when the illegal market is monopolistic, violence is likely to be less frequent because criminals do not face strong disputes from the outside; when they resort to violence it is often to discipline their members, harm civilians perceived as threatening, punish transactions gone wrong, or scare away (rather than openly fight) enemies; violence tends to be sporadic because the power of the organization deters revenge and retaliation. By contrast, when the illegal market is competitive, with disputes for turf and territory among two or more organizations, violence is likely to be more frequent, as criminals try to drive out competitors not by lowering prices but by using force against them.[50] Disputes for territorial control are unlikely to be solved with a single homicide, and violence may nurture retaliation that is unlikely to stop before competitors are eliminated or significantly diminished. Criminal organizations can sometimes coexist peacefully as a result of pacts or arrangements, such as those in which one organization charges another one for the right to operate in a given territory.[51] Yet, such criminal pacts tend to be fragile, and analysts like Stergios Skarpedas consider that competition constitutes an equilibrium in illegal markets and, therefore, violent competition is more often present than not. And as in civil wars, alliances among armed groups, although frequent, are unstable as they are susceptible to the balance-of-power logic.[52]

Paradoxically, a cohesive state more efficient in enforcing the law can also successfully protect criminals. The results are the same (less visibility) but the mechanisms are different. A cohesive protector state deters criminals from using visible violence that could force the state to act. A cohesive nonprotector state provides a credible threat—that is, criminals know the state can harm them, and they try to avoid its attention by reducing visibility. Visibility thus depends on the relation between criminals and the state, but it does not mean that it is used only against the state: once the incentive to hide violence disappears, criminals may decide, depending on their interests, to display violence to eliminate rivals, to retaliate or pressure the state, or to scare away civilians, rivals, and enforcers. This argument does not negate that the design of state interventions against crime can affect criminals' calculations about the use of violence, that state actions can effectively reduce crime, or that states not only intervene in reaction to violence but also in response to domestic and international pressures. Rather, it emphasizes that whether the intended objectives of anticrime policies can be achieved and what type of violent consequences they can generate depends on the state's

ability and internal coherence to implement such policies. When actions carried out by the state fragment criminal groups, violent intra- or interorganizational disputes may emerge. Such disputes may be less visible if the state conducting operations is cohesive. As Lessing contends,[53] when crackdowns on criminality are not conditional on the organizations' use of violence, enforcement can drive up demands for corruption and reduce the cost of violence. However, a promise of selective enforcement may not be deliverable when the state faces conflicts among elected authorities or enforcement agencies.

It is crucial to note that criminals have to consider both frequency and visibility when making decisions about violent strategies. In other words, if the market is competitive and market disputes emerge, criminals are likely to deploy violence, but they simultaneously decide, depending on the conditions of the state security apparatus, whether that violence should be publicly exposed or should be kept hidden.

Jointly, state power and competition in the drug market determine patterns of drug violence, which cannot be simply explained by looking at the market or at the state in isolation. A fragmented state creates conditions for visible violence, but such violence may not emerge if there is no market contention. Conversely, market disputes can increase violence, but if the state is cohesive, it may be hidden.[54] One may imagine situations where state fragmentation may also affect frequency and market competition may affect visibility. For example, a monopolistic crime organization may exploit state fragmentation to lower the price of corruption, thus generating violence among state actors. Likewise, competing criminal groups within a cohesive state may use visible violence because criminals benefit from a violent reputation when they try to eliminate rivals. Yet if criminals take advantage of a fragmented state but they enjoy a market monopoly, violence is likely to be sporadic because the power of the organization deters revenge and retaliation. And if competition creates incentives for visibility but criminals fear enforcement or losing protection, they may prefer to hide. Thus although each independent variable can affect both visibility and frequency, the direct effect of each variable is predominant on one dimension of violence. This is a static argument, yet over time, as we will see below, market competition may affect visibility indirectly, by contributing to the breaking up of state protection, and state structure may affect frequency by transforming criminal competition.

"Insourcing" and "Outsourcing" Violence

An often-overlooked element in criminal markets is the type of armed coercion criminals employ and, in particular, whether violence is *insourced* or *outsourced*. The internal structures criminals use to deploy violence vary significantly and can impact how violence is carried out, and, more specifically, they are crucial in helping us to understand upward spikes of violence. Criminals insource violence when they deploy personnel from within the organization to carry out violence. They outsource when they systematically draw from youth gangs to attack their rivals or the state.[55] While there are different definitions of the term "outsourcing" in the business parlance, here it is understood as a situation where business activities are allocated to an external source, and where lines of authority are fuzzy, but there is clear alignment between organization and contractor and some level of control. Outsourcing of drug violence thus implies that street gangs know who they work for—and they are punished if they don't remain loyal—but many layers of authority separate them from those giving them instructions. Thus when criminals outsource violence to youth gangs, they may increase their firepower but lose ability or willingness to control their "soldiers" because of the high transaction costs of dealing with many small organizations. In Phil Williams's terms, outsourcing creates a relatively autonomous "low level" violence.[56] Better-armed and more violent gangs can spread violence beyond criminal disputes. By contrast, if criminals insource, criminal soldiers can be easier to discipline and less likely to spread violence. Outsourcing primarily increases the frequency of violence, although it can also affect the visibility of violence because hiding may not be a strategic priority for gangs as it is for the direct protagonists of the illegal business. In fact, showing power can be crucial for the gang's symbolic appropriation of spaces and turf.[57]

Outsourcing can also make violence more complex. Up to this point I have discussed the use of violence in a way that assumes it is strategic and rational; however as studies of civil war have shown, the rationality of the higher echelons of organizations is not necessarily the same as that of soldiers. Emotions and individual motivations also drive violence, and highly contextual moments of "madness" can lead to outbursts of brutality.[58] But these individual motivations and emotions can be more easily controlled when the lines of command are stricter. There may also be intermediate situations when criminals subcontract activities to members of gangs but do it sporadically—without establishing long-term obligations or clear identity alignments. In these cases, traffickers may still be unable to control the youth who provide sporadic services, but their effect on making their violence more sophisticated or lethal can also be more limited.

When traffickers outsource coercion, they encourage gang proliferation as the expectations of the money that could be earned working for traffickers create incentives for gangs to compete for the more profitable jobs, even if such expectations are rarely fulfilled. Violence is likely to reproduce rapidly because gangs acquire abilities that they did not previously have, such as the use of firearms.[59] Marginalized youth, with little economic, educational, or social options, acquire abilities that can also be used beyond organized crime and trafficking disputes.

Although this process could be characterized as one of "violent" professionalization of gangs, the issue is precisely that most youth are not professional killers who follow the "rules" of violence specialists such as mercenaries, enforcement agents serving traffickers, or privatized security firms. Some gang members engage in a criminal career that takes them to the upper echelons of criminality, yet most of them only have momentary interactions with the upper criminal ranks. Cali and Medellín in the 1980s illustrate the importance of outsourcing: while the Cali drug-trafficking organization preferred to insource violence, the Medellín DTO actively hired and deployed youth gangs as paid assassins and, as a result, homicide rates were far higher in the latter city.

Outsourcing resembles the process that linked mafia groups to common and juvenile crime during a period when the demand for criminal labor expanded[60] and met the supply of marginalized youth generated by socioeconomic changes and crises that greatly increased unemployment. In drug trafficking, outsourcing occurs when supply of force meets demand. The supply—that is, the mere existence of gangs or marginalized young populations—does not imply that they will be used as criminal labor; outsourcing occurs if supply meets the demand, created by illegal market disputes.

Organizational preferences play a role in criminals' decision to outsource violence: outsourcing can expand the armed muscle of an organization relatively cheaply, but it also creates the risk of exposure. Organizations aiming to create a reputation as businessmen or operating within a cohesive state might prefer insourcing. By contrast, organizations may choose to outsource when entering unknown territories where they lack social or state support or where they are less concerned about state enforcement or protection.

I treat the type of armed coercion and illegal market competition as separate variables because gangs can exist independently of and uncontrolled by criminals. Gangs tend to remain subordinated when drug traffickers employ them[61] and thus do not simply become a competing actor in the drug market when outsourcing occurs. Outsourcing appears as an option only when traffickers face market competition or are engaging in wars against the state. In the absence of market competition, criminals may need to discipline gangs to consolidate power monopolies, but this is unnecessary when gangs are either peaceful or, in Hagedorn's terms,[62] not institutionalized. Of course the distinction between gangs and traffickers becomes blurry where highly localized and powerful gangs control the trafficking business, as occurs in Rio de Janeiro, but in most cases it is possible to distinguish large institutionalized criminal groups from local identity–based groups. Even in Rio's complex criminal structure the notion of outsourcing seems applicable. There, large prison-based gangs—"gang factions"—such as the Comando Vermelho (Red Command) control lower-level gangs—quadrilhas—through a decentralized and hierarchical structure, but they remain relatively independent from international drug wholesalers.[63] According to Luke Dowdney,[64] during the 1990s, when new prison-based factions emerged or broke apart from the dominant Comando Vermelho and disputes for the control of valuable cocaine markets heightened, demand for military protection and soldiers to wage war increased. This, in turn, led to increasing deployment by gang factions of children and adolescents in street gangs, nurturing an exponential increase in violence. Without the demand for force created by the competition between the gang factions and the capture or killing of older traffickers, the expansion of recruitment into the favelas (slums) perhaps would have not been as pronounced, and without the large involvement of local youth gangs, overall violence would have been more limited.

The analysis of outsourcing in this book shows that organized criminal groups can relate to more disorganized or lower-level delinquency, and to gangs in numerous ways, sometimes increasing and other times reducing violence. While outsourcing can explain the most extreme increases in violence, analyzing whether criminals have the ability to discipline gangs from the outside, when such gangs have some power to exert violence, is also crucial for understanding how peaceful scenarios emerge.

Figure 1.2 illustrates the interaction between armed coercion, competition within illegal markets, and state power. The front panel of the cube depicts the interaction between the state security apparatus and competition in the illegal market, and the right side represents the type of armed coercion criminals

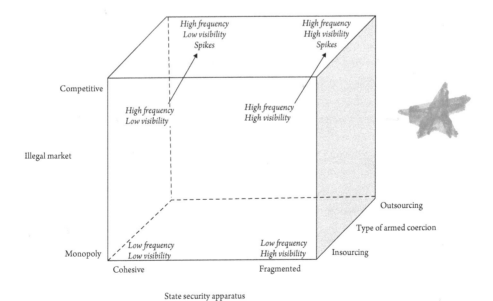

Figure 1.2 A Dynamic Depiction of Drug Violence. Source: Author's elaboration.

employ. Outsourcing is more likely when there is market competition; criminals may not need to hire additional armed muscle if they control the market. The upper right quarter of the cube depicts the possibility that high-frequency violence may explode if there is outsourcing. Criminals who receive reliable protection from cohesive states might prefer to avoid outsourcing because it risks exposure, and thus outsourcing is less likely in the left side of the cube. In this attribute space, the upper right quarter in the backside depicts the worst outcome: when state fragmentation, competition within illegal markets, and outsourcing lead to high frequency, high visibility, and upward spikes of violence. While visibility and upward spikes are closely related (most spikes occur in scenarios of high visibility), they are not the same, as illustrated by high-visibility scenarios that occur without spikes.

Assessing Competition in the Illegal Market

The assumption that drug-trafficking activities are highly organized and criminal organizations are extremely hierarchical, compact, and powerful has prevailed in policy discussions about the drug trade. Yet scholars of illegal activities have shown that the supply of illegal drugs may be highly disorganized, that organizations are often networked rather than hierarchical, and that trafficking organizations are unable to set prices, and therefore it is inappropriate to label them as cartels.[65] These insights highlight how depictions of extremely powerful organizations are often the result of media- or enforcement-driven agendas. There is, however, a wide variation in the organization of illegal markets, which in turn shapes the behavior of trafficking organizations.

Drug-trafficking organizations can sometimes create monopolies, but they also operate in highly competitive environments; there is variation even when they operate like networks.[66] The evidence compiled in this book shows that as the number of organizations competing for control of a territory or an illegal market increases, we can expect violence to be more frequent, and when one organization dominates the market, violence declines. The problem is that it is often difficult to assess an organization's real power and control over a market, considering that enforcers are usually interested in depicting extremely powerful organizations whereas traffickers may sometimes prefer to downplay an organization's power in order to avoid enforcement.

To address the difficulty of defining what an organization is, I assess whether one or more groups claim control over a territory, regardless of their internal consolidation or organization. Claiming control differs from simply assessing whether two organizations are present in a territory, because organizations sometimes coexist without attempting to invade each other's turf.[67] Internal organization is of course important, and it is possible that internal structures rather than competition determine the use of violence: small and decentralized organizations may have less capacity to engage in violence than large, centralized ones.[68] The case studies will show, however, that similar organizational types can be linked to different forms of violence: smaller organizations can be linked to less violence in Cali and Medellín in the 2000s but to more violence in Mexico.[69] As research on terrorism and suicide missions shows, high-impact violence can be carried out by diverse organizations including small organizations or splinter cells within extremist groups.[70] Additionally, even organizations with clear hierarchies and abilities to use violence may operate like networks to compartmentalize information and protect their operations.[71] The discussion of insourcing and outsourcing, however, highlights that command lines within an organization can partially account for the reproduction of violence, and fuzzier lines of command (if not necessarily of alignment) may reproduce violence more easily.

Assessing the structure of the drug market faces another complication, which is the transnational character of drug trafficking. This problem can be addressed partially because manifestations of violence are localized, and the same criminal organization can behave differently across locations because turf wars are often fought at the local level; so for the purposes of explaining violence it matters less whether the organization has transnational operations and more how it is organized locally.

Defining the State Security Apparatus

State actors and law enforcement should be at the center of understanding violence by nonstate actors, because violence challenges the state's monopoly of force. Since the 1990s, knowledge about law enforcement has proliferated but it is scattered among studies of democratization, citizen security, and police reform[72] that usually focus on the impact of policing frameworks on human rights and citizen security or on the endemic problems of police forces in countries with weak institutions. Studies rarely analyze the interaction between law enforcement, political competition, and broader institutional variables like regime type[73] and their impact on violence. Police corruption is often associated with violence and growing criminal behavior, yet most studies do not specify the mechanisms connecting law enforcement and violence. We can use the concept of the state security apparatus to address these issues, detailing the mechanisms that connect the power dynamics of law enforcement to criminal behavior and illustrating how corrupt enforcement can be associated with both high and low violence depending on how the state, and corruption, is structured.

Cohesion in the security apparatus depends on three components: intergovernmental relationships (vertical relations among government levels);

interagency relationships (horizontal relations across enforcement agencies); and time horizons of elected and enforcement officials (that is, how long they stay in office or in a given post). Fragmentation increases when there are conflicts between levels of government (e.g., the president and the mayor), conflicts across enforcement agencies (e.g., the military and the police), and when time horizons of officials are short due to processes such as rotation and purges in police forces or greater electoral competition.[74] This definition captures complex interactions between multiple scales of power that characterize urban politics and violence[75] and the various levels that interact in drug policy. The unit of analysis is thus local and subnational, in this case the city, but the assessment requires the consideration of national and even international politics. Paraphrasing Putnam's[76] summation of the interaction between foreign and domestic policy, such definition can be seen as a three level game between the local, the national, and the international. As chapter 2 discusses, national regimes constrain local outcomes, reducing or multiplying the centers of power that make decisions at the local level; international forces can also strengthen or weaken national centers of power. But as studies of subnational politics emphasize, within the same regime local areas can have radically different configurations of power.[77] The concept of state security apparatus thus captures two essential premises: that enforcement agencies do not operate in political vacuums, and that national and international politics certainly affect local dynamics but do not determine them single-handedly. At any rate, the concept can be scaled up or down to other units of analysis.

The three components of the security apparatus are interrelated, but do not necessarily co-vary: a purge within a given police agency affects time horizons by increasing uncertainty about who is a cop and about how long someone can remain within the purged agency, but it may not increase conflicts between different enforcement agencies or government levels. A change in one component is likely to increase the visibility of violence, even if other components remain stable. In short, the more changes there are along the three components, the larger the effect on visibility there is.

State cohesion thus depends on institutional arrangements that distribute government responsibilities, such as regime type (unitary or federal), on bureaucratic dynamics that determine rotation and responsibilities of enforcement agencies and on political and electoral dynamics and processes of democratization.

In federal systems, fragmentation can increase because local authorities have more power and conflicts among government levels are more likely. Federal systems usually have more police forces than unitary systems. For example, in Mexico there are more than 2,000 police forces,[78] thus making it more difficult to coordinate enforcement. Such fragmentation can be mitigated when political forces are hegemonic, as when the Institutional Revolutionary Party (PRI) successfully managed to control subnational political units and regulate relations with trafficking organizations.[79] Likewise, cohesion in a unitary system can be destabilized when decentralization augments territorial power, as occurred in Colombia after the popular election of mayors was introduced in 1986.[80]

Bureaucratic dynamics generate fragmentation when responsibilities in antinarcotics policies are assigned to new agencies or personnel rotation occurs. Assigning new agencies can create coordination problems, cause distrust among agencies, and break up existing protection arrangements, and personnel rotation can remove trusted allies for traffickers. As the case studies will illustrate, deploying the military in antinarcotic actions not only worsens human rights records (as many analyses document)[81] but also fragments the security apparatus—when the military is moved in to replace local police forces, it creates conflicts between military and police and discontent within the military itself.[82] Fragmentation can be exacerbated when support for military operations is uneven across authority levels and political actors.

Finally, political and electoral dynamics and democratization also affect cohesion in the state security apparatus. Democratization, for example, can produce fragmentation by multiplying the political forces that influence policymaking or that may provide protection. Open electoral competition can provide opportunities for political actors prone to establish relations with criminals to influence politics. It can also create opportunities for politicians committed to prosecute criminals, or at least willing to expose corruption for electoral purposes[83] to oppose them. Democratization can empower regional actors and provide renewed opportunities for criminals to establish political connections with state actors as occurred in Colombia[84] and for politicians to use criminals as a source of funding or even as tools to advance electoral power. Fragmentation, however, also reduces the state's ability to credibly protect criminals as occurred due to the declining hegemony of the PRI in Mexico.[85] Political competition can also increase the likelihood of anti-crime operations, which could be used to increase the incumbent's popularity or to attack political rivals.[86] Political competition thus reduces state cohesion although its effect may be mitigated when political actors cooperate beyond party lines.

More parsimonious analyses focused on just one component, such as electoral competition, could also help explain changes in violence. Yet a broad notion of the security apparatus illuminates important variability, for example, that even though urban military intervention is often associated with more violence, the rate of increase is not homogeneous, or as David Shirk and Joel Wallman[87] point out, that the timing of democratization does not necessarily coincide with upsurges in violence.

State and Market Interaction

pros &
cons to
enforcement
in terms
of violence

State interventions against crime can shape the criminal market and, in turn, violence. For example, heightened law enforcement can force cooperation among criminals who would otherwise work individually and create pressures for territorial expansion, but it may also force organizations to reduce their size to evade attention. Arrests and enforcement pressures can transform, fragment, or create leadership vacancies within criminal organizations, which can turn into violent market disputes.[88] State action can thus spur competition in the illegal market and increase the quantity of violence. States can sometimes succeed in eliminating criminal organizations, but given the incentives generated by the illegality of drugs, successful enforcement in one area is often paired with the relocation of trafficking activities or the dispersion of trafficking groups in what is variously labeled as the "balloon" or "cockroach" effect: Successful enforcement in one place can enable potentially violent criminals to appear in another place, much like when a balloon is squeezed on one end and all the air rushes to the other end. Similarly, when one organization is attacked, it may fragment into multiple groups that scatter to different places, just like when you swat at a group of cockroaches and they all run away in different directions to hide inside the wall, under the rug, and so forth. If criminal actors relocate or emerge in new places, the state structure in the new location can then explain the violent manifestations that end up emerging.

Conversely, criminal behavior can force the security apparatus to reform, expand, and modernize in its effort to confront criminality and violence. As in Tilly's classic ideas about war as state making, when states confront criminals for sustained periods of time, they are forced to improve the technological, logistic, and bureaucratic capacities required to handle specialized antinarcotic tasks. Given the emphasis on military responses within drug policies, such transformations often privilege the advancement of fighting capabilities and militarization at the expense of other aspects of the rule of law, but they nonetheless change the state's ability to fight. In Colombia, for example, the need to confront criminal organizations motivated crucial transformations in security agencies such as the creation of specialized elite units or the implementation of sophisticated intelligence capacities by the police. Criminal competition may also increase state fragmentation over time, when competing organizations penetrate different sectors or agencies of the state thus reducing cooperation between them.

These complex interactions illuminate the dynamics of the argument: when drug trafficking emerges within a cohesive security apparatus, violence is likely to be relatively hidden, and thus the state is less likely to react and transform itself in response to violence. This continuity contributes to predictable relations between state and criminals, and thus to relatively stable configurations of violence. Such stability can be disrupted by institutional transformations or by changes in criminal structures. By contrast, if drug trafficking emerges within a fragmented state where protection is unpredictable and enforcement inefficient, visible violence may emerge. The state, in turn will be likely to react and the relations between criminals and the state are likely to change constantly, generating volatile patterns of violence. In this context, enforcement actions are likely to exacerbate criminal fragmentation more quickly that in cohesive states. Governments can sometimes intervene against drug trafficking even if it is nonviolent due to international pressures (such as US politicized certification practices), domestic pressures for reform or for an iron fist approach to crime, or even legitimate concerns with crime, and these pressures can unsettle relatively stable interactions between states and criminals. Yet as chapter two discusses, violence is a key motivation for state enforcement, and even if enforcement is stepped up for other reasons, its immediate effects vary depending on state cohesion. In sum, when state institutions change, we are more likely to see transformations in violence than when the state is cohesive and stable, and violence, in turn, is likely to generate profound transformations within the state structure.

Patterns of Drug Violence

The interactions between competition (or monopoly), state cohesion, and type of armed coercion produce four patterns of violence that will be discussed throughout the book:

- Low frequency–low visibility (LF-LV)
- High frequency–low visibility (HF-LV)
- Low frequency–high visibility (LF-HV) and
- High frequency–high visibility (HF-HV)

Each of these patterns creates different incentives for outsourcing coercion, which in turn explains upward spikes in violence.

Relative Peace and Social Control (LF-LV)

This pattern occurs when the state is cohesive and the market is monopolistic. Market monopoly reduces conflicts for territorial control. State cohesion motivates criminals to use less-visible violence because they fear losing state protection, because they fear state prosecution, or both. In this context, if youth gangs exist, trafficking organizations are more likely to discipline them (to maintain their monopoly) than to outsource armed coercion to them, because they put a premium on low visibility. Violence may emerge to discipline members, to eliminate potential competitors, or to regulate "public threats" such as common crime, drug users, or social "undesirables," but it is usually hidden.

Quiet Wars (HF-LV)

High frequency–low visibility violence occurs when the drug market is competitive and thus generates violence aimed at gaining market control, but the state security apparatus is cohesive. The incentive for traffickers to make violence visible is reduced (or the desirability of hiding it is greater), and as result, this pattern may be overlooked by the media and enforcement agencies. Given the incentives of criminals to reduce visibility, outsourcing is not likely to occur.

Controlled Signaling (LF-HV)

This pattern results from a monopolistic market and an increase in fragmentation within a state that used to be cohesive and once protected criminals. It emerges when new enforcement agencies are deployed in a territory or when rotation and purges reduce the time horizons of enforcement agents. Traffickers then use visible violence mainly to retaliate against the state and to force it to refrain from enforcing the law. This pattern is uncommon and tends to be very short-lived because it is highly unstable and can easily evolve into HF-HV if the state or the market becomes further fragmented or if traffickers have a tradition in outsourcing coercion.

Extreme Violence (HF-HV)

The HF-HV pattern results from a competitive market and a fragmented state along all three components (conflicts among government levels, conflicts between enforcement agencies, and short time horizons of public officials). In this configuration incentives to outsource proliferate and if outsourcing takes place extreme spikes of violence are likely to occur.

Research Design and Methods

The book examines drug violence in Cali, Culiacán, Ciudad Juárez, Medellín, and Tijuana. These cities have been home to major DTOs throughout the entire study period (1984–2011) and highlight the variation in violence that occurs over time and both across and within territories. Given the limited development of theories on drug violence and of data amenable for large-N cross-national testing (that is, a comparison of a large number of countries or localities), cases were chosen to represent variation in the dependent variables: frequency and visibility.[89] However, cases also show variation along independent variables (state cohesion, market competition, and armed coercion) and other key variables such as the size of the illegal market and international influence. This method elucidates causal connections to better specify theories on a topic that is by nature difficult to study.

The unit of analysis is a period of violence within a city. I use subnational comparative analyses[90] across two countries and systematic paired comparisons to identify the simplest combination of variables that produce violence in each case, thus addressing a potential limitation of subnational analyses, which are usually focused on one country.[91] Pairing cities in the same country that experienced *contrasting patterns of violence,* as is the case in Cali and Medellín in Colombia or Ciudad Juárez and Tijuana in Mexico, provides a most-similar comparison. Pairing *similar patterns of violence* in different countries, as in Cali and Culiacán, provides a most-different comparison. Finally, pairing periods of violence *within* each city provides an even stronger, longitudinal most-similar research design. These systematic comparisons also account for the endogenous process of violence reproduction within cities over time.

The data derives from more than fifteen months of fieldwork conducted in the summers of 2008 and 2009 and between September 2010 and November 2011 in the five cities and from 196 semistructured interviews, including 42 police, enforcement, and intelligence officials; 34 politicians and public officials; 23 journalists; 43 human rights and nongovernmental organization (NGO) workers; 10 representatives of international organizations; and 38 academics. Due to security concerns, I conducted only a few interviews (7) with active criminals; though this poses problems for analyzing criminal incentives, I use judicial records and other firsthand testimonies to fill in this gap. I also created a data set that includes 6,497 violent events coded from the main local newspaper in each city for selected years.[92] Among the features coded that are relevant to visibility are the methods, the type of victims, and the number of victims for each violent event. As explained in detail in chapter 2, cases of low visibility entail less deliberate "publicizing" of violence, fewer collective (three or more victims) attacks and public targets, and no claims of responsibility. Cases of high visibility entail more publicly exposed methods, collective attacks, public targets, and claims of responsibility. Human-rights reports and interviews are also used to trace cases of low visibility in the years when the data set is not available. To assess frequency I use homicide rates, coding as "high frequency" cases with rates over 20 per 100,000 population.[93] Extreme upward spikes of violence are defined as years when homicide rates in a given city grow to be over three times the national average and any subsequent years when the rate remains as high.

The operationalization of independent variables combines data from official statistics, bibliographic material, government documents, newspapers reports, judicial records, and interviews. To assess cohesion in the security apparatus, I combine indicators of electoral competition such as electoral volatility and win margins for local executive elections, indicators of intergovernment relations (party coincidence between president, governor, mayor), and indicators of interagency relationships by coding whether military operations or rotations occurred in a given year. To assess market competition, I combine sources to determine how many criminal or armed organizations had territorial presence in each city-year. Triangulation of sources was essential to compensate for the recall problems that emerge in interviews referring to distant events; however, the distance of events was an advantage for collecting information on hidden violence that may not be noticed or reported at the time it occurs but that gets documented later on—when governments or human rights groups conduct investigations or when arrested criminals are summoned to court. Table 1.1 summarizes the definition of each variable, Table 1.2 describes coding details for assessing variables, and Table 1.3 presents the values of key variables for each city-period.

Table 1.1 **Definition of Variables**

		Definition
Dependent Variable	Frequency of Violence	Rate at which violent events occur. Spikes refer to years when homicide rates grow to be over three times the national rate and subsequent years where the rate remains this high.
	Visibility of Violence	Whether criminals publicly display the evidence or claim responsibility for the attacks they carry out.
Independent Variables	Market Competition	Number of organizations present in a territory competing for market control.
	Type of Criminal Armed Coercion	How criminal organizations carry out violence: from within the organization (insourcing) or by contracting out youth gangs (outsourcing).
	Cohesion in State Security Apparatus	Elected authorities and enforcement agencies that determine security and antinarcotics policies. Determined by (1) intergovernmental relations, (2) interagency relations, and (3) time horizons of public officials.

States, Trafficking, and Violence 27

Table 1.2 **Coding Details for City-Period Indicators of Violence, Cohesion in the Security Apparatus, and Market Competition**

Indicator	Values Min–Max	Coding	Sources
Homicide Rates	10.9–232.16	Total of homicides per 100,000 inhabitants, average for period.	Statistics agency INEGI (Mexico); Policia Nacional/ Medicina Legal (Colombia)
Visibility	19–287	Number of attacks with visibility score of 1.5 or greater.	Author's data set. Only selected years for each period were included, therefore the data set is not appropriate for full statistical analysis. This data was complemented with interviews and secondary sources to verify that the year was representative of the period
Win Margin Mayor	1.2–35.9	Difference between winning candidate and runner-up in elections for mayor.	IFE (Mexico); Congreso Visible data set based on Registraduria Nacional del Estado Civil (Colombia)
Electoral Volatility Mayor	2.8–50	Total net change in the percentage of votes obtained by all parties in an election compared to the previous election, in elections for mayor.	IFE (Mexico); Congreso Visible data set based on Registraduria Nacional del Estado Civil (Colombia)
Military Operations/ Purges	1.0–3.0	Total number of years with military incursions, massive purges in enforcement agencies, or both.	Analysis of secondary data (books) and interviews
Party Coordination	1–3	Party affiliation of the three levels of executive branch (president, governor, mayor). Coded 3 when all three are the same party affiliation. Average of values for the years in the period.	IFE (Mexico); Congreso Visible data set based on Registraduria Nacional del Estado Civil (Colombia)

(continued)

Table 1.2 **Continued**

Indicator	Values Min–Max	Coding	Sources
Win Margin governor	6.3–45.4	Difference between winning candidate and runner-up in elections for governor.	IFE (Mexico); Congreso Visible data set based on Registraduria Nacional del Estado Civil (Colombia)
Electoral Volatility Governor	3.5–58.25	Total net change in the percentage of votes obtained by all parties in an election compared to the previous election, in elections for governor.	IFE (Mexico); Congreso visible data set based on Registraduria Nacional del Estado Civil (Colombia)
Groups Present	1–7.6	Armed groups present in the city each year, average for period. The measure includes armed or criminal actors with territorial presence in the city, but not street gangs. Splinter groups within one organization are coded as 0.5	Based on interviews and secondary data, corroborated with the following sources that identify groups responsible for violence or homicides in a given year. Colombia: DNP data set on terrorism, CERAC data set on territorial presence of armed groups (1988–2009), Grupo de Memoria Histórica and DIJIN data on homicide 2003–2009. Mexico: Javier Osorio's data set on drug violence in Mexico 2000–2010.

Conducting Research on a Sensitive Topic

Drug trafficking and violence are highly sensitive topics that pose two main challenges for research: first and foremost, the safety and security of the researcher and her informants, and second, the reliability of collected information. To limit risks for my informants, I have taken many precautions to guarantee anonymity of interviewees except in cases of high-level public officials (although some officials explicitly asked me to anonymize their opinions, in which cases I did). Each interview is identified only by its location and date and, to provide some guidance for the reader, with the broadest and most generalized description that

Table 1.3 **Values of Indicators for Each City-Period**

| Period | Violence | | | | State Cohesion | | | | | Illegal market competition |
	Homicide rate (per 100,000 people)	Visibility (number of acts)	Win margin mayor (%)	Electoral volatility mayor (%)	Military operations/ Purges (number)	Party coordination (number)	Win margin governor (%)	Electoral volatility governor (%)		Armed groups present in city (number)
Cali 1984–1988	56.8	29			1	3				3.00
Cali 1989–2010	84.81	82.5	32.5	37.9	1	2.5	37.59	54.65		3.10
Medellín 1984–1993	232.16	287		50	2	2.8	34.88			4.20
Medellín 1994–2002	187.72		14.98	48	2	2.7	8.9	53.22		3.25
Medellín 2003–2007	50.97		20.4	37.3		0.8	11.59	41.57		2.00
Medellín 2008–2010	75.79	39	9.94	5.4		2	45.38	58.25		2.00
Culiacán 1984–2007	36.6	49.6	14.8	13.31	1	2.55	19.33	13.67		3.20
Culiacán 2008–2010	73.38	277.5	35.9	21.17	3	2	14.16	3.56		6.00
Ciudad Juárez 1984–1994	10.92	19	17.21	20.7		2.55	30.52	19.24		1.00
Ciudad Juárez 1995–2005	22.15		2.46	6.49		2	8.2	11.4		1.16
Ciudad Juárez 2006	17.3		9.45	5.11	1	2	15.09	3.9		3.00
Ciudad Juárez 2007	14.6		9.45	5.11		2	15.09	3.9		4.00
Ciudad Juárez 2008–2010	195.69	377	14.43	4.53	3	2	14.16	3.56		7.60
Tijuana 1984–1987	17.59	10	23.5	10.5		3	35.6			1.00
Tijuana 1988–1995	21.63	23	6.3	7.5		2.25	14.05	22.41		1.50

(continued)

Table 1.3 Continued

Period	Violence				State Cohesion				Illegal market competition
	Homicide rate (per 100,000 people)	Visibility (number of acts)	Win margin mayor (%)	Electoral volatility mayor (%)	Military operations/ Purges (number)	Party coordination (number)	Win margin governor (%)	Electoral volatility governor (%)	Armed groups present in city (number)
Tijuana 1996–1997	19.97		12.48	7.04	1	2	13.5	3.9	1.00
Tijuana 1998–2007	22.87	89	5.4	7.8		2.4	25.35	10.74	3.50
Tijuana 2008–2009	60.09	197	1.2	2.8	2	3	6.3	16.1	3.10
Tijuana 2010	52.5		1.4	5.5		3	6.3	16.1	6.00

characterizes the respondent without possibly risking his or her identity (e.g., police officer, journalist).

During fieldwork, I took several precautions to ensure my safety, which forced me to change plans constantly and be flexible with research schedules. In the most violent places (and even in apparently calm ones), gathering extensive information about the situation on the ground, reading newspapers, talking to experts, and especially talking with journalists, scholars, and practitioners who visited the research areas prior to my visits was essential. Establishing personal contacts beforehand was crucial in order to have a better sense of the security situation. Contrary to my initial plan, I did not spend long periods in each city but conducted several short trips, because this reduced the possibilities of being singled out for asking too many questions. In Mexico this was particularly important because I traveled between cities where rival organizations operate. Staying with local families who were known to me beforehand became a great source of protection. I used the snowball sampling technique for the interviews (in which respondents are asked to refer other people who may be relevant and willing to participate in the study), but I did not accept every interview that was offered to me. For example, on one occasion I could have interviewed high-ranking criminals, but I refused it because the person who offered the opportunity was not trustworthy; it turns out that this person was killed a week after our initial interaction, apparently for his connection to a trafficking group. Conducting interviews recommended by trusted people of course generated a bias, but ultimately only in one case were more than five interviews generated from the same contact (a group of twenty interviewees who could be traced to the same initial contact, although not directly). I was always clear about my research objectives and never misrepresented my work, but (in many cases) starting interviews by using the words "public security," rather than introducing a research project on drug trafficking and violence, facilitated breaking the ice without sounding too threatening. All in all, following common sense and, to a great extent, my gut feelings became the most important protection device.

Addressing the issue of data reliability is highly complicated. As Peter Andreas and Kelly Greenhill[94] point out while discussing the politics of statistics, data about transnational illegal activities is politicized, particularly difficult to come by, and plagued by morally charged debates. In William Finnegan's words,[95] in conflict- and crime-ridden societies it is difficult to know who is behind a murder, a candidacy, the uncovering of a corruption scandal, an enforcement operation; the truth is usually complex, fluid, and difficult. By nature, essential information on an illegal organization is hidden; official data on drug trafficking and drug violence is scarce, methodologically weak, and biased by government's efforts to show progress. Judicial reports are difficult to access, and if available, they do not necessarily ask questions the researcher wants to address, and in turn, traffickers' responses tend to be biased; interviews are biased by recall issues, opinions about the government and the traffickers, and perceptions. The best way to increase data reliability is thus to triangulate several sources for each piece of information and cross-validate all the characterizations presented in the book. Naturally, there is still room for ambiguity, biased information, and information gaps, but I have worked to the best of my abilities to use reliable information that can contribute in the expansion of a research field that is everyday more important in academia and that is crucial for political, economic, and social stability.

Road Map

The following chapters develop, test, and illustrate the political-economy framework for explaining drug violence as outlined in this chapter. Chapter 2 discusses how frequency and visibility conceptually allow us to tackle two crucial puzzles of criminal behavior: If some violence is inherent to the drug trade, can drug traffickers regulate its use? And why do drug traffickers decide to use visible violence if doing so can attract attention that can be detrimental for their business? The aim of chapter 2 is to locate the concepts within broader classifications and definitions of violence. I analyze how visibility is distinct from related concepts like brutality, symbolic violence, random or indiscriminate violence, and from media representations of violence. The chapter also discusses mechanisms for the reproduction of drug violence, how they affect its definition and operationalization, and the implications of visibility for researching violence.

Building on the paradox that a cohesive state that is more efficient in enforcing the law could also be a state that potentially protects criminals, chapter 3 discusses whether there is a tradeoff between state capacity to control violence and state autonomy from criminal influences. Using this framework it then discusses the evolution of drug trafficking and the responses to trafficking by state institutions in Colombia and Mexico. The discussion shows how state transformations have shaped the interactions between the state and criminals and illustrates how, while confronting criminal organizations, the state security apparatus grows. This chapter sets the stage for the subnational comparisons, showing that although national and international policies and processes are often necessary conditions for changes in criminal behavior, they are insufficient to explain contrasting patterns of violence across cities.

Chapter 4 explores Medellín, a city that has experienced sharp variations in criminal violence, with an initial period of extreme violence, followed by frequent but not visible violence, a subsequent phase of pacification, and then a fourth phase characterized by a gradual return of violence that again decreased beginning in 2012. The comparison within one city over time provides a controlled test of the argument about the impact of the relationship among the state security apparatus, illegal market competition, and the type of armed coercion on the frequency and visibility of drug-related violence because it holds crucial variables constant, such as the specific economic importance of Medellín, its history as a hub for early industrialization, and the particular characteristics of its urban landscape. The chapter shows how transformations in the organization of the criminal world and within the state affected violence, and it explains how a city once dubbed the most violent in the world during the 1990s saw a sharp decrease in homicide rates in the 2000s. The chapter also discusses how in 2008, despite improvements in living conditions and urban governance, violence increased again. To explain this resurgence, the chapter focuses on the growing competition in the criminal world.

Chapter 5 further tests the argument by comparing Cali and Culiacán, two cities that although located in different countries have experienced similar violent patterns, characterized by their low visibility. These cities illustrate how persistent and strong political elites can facilitate collaboration between state and criminals, thus creating incentives for the latter to hide violence even when facing criminal disputes. Cali and Culiacán also demonstrate that when criminals "insource" armed coercion, they can regulate violence more easily. The relative stability of patterns of violence allows me to assess how relatively minor changes in the state security apparatus can generate sporadic visible violence when a component of the security apparatus fragments—for example, when rotations or purges occur in enforcement agencies.

Chapter 6 focuses on Ciudad Juárez and Tijuana, highlighting how cities within the same country, similarly shaped by their shared borders with the United States, by the powerful influences of economic globalization, and by diverse migrant populations, can nevertheless experience diverging patterns of violence. The cross-city comparison challenges explanations that account for the violence in these cities, focusing mostly on their proximity to the border. This chapter also illustrates how, when the drug war exploded in Mexico, insourcing and a more cohesive security apparatus in Tijuana led to a different dynamic than in Ciudad Juárez, where outsourcing and fragmentation prevailed. Even though both cities experienced sharp increases in the frequency and visibility of violence in 2008, they were more limited and short-lived in Tijuana than in Ciudad Juárez.

The conclusion summarizes the arguments and explores their potential to explain violent criminal behavior in other places. It identifies avenues for future research as well as implications of the book's theory for research on issues such as the origin and consequences of violence, the definition of state power and its limits, the causes of institutional change, and the impact of democratization on public security. The conclusion also discusses policy implications of the argument for violence reduction and drug control.

2

Conceptualizing Drug Violence

On November 6, 1986, a group known as Los Extraditables (The Extraditable Ones), founded by the Medellín DTO, officially appeared before the Colombian media, releasing a document calling for the end of the extradition of Colombian nationals to the United States "in the name of national sovereignty, family rights, and human rights."[1] Over the following five years, the organization was responsible for a deadly period that claimed the lives of hundreds of civilians, judges, politicians, and police officers. The evolution of Los Extraditables was marked by its intriguing willingness to claim responsibility for attacks, usually through communiqués that conveyed its rationale for the use of violence.[2]

Los Extraditables' interest in publicity stands in sharp contrast to the efforts of another DTO, the Arellano Félix organization (AFO) in Tijuana, Mexico, to hide its violent acts in the late 1990s and 2000s, exemplified by the use of acid to render unidentifiable the corpses of people killed by traffickers. The remains of the bodies would then be dumped into sewage systems or buried on the outskirts of the city. Such techniques of hiding attacks only became public in 2009 when Mexican authorities captured the criminal Santiago Meza López, known as El Pozolero[3] (The Stew Maker). Meza acknowledged to the Attorney General's Office of Mexico that for over ten years he and other collaborators had dissolved more than three hundred bodies as they worked for the AFO, especially for the organization's top enforcers, men known as El Efra, and El Teo.[4] Rather than publicly claiming responsibility for deaths as Los Extraditables did, the AFO hid its attacks. In fact, since the mid-1990s some human-rights organizations had been denouncing the tragedy of disappeared people thought to be victims of drug traffickers in the state of Baja California, and some of those missing could perhaps have been disappeared by *pozoleros.*[5]

The contrast between Los Extraditables and El Pozolero highlights two crucial puzzles that have not been systematically analyzed in existing studies of drug violence: Why would DTOs use visible violence, like that employed by Los Extraditables, which can attract detrimental law enforcement and media attention? And if, as stated in chapter 1, violence is sometimes unavoidable to regulate illegal transactions, how can traffickers regulate its use, as occurred in Tijuana? An analysis solely focused on the quantity of violence would not capture the variation illustrated by these examples or the complex—and sometimes contradictory—incentives that drive traffickers' violent behavior. As chapter 6 discusses, a powerful trait of violence illustrated by El Pozolero is that the same traffickers' violent strategies can change over time: Meza's testimony revealed that, for almost a decade, his job was to eliminate evidence of violence. Later, in 2008, instead of hiding the bodies, he was specifically instructed to place them in the middle of a busy street along with a note: traffickers had decided to change their strategy from hiding to exposing violence.

This chapter conceptualizes drug violence along its frequency and visibility. The growing literature on drug violence tends to focus on explaining high levels of violence and is usually based on body counts, but it does not explore systematically the methods used to carry out violence, which are often presented in public depictions merely as an illustration of criminal brutality. The conceptualization this book advances provides, in Giovanni Sartori's terms,[6] precision to capture subtle variation, while maintaining a level of abstraction and a common taxonomy across the multiple ways in which drug violence can be carried out.

The goal of this chapter is to place the discussion of frequency and visibility within a broader discussion about the definition of drug violence. It first explains the practical relevance of assessing the frequency and visibility of drug violence, explores its relation to other classifications of violence, and then discusses how visibility is distinct from related concepts like brutality, symbolic violence, random or indiscriminate violence, and from media representations of violence. The second part of the chapter outlines causal mechanisms explaining the reproduction of drug violence. The third explains the operationalization of concepts—that is, the indicators and information collected to measure and assess these concepts. The conclusion discusses implications of using the concept of visibility.

Defining Frequency and Visibility

Literature on violence by nonstate actors and during civil wars provides the crucial insight that variation in levels and types of violence is not purely irrational but rather purposeful.[7] Criminals' apparently irrational use of excessive violence that attracts enforcement attention can therefore be seen as a strategic decision. Of course, violence is not always rational, and not all perpetrators are strategic thinkers, but many behaviors that appear gratuitous result from complex interactions between states and traffickers. Although some literature on illicit markets has explored why violence can change and reach extreme levels, it rarely considers how particular forms of violence can meet different strategic needs.[8]

"Visibility" refers to whether criminals expose or claim responsibility for their attacks, and it can be useful for criminals to scare away enemies, retaliate against government action, attempt to modify the behavior of governments, or bargain the price of protection.[9] Visible violence is thus similar to the signaling used in civil wars and terrorist actions. In civil wars, armed actors can deploy violence strategically to elicit civilian collaboration and allegiance, because violence can signal power or strength, infuse fear, and serve as a powerful coercive tool. Yet not all forms of physical violence generate the same reaction, and consequently insurgents use symbolic violence and manipulate violent images to mobilize the population's support because, as described by the scholars Gordon McCormick and Frank Giordano, "different types of actions, against different types of targets, carried out under different circumstances, at different times will not only elicit different impressions on those who witness them, they will also influence the level of exposure these attacks can expect to receive in the first place."[10] Similarly, terrorism can be a signaling strategy that emerges when rebels are weak and do not have the power to extract concessions or impose their will on rivals but want to show power, resolve, or provoke state reactions that help them expand their support base.[11]

As Tilly contends, different forms of collective violence tend to cluster, to respond to similar processes, and to belong to wider repertoires of contention.[12] Indeed, criminals sometimes behave in a way akin to social movements or to lobbyists when they try to mobilize support for policy changes, or they can, like insurgents, attempt to create new social orders that bypass the state and that actively involve civilians. The boundaries between actors engaged in collective violence are thus often more blurred than usually acknowledged, and similarities tend to be more evident across subgroups of violent nonstate actors than within them. Yet, in an ideal sense, traffickers can be thought of as differing from other violent actors not only because of their goals—goals not politically open in nature—but also because of their relations vis-à-vis the state and communities. The survival of trafficking actors may benefit from, but is not defined by, civilian support of their objective, as can be the case for social movements, armed actors in civil wars, and organizations that deploy terrorist tactics. To be precise, criminals often establish social orders providing benefits for communities in exchange for protection and support,[13] but establishing the legitimacy of their cause is not their primary concern. Most importantly, criminals depend on the direct or indirect support of state actors to survive. As Paul Staniland contends, rebels sometimes collaborate with states, too, but doing so is not inherent to their nature.[14] In consequence, a criminal's violent act that signals power increases the risk of detention and may motivate state repression, as terrorist actions do,[15] but it may also risk losing state protection. A characterization of violence in criminal markets should, then, account for the effects of violence on the relationship between criminals and states, which can be both confrontational and collaborative. It also requires explaining the range of violent strategies criminals can use, something usually overlooked when terrorism or extreme forms of violence are analyzed as isolated strategies and not as part of a wider repertoire of violence.

Traffickers vacillate between using violence that serves functionally to solve disputes and show power and avoiding violence that can be detrimental for the business while attracting enforcement attention,[16] because different forms of drug violence elicit different state reactions.[17] As Kent Eaton points out, the international "war on drugs" has constrained possible state responses to drug trafficking by privileging supply reduction and militarized responses, consequently undermining state institutions and democracy.[18] Yet, the strength and specific type of responses has varied, and the type of violence is one factor accounting for this variation. In Colombia in the 1990s, the government hunted down Pablo Escobar and the Medellín DTO more forcefully than its rival Cali DTO. As a former Colombian minister of defense acknowledged, the government's focus on Escobar was a response to his extreme violent techniques because "a group placing bombs generates more social rejection"; unlike individual murders committed in marginalized areas, bombs are likely to affect the public at large and generate opposition even among those who are not directly victimized.[19] Similarly, following the Mexican government's declaration of war against trafficking organizations that initiated a deployment of federal and army troops to cities beginning in 2006, certain forms of violence precipitated decisions about where to mobilize federal troops. A high-level official described to me, for instance, that when masked gunmen stopped traffic on a busy highway in the state of Veracruz and dumped thirty-five bodies in broad daylight in September 2011, the federal government decided to deploy troops to the area. This was not the first violent event in the region, but it was particularly visible: before that event, according to this official from Mexico's federal Secretariat of Public Security, the state of Veracruz "did not report kidnappings and kept the statistics hidden. People didn't know [about violence], but then, to make people aware, traffickers dumped thirty-five corpses. Those are clear images that say 'I'm the boss.' Of course, we hurried and we had to react to that. That's how we have to operate."[20] Visibility affects not only the state's reaction but also people's perceptions: Mexicans tend to see violence before 2006 as respectful of honor codes and limited to "them" (criminal elements), in sharp contrast to violence that ensued afterward, seen as generalized, random, and dishonorable because it was perceived to affect "innocent" people.[21] States may attack criminals in the absence of visible violence as a way of preventing, rather than reacting to public security crises or as a response to international pressures or domestic ideological agendas. Yet, when visible violence grows, enforcement becomes unavoidable.

The concepts of frequency and visibility are useful in capturing the tradeoffs criminals face in using drug violence. As explained in chapter 1, frequency refers to the rate at which violent events occur and it can increase as competition in the illegal market increases. When the market is competitive, disputes for territory or control among rival organizations, or within the same organization for leadership, generate more violence, as they are unlikely to be solved with a single homicide. In a competitive market, violence can beget violence because violent acts may nurture retaliation that is unlikely to stop before competitors are eliminated or significantly diminished.[22]

By contrast, if a criminal organization holds a monopoly, violence can be used to solve internal disputes, enforce contracts, discipline members of the organization, punish transactions gone wrong, punish treason, or scare away enemies, but the violence is more contained because it is unlikely to generate retaliation. The organization's power deters revenge and may persuade rivals not to react. The goal of using violence, such as punishing a traitor, can be achieved with a single violent act. This may occur when a criminal organization holds a quasi-monopoly but is challenged by internal and external competitors. Chapter 5 shows how, for example, the Juárez DTO faced challenges in the 1980s and 1990s, but its power allowed it to control spirals of violence when market disputes emerged. As control declines, the organization also loses its power to persuade other actors not to react or imitate its own violent actions. An analysis of frequency can accordingly help assess situations of declining violence and, consequently, scenarios that challenge the idea that violence is inherent to illegal markets.

Using visible violence provides criminals with a key advantage, which is the ability to show power or to inspire fear, but it has the disadvantage of generating state attention and for this reason its use depends on the interactions between states and criminals. The concept of visibility can consequently be used to explain why traffickers decide to be either visibly brutal criminals or "narcotraffickers in silence," as one interviewee put it.[23] As explained in chapter 1, visibility is primarily affected by state cohesion, which shapes the ability of the state to attack or, alternatively, protect criminals. This in turn affects the criminals' calculation about how costly it can be to expose violence or use it as a pressure tool. This does not mean that the state is simply a passive regulator of crime or that its actions cannot directly affect violence: the point is rather that the structure of the state security apparatus mediates the consequences of state interventions and the type of violence they unleash or inhibit.

Publicizing violence may be crucial in at least three situations: when criminals fight for internal leadership, when two or more organizations fight for turf within the same territory, and when criminals react to state anticrime interventions or want to persuade state officials not to enforce the law against them. Accordingly, it may appear that competition in the criminal market, and not just state cohesion, determines visibility because criminals benefit from intimidation and from a violent reputation when they need to eliminate rivals. Indeed, research has shown that armed political groups can use gruesome attacks to distinguish themselves from other rebel groups.[24] Yet, as shown in the case studies, if illegal market competition creates incentives to display violence but criminals fear state enforcement, or fear losing state protection, they may prefer to hide their disputes. This explains why criminal disputes in Medellín after 2008, as described in chapter 4, have made violence more frequent but not visible: criminals have learned that visible violence, like that deployed by Los Extraditables, makes them vulnerable to state action.

Confessions made by paramilitary leaders after a demobilization process was carried out in Colombia in 2003 illustrate the tradeoff between exposing or hiding violence and how relationships with the state determine the calculus about how to deploy violence.[25] The confession of one paramilitary commander, Jorge Laverde, before a judge captures the tradeoffs of exposing violence:

LAVERDE: Sir, in Villa del Rosario, where the sugar mill used to be, near the river, we built an oven where approximately forty or fifty people could be cremated after they were killed . . .

JUDGE: Aside from that oven, those ovens used to dispose of bodies or the remains of people that the paramilitary assassinated, did you use any other method to dispose of the bodies?

LAVERDE: Yes, sir. They were thrown in the river.

JUDGE: Which river?

LAVERDE: The Zulia River.

JUDGE: Who made the decision to get rid of the people? Why get rid of the people? Why not simply kill them?

LAVERDE: That began a long time ago in Urabá. The commanders in Urabá ordered [us] to disappear those who had been killed. Salvatore Mancuso said, "There's a reason they're killed. Let the community see who was killed and that we are cleaning up the area." But Commander Castaño disagreed. He said, "*If dead bodies start piling up, it would make the authorities look bad. And it could be detrimental to us as well.*"

Referring to a similar effort to bury bodies in mass graves, the paramilitary commander Ever Veloza described how hiding violence might be essential when criminals collaborate with state authorities:

JUDGE: When did you stop leaving bodies in plain sight and start digging mass graves?

VELOZA: The commanders were responsible for that. More and more people were killed in Urabá every day. The homicide rate was going through the roof.

JUDGE: Under which commanders?

VELOZA: Police or army commanders. The homicide rate kept rising. They started being pressured by their superiors or the media or various government organizations or NGOs because violence was happening right under their noses. *So they asked us to please get rid of the dead bodies, to bury them to keep the statistics from rising. That's when the mass grave system began to be implemented and used. They authorized killings but only with the understanding that the bodies would disappear.*[26]

The strategic interest in covering violence up was also evident in the declaration of Santiago Meza, El Pozolero, before Mexican authorities. He claimed that the main objective of the brutal technique of putting corpses in vats of acid was to disappear bodies. He did not kill the victims and he received the corpses after the murder had taken place. His only function was to destroy the corpses in acid and bury them; allegedly he did not know the cause of the killings or the identity of the victims and his task was only instrumental: to hide the evidence.

In this light, measures of frequency and visibility help capture instrumental changes in the use of violence, and their combination unveils a wide range of manifestations of drug violence. Of course, forms of violence intermix and there are always ambiguities in any classification;[27] consequently, each possible pattern of violence combines both visible and nonvisible events. In fact, the database on drug violence constructed for this book, explained in the third section of this chapter, illustrates that visible violence may not cause the majority of deaths in a given location; given their nature, a few visible lethal attacks can be enough to elicit media and enforcement attention. For any period, there are fewer "highly visible" than "low visibility" attacks. Yet there are periods when visible acts become more recurrent even if they still represent a minority, and these constitute the "high visibility" patterns.

The dimensions of frequency and visibility may not be completely independent from each other. Frequent violence can be visible in and of itself: for example, when a city reaches a very high homicide rate, violence can gain media attention and sound the alarms of governments and civil organizations. Visible acts can sometimes deter violent retaliation and thereby reduce the amount of killings by instilling fear, particularly when the organization perpetrating violence holds a market monopoly. But visibility can also further reproduce violence and induce retaliation if the market is competitive, as criminals imitate existing killing techniques. Despite these interconnections, a separate understanding of the two dimensions is important because fewer people witness low-profile violence than its visible counterparts. Most importantly, criminals consider both dimensions when making decisions about violent strategies.

Alternative Classifications of Violence

The dimensions analyzed in this book differ from existing classifications of violence and from similar concepts. In criminological studies, for example, a well-known classification of drug violence put forward by Paul Goldstein differentiates between psychopharmacological, economic-compulsive, and systemic drug violence.[28] Such classification separates violence derived from drug use, from the need to find money to buy drugs, and from interactions within drug-distribution systems. This useful classification, however, does not capture variation within systemic drug violence (the focus of this book) that is more connected to societal, political, and organizational factors and more common than violence directly derived from drug use.[29]

The dichotomy of selective versus indiscriminate violence advanced by Stathis Kalyvas in the study of civil wars[30] could be helpful in explaining the puzzles and patterns of drug violence explored in this book. Such classification however, does not capture the fundamental questions about visibility and frequency described above because selective and indiscriminate violence can be both exposed and concealed. Indiscriminate violence tends to be highly visible, as was the case of car bombs during the period of narcoterrorism in Colombia, yet it can also be hidden, for example when victims of massacres are buried in mass graves. Similarly, selective violence can be both visible and hidden: in Mexico after 2006 criminals carefully selected many of their targets (as occurred during the relatively peaceful 1980s) but attacked them in highly public events. For many observers, the increasing victimization of civilians in Mexico since 2006 could be seen as a reflection of a higher recurrence of indiscriminate violence. While this may be true in some cases, attacks against civilians also reflect selective targeting of victims of extortion and of those perceived as enemies both by criminals and by corrupt authorities, targeting mistakes by authorities and criminals, and cases of "stray bullets" that are more likely to occur in visible events like shootings.[31] Thus violence that appears to be indiscriminate may reflect a change in the method, rather than the target, of violence.

Drug violence could also be differentiated according to the purposes it serves, such as solving contractual disputes or territorial, disciplinary, or succession issues.[32] The problem with a classification based on the goals of violence is that similar tactical or strategic goals can be met with different forms of violence. As Kalyvas has noted a single violent event can mix multiple motivations (from ideological to pure revenge or sadistic impulses) and multiple uses (from intimidation to provocation),[33] and this also occurs in drug violence. We can hypothesize the motivations behind an observed act of violence, but we cannot directly observe the purposes behind a particular act. For example, transactional violence, used to regulate transactions in a contractual environment that cannot be officially regulated by the state, can be both frequent and infrequent. It may target rival traffickers or members of the organization retrospectively, when transactions go wrong, when members of organizations try to cheat or steal merchandise, or when they provide information for enemies or for the state. If one organization holds market monopoly, this violence can be sporadic, used to discipline members; but if market competition increases, transactional violence can grow as the perpetrators lose capacity to prevent retaliation. Transactional violence can also be visible or hidden. In the 1980s Mexican traffickers punished traitors by disappearing them or their remains, but punishments became more public in the late 2000s, as criminals employed a whole system of coded meanings in mutilated bodies that exposed violence and signified the reasons for a transactional killing. A corpse with a mutilated finger, for instance, was used to indicate that the victim had been a *dedo* (a "finger")—someone who provided information to enforcement authorities.

The victimization of marginalized civilians as a way of imposing social order, especially when criminals receive state protection, is another illustration of how the concept of visibility tackles variation that does not relate to the purpose served with one violent act. DTOs may repress vulnerable sectors of the population seen as "public hazards"—such as petty criminals, drug users, prostitutes, and beggars—to gain legitimacy before certain sectors of the community and the state. As Pino Arlacchi noted in the case of Mafiosi in Italy, this type of social-control violence can be used to collaborate with the state in maintaining the "established order."[34] Social control is often hidden because the pool of "undesirables" is limited, they do not have the power to retaliate, and if criminals receive state protection they prefer to hide these acts of "social control." Yet in some cases, social control can be publicly displayed: in Culiacán in 2009, out of thirty-five messages found on dead bodies, thirty were directed to petty criminals and car thieves; the notes, which were also accompanied by toy cars, threatened other car thieves with the same treatment if they did not stop stealing.[35] Visible violence sometimes affected other "social maladies," such as rapists or even unfaithful husbands.

The examples of transactional violence and social control show how classifications of violence based on its instrumental objectives are difficult to observe and for that reason may be less useful in terms of understanding why and when criminals change their performance of violence. Furthermore, because a single violent act can serve multiple objectives and similar objectives can be fulfilled with both visible and hidden violence, a classification based on motivations or objectives tends to be ad hoc and provides little basis to predict what forms of violence are likely to prevail in different circumstances. By contrast, frequency and visibility unveil criminal incentives that can be then systematically connected to factors essential for criminal existence, such as their relation with the state and with rivals.

It is worth mentioning that other studies differentiate between visible and nonvisible violence or (as Jeremy Weinstein does in his analysis of rebel groups[36]) look at the difference between the character and the quantity of violence. These studies aim to differentiate between the lethal violence that often attracts attention and the nonlethal forms of social control and physical harm that tend to be ignored.[37] My analysis in this book focuses on lethal violence, although, as the cases of apparent peace in criminal markets suggest, nonlethal forms of physical harm and social control may be correlated with lethal, low-visibility violence. A separate differentiation across lethal forms of violence is crucial, however, because it does not necessarily depend on how people perceive forms of bodily harm but, rather, captures different criminal intentions.

Symbolic Violence, Brutality, and Media Representations

The concept of visibility is connected to ideas about the semantic and symbolic uses of violence, which stress the power of violence as a communication tool.[38] María Uribe, for example, analyzed and described the symbolism and rituals in massacres and mutilations in Colombia during the period of civil war known as La Violencia (1948–1964).[39] She described how parts of the body were separated and sometimes relocated (for example, the legs would be placed where the head should be) to desecrate the victims, bodies were disposed to scare away communities, and notes would be placed in massacre scenes to let people know who the perpetrators were. More recent analyses of violence in Mexico have also focused on understanding why methods such as the use of beheadings became prevalent after 2006, emphasizing the combination of cultural and technological factors (such as the spread of communication technologies), and the varied meanings and symbols associated with different killing methods.

Unlike concepts of symbolic violence, visibility emphasizes not unique cultural manifestations but rather the instrumental character of violence. For

example, Uribe and Teófilo Medina explain recurrent massacres and mutilations among peasants with shared identities during Colombia's La Violencia
as a result of a latent aggressiveness, a tendency to retaliate and defend honor
codes, and superstitious ideas about the adversary ingrained in peasant loyal-
ties and culture.[40] They clarify that these practices were not simply pathological
but occurred under particular political circumstances, motivated by revenge and
other instrumental objectives such as the elimination of opposing political parties. Yet they do not elaborate systematically on why cultural propulsions to kill
in barbaric ways were activated only under certain conditions.

The problem of explaining symbolic violence as being the result of cultural
predispositions is that it simplifies the motivations for violence and stigmatizes
certain cultures. For example, their so-called familiarity with death, as Claudio
Lomnitz puts it, has led to the characterization of the Mexican lower classes as
potentially barbaric.[41] Casualness about death has also been tied in conceptually with brutality and violence as a product of cultural influences, such as Aztec
indigenous practices or, in more recent years, the cult of the Santa Muerte (Holy
Death) followed by some proletarian and criminal elements of Mexican society.[42] Cultural influences may inform brutal practices such as beheadings, but
they cannot explain why such practices are only employed at certain times or
why criminals may both use and refrain from using these methods. This book
thus focuses on analyzing when and why visibility appears rather than on disen-
tangling the meanings, rituals, and cultural practices attached to different forms
of killing—although such analysis is equally interesting.

Media Representations of Violence

Visibility is also connected to research on media representations of violence
and their impact on perceptions of insecurity, which emphasizes how different
acts can shape perceptions of security among those who are not direct victims
of violence.[43] Such research also explores how media prerogatives affect coverage of violent events. Media prerogatives may indeed manipulate and create
the visibility—or invisibility—of violence. In Medellín, for example, since the
mid-2000s local media has worked to reduce the prominence of violence in
the news. Similarly, in Tijuana, Mexico, authorities and business leaders have
actively shaped security perceptions by manipulating media coverage of violence. Indeed, a businessman in Tijuana explained to me that a leading objective of the business sector's active engagement in security policies was to change
perceptions of the city as a dangerous place: "We started to monitor TV stations;
we looked at each newspaper to see how many beheadings and deaths appeared
in the headlines, and then we identified who was the main advertiser in each of

them. We sat with the newspaper owners and told them, 'If you continue pub-lishing violence, your advertisers will stop buying publicity.' "[44] Media coverage of violence is not neutral or objective, and media outlets can be pressured to downplay reports of violence when it is in the government's or business sector's interest to reduce perceptions of insecurity. Media coverage may account for the divergence between realities and public perceptions of violence, yet it does not explain why criminals change violent strategies. A focus on media coverage also tends to favor the analysis of excessive portrayals of violence, rather than cases where media refrain from reporting violence.

Criminals' changing strategies for perpetrating violence can also affect or shape media coverage. Some forms of violence are more likely to be covered than others (for example, a display of a beheaded body in a public place ver-sus someone being shot on the outskirts of the city). A freelance journalist in Tijuana explained to me how her priorities in covering violence shifted as the criminals' violent techniques changed. In 2008–2009 "high impact" violence (such as shootouts and beheadings) rose, but by 2010 it had declined. Even though less-visible violence still occurred, especially in poor neighborhoods, she could not hope to sell stories about "low impact" violence while her col-leagues in other parts of the country could offer news agencies far more lurid stories of beheaded bodies or "terrorist" acts. Her decision not to report hidden violence was therefore a response to media interests, but such interests did not create the changes in violent techniques motivating her decision.

Of course, media coverage decisions can be affected by different reporting standards. For example, in 2010, as the number of journalists killed and threat-ened in Mexico kept growing (at least thirty journalists had been killed since 2006 because of their profession),[45] heated debates divided Mexican media out-lets. Some considered that brutality should not be reproduced in the media while others considered that journalists did not create violence and could not be held responsible for reporting reality and informing the public. Many journalists told me that they could not ignore reality and their responsibility was to analyze, rather than simply reproduce, grisly scenes. The point is that even though media plays a key role in publicizing some attacks more than others, and even though journal-ists are sometimes manipulated to report in favor of or against certain actors, such as criminal organizations, government bodies, or business groups, reporting deci-sions also respond to objective changes in the performance of violence.[46]

Brutality

Visibility is related to, but different from, brutality. Brutality as a category is often used in academic and nonacademic analyses, but it is rarely clearly defined and is often used synonymously with irrationality, cruelty, sadism, barbarism, or savagery—making "brutality" a difficult concept to explore with systematic analysis. In this book I identify brutality as instances of violence where the corpses are manipulated or desecrated (without any assumption as to why the bodies are treated in such ways).[47] Research on traditional Mafia organizations illustrates the difference between brutality and visibility. Italian Mafiosi used highly brutal methods to impose sanctions, retaliate against offenses, gain prestige, and overpower rivals. Yet the "honor dimension of murder" led Mafiosi to show brutality only to direct victims, the members of the group, or rivals. According to Arlacchi, the change from the traditional to an entrepreneurial Mafia was marked precisely by an increase in violence, which was no longer held in check by traditional honor codes and which became visible to a wider public.[48]

The behavior of the Cali DTO, considered less violent than its Medellín counterpart in the 1980s, further illustrates the point. The Cali DTO used brutality, but mostly in private spaces and usually as an instrument to hide violence. Chapter 5 recounts how when the Cali organization operated, it allegedly threw tortured bodies in the Cauca River and their fingerprints were destroyed, thereby making it difficult for authorities to find and identify the victims and the perpetrators of the violence. According to criminal investigators analyzing a similar episode of bodies found in the Medellín River in 2011 and quoted in a newspaper article, "criminal organizations throw the corpses with the aim of disappearing them and, thus, eliminating the possibility of identifying the perpetrators."[49] In other words, brutality can sometimes be used as a signal, or even reflect irrational impulses, but it can also be instrumental in destroying evidence of responsibility and can be deliberately used to this effect—to conceal violence precisely by making it more difficult for authorities to find victims and perpetrators. The concept of brutality, consequently, does not capture tactical or strategic changes in the use of violence. Visible violence can be, and usually is, brutal, but hidden violence can be brutal, too. There can be different audiences for violence, and violence is always evident for direct victims, but visibility implies that brutality and the experience of violence transcends direct victims and is communicated to the general public. When brutality is publicized, it becomes visible, as occurred with beheaded bodies exhibited in public spaces in Mexico since 2006.

Violence as a category can be further disaggregated by considering who the intended audiences are (e.g., the state, rivals, citizens). But as in the case of motivations, it may not be obvious who the audience is, and the concept of visibility does not assume who the intended audience is for a particular act. Visibility, however, is not absolute: civilians and states react differently to "hierarchies" of violence. Class, gender, and ethnicity, therefore, can influence whether people pay attention to the events or not, and such perceptions can change over time and space. It is possible that an act deemed visible according to this theory may not attract public attention. While effectively attracting attention is not necessary to render an act visible, the key for the operationalization of visibility presented below is that nonvictims and those not directly related to the victim can notice the events and that the methods suggest either an intention to display attacks or lack of interest in concealing them. Not all visible acts may attract public attention, but it is fair to assume that hidden acts are less likely to be noticed by the general public than visible ones.[50]

Mechanisms for the Reproduction of Drug Violence

This book has so far discussed drug violence as resulting from market disputes and the exposure of violence as a function of how criminals interact with the state. Yet when criminal disputes emerge or when criminals confront the state, violence can reproduce outside neatly defined categories of criminals or enforcers. The theory in this book includes one crucial mechanism for violence reproduction, which is when traffickers outsource violence to youth gangs that provide cheap soldiers. When outsourcing takes place, youth gangs may appropriate violence for their own purposes, which range from the commission of other crimes (such as robbery or extortion) to the use of a violent reputation to assert their territory and identity. The following discussion explains three additional channels through which the reproduction of violence takes place, which justify the broad operationalization of drug violence I propose. Ultimately, however, the discussion asserts that the three key variables of the book's theory— state cohesion, market competition, and type of armed coercion—can account for the activation of these channels at different times.

First, drug violence may be reproduced when criminals and states intentionally target or unintentionally attack civilians. To protect their turf, criminals may target civilians whom they suspect to be members of rival gangs or informants for the state or for rivals. Likewise, state authorities may target civilians whom they suspect to be criminals, or they may victimize civilians simply to show operational results. When state authorities collaborate with criminals, they may victimize civilians who are suspected of opposing criminal interests. Furthermore, when drug-trafficking organizations engage in other criminal activities, such as extortion or human trafficking, they may be more likely to attack civilians to extract profits from them. In Ciudad Juárez, for example, extortion reportedly did not exist before drug disputes exploded, military and federal forces moved in,[51] and gangs became a crucial asset for criminal organizations—but after these events, the refusal of civilians to pay extortion fees became a source of violence.[52] Finally, when both criminals and state employ force more indiscriminately, the chances of civilians becoming "collateral" damage or becoming unintended casualties of "stray bullets" increase.

A second mechanism that reproduces violence into realms beyond trafficking disputes is the attempt by different social and armed actors to protect themselves or society from criminals. Drug violence can generate retaliation by militias or vigilante groups that are attempting to "protect" citizens from high-level and common criminality, ultimately unleashing cycles of revenge. Since this privatized protection is unregulated and not based on a legal assessment of who is a criminal, it often targets innocent or marginalized people. The attempt by non-trafficking actors to benefit from the violent reputation of criminals, or to throw the authorities off the trail by copying traffickers' methods, can also reproduce violence. A common criminal may behead the victim of a robbery in hopes that authorities will automatically pronounce the crime to be a drug-related homicide and stop investigating. For example, in Mexico a criminal syndicate that goes by the name Los Zetas was considered by the state, media, and academics as the country's most brutal drug-trafficking organization. Los Zetas became infamous for visible killing methods such as beheadings,[53] and the group's actions spawned imitation and the emergence of copycat groups that benefited from developing a violent reputation while conducting other crimes such as extortion.[54] Los Zetas themselves learned from other groups: their first live broadcast of a torture in 2005, widely reproduced throughout the Internet, allegedly mimicked a similar video posted by Hamas months before.[55] Authorities and media were quick to blame the Zetas for brutal attacks even before a proper investigation had been conducted because of the Zetas members' military backgrounds and their proved brutality, thus benefiting the copycats.[56]

Finally, the complex connections between drug resources and armed conflict may also augment drug violence. In locations where nonstate armed actors with political or ideological motivations have opposed, or allied with, trafficking organizations and where illegal activities like drug trafficking fund warring factions in the armed conflict, violence is likely to be reproduced more quickly and for longer time periods, as has occurred in Colombia. The acquisition of drug money increases the capacity of armed groups to wage war, and traffickers can also use rebels as protectors of drug routes and crops. In turn, states can wage more comprehensive wars by fusing counterinsurgency and counterdrug objectives. This makes it even more difficult to determine whether a particular attack is aimed at facilitating drug-trafficking activities, at eliminating political enemies, or at securing territorial control. Often the reality is that violence affects both politics and the organization of the illegal enterprise.[57] While theorizing on the connections between drugs and armed conflict exceeds the purpose of this book, the key here is that such connections may expand and complicate drug violence.[58]

In places like Mexico, where the connections of criminals with rebels or with ideological agendas are weaker than in Colombia,[59] drug violence may acquire political undertones when the state and criminals attack prominent state officials either to retaliate, to bargain for protection, or to scare away enforcers. In these circumstances, drug violence becomes more political in the sense James Fearon and David Laitin define political violence,[60] because criminals are more likely to seek changes in state policy or in the severity of law enforcement through violence. For some observers, this suggests a comparison in which criminals are behaving like insurgents who challenge the existing power structure.[61] What the label of "criminal insurgents" ignores, however, is that, unlike rebels in civil wars, criminal actors may not seek to replace or conquer state power[62] and, most importantly, that such insurgent behavior is not inherent to criminals but is more precisely a response to changing state structures that affect the price and the risk entailed in using violence. Whether and how violence reproduces outside trafficking disputes is largely a function of state cohesion and criminal-market structures.

All the aforementioned mechanisms show that a minimalist definition of drug violence limited to disputes among traffickers and between criminals and state officials may overlook how drug violence affects multiple sectors of the population. A more extensive definition including victims and events associated with all the issues described above, however, could raise a question about the validity of the argument that frequency and visibility of violence result from interactions between the state and traffickers and from the type of armed coercion that criminals employ. However, these mechanisms of violence reproduction are more likely to emerge when, as my theory suggests, criminal competition increases, the state fragments, and criminals outsource violence to gangs. Retaliation by nontrafficking groups, imitation by copycats, or violence derived from other criminal activities may emerge when several criminal organizations compete, but they are unlikely to emerge if the market is monopolistic. Imitation may proliferate when the market is competitive because criminal organizations may have less power to discipline members or they may benefit from the reputation spread by imitators. By the same token, gang interactions are likely to become deadly when traffickers outsource violence to youth gangs, and this, in turn, is likely to spur vigilantism; this is why outsourcing explains upward spikes of homicides. In the absence of competition, traffickers may instead attempt to discipline gangs or may simply not engage in the direct interactions that could increase gangs' violent capacity. Similarly, as explored in chapter 3, when rebels or warring factions within a conflict fuse with drug-trafficking actors, allowing the creation of a monopoly, violence may decrease, as occurred in regions of Colombia in the late 1990s when paramilitaries centralized their structures and engaged more heavily in drug trafficking. Conversely, when trafficking actors create multiple and parallel alliances with different sides within a conflict, or directly compete with them, violence increases as a result of the intensified competition among armed actors.

Likewise, changes in state structures that transform criminal incentives, leading them to expose attacks, can also make them less willing to control the reproduction of violence. When criminals lose incentives to lower the profile of violence, they may also be less concerned with deterring imitators or common criminals. Conversely, criminals' concern with maintaining state protection can lead them to attempt to regulate common criminality and engage in violent— but hidden—social cleansing practices. Furthermore, the imitation of highly violent techniques may only emerge when criminals are less willing or able to control copycats. Finally, when states are fragmented and lose coercive capacity, the space for violent groups and for privatized protection is likely to expand. For this reason, even though state fragmentation primarily affects visibility, it can also contribute to increased frequency. Considering the dynamics of violent reproduction that I have just described, the case studies in this book adopt a broad characterization of drug violence that is attuned to the multiplicity of both victims and dynamics that—even if not drug-related in the strict sense—is fueled by trafficking disputes and state antitrafficking actions.

The importance of using a broad definition of drug violence is illustrated by examining the violence that exploded in Mexico after President Felipe Calderón declared war against trafficking organizations in 2006. The government initially claimed that most violence involved criminals, but it was forced to start changing this rhetoric after the famous Mexican poet Javier Sicilia, whose son was killed in April 2011, organized a victims' movement called the Movimiento por la Paz con Justicia y Dignidad (Movement for Peace with Justice and Dignity). The massive victim gatherings promoted by Sicilia made evident that drug violence affected many civilians who died as a result of abuses of force by state officials, of extortion, of "stray bullets" (being in the wrong place at the wrong time), and of a variety of causes that transcended, but were not detached from, trafficking disputes. The next section discusses how a broader notion of violence that acknowledges these complexities is operationalized—that is, how it is assessed and measured throughout the book.

Operationalizing Frequency and Visibility

Analyzing drug violence from a minimalist viewpoint, limiting it to instances when criminals kill each other or state officials in their quest for market control, raises the problem of how to determine and count those instances accurately. This problem was painfully evident after the upsurge of violence in Mexico in 2006, which generated many controversies around efforts to count the victims of vio-lence associated with organized crime. The newspaper *Reforma* started counting crime deaths by tracking the numbers of executions by organized crime (*nar-coejecuciones*). Then, in 2011, the government released a database on homicides presumably related to organized delinquency (*Base de datos de homicidios presun-tamente relacionados con la delincuencia organizada*) that included drug-related homicides from 2006 up to 2010. In 2012, the government officially abandoned the effort to produce these statistics, acknowledging that it was very difficult to determine a drug-related murder. *Reforma* on its part also briefly stopped the counting in 2012, and then resumed it with a different methodology.[63]

The government's database made evident the difficulty and danger of assum-ing motivations and perpetrators based on characteristics or a murder in a con-text of weak justice and low-quality criminal investigations where few cases lead to a clear determination of facts or culpability in drug-related homicides.[64] Without finalized judicial investigations and sentences, it is impossible to fully determine if a given murder is associated with organized crime or not. The government database classified killings based on aspects such as the method employed in the homicide (for instance, the corpse had suffered shots from a high-caliber or long-arms weapon; showed signs of torture; was found with ele-ments characteristic of organized crime such as blankets, duct tape, or notes; had some possible link to organized crime; or some combination of these factors).[65] Victims of such homicides were assumed to be members of criminal organiza-tions. Not surprisingly, the government statistics angered relatives who found it unfair to stigmatize victims as involved in trafficking simply because they had been killed in a certain way. Human rights activists also criticized these numbers for underestimating violence perpetrated by state officials against civilians as they tried to generate results for the government's "war against drug traffickers."

The difficulties for counting drug-related deaths also exist in Colombia, where several efforts to count victims have been carried out over the course of nearly six decades of armed conflict. Government, NGOs, and academ-ics have created sophisticated databases to count violent events related to the ongoing armed conflict,[66] but given the difficulties of separating drug and polit-ical violence, many murders that can serve both drug-trafficking and political objectives have been classified as politically related. In the 1980s, an academic commission conducted one of the first comprehensive analyses of violence in Colombia and argued for the need to recognize the multiplicity of violent mani-festations, to separate different forms of violence (economic, cultural, interper-sonal, common criminal) and to recognize that political or organized violence were not necessarily the most common.[67] Later studies questioned a neat sepa-ration between criminality and political violence and of different forms of vio-lence.[68] Over the years, official data produced by the Colombian National Police, the Forensics Institute, and the Presidency of the Republic, among others, has improved, and some sources such as the National Police disaggregate aspects of deaths that could potentially help identify violence perpetrated by traffickers. All this data, however, generates the same questions that the database on organized crime–related homicides generated in Mexico: short of investigation, is it fair to assume that a homicide carried out in a certain way is drug related? How should we classify the purpose of a murder that can serve multiple objectives or benefit an actor that cannot be clearly classified? How can we acknowledge that all forms of violence can have direct and indirect effects on each other?

No easy solution is available for identifying drug- related murders even when we employ a minimalist definition. In a more expansive definition, identifying the boundaries between drug-motivated violence perpetrated by political actors, political violence perpetrated by criminals or state actors, violence aimed at protecting illegal profits, or violence perpetrated by common criminals attempting to enjoy the reputation of larger organizations is also a daunting task. To address this problem I define drug violence as *acts of lethal violence that emerge in the functioning of drug markets and can affect civilians, state officials, and criminals alike.*[69] Drug trafficking thereby becomes a lens through which to analyze the dynamics of violence in a given city without assuming that every single attack emerges directly from a trafficking dispute and involves only criminals. Instead, the framework analyzes how the interaction between criminals and the state can inhibit or fuel broader dynamics of violence. This choice may overestimate drug violence, but it helps distill the incidence of drug trafficking without conceptualizing it as independent from other violence.

To assess frequency, I use homicide rates from official government statistics: the National Statistics and Geography Institute in Mexico (INEGI) and the Forensics Institute (Medicina Legal) and the National Police in Colombia. Not all homicides in a given city can be attributed to trafficking, but given the broad definition presented above, the homicide rate is a good indicator. Raw homicide rates alone cannot be an indicator of drug violence and thus they are analyzed in tandem with all other primary and secondary materials to determine whether up and down trends in homicide can be safely attributed to drug trafficking.

Figures 2.1 and 2.2 show that the cities analyzed in this book have experienced a puzzling variation in homicide rates over time and compared with their country counterparts. To characterize high and low frequency, I compare a city's homicide rate with the national average, with its country counterparts, and with its own rate over time. This comparison is important because national and local dynamics can affect the absolute number of homicides. For example, between 1984 and 2008, on average, Culiacán had a homicide rate (29.5) that was significantly higher than Mexico's national average (15.19) but significantly lower than Cali's rate (80.0). If one takes into account the armed conflict and the fact

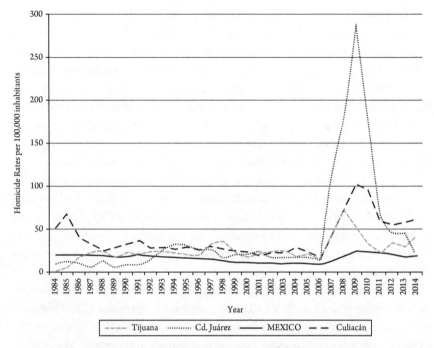

Figure 2.1 Homicide Rates 1985–2015, Mexican Cities (per 100,000 Inhabitants). Source: Author's elaboration, based on data from INEGI. My analysis formally ends in 2011 but I report more recent rates to provide a broader context.

that even within Latin America, Colombia exhibited extremely high homicide rates,[70] 29 is indeed a very high homicide rate by international standards but also compared to the country average. I operationalize extreme upward spikes of violence caused by outsourcing determining years when homicide rates in a given city grow to be more than three times the national average and any subsequent years when the rate remains this high. In this sense, "spikes" refer to extreme quantities—that is, extreme frequency of violence.

To operationalize visibility, I constructed a database on drug-related homicides coding newspaper clips in each city for selected years.[71] Given the detailed coding involved and resource constraints, the data set includes only one year for most city periods. Interviews and secondary data helped define these periods. This information then guided decisions about what years to collect information from in the data set, as the objective was to collect detailed information for at least one year in each city period. The process was dynamic and as fieldwork evolved, I made new decisions about the need to collect information for a particular year.

The data set comprises 6,497 violent events disaggregated along sixty variables. The basic selection criteria was to include events directly attributed to drug

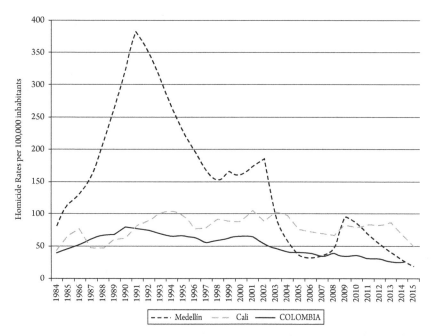

Figure 2.2 Homicide Rates 1984–2015, Colombian Cities (per 100,000 Inhabitants). Source: Author's elaboration, based on data from Medicina Legal and Policia Nacional de Colombia. My analysis formally ends in 2011, but I report more recent rates to provide a broader context.

traffickers or that could be reasonably linked to them given the methods used, the victim, or the background provided. This selection can overestimate or misclassify many events as drug related, but I decided to err on the side of overestimation by excluding only events that could unmistakably be attributed to other causes such as domestic violence or common crime. The advantage of this choice within my definition of drug violence is that it does not assume all victims to be criminals or law enforcers. News accounts do not provide an accurate source for the number and motivation of killings but do offer rather substantial information to characterize how violence is carried out. Reporting biases, incomplete information, and over- and underreporting are obvious limitations for using press sources to code violent acts. In certain areas of Mexico for instance, local journalists may be forced to report attacks by one organization in a way that contributes to bolstering its reputation to the detriment of other organizations,[72] or alternatively they may be persuaded not to report at all. Given these limitations, the data set is only one of the various sources used to characterize visible violence. The full coding criteria for the data set are presented in the Appendix.

Table 2.1 breaks down four indicators included in the data set that help characterize visibility: (1) whether criminals claim responsibility for their attacks, (2) the type of victims, (3) the number of victims per violent event, and (4) whether the methods used to perform violence are designed to draw publicity. The type of victims indicates visibility, because when criminal actors target public officials, enforcement officials, and public personalities such as journalists, they know they are exposing themselves to public attention. Coding the type of victim as an element of visibility does not assume the motivation or the audience of a violent act. For example, targeting public officials can signal a deliberate attempt to challenge the state, but state officials can also be targeted as an individual retaliation when they are supposed to protect criminals and somehow fail to deliver protection. One does not have to assume that criminals target public officials to seek state or media attention, yet it is clear that killing a rival does not expose violence in the same way that killing a politician does.[73]

The number of victims can also indicate visibility, because the more victims there are the more likely an event is going to be noticed by the public. Therefore, if criminals lose incentives to hide violence, they may also lose incentives and capacity to avoid collective attacks. It is crucial to note, however, that many visible attacks may generate only one victim, as when a single body is mutilated and exposed publicly. Yet collective attacks may also reflect identification problems that emerge when criminal markets are competitive, because if there are rivals invading territory it becomes more difficult for criminals to differentiate friend from enemy.[74] Chapter 6 shows how some massacres after 2008 in Ciudad Juárez reflected this problem: perpetrators looking for a rival, but not knowing exactly who the rival was, attacked groups in parties or even all patients in a rehabilitation center. Collective attacks can indicate visibility in the sense that criminals may avoid them when they fear state reaction or fear losing state protection. It is important to note, however, that some collective killings may be meant to be invisible: an example is the disappearance of forty-three Mexican students from the rural town of Ayotzinapa-Guerrero in September 2014, which sparked national and international protests. The students were taken away by local police during protests, and according to the official investigation, they were handed over to organized crime groups upon orders of the local mayor and his wife. Further analysis by experts from the Inter-American Commission on Human Rights (IACHR) determined that the official version of the events could not be corroborated and that officials ignored the role that the federal police and army played while witnessing the kidnapping and attacks against the students. The IACHR experts could not establish a final explanation for the events because, among other reasons, the bodies could not be found. Disappearing the students was certainly meant to make this an invisible attack, but the number of victims, as well as the display of repression before the disappearance, made it impossible to cover up the attack, even if justice continues to remain distant for the victims.[75] This example demonstrates that although the number of victims does not necessarily signal an intention to expose violence, attacks as blatant as these are difficult to ignore—and the number of victims is therefore a relevant dimension to consider.

The methods used to carry out violence expose attacks in different ways; a corpse bearing gruesome evidence of torture and mutilation is far more visible than one with a single bullet to the head. The list of methods outlined in table 2.1 was not established a priori but constructed as information was collected.

Finally, criminals' claims of responsibility can also indicate visibility, because such claims signal their interest in gaining the violent reputation associated with an attack; this is perhaps the most straightforward dimension of visibility. Yet since visibility can entail both a direct interest in exposing violence or lack of concern for attention, claiming responsibility is not necessary for an event to be visible. (Note, for example, in table 2.1. that the use of corpses with notes can be classified as high visibility both as a method and as a direct claim of

Table 2.1 **Indicators of High- and Low-Visibility Violence**

Indicator	Events Included	High, Medium, or Low Visibility
Criminals claim responsibility for attacks	Communiqués, banners, notes on corpses	HV (3)
Type of victim	Public officials, enforcement officials, journalists, human rights workers	HV (3)
	Civilians, members of DTOs	MV (2)
	Members of the underworld, "undesirables" (prostitutes, drug addicts, street criminals)	LV (1)
Number of victims per attack	Three or more	HV (3)
	One or two	LV (1)
Methods	Car bombs and explosions, mutilation or incineration exposed in public spaces, corpses with notes	HV (3)
	Combats in the street, forced disappearance in which the victim is taken in public, drive-by shooting	MV (2)
	Simple use of firearm, blunt object, or knife; strangulation	LV (1)

responsibility; in cases of corpses with notes that do not entail a clear claim of responsibility, the event can still be considered high visibility because it displays violence.)

Each of these four variables takes a value of 1, 2, or 3 for low, medium, or high visibility, as detailed in table 2.1. For each event, the scores on these variables were summed and divided by the number of variables for which there was information to standardize the measure. This yields an index ranging between 0 and 3. (Variables lacking information were coded with 0; therefore, an event with no information on any variable can have a value of 0 on the index.)

Table 2.2 presents general findings of the database, summarizing the values for an indicator in each of the city-years available. Cases of low visibility entail less deliberate "publicizing" of violence, fewer collective attacks and public targets, and no claims of responsibility. Cases of high visibility entail more publicly exposed methods, collective attacks (three or more victims), public targets (politicians, police officers, journalists), and claims of responsibility. The second-to-last column indicates how many attacks in each city had scores of 1.5–3. High-visibility city-years were defined as having more than one hundred high-visibility events. Note that periods of high visibility also tend to have a higher proportion of attacks in urban areas than in the outskirts of the city and in public spaces.[76] Events occurring in the center of cities and public spaces expose violence more than those in the outskirts of the city, or in abandoned lots.

To characterize patterns of violence in each city, I triangulate information from homicide statistics, secondary sources, human rights reports, and interviews to check the validity of all characterizations and to complement the information for years for which the data set is not available. Human rights reports and interviews with human rights workers were crucial to identify the common, but not officially reported, practice of disappearing people. Naturally, human rights reports also carry biases, but they are particularly useful for characterizing hidden violence, which is otherwise difficult to identify precisely because criminals are covering up their actions.

The consideration of homicide rates along with the data set unveils different combinations of frequency and visibility. For instance, Culiacán in 1992 and 1996 had high frequency, with homicide rates of 35 and 29 per 100,000 inhabitants, yet visibility was low (few methods for carrying out violence, few collective attacks, few public targets, and a high percentage of attacks in the outskirts of the city). These years are characterized as quiet wars (HF-LV). By contrast, Medellín in 1989 and Ciudad Juárez in 2010 present some of the highest homicide rates for all the city-years (258 and 250 respectively) and the highest values in all the indicators of visibility, thus constituting a pattern of extreme violence (HF-HV).

Table 2.2 **Acts of Visible Violence in Colombian and Mexican Cities**

City	Year	Events with High-Visibility Methods*	Collective Events (Three or More Victims)	Number of Public Targets (Politicians, Police, Journalists)	Events with Direct Claim of Responsibility[†]	High-Visibility Events	Total Violent Events
Cali	1984	4	2	2	0	28	41
Cali	1989	23	10	8	1	101	199
Cali	2009	8	3	4	0	24	79
Culiacán	1984	8	4	3	0	33	66
Culiacán	1986	15	4	12	0	60	140
Culiacán	1992	13	3	4	0	37	85
Culiacán	1996	9	1	2	0	37	120
Culiacán	2002	11	1	3	0	49	99
Culiacán	2009	71	11	8	13	213	252
Culiacán	2010	136	19	22	14	370	558
Juárez	1984	7	0	1	0	25	131
Juárez	2010	86	101	61	4	353	689
Medellín	1984	21	2	16	0	106	257
Medellín	1989	110	26	27	3	261	1281
Medellín	2009	6	11	2	0	24	73
Tijuana	1984	3	0	2	0	9	33
Tijuana	1992	5	3	1	0	21	127
Tijuana	2002	52	1	5	0	99	189
Tijuana	2010	93	20	9	9	205	405

* Car bombs and explosions, mutilation or incineration in public spaces, corpses with notes.

[†] Notes and messages do not necessarily entail a direct claim of responsibility, i.e., an organization signing. Only events with a direct claim are included.

One interesting finding of the data set, shown in Figure 2.3, is that one of the less-visible methods for killing, the simple use of firearms, is the most common, and the most visible methods, such as mutilations with notes, represent only a small proportion of total violent events, even in scenarios of high visibility. Yet studying visibility, even if high-visibility violence does not generate the most victims, is crucial because a few visible acts can affect public responses and perceptions more directly than many hidden acts of violence. For instance, the Colombian

PROPORTION OF VIOLENT EVENTS BY METHOD

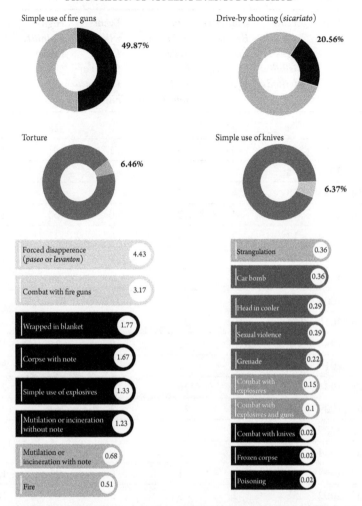

Figure 2.3 Proportion of Violent Events by Method (percentage of total events in the dataset where a method was identified n = 5,867). Source: Based on author's data set. Infograph by Nancy Durán, copyright © 2016.

government enforced extradition treaties for traffickers after the assassination of Minister of Justice Rodrigo Lara Bonilla in 1984. Likewise, the Mexican president Felipe Calderón officially deployed troops in his home state of Michoacán in September 2006, after the DTO La Familia Michoacana threw the severed heads of five bodies on the dance floor of a club along with a note that read, "La Familia doesn't kill for money, it doesn't kill women, it doesn't kill innocent people, only those who deserve to die. Everyone should know: this is divine justice."[77]

Visible violence does not need to cause the majority of victims to reflect a change in the criminals' incentives and to motivate state reactions. This also

Table 2.3 **Prominence of Newspaper Coverage of Murders by Visibility Index**

Visibility Index	Reported on Front Page			Reported in First Section		
	No	Yes	Total	No	Yes	Total
0	372	0	372	327	45	372
%	95.3	0		87.9	12.1	
1	2944	7	2951	2685	266	2951
%	99.76	0.24		90.99	9.01	
1.5	906	13	919	821	98	919
%	98.59	1.41		89.34	10.66	
2	862	14	876	741	135	876
%	98.40	1.60		84.59	15.41	
3	121	8	129	116	13	129
%	93.8	6.20		89.92	10.08	
Total	5205	42	5247	4690	557	5247
%	99.2	0.8		89.38	10.62	

means that most victims of drug violence can be routinely ignored and a relatively small number of attacks can create an image of extreme brutality. The common stigma associated with victims of drug violence by the media and the general public (they died because they deserved it or because they were engaged in something bad) perpetuates the invisibility of many victims of violence, the creation of what Noam Chomsky has labeled as "worthy" and "unworthy" victims.[78] The key point to highlight is that the worthiness of victims is not only the result of media manipulation but also of how violence is carried out. To further illustrate this point, table 2.3 illustrates how visibility impacts media coverage, by comparing events covered in the first page or first section of newspapers when they first occurred, across levels of visibility. The visibility index has been aggregated into categories for ease of interpretation. The results show that even though a small fraction of events were covered on the front page, visible events were more likely to receive prime coverage.

Conclusion

The multidimensional approach to drug violence captures complex violent behaviors that force us to transcend a predominant focus on extreme violence.

As discussed throughout this chapter, visible cases are as puzzling as those where criminals seem to be peaceful. Visibility has several implications for the analysis of criminal violent behavior, as well as methodological and policy implications that will become more evident throughout the book.

Visibility shows that low-violence statistics sometimes mask situations where criminals have not abandoned violence altogether but rather have engaged in less-visible forms of violence. Low visibility should not be equated with the absence of violent criminality because peaceful situations may result instead from the dominance of strong criminal powers or from symbiotic relations between states and criminals when the latter prefer to hide violence. While considering visibility we can also better understand citizen and state reactions to violence. States and citizens typically react more strongly to visible violence. Quiet wars may not generate strong state and civil society reactions, even if they produce many victims, because they may not instill a sense of insecurity and victimization in the population or represent a threat to national security for government officials. The public can often normalize low-visibility violence. By contrast, states and citizens may react more strongly to visible violence, further reproducing it because state interventions, especially militarized responses to criminality, may generate more insecurity. It is possible, however, that the public outrage generated by visible violence can motivate civilians to mobilize, demand state action, and mitigate the stigma that often falls on those who die in criminal violence.

Taking visibility seriously requires that evaluations of drug violence do more than analyze homicide rates. It calls for a diversification of sources of information and an attention to how violence is performed. If criminals successfully eliminate all evidence of a criminal act, it may never be recorded. Data on disappearances and human rights reports are essential to document low visibility, but that information may emerge long after the violence occurs. The characterization of violence may become more time-consuming if it requires collecting and analyzing information from multiple sources, but doing so is critical for understanding the impacts and dynamics of violence.

The conceptual discussion in this chapter suggests that policies aimed at reducing violence should start with analyses that encompass varied manifestations of violence and pay attention to apparently peaceful situations. As I discuss in the book's conclusion in more detail, one option to rationalize drug policy and improve interventions to reduce violence would be to target law enforcement resources toward the most violent consequences of drug trafficking,[79] yet for this option to be effective, it is necessary to consider that many difficult security situations can be overlooked if authorities focus only on the most visible forms of violence.

The following chapters will show that the disaggregation of violent behavior reveals varied and complex interactions between criminals and state actors.

Only by unpacking the nature of the state security apparatus and of the power relations among criminal groups can we understand those varied interactions. Before turning to detailed case studies that develop the theory, the next chapter discusses the evolution of drug trafficking in Colombia and Mexico framed as a discussion about the potential tradeoff between a state's coercive capacity and a state's autonomy from criminal influence. The chapter emphasizes the complex interactions between states and criminals at the national level but also explores why a subnational perspective is necessary to understand violence.

3

Democratization and State Capacity to Control Violence

Since the 1990s, Latin American countries have experienced two crucial and paradoxical processes. On the one hand, the region has become more democratic, seeing the establishment of competitive elections and civil liberties. On the other, there has been an upsurge in violence with complex roots and dynamics, which is related in several countries to criminal groups and illicit markets. Although Latin America makes up only 9 percent of the world's population, about 30 percent of homicides in the world take place there, so it ranks far above regions with armed conflicts such as Africa and the Middle East. While there is wide intraregional variation both in the quality of democracies[1] and in the dynamics of violence, the convergence of these two processes generates a troubling question: have states with stronger—although imperfect—democratic institutions become less capable of enforcing the law? In Colombia[2] and Mexico this question takes on significant relevance because since the late 1980s both countries have witnessed crucial transformations in their political regimes and also sharp variation in drug violence, with higher violence loosely coinciding with crucial institutional changes.

This chapter argues that democratization and institutional change may potentially—though not inevitably—increase criminal violence. Building on the book's central argument that the visibility of violence increases when the state is fragmented and thus less efficient in enforcing the law or in reliably protecting criminals, I argue that democratizing states that are becoming more fragmented may face a trade-off: while increasing their autonomy from criminal influences they may lose their ability to control violence and produce order. To put it differently, democratizing states may be less likely to be symbiotic with criminal interests but also less capable of controlling their violence. Throughout this chapter I build on Theda Skocpol's and Peter Evans's definitions of autonomy as the ability of the state to make policy decisions independent from social actors.[3]

This argument does not imply that the only tool that states have to control violence is by corruptly accommodating criminals and maintaining authoritarian structures, for two reasons. First, democratizing states may be less capable of enforcing the law in terms of controlling violence, but their enforcement agencies may become more professional and accountable. In other words, controlling violence is one critical dimension of enforcing the rule of law, but it is not the only one. Authoritarian states may be better at controlling violence but not at advancing the rule of law more broadly. Second, democratizing states are not necessarily less corrupt. They are simply less prone to being taken over by criminal interests.

Building on this argument, the chapter presents an overview of drug trafficking and the responses to it by state institutions in Colombia and Mexico that illustrates why national processes and policies as well as international drug policies are essential but insufficient to explain local dynamics of violence. Thus, it sets the stage for the city case studies and the subnational comparisons developed in subsequent chapters. This overview also shows how criminal violence and state confrontation with criminal organizations may contribute to the growth of the state security apparatus over time, thus building the state in a process that echoes Charles Tilly's classic idea about the state-making potential of war.

The chapter first reflects on how to conceptualize state capacity to control violence in contexts of institutional change. Next, it explains how drug trafficking in Colombia consolidated within a fragmented state and how it has evolved through complex interactions with the armed conflict. Over time, the fight against drugs and conflict contributed to increase the state coercive capacities and shaped criminal behavior, although drug trafficking persists and local state capacity is uneven. It goes on to describe how drug trafficking in Mexico became consolidated through attachment to the centralized one-party rule of the Institutional Revolutionary Party (PRI), and then changed over time as democratization and institutional transformations revamped the relationship between criminals and state, reaching an extreme condition of disorder where state capacity to enforce the law remains elusive.

State Capacity and Autonomy from Criminal Actors

Chapter 1 argued that a cohesive state that controls violence more efficiently could, paradoxically, also provide predictable protection for criminal organizations. Institutional changes that redistribute power among state elites—such as democratization or bureaucratic reforms—may reduce state cohesion.

Democratizing states are less cohesive than authoritarian ones and therefore less likely to control violence or to protect criminals in a stable fashion. Authoritarian states can be more cohesive and thus more able to establish a monopoly of force, but they can also be less autonomous from criminal influence—that is, more prone to be constrained in their policy decisions by criminal interests, especially when they are facing a powerful criminal counterpart. The argument does not imply that states simply react to violence or solely act as regulators of criminal activity: states shape criminal activity both by informally regulating it and by directly intervening in crime control. Rather, it underscores that how a state shapes crime is not only a function of its decision to protect or fight criminals, or of its decision about how to fight criminals and design crime interventions, but also of the power relationships underpinning such decisions.

One caveat is important here: not all authoritarian states are cohesive, and not all democratic states are fragmented. Many African states in the 1990s fit the definition of an authoritarian regime, yet they were very fragmented in their coercive capacity.[4] Additionally, as this book's definition of state security apparatus emphasizes, bureaucratic dynamics can alter power distribution even in authoritarian states, as occurred in Mexico, where power was fragmenting in multiple ways before there was party alternation at the national level. This does not undermine the gist of this chapter's argument, which is that regimes with fragmented power are less capable of enforcing coercion and that democracies tend to multiply channels of power by introducing electoral competition, restrictions on the use of force, and institutional checks and balances—conditions not readily available in authoritarian regimes. Ultimately, as the rest of this book contends, national dynamics are one part of the story: to fully understand criminal violence one needs to scale down from the national to the local, and analyze the interplay between politics and bureaucratic dynamics in the security realm.

The idea that democracy, and particularly elections, can erode state coercive capacity, has been prominent in some analysis of democratic transition and civil war. One strand of literature has analyzed how democratic transition can lead to increases in violence, arguing that when central authority collapses, actors that were formerly intimidated may gain space while states lose capacity to repress, as occurred with the collapse of the Soviet Union.[5] The literature on civil wars has further disentangled multiple mechanisms connecting elections and violence.[6] It has argued that violence can be used by armed actors to force allegiance among voters or potential political allies, and thus advance electoral interests, or that results of elections can reveal politico-ideological preferences that are then used to violently target real and perceived enemies. Elections can also motivate violence among those who perceive the electoral process as illegitimate, and in the wake of fragile peace agreements, winners of elections can use violence to oppress groups they still fear.[7] A growing strand of research has shown that both in war and peacetime state actors empowered by elections, but also uncertain of their political tenure, can tolerate or directly support the action of violent nonstate actors, or certain forms of communal violence, if it benefits them electorally.[8]

Of the mechanisms suggested in the literature connecting democratization and violence, three seem particularly relevant for the study of the relations between criminal actors and the state. Democracy can complicate the state's capacity to use force; it may also multiply the channels through which state actors deal with nonstate opponents; and it also provides nonstate actors more opportunities to access the state. The paradox for criminal actors, which are not necessarily opposing states ideologically as rebels or other social actors do and therefore are more likely to seek state protection, is that even if they gain channels to access the state, protection also becomes less predictable. Criminals may find new channels to gain politicians' protection, but they can also become more vulnerable to other politicians, thus making violence a more attractive option to influence state policy. In the case of criminal actors, unlike rebels in civil wars, violence is not likely to result from the mobilization of particular grievances for electoral purposes and is less likely to be related to attempts to shape civilian ideological support. But as in civil war, it can be used to force or gain candidates or elected politicians' support. The state capacity to control violence is thus further complicated because some politicians can benefit from the funding provided by illegal actors in campaigns. In return they may protect their criminal funders by not enforcing the law against them, they may allow criminals to carry out some violence, or they can selectively enforce the law to punish political opponents. The argument in this chapter builds on these insights, discussing how democratization and institutional change affect law enforcement and state autonomy, something existing theoretical developments do not delve into.

Literature analyzing the paradox of increasing violence in an era of democratization in Latin America also highlights the possible trade-off between the state ability to control violence and state autonomy from criminal influences as democratization advances. Enrique Desmond Arias and Daniel Goldstein coined the term "violent pluralism" precisely to denote that multiple violent actors operate in Latin American democracies and maintain diverse and changing connections with state institutions;[9] one thus can say that no single violent actor is controlling the state, but multiple actors use varied channels to obtain benefits. Douglas North, John Joseph Wallis, and Barry Weingast also present an argument about why there can be a trade-off between autonomy and coercive capacity: they contend that states discourage violence by providing opportunities for elites to access higher rents under peace than under conditions of violence.[10] These arrangements may thus reduce violence but do not necessarily bring elites (or criminals, for the purposes of this analysis) under direct government control. Mexico under PRI rule illustrates this: the state had authority to regulate criminals but was unlikely to confront them.

Following these insights we can assert that an authoritarian and centralized state that decides to regulate criminals' violent behavior without necessarily confronting criminals can reduce its autonomy. This is not necessarily because democratic states are less corrupt than authoritarian ones, but rather it is because, along the lines of Mancur Olson's stationary and roving bandits model,[11] in authoritarian states corruption networks can be more centralized and coherent than in democratic states. Corrupting influences in democratic states may permeate the state at different levels and even impose contradictory demands on state actors. Furthermore, considering that (as argued in chapter 1) violence is the joint result of state cohesion and criminal competition, if states want to regulate violence they may become stakeholders in one criminal group's hegemony or, at least, in an equilibrium between a relative few crime groups. Autonomy is thus reduced, because state structures as a whole may establish symbiotic relations with one or a few, rather than multiple, criminals.

This argument is aligned with works showing that authoritarian states may need to either negotiate with or tolerate local elites or nonstate actors in order to maintain national unity and shore up their hierarchical control. This occurred in cases such as the Congo under Mobutu Sese Seko's authoritarian rule, the Soviet Union after Nikita Krushev's decision to eliminate Stalinist-type repression, or even during the PRI's rule in Mexico.[12] To put it another way, that centralized states can better control violence does not mean that they do away with violent actors altogether or that they do not need to negotiate their power. Rather, it means that state actors are in a stronger position to regulate, oversee, and dictate the terms of interaction with potentially violent actors while becoming stakeholders of those actors' power.

Institutional transformations are not the only channel through which states lose coercive capacity, and although closely connected, state capacity and democracy do not always vary together. As William Reno argues in the Congo's case, declining international support or economic crises can also force states to change how they deal with societal actors and especially with regional elites and potential violent challengers.[13] Similarly, Kent Eaton argues that in Latin America, in addition to democratization, neoliberalism and decentralization also have challenged the state: by changing what it does in relation to the market and by redistributing responsibilities for service provision.[14] In the security realm, this has meant redistributing responsibilities for law enforcement. While such processes per se are not the focus of this book, they are consistent with the cohesion-fragmentation argument just proposed: economic crises or waning international support can decrease the ability to control violence when these variables force states to fragment and decentralize patronage networks, allowing local elites a free reign in regulating illicit trades because the central state can no longer fund and sustain the cooptation of those elites. In other words, besides institutional change, other economic and social processes could undermine coercion when those processes fragment state power.

A full theorization of the connections between international drug policy and state cohesion and capacity supersedes the objectives of the book, yet because drug traffickers operate within a global prohibition regime, a brief discussion of how foreign drug policy affects state cohesion is warranted. Prohibition as a whole has increased the vulnerability of state security agencies and of politicians to corruption, and it has also made states more prone to violate human rights and to privilege the use of force, thus reducing both state capacity and the quality of democracy. These effects permeate both democratic and authoritarian regimes, as racialized mass incarceration in a democracy like the United States illustrates.[15] Yet corruption and militarized policing vary across cohesive and fragmented states, and three processes may explain how foreign influence mitigates or exacerbates state fragmentation.

The first process is when the priorities of foreign powers—and more precisely, the priorities of the United States, the foremost enforcer of the prohibition regime—change, leading to the stepping up of pressure over other countries. This pressure consequently reduces the subordinate state's ability to sustain promises of protection to criminals or unleashes conflicts between enforcement actors within a country, thus increasing fragmentation and the potential for violence. For instance, during the Cold War drug policy was not the first priority for the United States, and drug trafficking could even be tolerated if it served Cold War objectives.[16] In Mexico, however, changing Cold War priorities led the United States to step up counterdrug initiatives, which in turn contributed to reducing the state capacity of the Mexican state to protect criminals in the mid-1980s.[17] The second process relates to how international pressure can increase fragmentation when foreign aid is given to some state agencies, deemed to be more trustworthy, at the expense of other agencies, creating conflicts between state institutions. By contrast, foreign aid and intervention can increase state cohesion when aid is targeted at particular enforcement agencies that grow, expand, and become a node of state enforcement, often privileging coercion over other aspects of law enforcement—as has been the case with the US-supported expansion of the Colombian police and military. The last process explaining the relation between foreign pressure and state fragmentation is when different foreign policy agendas merge—as occurred with counterterrorism, counterinsurgency, and antinarcotics agendas in the United States after the al-Qaeda terrorist attacks of September 11, 2001 (9/11). This may increase cohesion by reducing channels of bureaucratic tension both at the recipient and sending ends of foreign aid. International drug policy tends to simplify complex realities and build up coercion at the expense of justice, development, and the reduction of socioeconomic inequalities; yet as the processes briefly described show, these prohibition-driven problems can sometimes mitigate or exacerbate state fragmentation. The relation between state cohesion and foreign drug policy is a two-way street, and the implementation of antinarcotics aid also changes depending on domestic configurations of state power and on foreign perceptions of how "collaborative" domestic elites are.[18]

Keeping in mind that multiple forces affect state cohesion but that democratization is a prominent one of these forces, one crucial implication of the argument is that the absence of violence does not necessarily equate absence of criminality or a triumph of the state in controlling criminals, because peaceful scenarios sometimes result from criminals' regulated behavior. This does not negate that peaceful scenarios under cohesive states can result from the elimination or significant reduction of drug trafficking. Indeed, if authoritarian states decide to crush criminals, they can do it more efficiently (and potentially more ruthlessly). This occurred at the beginning of the Cuban Revolution, when well-established trafficking networks based in Cuba were forced to relocate, partially in response to the revolutionary government's commitment to create a "new man" with higher moral standards that ceded no ground to drug use or trafficking.[19] Similarly, an anti-opium campaign motivated by ideology but also by a nationalistic sentiment that defined drug trafficking as a foreign imposition was initiated in China after the 1949 Communist Revolution.[20] The initial antidrug campaign was not entirely successful because the Communist regime still had other political priorities and was not completely consolidated.[21] A second campaign in 1952 was far more efficient, as the central government acquired greater control over local governments, increased its resources, and used its mass-mobilization machinery to carry out an antidrug campaign that drastically reduced opium trafficking and use,[22] displacing it to other Southeast Asian countries like Burma (today's Myanmar). These examples illustrate that centralized authoritarian governments can carry out antidrug operations more swiftly and rapidly than fragmented democratic states. Yet, given the economic and coercive benefits that can be gained from tolerating criminals, enforcement and coercion are likely to go hand in hand with collusion. Furthermore, because successful operations displace rather than completely eliminate drug trafficking, even after successful antidrug campaigns, drug trafficking can reemerge—as indeed seemed to have occurred in China after the 1980s. The key point of this discussion is that authoritarian and cohesive states have different resources with which to confront or regulate criminality than do democratic and fragmented states. Yet because governments' coercive efforts to attack drug trafficking often coexist with collusion and corruption, a peaceful scenario in a cohesive state can often reflect a form of collusion.

A second crucial implication of this chapter's argument is that violence does not necessarily reflect state absence or state collapse, but rather it follows from transformations in the interaction between criminals and states. Of course, in rural isolated communities, violence and criminal control may reflect lack of state presence, state collapse, or criminal monopolies,[23] but in many other places, including the cities analyzed in this book, violence cannot be equated with state absence. Violence thus not only reflects an erosion of the state's coercive capacity but also a fragmentation of the channels through which the state deals with criminal actors.

Despite the potential trade-off between control of violence and autonomy from criminal influence in cohesive states, some theoretical reasons explain why we cannot simply assert that authoritarian or corrupt states are better in controlling criminality than democratic ones. First among these reasons is that, during democratization, states may increase their law enforcement capacities. Daniel Brinks identifies two dimensions of law enforcement: horizontal (regulating relations between citizens) and vertical (regulating relations between the state and citizens).[24] He argues that democratizing states can improve vertical law enforcement, as leaders become more accountable to their citizens and less likely to repress them. Yet states may face more limitations in horizontal law enforcement, precisely because of the reduced capacities for repression, thus explaining increases in violence. To put it differently, democratizing states do not inevitably become less capable of enforcing the law altogether, but they do become less capable—or willing—to coordinate enforcement and to control violence generated by nonstate violence specialists.

A cohesive authoritarian state does not rely on modern, professionalized, enforcement agencies to control violence. Conversely, democratic states can progressively—but not necessarily—acquire professional enforcement agencies and more accountability over enforcement actions, but because of fragmentation, enforcement may be less effective. As a result, attempts at eliminating criminals through enforcement operations in democratizing states may be difficult even if the attempts are properly designed or targeted, because coordination and implementation of anticrime policies are more difficult in a fragmented state. Democratizing states cannot simply abandon the idea of confronting criminals, but they require more careful planning in doing so. Democratizing states not only need to design good anticrime interventions, but they also need to put extra effort in coordinating those interventions and in promoting other dimensions of law enforcement (not simply eliminating illegal actors): otherwise violence may be exacerbated by anticrime efforts, as occurred in Mexico after 2006.

A second reason that explains why we cannot simply assert that authoritarian or corrupt states are better in controlling criminality than democratic ones, or believe that it is better so simply tolerate criminals, is that democratic states are not necessarily free from corruption, but rather less likely to be coherently permeated by, and protective of, criminals. As a result not all states can successfully use corruption to control violence. Democratization can increase opportunities for criminals to access and influence the state, although it can also multiply the actors willing to prosecute criminals. Collusion in democratizing states is thus unlikely to bring about stable violence reduction pacts. Yet, because completely abolishing drug trafficking may be an unrealistic objective as long as it remains a profitable illegal enterprise, states may need to consider the possibility of negotiating with—not tolerating—criminal actors, just like they negotiate with rebels in civil wars. Here again, the decision for democratizing states may not be simply about the pros or cons of negotiating but rather about assessing how to successfully coordinate such negotiations.

With these caveats in mind, I next discuss how the potential trade-off between controlling criminal violence and maintaining autonomy from criminal influences has shaped institutional transformations and the evolution of criminal violence in Colombia and Mexico. Changes in political competition, institutional reforms, and anticorruption policies have made criminal-state interactions unpredictable, generating incentives for criminals to use visible violence and reducing governments' ability to carry out successful anticrime policies as democratization advances. In the long run the key challenge for democratizing states is to build up their broad enforcement abilities and to carefully plan crime-control strategies to compensate for their coordination problems. As Arias and Goldstein contend, there is no easy path to reduce violence, because violence is not simply the result of state failure or of disorder.[25]

Drug Trafficking and Institutional Transformation in Colombia

The history of drug trafficking in Colombia dates back to the 1960s when marijuana production emerged as a highly profitable commodity.[26] As marijuana profits started to decline in the late 1970s and early 1980s, the country became a major player in the world's cocaine-trafficking chain, representing the main source of cocaine bound for the United States. Over the following five decades, the organization, geography, and behavior of illicit drug markets has been shaped by the policies enacted by the Colombian government and largely determined by US enforcement priorities and aid flows. The coexistence between a

long-standing armed conflict and drug trafficking in Colombia has created particular challenges in enforcement operations and complex interactions between
various nonstate armed actors. In this context, regime transformations and local
power dynamics have shaped the violent behavior of trafficking groups; because
drug trafficking emerged within a fragmented state that was democratizing, its
initial potential for violence, especially visible violence, was far greater than in
Mexico. The challenge of violence, in turn, has had greater state-making potential in Colombia, while forcing constant institutional transformations, especially
in the police and the military.

The Consolidation of Drug Trafficking and Democratization (1980–1998)

In the early 1970s, marijuana became a highly profitable and often violent market[27] that infused the economy with extraordinary amounts of cash. In an effort
to capture these revenue streams, the government eased controls on exchange
houses known to deal dollars derived from the marijuana trade. This process,
colloquially known as the *ventanilla siniestra* (sinister window), allowed marijuana profits to enter the legal economy. In the late 1970s, policies of the government of President Julio César Turbay (1978–1982), in tandem with increasing
marijuana production in Mexico, led to the decline of the *bonanza marimbera*
(marijuana boom), thus illustrating how drug-enforcement policies can generate balloon effects within and across countries: the deactivation or elimination
of trafficking groups or crops in one location can be offset by its emergence in
another. As Paul Gootenberg, a prominent historian of cocaine has carefully
documented, while marijuana production lost prominence, Colombians' centrality in cocaine trafficking skyrocketed as they replaced the Bolivian, Cuban,
Chilean, and Peruvian cocaine smuggling networks that dominated a nascent
illegal cocaine trade in the 1950s and 1960s.[28] Interestingly, cocaine trafficking
did not develop mainly through the marijuana trade networks but through other
illegal traditions such as cigarette smuggling.[29]

By the early 1980s, two organizations dominated the international cocaine
market: the Rodriguez Orejuela brothers (the Cali DTO), and Pablo Escobar
and the Ochoa brothers (in the Medellín DTO). These two organizations fed a
stereotype that became dominant among enforcement officials and journalists:
that of drug-trafficking organizations as "cartels" that were centralized, hierarchical, and omnipotent in their control of the illegal market. Over time, it has
become clear that these organizations operated more like networks than like
highly centralized and organized groups, and thus, the label "cartel" is often mis-
leading, as Michael Kenney has documented.[30] Yet these pioneer organizations

were very powerful and more centralized than the drug-trafficking groups of the twenty-first century.

In the 1980s, when cocaine networks consolidated, Colombia was not yet the world's main producer of coca leaves. Traffickers processed coca grown in Peru and Bolivia and the potential cocaine production from Colombian coca was low. As shown in Figure 3.1, coca cultivation and cocaine production peaked after early trafficking groups were dismantled in the 1990s in response to eradication efforts conducted in Bolivia and Peru. Thus, the influx of drug-trafficking resources was huge in the 1980s and 1990s, but the power achieved by traffickers and the violence they generated in these early stages did not simply result from the illegal market's size but from the interaction between a new and shocking stream of resources that empowered different sectors of the society, together with a democratizing political system.

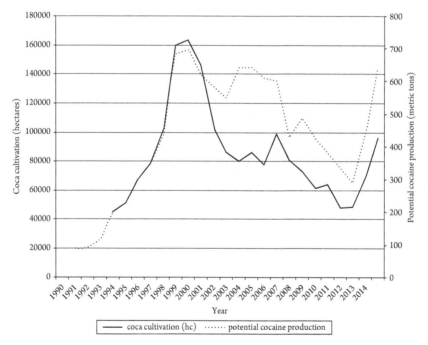

Figure 3.1 Coca Cultivation and Potential Cocaine Production in Colombia.
Source: Author's elaboration. Cocaine production refers to cocaine hydrochloride. Based on UNODC data from *Colombia Monitoreo de Cultivos de Coca 2010*, June 2011; *Colombia Monitoreo de Cultivos de Coca 2014*, July 2015; *Colombia Monitoreo de Cultivos de Coca 2015*, June 2016. Coca cultivation between 1994 and 1998 is from the US Department of State, cited in the UNODC 2010 report. Methodologies for the calculation of both coca leaf acreage and cocaine production have changed over time, as well as the technologies for cultivation and production. This complicates strict comparisons, although the trends with UNODC data appear consistent over time.

Early cocaine traffickers consolidated their power while the political system was democratizing, setting the stage for a highly violent and unstable interaction between the state and criminals. For almost two decades (1958–1974), the political system in Colombia had functioned under a power-sharing agreement known as Frente Nacional (National Front). Designed as a conflict-mitigation strategy, this agreement evenly distributed electoral posts and bureaucracies between the two main political parties (the Liberal and Conservative Party) that had been the center of a civil war since the 1950s. The scheme excluded other political forces, and thus, even though the country was democratic in a minimalist sense (there were regular elections) and more democratic than other Latin American countries at the time, there were serious restrictions on electoral participation. In 1974, the National Front came to an end, thus paving the way for further democratization to take place. The government of President Belisario Betancourt (1982–1986) initiated a decentralization process that established the popular election of mayors and effectively reshaped the country's territorial bases of power.[31]

The institutional reforms of the 1980s fragmented political power in Colombia, creating contradictory opportunities for emerging traffickers: on the one hand, power fragmentation increased opportunities for them to access the political system, but on the other, it empowered politicians willing to oppose their growing influence, thus making state protection unpredictable. This contradiction is illustrated vividly by the political behavior of traffickers such as Pablo Escobar and Carlos Lehder, who formed their own political movements. As explained in chapter 4, Pablo Escobar ran as a candidate for Congress and was elected as an alternate member for the Lower Chamber of Congress in 1983. His infamous attempt to become a politician illustrated the doors that democratization was opening for traffickers to access the state. Yet the fierce opposition by other recently formed political actors (such as the party Nuevo Liberalismo) to Escobar's political strategy reflected that democratization could also undermine traffickers' interests.

Criminals Confront the State (1984–1993)

The state's difficulties while confronting and protecting criminals paved the way for one of the most visible manifestations of violence in Colombia's history—the so-called narcoterrorist war. Justice Minister Rodrigo Lara Bonilla, a member of Nuevo Liberalismo, became a leading voice in opposition to Escobar's participation in Congress and championed an enforcement campaign against the Medellín DTO. His efforts led to Escobar's ousting from Congress in 1983 and to the discovery and destruction of a vast cocaine-processing facility known as Tranquilandia, located in the southern Amazon region, in 1984.

In Tranquilandia, the Medellín DTO established housing, landing strips, and laboratories for processing coca leaf that was grown in Peru and Bolivia (later the organization expanded coca cultivation in Colombia). At the time, the operation constituted the largest drug bust ever.[32] In retaliation for these actions, Escobar ordered the assassination of Lara Bonilla on April 30, 1984, and the Colombian government in turn sought to enforce extradition treaties against the nation's drug traffickers. Since it was first approved in 1979, the extradition of Colombian nationals to the United States had been controversial, and President Betancourt had refused to extradite any Colombian nationals in 1982 and 1983, mostly arguing sovereignty issues; his position changed radically after Lara Bonilla's death and extraditions were actively enforced after 1985. Ending extradition became the end goal of the traffickers' violence and war against the state. In 1986, the Medellín DTO created Los Extraditables, an armed branch aimed at fighting extradition. In the following years, narcoterrorist violence left thousands of civilians and police members, hundreds of judges, and several prominent politicians and journalists dead, and was imprinted in the memories of Colombians with terrorist attacks such as the bombing of a major national newspaper and the headquarters of Colombia's civilian intelligence agency, DAS (Security Administration Department).

Lara Bonilla's assassination led the government to define drug traffickers, especially the Medellín DTO, as a national security threat. Yet the state security apparatus was weak and unprepared to face the threat. Police forces were unprofessional—plagued by corruption, inefficiency, and lack of coordination. The state, even though potentially more autonomous from criminal influence than a more authoritarian state, had little capacity to effectively enforce the law, reassert its coercive capacity, and contain the violence of the emerging narcoterrorist threat. It was also caught within the narrow range of options privileged by US antinarcotics support, aimed at eliminating drug supply through repression. This did not mean that state actions were inconsequential, and indeed the first years of heightened drug enforcement after Lara Bonilla's assassination shaped criminal behavior but without containing criminal incentives to display violence and to attack the state.

In 1983, General Procurator Carlos Mauro Hoyos expressed that extreme fragmentation in state enforcement was a grave hindrance for the fight against drug trafficking in Colombia. According to Hoyos,

> The judicial police lack coordination. The law gives the procurator the mission of overseeing and coordinating the judicial police, but the reality is that this police is made of autonomous contingents that answer to their own commands and that come from the police, the Security Administration Department (DAS), from the procurator's office

itself. . . . As long as there is no specialized policing body responding to one command and with unity in terms of hierarchy, direction, and policy, and as long as it does not have specialization in the drug-trafficking function, . . . we won't be able to have a policing mechanism that corresponds to the gravity and urgency of our problems.[33]

Thus, although it had been nominally centralized since 1950, the Colombian police department lacked the capacity and coordination to combat the threat that had emerged from drug-trafficking violence by the mid-1980s.

The first governments that confronted the visible attacks by the Medellín DTO faced a dilemma: they could not use a police force perceived to be corrupt and inefficient, and thus they attempted to use the military against drug traffickers, but the military did not warm to the idea of participating in antinarcotic responsibilities, especially in urban areas.[34] The military preferred its role in combating guerrillas in the context of the armed conflict that had affected the country since the 1960s. In the early 1980s, trafficking organizations were relatively independent from the leftist guerrillas, and thus, the military did not see the combat against drug trafficking as a way to achieve the greater objective of eliminating guerrillas.

Early drug traffickers interacted with armed actors in varied ways. Traffickers sometimes hired guerrillas to provide security for coca crops,[35] but paradoxically, they also allied with, and actively supported, paramilitary groups that opposed guerrillas and protected landowners. As traffickers accumulated more land they had a stake in preventing the guerrillas' land-redistribution objectives. One precursor in mixing trafficking violence and antiguerrilla actions was the group Muerte a Secuestradores (Death to Kidnappers), formed after guerrillas from the M-19 (19th of April Movement) kidnapped the daughter of Jorge Luis Ochoa, a leader of the Medellín DTO. Paramilitaries, traffickers, landowners, and sectors of the military also allied strategically against guerrillas,[36] but alliances were unstable and changed constantly, contributing to a general fragmentation of illicit violent actors. Despite these complex connections between trafficking and armed groups, until the 1980s the government still perceived conflict and trafficking as separate threats, and (as noted) the military was reluctant to fully engage in the fight against drug trafficking. This situation eventually changed in the mid-1990s.

In 1986, as narcoterrorism intensified, President Virgilio Barco (1986–1990) centralized antinarcotics responsibilities in the military because he did not trust the nation's police forces. The decision generated discontent in the military, conflicts with police forces, and a grim record of human rights violations, especially in the urban operations carried out in Medellín in the late 1980s, which, rather than controlling criminal groups, contributed to their fragmentation.

The security apparatus of the democratizing state grew increasingly fragmented and weak in the wake of political conflicts, corruption, and lack of capacity in enforcement agencies. The first election of local mayors in 1988 added complexity to the decision-making process in security policies. Furthermore, the Barco government adopted a political arrangement known as the "government-opposition scheme" that further complicated the government's capacity to coordinate its security programs. As explained by a defense minister from the period, the scheme was aimed at protecting political opposition by clearly separating public posts that belonged to the opposition and the government, but it ended up preventing the creation of political alliances that could approve any new policy proposal during a convoluted security period that required rapid, but difficult, decisions.[37] Paradoxically, as the state was working to strengthen its security apparatus, it was also facing a huge challenge in its capacity to control violence.

Problems generated by the military deployments, particularly mounting complaints about human rights violations and corruption, led President Barco to experiment with an alternative enforcement scheme in 1989, creating "islands of efficiency" such as the Cuerpo Élite (Elite Police Force) within the weak and delegitimized police. This approach also proved limited when scandals of corruption and abuse plagued the Cuerpo Élite. By the end of Barco's term, Colombia was undergoing one of the most violent crises in its history, and the narcoterrorist war had taken a more extreme turn in 1989 with the assassination of Luis Carlos Galán, the presidential candidate of the Nuevo Liberalismo party, who actively opposed drug traffickers and Pablo Escobar.

Constitutional Reform in the Midst of Crisis

In 1990 César Gaviria, appointed by the Nuevo Liberalismo party to succeed Luis Carlos Galán as its candidate, was elected president by popular vote. Gaviria summoned a constitutional assembly and eventually sanctioned a new constitution in 1991, thus completing a political process initiated during the Barco administration. The 1991 Constitution introduced critical political changes and transformations in the structure of law enforcement, such as the creation of the Attorney General's Office and the introduction of multiple mechanisms protecting individual rights. Crucially, the Constitution also banned the extradition of Colombian nationals, and thus it removed the motivation for the visible violence of the narcoterrorist campaign, although inter- and intraorganizational disputes continued to generate violence.[38]

The profound institutional changes in 1991 enabled Gaviria's government to experiment with specialized police units again, with the expectation that new institutional checks and balances would prevent abuses like the ones that occurred with the Cuerpo Élite.[39] In 1993, the government created a joint military-police command called the Search Bloc (Bloque de Búsqueda) to dismantle big trafficking organizations and specifically to hunt down Pablo Escobar. This unit received ample military training and funding from the United States[40] and also facilitated the coordination and channeling of US aid, which up to that moment had been fragmented between several US and Colombian enforcement agencies.[41] The Search Bloc eventually brought Escobar down in 1993 and its actions were presented as a success story for Colombian law enforcement. The Search Bloc received support and information from Escobar's trafficking enemies, so the success was not simply derived from effective enforcement. The operations against Escobar reshaped the panorama of trafficking groups and illustrated the crucial role that US support and drug policies play in shaping the organization of illicit markets.

The model set up with the Search Bloc became a blueprint for subsequent enforcement operations. In fact, another Search Bloc was set up to dismantle the Cali DTO, but due to pervasive police corruption, it depended more on the army than on the police (as will be explained in chapter 5). The impact of the Search Bloc's operations on violence in Cali was thus different than in Medellín partially because the reaccommodation of trafficking actors after the main DTO was dismantled was not as radical in Cali. The operation of this new Search Bloc illustrates how, even though framed by national antinarcotic strategies, drug traffickers' behavior and their relationships with local and national governments varied across regions; the impact of enforcement operations also varied depending on how local and national governments coordinated their efforts.

The Transformation of the National Police

In the aftermath of Pablo Escobar's death, the state gained cohesion through the reform of the National Police. The national and international pressure to dismantle the Cali DTO increased as its corruptive power became increasingly evident, even though the organization did not pose a security threat similar to the Medellín DTO. During the presidency of Ernesto Samper (1994–1998), the extensive links between the Cali DTO and sectors of the police and the political class came to light; accusations emerged that Samper's presidential campaign had received funds from the Rodríguez Orejuela brothers, drug lords in the Cali DTO (as chapter 5 describes). The judicial process initiated with these accusations, known as Proceso 8000 (the 8,000 Process, named for the case number assigned to the investigation by the Prosecutor General's Office), linked twenty-one senators and representatives of Congress,[42] hundreds of police officers, private companies, and national authorities such as the general comptroller of the nation and the general procurator, with Cali traffickers. President Samper himself was exonerated, but the scandal seriously undermined his authority.

In 1996, in a display of its influence on drug policy, the US government decertified Colombia's counternarcotic efforts. Since 1986 the US president is required by the US Congress to certify every year that major drug-producing and trafficking nations are fully cooperating with US counternarcotic measures. Decertification entails economic punishments such as loss of aid, access to loans, and trade preferences. The process is highly controversial (and changed names in 2002), as it encourages abusive practices by governments that want to be certified and because it has been highly politicized[43] and less strictly enforced on US allies. In this case, along with the decertification came the revocation of President Samper's visa to the United States. As Russell Crandall documents[44] US policy during that period thus contributed to maintaining a fragmented Colombian state because it worked to bring Samper down while collaborating closely with the National Police. Paradoxically, Samper had no option but to keep implementing the United States preferred antinarcotics policies to maintain some legitimacy at home. In the midst of the diplomatic crisis, the director of the National Police, General Rosso José Serrano, emerged as the most credible interlocutor for the US government. The US prioritized relations with the National Police because it perceived Serrano to be a champion against corruption.[45] Serrano took up the task of "cleaning up" the police forces and dismantling the Cali DTO, and by the time he stepped down, the international image and power of the National Police had been revamped.

Under Serrano's leadership, the National Police was recentralized to conduct the massive firing and rotation of about seven thousand police officers between 1995 and 1998.[46] The institution also became more independent from civilian oversight, police roles more militarized,[47] and its investigative and technical capacities increased. This process reversed an earlier reform initiated in 1993 aimed at strengthening the civilian nature of the police force, professionalizing it, decentralizing it, and increasing community oversight over it. The scandals of trafficking-related corruption, especially in Cali, and the need to effectively dismantle the Cali and Medellín DTOs, countermined the democratizing impetus of the previous reform. In the mid-1990s the police force thus gained more enforcement capabilities, although it did not necessarily become more democratic. By 1995, the National Police could present itself as a highly effective institution that had eliminated the most dangerous man in Colombia (Pablo Escobar) and incarcerated the highest echelons of the Cali DTO.[48]

To recapitulate, during the period of consolidation and demise of the first trafficking organizations between 1980 and 1998, fragmented political power, democratization, and corruption in enforcement agencies made it impossible for politicians to centralize control over trafficking networks (as occurred in Mexico[49]) or to enforce the law efficiently. Initial enforcement operations shaped trafficking dynamics but did little to deter criminals from confronting the state, partially because the operations did not generate a credible threat of elimination. However, state responses to the rising threat of traffickers, along with the US support for (and pressure to implement) militarized responses to drug trafficking, radically transformed the security apparatus, and police forces emerged as more powerful and legitimate at the end of this period. Coordination between police and military increased, and the police's technical capacities grew significantly.

The pressure to confront narcoterrorism extended the power of both the National Police and the military over the course of a decade, thus highlighting the state-making potential of the war against drug trafficking. US pressure and the constraints of prohibition played key roles in state transformation, encroaching militarized antinarcotics control, but in slightly different ways in each period. Before Samper, funding was relatively low and fragmented through various agencies, and for that reason it did not change the state structure radically. As US funding increased, however—from US $2.8 million in 1982 to $26 million in 1994[50]—so did this funding's capacity to alter the state apparatus. During the Samper years, the United States distrusted Colombia's political leader and other governmental sectors. Yet it supported what would become a pillar of state cohesion later on, the growth and militarization of the National Police. Such ambiguous relations deepened state fragmentation, a situation that would change a few years later.

Within the framework of foreign pressures that augmented state fragmentation, realities at the local level were diverse. In Medellín, as will be seen in chapter 4, a fragmented security apparatus made it very difficult for criminals to establish predictable arrangements with state officials. While many cops and politicians collaborated with Pablo Escobar and the Medellín traffickers, others opposed them actively. By contrast, in Cali traffickers secured protection within a more cohesive local state and thus privileged less visible violence. This subnational variation illustrates two points: First, a fragmented national state operated differently across regions, and subnational authoritarianism coexisted within the democratizing state.[51] Second, even though cocaine trafficking thrived under the state weakness of a war-torn country with limited ability to reach all corners of national territory,[52] drug-trafficking networks did not simply emerge where the state was absent. Especially in the urban areas where DTOs located their operational bases, the state was present, even if fragmented and weak.

The Aftermath of the Big "Cartels": 1998–2006

Three changes marked the mid-1990s: the big trafficking organizations had been dismantled; guerrillas and self-defense groups became more actively engaged in cocaine production and trafficking; and the security apparatus became more sophisticated, coordinated, and cohesive, largely aided by US funds and militarized guidelines. At a first glance, antitrafficking operations seemed successful because the threat of narcoterrorist violence disappeared and trafficking organizations fragmented into many small organizations, colloquially called *microcartelitos* (microcartels).[53] In practice, however, the situation was more complex. Trafficking networks had been incapacitated but not eliminated, and the successors engaged in complicated interactions with guerrillas and especially paramilitaries. Rather than pure fragmentation, there was a reaccommodation that intensified the armed conflict, associated with the expansion of paramilitary groups and their attempt at winning territorial control over guerrillas. This process illustrates that state enforcement can directly affect violence by altering power configurations among trafficking groups, but the forms that violence takes are in turn affected by the underlying power structure in the state. Indeed, as the state gained cohesion in Colombia, traffickers became more discrete in using violence. The fusion between traffickers and paramilitaries and the connections of the latter to political actors, reduced violence in some areas of the country, demonstrating how the dynamics of the armed conflict interact with both state cohesion and competition in the illegal market.

In the mid-1990s, Colombia's main guerrilla group, the Fuerzas Armadas Revolucionarias de Colombia (Revolutionary Armed Forces of Colombia), known as the FARC, significantly increased its involvement in taxing coca crops. The FARC found in drug trafficking not only funding but also a mechanism for social control and for creating bases of support among peasants and coca growers.[54] Yet domestic and international voices emphasized the narco-guerrilla discourse—that is, the idea that guerrillas were not motivated by ideological grievances but by pure greed. This discourse enabled the US and Colombian governments to merge drug enforcement with counterinsurgency, thus transforming the nature and strength of enforcement and the dynamics of the civil war.

Guerrilla involvement in coca cultivation provided the motivation that the army needed to fully engage in antitrafficking operations. Coordination between army and police increased, reducing state fragmentation. A military colonel deployed in the 1990s as the commander of an elite unit in charge of dismantling the Cali DTO summarized the changing relation between military and police as follows: in the 1980s, "the relationship with the police was respectful but distant," he said, and "institutional distrust was a clear obstacle." But "nowadays the relationship is more fluid and it is easier to work together, perhaps because when you introduced guerrilla to the narco equation it became more difficult for the military to be bribed."[55]

During this period, radical transformations followed Plan Colombia, an initiative launched in 1999 by President Andres Pastrana (1994–1998) with the aim of reducing cocaine production by 50 percent in six years and restoring security in areas controlled by illegal armed groups.[56] In 2000, the US government

officially committed resources to Plan Colombia, thus making it one of the largest antinarcotics plans funded by the United States and the blueprint that the
United States still promotes as a success story. The military component of the
plan[57] totaled US\$ 5.3 billion dollars provided by Colombia and US\$ 4.3 billion
provided by the United States.[58] US funding was initially presented as focused
on antinarcotics because many sectors within the US government were reluctant
to support the antiguerrilla components. After the 9/11 terrorist attacks, the
designation of the FARC as a terrorist organization gave the United States the
platform to support the counterinsurgency component of Plan Colombia. By
the early 2000s, Plan Colombia had successfully merged antinarcotics actions
with counterinsurgency operations and policy discourses.

Plan Colombia radically transformed the geography and operation of trafficking organizations within and outside Colombia in four major ways. First, it
changed the geography of coca production. Although measurement problems
abound, it is possible to assert that the area of coca cultivated decreased from
its peak of 161,700 hectares in 1999 to 86,000 hectares in 2005–2008,[59] and
then to 48,000 hectares by 2012 (although cultivation area increased again
beginning in 2014). The decrease in established production areas was offset by
increases in Peru and Bolivia and by increasing concentration of coca crops and
cocaine production within areas of Colombia that were previously marginal in
drug trafficking, such as the Nariño department on the Pacific Coast. Second, as
Winifred Tate documents, Plan Colombia privileged attacks on guerrillas while
ignoring the expansion of paramilitary groups, thus contributing indirectly to
their consolidation in the early 2000s.[60] Oeindrila Dube and Suresh Naidu find,
for example, that US military aid was associated with increases in paramilitary
presence and violence.[61] Paramilitaries and remnants of older drug-trafficking
groups benefited from the dual antinarcotics-antiguerrilla campaign, and their
alliances facilitated the creation of illegal market monopolies in some areas of
the country. Third, a greater emphasis on interdiction of cocaine en route to
major consumer markets—especially during the late phases of Plan Colombia
after 2006[62]—along with the demobilization of paramilitary groups—explained
below—changed the nature and behavior of trafficking actors. As the marginal
profits for cocaine decreased for Colombian groups, they became more prone to
engage in alliances with domestic and international actors[63] and to prefer more
silent violence. The scarcity generated by interdiction in Colombia could have
contributed to the violent explosion in Mexico, although such effect may not
be as great as that of the Mexican enforcement campaign.[64] Fourth, and crucial for this book's argument, Plan Colombia increased the funding, technical
training, and mobility of armed forces throughout the territory and promoted
cooperation between military and police forces, thus increasing militarized state
cohesion.

Plan Colombia transformed trafficking dynamics and state power, thus affecting general violence trends. Paramilitary violence and human rights violations increased especially in the first stages of the plan, but by 2003 general security indicators such as homicide rates and kidnappings had improved. In the early 2000s, the reaccommodation of forces in the armed conflict allowed paramilitaries to become the main authority in many territories and, consequently, in criminal markets.[65] Violence initially increased as paramilitaries fought for territories with guerrillas and other armed actors, but decreased as they consolidated monopolies. By contributing to a recentralization of state power, the plan helped reshape the incentives of criminals to use violence, forcing them to become more covert in their violent techniques.

While Plan Colombia accounts for crucial transformations, it cannot fully explain regional variation in criminal behavior. For example, older trafficking groups remained strong in the Valle department, where the Norte del Valle DTO, which was far from being simply a *microcartelito*, generated significant violence. According to one army officer from the period, "Between 1995 and 1998, the main problem started to be the guerrillas and the Norte del Valle cartel benefited from that."[66] Paramilitary power and connections with drug trafficking changed nationally, but they took on very different local dynamics.

Álvaro Uribe's Presidency and the Paramilitaries' Changing Role

Central to the consolidation, expansion, and centralization of military power was the election of the right-wing politician Álvaro Uribe as president in 2002. Uribe got elected on an agenda of all-out war against guerrillas that reflected, among other things, the citizen's disappointment with a failed peace process undertaken by former President Pastrana, which contributed to the expansion of FARC's power in southern Colombia.

Uribe expanded the territorial reach and capacity of both the military and the police. Military investment increased under a plan aimed at gaining territorial control known as the Politica de Seguridad Democrática (Democratic Security Policy). Military forces grew from 145,000 personnel in the late 1990s to 431,253 by January 2009. In 2003, the government also established the Comandos Conjuntos (Joint Command Forces), which improved the operational coordination of state forces. The close relationship between Uribe and the US government meant that, unlike in the Samper years, US policy facilitated state cohesion while still advancing the same priorities of the past.[67]

Uribe's policy, facilitated by Plan Colombia's resources, effectively reduced kidnappings, civilian and combat deaths, and weakened guerrillas.[68] Both political power and enforcement coordination concentrated around the president, and thus the state gained cohesion. Meanwhile, paramilitary groups acquired prominence in international distribution, the most profitable part of the drug-trafficking chain, and they consolidated relations with sectors of the political establishment in temporary protection rackets.[69] In 2006, the Supreme Court of Justice and the Attorney General's Office started investigating such links between politicians and paramilitaries through a judicial process known as Parapolitica. The proceedings of this large-scale process, which by 2012 had investigated 943 politicians including 139 legislators, 41 mayors, and 20 governors,[70] unveiled how paramilitaries established symbiotic relations with large sectors of the political class. Perhaps for the first time in the history of drug trafficking in Colombia, the state achieved a centralization that facilitated predictable protection to paramilitary groups, by then as much political actors as drug traffickers. The trade-off between state autonomy from criminal influence and state coercion appeared: more security went in tandem with less autonomy. However, police and military were significantly more professionalized than in the 1980s, and as a result, antinarcotic and security policies were more efficient. Such efficiency underscores, along the lines of this book's argument, the importance not just of how security policies are designed but of the correlation of forces that allow their implementation. The antidrug policies of the Uribe era, as in the past, were militarized and mainly concerned with capturing major trafficking leaders, and leadership decapitation often unleashed criminal competition and violence. Yet explosions of drug violence or increases in its visibility did not occur, partially because in a more centralized and powerful state where criminals sometimes received protection, they had more incentives to hide. Traffickers also became more wary of attacking the state or their rivals in a way that could make them vulnerable to enforcement.

In 2002, paramilitary groups entered a peace negotiation with the government that led to the demobilization of approximately thirty-two thousand combatants.[71] The process lacked a clear legal framework to guarantee transparency, justice, and reparation for victims of crimes against humanity.[72] Once such legal framework was created, there were also concerns about impunity.[73] An analysis of the consequences of this process exceeds the purpose of this book,[74] but the crucial point is that the consolidation of paramilitary forces, their successful engagement in drug distribution, the protection provided both by the peace process and the networks of political protection, and the greater efficiency of security operations together created a context for drug violence to decrease and become less visible at the national level.

Within this national context, subnational dynamics were diverse. Paramilitaries successfully merged with trafficking actors in Medellín, as described in chapter 4, and contributed to the creation of a criminal monopoly and a reduction in both the frequency and the visibility of violence. Conversely, in Cali traffickers did not merge with paramilitary actors, and as a result, violence remained frequent.

Drug Trafficking in the Twenty-First Century (2006–2012)

At the beginning of the twenty-first century, drug trafficking had changed radically in Colombia, with a combination of more decentralized illegal actors including new traffickers, nondemobilized paramilitary forces, recidivate demobilized soldiers, and older criminals. The illegal market thus became more competitive and, combined with greater state cohesion and enforcement capacity, created situations where violent disputes were less likely to be highly publicized.

In the mid- to late 2000s, coca cultivation, and to a lesser extent cocaine production, declined. Colombian traffickers relinquished some hierarchical control over the international drug-trafficking chain while the power of Mexican trafficking organizations increased. Yet drug trafficking remained important for Colombians. The institutional transformations previously described forced traffickers to adapt, becoming less open in their operations and more attentive to avoiding media and enforcement attention. Many criminals exerted control within local niches and were thus less likely to pose a "national security" threat, yet they retained destabilizing power,[75] links with security forces, and political and electoral connections.[76]

The paramilitary demobilization dismantled the national network of the Autodefensas Unidas de Colombia (AUC; the United Self-Defense Forces of Colombia), yet soon after demobilization newly armed structures emerged, especially in areas with history of paramilitary presence. The nature of these groups remained controversial at the time of writing this book. Some scholars and observers emphasize their continuities with paramilitary forces; others emphasize their criminal motivations, an emphasis reflected in the initial labeling of these groups as *bandas criminales* (BACRIM, that is, criminal gangs). Although demobilized combatants do not make up the majority of members of these groups, remnants of paramilitary structures, especially middle ranks that did not demobilize, play a key role in their configuration. Assessments about the nature and size of new groups vary widely depending on the source. By 2012, their reported geographic reach ranged from estimates of 4,800 members present in 167 municipalities to 8,000 members present in 406 municipalities.[77] These groups, although geographically dispersed and less able to challenge national security, acquired significant territorial presence and became crucial both in the armed conflict and in illegal markets.

These criminal structures diversified their illegal portfolios, engaging in other illicit and semilicit activities, such as illegal gold mining, gambling, and extortion.[78] Alliances between former enemies, such as guerrillas and neoparamilitary groups, also became more common, although they were not entirely new or homogeneously present across regions.[79] Diversification of illegal activities was not new, either, but trafficking groups became more active in controlling other

illicit markets because their direct income from drug trafficking, even though
still large, had decreased, partially as a result of the government's interdiction
policies.

Traffickers' power declined but did not disappear and drug trafficking
remains a crucial source of income for illegal actors as well as a grave security
issue. Some criminal groups operate as security providers for owners of cocaine-
processing facilities rather than as controllers of international distribution.[80]
Others supply cocaine for powerful Mexican traffickers and play decisive roles
in cocaine trafficking to Europe. Although the initial balloon effect produced by
Plan Colombia displaced coca cultivation to Peru and Bolivia, Colombia still
plays a major role in the coca and cocaine supply. Statistics are controversial and
imprecise, but comparable estimates from the United Nations Office for Drugs
and Crime suggest that in 2010 Colombia produced as much coca as Peru and
more than twice the amount produced in Bolivia. By 2015, coca acreage had
again almost doubled from the lowest level seen in 2012.[81]

Criminal Adaptation and Silent Traffickers

After decades of interaction with state actors, traffickers have learned to lower
their profiles, reducing visible violence and thus the possibilities of being
captured by enforcement agents. In the words of one intelligence officer,
"Traffickers are no longer flashy [*dan pantalla*]. You don't see many flashy traffickers [*traquetico*] but they do extort and threaten people. It's a very strong phenomenon. . . . Trafficking is a time bomb, not like Mexico, but the BACRIM are
uncontrollable; this hidden criminality has a strong ability to penetrate [state
institutions]."[82]

The intelligence officer's remarks about the criminal ability to penetrate institutions summarize the consequences of the institutional transformations since
the late 1970s. On the one hand, as a result of enforcement efforts, drug policies, and the combat against nonstate armed actors, military and police forces
are more sophisticated and have more territorial reach than in the 1980s. To
some extent, Colombia has reduced the trade-off between democracy and state
coercive capacity by professionalizing its enforcement and extending military
presence. On the other hand, there are still vital challenges to the state capacity
to enforce the law, especially at the local level; other areas of law enforcement—
like justice provision—are plagued with problems; and drug policies remain
constrained within the framework of prohibition.

The enforcement officials' confidence in their own operational capacity
reflects the growth and power of the security apparatus, a situation that stands
in sharp contrast to the fears and distrust of the 1980s. In the words of Oscar
Naranjo, former director of the National Police: "Police forces in the world are

threatened by four monsters: inefficiency, police brutality, lack of solidarity, and corruption. We have combated all of them. Today the penetration of corruption is minimal. Today, drug traffickers do not feel at peace in Colombia, although it does not mean that there is nothing left to do."[83] Naranjo's remarks reflect the legitimacy and self-confidence that police forces have gained.

The security apparatus has grown more complex, with multiple specialized units, and the National Police represents its node of cohesion. Institutional jealousies exist, and as many police officers and intelligence officials I interviewed put it, there is always confrontation about "who will appear in the picture"—or in other words, who will take credit for a particular enforcement operation, arrest, or seizure. Yet the National Police is the nation's leader in antinarcotics operations and has the most comprehensive territorial reach and resources. As one police commander put it: "Institutions work alone, and the one that has the most power and reach is the police. With the CTI [intelligence police of the Attorney General's Office] we divide cases, but they are inefficient. The DAS [extinct civilian intelligence agency] is weakened . . . . The army is not that efficient, because they want to use their spirit d' corps to hide things. The army has many scandals . . . . But because of hypocrisy and because of the power of the president, forces must be united."[84]

The Colombian security apparatus has thus acquired abilities to react more quickly to criminals, especially those that concentrate too much power. There are also well-functioning higher courts[85] critical in investigating large corruption scandals that connect sectors of the political class with illegal armed and trafficking actors. Yet impunity rates are very high and many traffickers have managed to get light sentences,[86] a situation that also occurs in the United States.[87]

Key challenges to the state's coercive and law enforcement capacity remain. In some regions the state is fragmented or symbiotic with criminal actors. For example, in Cali, violence does not recede but is not very visible because criminals have adapted their tactics and still receive state protection. In fact, in 2012, Cali was ranked as the seventh-most violent city in the world[88] but this situation did not attract significant media attention. In Medellín, a modern and progressive political coalition governs, but local police forces still collaborate with gangs (*combos*). Corruption networks are not necessarily linked to the highest ranks of police authority, yet they greatly affect the well-being of local communities, as expressed by a young inhabitant of a violent neighborhood in Medellín: "There have been some corruption cases, but those that get discovered are the unlucky ones. The cops [*tombos*] are the ones that handle the black market in arms, the robberies, the drugs. The police are highly corrupt."[89]

Other regions, such as the Pacific Coast in the departments of Chocó[90] and Valle del Cauca, face dangerous security situations associated with drug trafficking. For example, since 2006, the port of Buenaventura has been besieged by increasingly brutal but silent violence derived from the confrontation between several rearmed paramilitary and criminal groups such as La Empresa, Los Urabeños, Los Machos, and Los Rastrojos.[91] Such criminal organizations destabilize local public security even if they are not deemed a national security threat. These challenges tend to be overlooked in the optimist atmosphere of declining violence nationally.

One of this book's key contributions is to show that the number of killings in a given location cannot be the only indicator used to gauge the power of drug-trafficking organizations. Less violence does not necessarily equate to weak organizations or more capable state enforcement. Colombian enforcement agencies have increased their capacity to control territories and establish the monopoly of force, but trafficking organizations have adapted to enforcement changes by reducing visible violence. Additionally, state capacity is not evenly distributed throughout the territory. Even if they are weaker, more territorially fragmented, and more diversified than in previous periods, trafficking organizations still retain capacities for violence, and they derive significant income from illegal activities. The persistence of violence and corruption means that the Colombian state still has a long road to travel to consolidate both its capacity to enforce the law and its autonomy from criminal influences.

Two accomplishments during Juan Manuel Santos's second term as president of Colombia (2014–2018) may, however, contribute to the state's ability to control the challenges of organized crime in a more democratic and less militarized way. First was the historic signing of a peace accord between the government and the FARC. Second was Colombia's role in leading a global discussion about the need to reform drug policies, a discussion that may serve to initiate a reevaluation of policies that have exacerbated the negative consequences of the drug trade. These domestic changes, coupled with a changing role of the United States in Latin America, can transform the predominant focus of drug policies. How exactly these trends will affect drug-trafficking dynamics in Colombia will depend largely on how armed and criminal actors reconfigure in a postconflict situation, how the state responds to them, and especially how willing the state is to move from the rhetoric to the practice of drug reform, which would imply scaling back the ingrained militarization of law enforcement.

Mexico: From State-Sponsored Protection to Incomplete Democratization

Drug trafficking in Mexico, as Luis Astorga[92] has documented, has a long history linked to early marijuana and opium production. As in Colombia, national and international drug policies have shaped the flows, geography, and organization of trafficking actors. Marijuana eradication efforts in the 1970s dispersed trafficking networks, and in the 1980s, US policing over trafficking routes in the Caribbean increased Mexico's role in cocaine trafficking, a role that further expanded in the 2000s due to greater policing over cocaine production and distribution in Colombia. The following discussion shows how, within such context, institutional transformations and market competition have shaped violence patterns over time and throughout the territory. The control of a hegemonic party—the Institutional Revolutionary Party (PRI)—along with the centralization of enforcement responsibilities in the Mexico Attorney's General Office—provided the state with the cohesion and coercive capacity necessary to regulate drug trafficking both through corruption and selective enforcement. As a result, at least up to the 2000s, the state transformed not in response to the violent challenge of drug trafficking (as in Colombia) but rather to demands for democratization. Since the late 1980s, bureaucratic reforms and a slow political opening started to fragment such regulation, but cohesion was still retained through the power of the PRI and the Attorney General's Office. In the mid-2000s, the declining power of the Attorney General's Office, deepening electoral competition, and the military efforts to crack down on trafficking organizations by President Felipe Calderón further fragmented the state and contributed to the generation of one of the most violent periods in Mexico's history.

Origins of Drug Trafficking and PRI Rule

Opium and marijuana production in Mexico date back to the late nineteenth century, when these products were cultivated in small amounts to satisfy a demand for these drugs for medicinal purposes along with a growing but increasingly criticized recreational use. As worldwide efforts to control drugs intensified in 1909 with the Shanghai opium convention, the 1912 Hague Convention, and the US 1914 Harrison Act, the Mexican government also increased pressure on drug use and production.

In the 1940s, two important transformations occurred. First, in 1947, narcotic drugs started to be treated as a national security issue, and policing responsibilities were centralized in the Attorney General's Office. Second, global demand for marijuana, and especially opium, increased during and after World War II, presenting an opportunity for Mexico to become an important opium and marijuana supplier. Illegal crops proliferated, and the state of Sinaloa, on the Pacific Coast, became a new center for trafficking organizations. Unlike Colombia, drug trafficking emerged and consolidated within a system of centralized political power created by the decades-long rule of the PRI, which determined interactions between traffickers and the state.[93]

Drug trafficking initially concentrated on opium and marijuana, although Mexicans had early incursions into the cocaine market in the 1960s.[94] Mexican traffickers created a seedless (*sinsemilla*) variety of marijuana that had stronger psychoactive potency. In 1977, and with the support of the US government, the Mexican military carried out Operación Cóndor, aimed at eliminating marijuana production. The operation did not eliminate trafficking groups, but it dispersed trafficking networks from Sinaloa into other Mexican states, generating violence between trafficking groups and also against authorities, especially officials from the Attorney General's Office, as traffickers resisted eradication operations.[95] Yet for the most part the interaction between traffickers and state officials remained stable and not violent.

In the 1980s, US authorities cracked down on cocaine transportation routes in the Caribbean, and Colombian traffickers started to use transportation routes inland through Mexico. The incidence of Mexicans in cocaine trafficking subsequently increased.[96] Initially, Colombians paid Mexican traffickers a fee for their help in smuggling drugs, but over time Mexicans started to be paid in kind, or with a percentage of the profits, thus changing the nature of criminal organizations. By the mid-1980s, drug trafficking had become a great concern for national and international audiences; the cases analyzed in this book focus on transformations occurring after this juncture when trafficking became prominent in public security discussions. To be precise, drug trafficking had been a contentious issue in domestic politics and especially in bilateral relations since the escalation of prohibition in the 1960s. Operation Intercept in 1969 and Operación Cóndor in the 1970s were early and prominent manifestations of such tensions.[97] Yet, until the late 1980s a tradition of downplaying security threats was ingrained among Mexican authorities,[98] and for the United States the primacy of Cold War concerns made drug enforcement a priority only to the extent that it served the anti-Communist agenda.

As a result of their greater involvement in cocaine trafficking, Mexican organizations became more powerful and prone to using violence. Yet this market transformation alone cannot account for the variation in violence across cities where traffickers operated, or for the fact that violence did not explode immediately after cocaine trafficking became more important. For instance, Amado Carrillo and the Juárez DTO, who since the early 1990s mastered relations with Colombian traffickers and pioneered the idea of demanding a direct share in profits, regulated violence or preferred to hide it when necessary. Allegedly, Carrillo promised the Mexican military that his DTO would control disorganized traffickers, ban domestic drug sales, and limit violence in exchange for the freedom to conduct business.[99]

President Miguel de la Madrid (1982–1988) declared drug trafficking a national security priority and, as a result, enforcement agencies engaged more in policing drug trafficking. At the same time, shifting priorities led the United States to step up drug-control pressures in Mexico, contributing to the initial fragmentation of state protection. The Attorney General's Office assumed policing and judicial responsibilities and remained the leader of antinarcotic operations. Other agencies, such as the military, were subordinated to the Attorney General's Office. Within the Attorney General's Office, police units such as the Federal Security Directorate (DFS) became nodes of protection and interaction between the state and criminal actors.[100]

The Camarena Case and Its Implications

In November 1984, the Mexican Army, in collaboration with the US Drug Enforcement Administration, discovered and dismantled the Buffalo Ranch, a large marijuana plantation in northern Mexico, seizing thousands of tons of marijuana.[101] A few months later, on February 7, 1985, and in retaliation for this operation, the traffickers Rafael Caro Quintero and Miguel Ángel Félix Gallardo kidnapped the DEA agent Enrique Camarena and his Mexican pilot Alfredo Zavala, who were later found dead on March 6. Camarena's death unleashed an aggressive response from the United States. Days after the kidnapping, the DEA acknowledged that thirty of its agents worked in Mexico, that Guadalajara— Caro Quintero's turf—was the epicenter of national and international drug trafficking, and that seventy-five major drug traffickers controlled the drug business in the country, often protected by state authorities. These assertions angered government authorities, who denied that Mexico was a launch pad for international drug trafficking, asserted that only seven traffickers operated in the country, and maintained that Mexico had no police corruption.[102] Tensions between US and Mexican authorities ensued, with accusations of corruption and foreign intervention flowing from both sides.

In 1985, Mexican authorities responded to international pressure by capturing Rafael Caro Quintero and dismantling the DFS due to the pervasive corruption that affected it.[103] The initial reluctance of Mexican authorities to recognize the incidence of drug trafficking and corruption, as well as their ability to quickly conduct operations in response to public pressure, demonstrated the state's ability to regulate, and protect, when possible, criminal interactions. Despite the scandal and the dismantling of the DFS, the centralized structure of enforcement was promptly recovered.

The Camarena incident illustrates that the state protection that may emerge when a state is cohesive, as occurred during the PRI rule in Mexico, does not necessarily imply that enforcement actions cannot occur or that criminals cannot retaliate against those actions. Even very corrupt states may be forced to conduct enforcement operations in response to international pressure. The key is, rather, that at least in the short run cohesive states are better equipped than fragmented states to control the spillover effects of anticrime operations and to deter violent criminal retaliation.

Up to the mid-1980s, the situation in Mexico illustrated the trade-off between state capacity to control violence and state autonomy from criminal influence. The concentration of power in the PRI and of enforcement responsibilities in the Attorney General's Office allowed the state to maintain its monopoly of force, even with corrupt and unprofessional police forces, while maintaining strong formal and informal links with trafficking organizations. The PRI held the upper hand in dominating criminals, but it also conceded benefits that empowered them, and thus the state was not autonomous. Criminals were powerful, but the state's capacity to coordinate enforcement made it too costly for traffickers to confront the state, as reflected in Caro Quintero's quick capture after Camarena's death and the lack of a strong retaliatory response to that arrest. The PRI-dominated government was efficient not necessarily because it designed or targeted enforcement better, but because it was capable to swiftly coordinate its responses.

Centralized political power effectively motivated traffickers to regulate violence without eliminating it completely, yet the behavior of traffickers varied across regions. In the 1980s, while Culiacán experienced violence well above the national average, Ciudad Juárez and Tijuana experienced violence below the average, at least up to the mid-1990s. Interestingly, higher violence in Culiacán occurred precisely in a PRI-dominated state, thus showing that state cohesion was primarily consequential for visibility, rather than frequency, of violence. PRI control did not always eliminate violence from intra- and interorganizational disputes, but instead it tended to make violence less visible; indeed, arrests, drug seizures, and other anticrime operations could unleash violent competition among criminals.

Initial Transformations in the Security Apparatus (1988–2000)

Beginning in the early 1990s, reforms to the Attorney General's Office, the creation and re-creation of police forces, and attempts at redistributing enforcement responsibilities proliferated. This, in turn, increased institutional fragmentation, reduced the state's ability to fully regulate an increasingly competitive drug market, and multiplied corruption channels. The pattern of US antinarcotics support and pressure officially aimed at completely eliminating drug supply further reduced the reliability of state protection, because mutual distrust largely fragmented bilateral interactions. Yet because the Attorney General's Office retained power and the PRI remained powerful, sustained increases in violence did not occur in this period. Throughout the 1980s, the main opposition party to the PRI, the PAN (National Action Party) had won mayoral offices in a few municipalities, especially in the northern states of Baja California, Chihuahua, and Sonora. In 1989, the slow opening of electoral competition in Mexico took on a new dimension when the PAN won a governorship for the first time, in Baja California, followed by other successes in the states of Chihuahua (1992), Guanajuato (1991), and Nuevo León (1997) and by the first opposition-dominated national legislature in 1997. These opposition successes created a more heterogeneous political landscape and curtailed the power of the federal government and the PRI, representing a watershed moment for democratization. In the short run, however, these changes had a contained impact on the structures of intermediation between state officials and traffickers. Transformations were accumulating but the old power structure, and the prevailing channels for dealing with security problems, were still deeply ingrained.

The PRI candidate Carlos Salinas de Gortari was sworn in as president of Mexico in 1988, amid accusations of electoral fraud. Drug trafficking had become more public and accusations of corruption and state protection proliferated, forcing the government to carry out more aggressive institutional and anticorruption reforms. In 1989, the Federal Judicial Police (PJF) captured Miguel Ángel Félix Gallardo, who was at the time Mexico's most powerful trafficker. Upon his incarceration, Félix Gallardo divided drug trafficking into regions separating traffickers from Sinaloa (Joaquin "El Chapo" (Shorty) Guzmán and Ismael "El Mayo" Zambada), Baja California (the Arellano Félix DTO), and Chihuahua (Amado Carrillo). Félix Gallardo retained command over these groups for some time, but by the early 1990s, confrontations between regional groups increased, thus changing the geography of trafficking. This episode illustrates how state enforcement operations can transform the organization of illegal markets by forcing realignments, leadership changes, or the relocation of operations. Yet the violent effects of such transformations vary depending on the underlying structure enforcing the law: criminal competition in the early 1990s was less visible than disputes generated by the war against cartels declared in 2006.

The growing competition among factions within a still somewhat coherent criminal network started to generate more violence. During Salinas's presidency, the high-level assassinations of Cardinal Jesús Posadas Ocampo in 1993, the presidential candidate Luis Donaldo Colosio in March 1994, and the general PRI secretary José Francisco Ruiz Massieu in September 1994 seemed to be connected to drug trafficking and thus prompted some institutional reforms and operations against traffickers. The cardinal's assassination was allegedly accidental, when the clergyman got caught in the crossfire as hitmen of the Arellano Félix organization tried to kill rival Joaquín Guzmán. The circumstances of the other cases were never clarified, even though both seemed to weave political and drug-trafficking interests, to the extent that the Ruiz Massieu case led to the imprisonment of the president's brother, Raúl Salinas. These events could be seen as early manifestations of visible violence that resulted from growing splits within trafficking factions—in this case the Arellano Félix DTO and Guzmán—which in turn were starting to face less-reliable protection and were bargaining to restore it. The high-level murders and a general sense of corruption within the Attorney General's Office led Salinas to constantly rotate heads of the office,[104] and each new attorney general arrived with new collaborators.

In the last year of Salinas's *sexenio*,[105] the infamous National Liberation Zapatista Army (EZLN) led an armed uprising in the southern state of Chiapas that shook up the country precisely the same day that the North American Free Trade Agreement (NAFTA) went into effect. When President Ernesto Zedillo (1994–2000) took office in December 1994, the regime's legitimacy was questioned as the PAN opposition party was gaining ground. Zedillo gave more concessions to the opposition. One significant concession was to name for the first time a PAN official, Antonio Lozano, as attorney general in 1994, thus breaking down a tradition of PRI leadership in this agency.[106] During his brief tenure, Lozano promoted reforms to decentralize the Attorney General's Office and to reduce corruption.

In 1995, Zedillo issued a law to create a system of national public security[107] partially aimed at providing a renewed role in public security to the Secretariat of Governance and reducing the role of the Attorney General's Office. Attorney Lozano, in turn, designed a reform to change the geographic organization of the office, and his successor, Jorge Madrazo, implemented it in 1997. The reform replaced the centralized, functionally based division of power of the Attorney General's Office with a decentralized, geographically based approach, which created three jurisdictions (*subprocuradurías*) grouping noncontiguous states. The logic behind the reform was that in contiguous jurisdictions corruption could spread out easily, while dispersed jurisdictions curtailed corruption.[108] The new organization separated geographies of enforcement and geographies of criminality,[109] multiplied enforcement actors, and made it more difficult for them to coordinate. The reform was short-lived precisely because it generated coordination problems and sharp divergences in conducting judicial processes and in evaluating procedures in each *subprocuraduría*.[110]

Attorney Madrazo continued the transformations of the office by dismantling the National Institute for Combating Drugs (INCD) and the Center for Drug-Control Planning. He created two new specialized units, the FEADS (Special Attorney for Crimes against Health) and the UEDO (Specialized Unit for Organized Crime) in April 1997. These reforms came after General José de Jesús Gutiérrez Rebollo, head of the INCD, was investigated and sentenced to prison for collaborating with the trafficker Amado Carrillo. In 1999, President Zedillo created the Federal Preventive Police (PFP), unifying the federal roads police, the fiscal police, personnel from the national intelligence agency, and the military police. The PFP generated criticisms among sectors that feared excessive federal intervention in municipalities and states and preferred to avoid duplication of roles between the Attorney General's Office and the newly created police. In 2002, the attorney general's organization changed again to one combining deconcentration and specialization by strengthening the regional offices (*delegaciones*) of the Attorney General's Office in each state and at the same time creating specialized *subprocuradurías* for crimes such as organized crime, electoral crimes, and piracy.

The dismantling of old police forces such as the DFS, and the reforms of the 1990s rotating personnel and creating and re-creating offices, added instability to the Attorney General's Office without solving its core problems, but it remained as the cornerstone of the security apparatus. Newly created police agencies, guided by the same policy frameworks, eventually became plagued by corruption, as in the case of the Federal Judicial Police (PJF), which became the most powerful unit under the attorney general, and as its predecessor the DFS, the central node for criminal-state interactions.

Nationally, violence declined, although in some regions these institutional changes affected the interactions between criminals and state, as occurred in Tijuana, where anticorruption reforms and enforcement operations generated visible violent reactions by the Arellano Félix Organization (AFO). At the national level the AFO had little concern for hiding its dispute with El Chapo in some critical moments, especially as federal enforcement increasingly targeted the AFO.[111]

Governments seeking to contain challenges to public security throughout the mid-1990s increasingly engaged the military in public security. As in Colombia in the 1980s, governments thought the military could counteract the weakness and corruption of police forces.[112] This perception was strengthened and extended as US security agencies also saw the military as the only reliable partner and militarization of the fight against drugs as the only policy option.[113] Attorney Lozano, for instance, named a military official as the director of the PJF and involved the military in antinarcotics operations. Yet, military commands remained formally subordinated to the attorney general and thus were not an open source of conflict within the state.

Protection Starts to Break Down

During the Salinas sexenio, the Gulf DTO led by Juan García Ábrego had become more powerful and independent from Sinaloan traffickers.[114] By the beginning of President Zedillo's sexenio, suspicions that the Gulf DTO enjoyed protection from the highest echelons of power and public pressure led to the indictment on money-laundering charges of President Salinas's brother, Raúl,[115] and to the detention of García Ábrego in 1996. These operations reconfigured drug-trafficking groups.

Ábrego's successor, Osiel Cárdenas, was determined to violently take over his rivals, and in 1997 he created a quasi-paramilitary armed branch of the Gulf DTO, the Zetas, as two processes coincided: on the one hand, García Ábrego's capture, after being protected by high-ranking officials, signaled that state protection was less predictable and motivated Cárdenas to scale up military capacities. On the other hand, starting in 1997, many well-trained soldiers deserted from the GAFES (Grupos Aeromóviles de Fuerzas Especiales), the airborne military special forces units created in 1994 to fight the EZLN uprising.[116] These deserting soldiers joined criminal groups and brought considerable skills to bear in the drug battles of the era. Former Kaibiles, special forces of the Guatemalan military trained for antiguerrilla operations and eager to work for the most profitable employer, supplied additional military skills for the Zetas.[117] The growing power of the Gulf DTO as well as the creation of the Zetas heightened criminal competition by the early 2000s.

A System on the Brink of Transformation

The Zedillo government took prominent steps to tackle drug trafficking, motivated in part by the high-level assassinations that occurred during Salinas's term, Zedillo's own concerns with widespread corruption, and the need to please the United States. Such measures included arrests of traffickers and corrupt politicians, the expansion of the military's role in drug control, and the institutionalization of drug-control cooperation with the creation of a high-level contact group with the United States. Yet public security, at least in its most public face, while far more important than in the previous decade, was less prominent both in Mexico and in the United States than what it would become by the mid-2000s. Despite institutional reforms and transformations in the criminal market, President Zedillo prioritized economic liberalization, the consolidation of NAFTA, and the political consequences of the Zapatista uprising over attention to organized crime and drug trafficking[118] although the pressure, especially from the United States to step up the militarization of the so-called war on drugs, was growing.[119] New trafficking challenges were publicly downplayed; the US and Mexican governments shared an interest in the success of NAFTA, and as a result, official government reactions to drug-related corruption and violence were minimized, even though conflicts abounded. The US government did not decertify Mexico, yet (as discussed earlier in this chapter) similar corruption scandals led to Colombia's decertification over the same period. In the 1997 report of the binational contact group it was even stated that Mexican traffickers had not translated their economic power into political power, and that they lacked capabilities to operate independently at the international level.[120] The corruption scandals and political assassinations forced Zedillo to restructure security practices,[121] but these changes were limited, even though they constituted the seeds of further bureaucratic transformations. By the end of Zedillo's term, criminals understood that protection was not as predictable as it was before, as the creation of the Zetas suggests. Yet criminals still seemed reluctant to confront the state or to deploy full-scale violence. In fact, it was not until 2003 that the Zetas came to the attention of the media. With the election of a PAN candidate as president in 2000, Mexico's democratic transition was formally completed at the national level, and politicians' and traffickers' incentives changed radically.

The End of the PRI Hegemony

During the 2000s, security agencies changed more rapidly and profoundly than in the 1990s, thus opening up opportunities for criminals to challenge the state as protection crumbled and enforcement was escalating without deterring violent reactions. This process was deepened during Felipe Calderón's presidential tenure, as the end of the PRI's hegemony, the deployment of military troops to fight criminals, and radical changes in security responsibilities led to extreme state fragmentation, which worsened the security crisis that was borne out of trafficking disputes. Enforcement operations of all sorts (seizures, arrests, combats) proliferated and deepened the criminal fragmentation that had been slowly growing since the mid-1990s.[122]

In 2000, the election of PAN's Vicente Fox as president marked the democratic transition at the national level, even though perhaps some of the most radical openings of political competition had occurred in the previous decade. The national transition increased intra- and interparty elite conflict[123] and accelerated bureaucratic changes. Fox appointed an army general as the head of the Attorney General's Office, thus changing the power balance between civilian and military law enforcement and giving more formal power to the military. During Fox's term, the secretary of defense and secretary of the navy engaged more directly in public security, and carried out joint operations with the attorney general. The Attorney General's Office was weakened as the military acquired greater de facto power in controlling operations and deployed more personnel in anti–organized crime operations than did the office of the attorney general.[124] This stood in sharp contrast to previous militarized operations where the Attorney General's Office deployed military personnel temporarily but maintained operational control. The replacement of the Federal

Judicial Police with the Federal Investigation Agency (AFI) added to changes within the Attorney General's Office.

Fox created the Secretariat of Public Security (SSP) and moved the Federal Preventive Police (PFP) from the Secretariat of Governance to the SSP, thus giving more independence to the federal police by formally separating preventive policing, investigation, and prosecution. In addition, the judiciary became more influential in the political system.[125] These reforms generated horizontal conflicts across agencies: federal and other police forces resented that the judicial police (*ministeriales*) did not communicate the results of investigations on people they had previously arrested. Before the creation of the SSP, the police did not have a voice[126] and thus conflicts with the Attorney General's Office were uncommon, but these reforms broke down the concentration of policing and investigative responsibilities under the attorney general and generated more conflicts.

The election of the first non-PRI president motivated law enforcement reforms during Fox's term. Up to that point, unlike Colombia, state enforcement institutions had changed not while responding to criminal violence but rather in response to domestic and international pressure to democratize and reduce corruption. The threat of violence, however, increased shortly after the election, as criminal organizations grew more fragmented and competitive.

The Slow Increase of Drug Violence

In the first years of Fox's sexenio, the government publicly acknowledged the existence of the Zetas, as their power, capacity for violence, and territorial reach were rapidly growing. In 2003, the Attorney General's Office reported grenade attacks by the Zetas in the state of Tamaulipas, and they were increasingly associated with methods of violence such as beheadings, placing messages on corpses, and using army weapons and gear. On September 11, 2004, members of the Sinaloa DTO assassinated Rodolfo Carrillo, of the Juárez DTO, deepening territorial confrontations, leadership reaccommodations, and violence. The available data, although imperfect, suggests that drug-related homicides started to increase in 2005,[127] although general homicide rates were showing a downward trend.[128] Visible violence appeared, but for the most part it was sporadic and scattered across the country.

The Mexican government claimed that criminal behavior changed after the 9/11 terrorist attacks on the United States. Increasing border controls, officials argued, made it more difficult for criminals to move drugs into the United States and motivated them to diversify their portfolios into internal drug distribution, which required control of micro-territories and thus more violence. Evidence from drug use surveys in Mexico does point to an increase in internal drug consumption after 9/11, which may reflect the criminals' diversification to internal markets. Yet survey data also suggests that an upward consumption trend preceded 9/11, as seen in Figure 3.2.[129] Likewise, data suggests that seizures increased on the border after 9/11, but they also spiked in 1999,[130] thus making it difficult to clearly connect drug flows and 9/11 policing. Even if heightened border controls after 9/11 reduced profits and contributed to increased internal drug distribution, border controls alone cannot account for changes in violence, especially because other enforcement trends, such as growing cocaine interdiction in Colombia, may have increased profits. It appears then, that in addition to the changes generated by drug policing, incentives to use violence changed as trafficking organizations became more geographically differentiated and prone to fight each other and as the state security apparatus lost capacity to regulate and coerce criminals.

The worsening security situation toward the end of Fox's government, especially in border regions, led the president to initiate a military operation known as México Seguro (Safe Mexico), a plan that deployed military troops to five cities in the states of Baja California, Sinaloa, and Tamaulipas in June 2005 and was later extended to Coahuila, Sonora, Chihuahua, and Veracruz. The operation was conceived as a joint operation to deal with growing violence from "confrontations between organized criminal gangs."[131] The operations formally involved

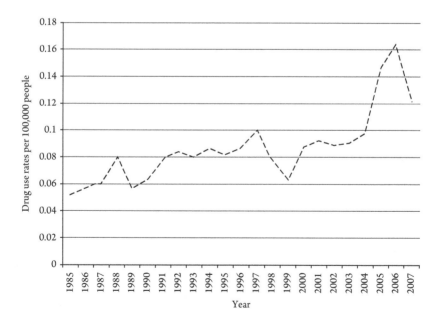

Figure 3.2 New Drug Users in Mexico 1985–2008. Source: Author's calculations based on National Addiction Survey (ENA 2008). These numbers correspond to new users of marijuana, cocaine, and methamphetamines in a given year based on the reported age of first drug use. They provide only a rough calculation of drug use.

all agencies of the public security system: the Secretariat of Governance, the Secretariat of Public Security, the Attorney General's Office, the army, the navy, and even the Secretariat of Finance as well as federal, state, and municipal forces. The plan formally dispatched soldiers to regions where drug trafficking was operating, and thus represented a precursor of the large-scale military display Felipe Calderón initiated in 2006, although this first mobilization did not have the same fragmenting effect on the state security apparatus partially because it was more limited both in size and in duration.

Breakdown and Transformation

In 2006, PAN's candidate Felipe Calderón won the presidency by a thin margin: he took 35.89 percent of the vote compared to 35.31 percent that went to his main opponent, Andrés Manuel López Obrador from the Democratic Revolution Party (PRD). With serious doubts hanging over his electoral victory, Calderón was in dire need of a legitimacy boost, and a declaration of war against trafficking organizations became a crucial strategy for legitimizing his election.[132] After this declaration, violence skyrocketed. The government's tactic of neutralizing low-, mid-, and high-level trafficking leaders generated succession struggles and inter- and intracartel fighting[133] that worsened existing criminal disputes. The effects of these operations, unlike previous arrests that also fragmented trafficking groups, were augmented and more visible not only because of the sheer number of enforcement actions but also because military deployments throughout the country deepened the ongoing state fragmentation by giving more power to the military and federal police at the expense of local and state police, thus completely destabilizing protection rackets and channels of authority. While criminals were exposed to an unprecedented number of antinarcotics operations, they had few incentives to hide or to refrain from attacking the state in retaliation. Perhaps the most vexing paradox of Calderón's war was that a government that claimed to assert its supremacy over violent competitors lacked the capacity to do so, because of the bureaucratic fragmentation among security actors, the extreme polarization among party elites that increased after Fox's election but reached extreme levels after Calderón's election, and the lack of political alignment between government levels. Indeed, as Trejo and Ley[134] show, between 2007 and 2012 only 10 percent of municipalities had a mayor with the same political affiliation of the governor and president.

Calderón's war fragmented criminal structures in the same way that early enforcement operations such as the capture of Félix Gallardo did, yet it generated far more frequent and visible violence. This illustrates that the coercive capacity is essential to explain both how efficient the state is in carrying out enforcement plans and how criminals react to the organizational transformations brought about by enforcement actions. The militarization undertaken by Calderón impacted both dimensions of violence not only because the operations were indiscriminate in their design as Lessing argues[135] but also because state forces were unable to collaborate in implementing their plans. As Trejo and Ley[136] contend, Calderón may have deliberately used military operations to punish political opponents, particularly the PRD, but this was especially the case after 2007 when the violent effects of the initial military deployments—and thus the inability of the federal state to control violence—became evident. Early military operations occurred in PAN strongholds such as Baja California and violence skyrocketed, suggesting that at least initially the government planned, but was unable, to reduce violence through its crackdown. Variation in local state cohesion explained why the military operations did not have the same impact across the territory, either because governments were unable to coordinate or because enforcement was used as a political tool, a result of a politically fragmented state.

The first joint military operation started ten days after President Calderón took office in his native state of Michoacán; military deployments continued in Tamaulipas in December 2006; Tijuana in January 2007 (more than 3,000 military elements); and in Chihuahua in March 2008 (5,000 military troops and 2,700 federal police officers). An extreme and tragic increase in violence followed Calderón's declaration of war: over his sexenio there were at least 80,000 deaths related to drug violence and over 120,000 total homicides. According to a tally kept by the newspaper *Reforma*, drug-related killings increased from 2,280 in 2007 to 5,153 in 2008, with a notable, although changing, pattern of geographic concentration. In 2008, for example, Baja California, Chihuahua, and Sinaloa comprised more than half of all drug killings in the country.[137]

After almost two decades of constant decline, general homicide rates increased from 8.5 per 100,000 inhabitants in 2007 to 13.5 in 2008, and to 24.22 in 2011. In 2010, there was a peak in drug killings (15,273 according to government figures) as violence dispersed throughout the country.[138] By the end of Calderón's term in 2012, violence seemed to have leveled off and its geographic dispersion decreased,[139] yet it had surpassed the lethality of many civil wars and many regions continued to experience extremely high levels of violence. Additionally, other violent crimes such as disappearances, kidnappings, extortion, and violent robberies skyrocketed.[140]

The initial violent hot spots were precisely areas where military troops were deployed, and although those areas were already violent, the homicide rates increased in a proportion far higher than would have been the case in the absence of military operations.[141] Paradoxically, the state's inability to establish the monopoly of force became evident in those locations where it displayed most publicly its coercive capacity through military operations. This paradox illustrates that violence is not synonymous with state absence and that it can actually emerge where the state has attempted to perform its authority more viv-idly. The military deployments increased violence in the entire country, but local dynamics differed depending on the cohesion of the local state apparatus before the deployments and on the correlations of force between trafficking groups. For example, while Ciudad Juárez experienced an increase of more than 700 percent in homicides between 2007 and 2008, the increase in Tijuana was 259 percent and in Culiacán 205 percent.

In addition to the military deployments, other reforms further reshaped the security apparatus. The most important was a shift of power away from the Attorney General's Office in antinarcotics operations toward the National System of Public Security. The Federal Investigation Agency (AFI) created under Fox was dismantled and merged with the Federal Preventive Police, becoming known simply as the federal police (PF). This shift locked in the fragmentation the Attorney General's Office had previously experienced. The growth of federal police forces, from just over six thousand members to about thirty-five thousand in six years (2006–2012), was essential for this process.

The Mérida Initiative, announced by the United States in 2007—an agree-ment aimed at providing $2.5 billion dollars for criminal-justice reform, training, equipment, and technical and military resources to support the combat against drug trafficking in Mexico—furthered law-enforcement expansion and militari-zation of the fight against trafficking organizations. The initiative also included aid for Central America, Haiti, and the Dominican Republic.[142] Implicitly, the United States and Mexico hoped that the Mérida Initiative could generate a "suc-cess" similar to Plan Colombia, and although the initiative seemed to put more emphasis on social issues and justice reforms, it shared Plan Colombia's focus on punitive measures and militarization. Yet the Mérida Initiative has been less consequential for the recentralization of the enforcement apparatus than Plan Colombia. This partially reflects that the US official relation with Mexico has been tenser than with Colombia. Though such historical tensions eased after Fox's presidency, the Mérida Initiative has not had clear political and enforce-ment allies in the way that Plan Colombia did, and as a result the channels of interaction between the United States and Mexico remain fragmented and not completely transparent. Still, resources and intelligence from the US govern-ment have been crucial in many notable arrests and raids.[143] The US support for the war against trafficking organizations[144] has been essential to maintaining militarized policies even in light of the mayhem they have generated.

State fragmentation and confrontations between criminal groups emerged before Calderón's term, but violence exploded after 2006 because the policing decisions of the government exacerbated both processes. On the one hand, the rapid mobilization of the military and growth of the federal police forced local authorities and police forces to either support or boycott these actions. On the other hand, fragmented protection networks, together with leadership vacancies generated by the capture of at least 25 drug leaders and 160 lieutenants, turned confrontations between criminal groups into all-out wars for territory.[145] In Ciudad Juárez, for instance, the confrontation between the Juárez DTO and the Sinaloa DTO worsened during the early 2000s, but it was not until late 2007 that there was a territory invasion by the Sinaloa DTO. In 2007, the government officially recognized six criminal organizations operating in Mexican territory. By 2008, there were eight organizations as the Tijuana DTO and the Sinaloa DTO split; by 2010 at least twelve organizations resulting from splits within the original six groups operated alongside smaller local organizations. By 2011, two major organizations seemed to be growing stronger—the Zetas and the Sinaloa DTO—while smaller groups still operated throughout the territory.[146]

One aspect of this situation that deserves comment is the growth of the Zetas. Many government officials, academics, and observers attributed to this group a substantial transformation in the methods of violence, and therefore, a great responsibility in the brutality of violence. Without a doubt, the Zetas represented a different breed of criminal organization because of their military origins and to their willingness to expand into other illicit ventures such as migrant smuggling.[147] It is also undeniable that the Zetas were responsible for horrifically violent acts such as the massacre of seventy-two Central American migrants in Tamaulipas in 2011 and the incineration of a casino in Monterrey that caused the death of fifty-six people in 2011.[148] However, reducing blame for Mexico's explosion of violence solely to the Zetas ignores the multiple causes driving strategic changes in the use of violence. In fact, the cities that became more violent in 2007 and that are the focus of this book—Ciudad Juárez, Culiacán, and Tijuana—did not have permanent Zeta presence. Even though the Zetas allied with rivals of the Sinaloa DTO in these cities, they were not the origin of the criminal disputes.

The Impossibility of a New "Pax Priista"

In 2012, the PRI candidate Enrique Peña Nieto was elected president. His relatively narrow win, with 38 percent of the vote, reflects multiple factors[149] including the still-effective electoral machinery of the PRI (which attracted both sincere voters and others mobilized by clientelistic exchanges), the support of mainstream media for Peña Nieto, and, importantly, a backlash against the explosion of violence during Calderón's administration. At least some voters expected that the PRI would be able to "rearrange" relations with drug traffickers and reestablish order in the country establishing a nex "Pax Priista. But the postelection performance of the Peña Nieto administration showed not only the impossibility of going back to the centralized pacts of the PRI era but also the enormous challenges that exist in terms of reforming the Mexican security apparatus.

Peña Nieto vowed to change Calderón's militarized antinarcotics and antiviolence strategy, and indeed he shifted public discourse from security to the economy. Yet in practice his actions were not much different from his predecessor's. In the first three years of the sexenio, homicide rates decreased slightly for the country as a whole,[150] and some regions in the north (like Ciudad Juárez), which had seen the worst violence during Calderón's term, saw a decline. At the same time, violence increased sharply in central regions of the country, and states like Michoacán and Guerrero saw an even further deterioration of public security, with the consolidation of vigilante groups created allegedly to confront criminal organizations.[151] In 2015 homicide rates started to increase again. Throughout Peña Nieto's term, visible violence seemed to become less common, but it also shifted throughout the country, becoming less prevalent in some areas that were the core of the violent explosion but shifting to others. As the security apparatus remained fragmented, local correlations of power became much more central in determining interactions between states and criminals than they had been during the PRI hegemony.

The credibility of the Mexican government plummeted as the involvement of security agents in human rights violations[152]—and the government's ineptitude and corruption in handling them—was exposed with major nationwide scandals. One of those was the extralegal execution of twenty-two suspected criminals by army soldiers in Tlatlaya, in the state of México, in June 2014. But perhaps the biggest blow to the government's credibility was the disappearance of forty-three students in Ayotzinapa, in the state of Guerrero, in September 2014. According to the official version of the events, the students were turned over by municipal police to the criminal group Guerreros Unidos at the request of the town's mayor and his wife. An expert report and concerns raised by the students' families and activists revealed a far more complex story that also involved federal authorities. Yet the government was unwilling to unearth all the necessary information to fully clarify the events and confirm the whereabouts or fate of the missing students. The government's inability to reduce corruption or increase enforcement capacities was further exposed when, after his arrest in February 2014, Joaquín Guzmán—El Chapo—escaped from prison in July 2015, to be eventually recaptured in January 2016. The government's general lack of transparency, and in particular its strategy of denying increases in violence and hiding the wrongdoing of security agents, further undermined public trust and tarnished the legitimacy of the state.

The inability of the PRI to reestablish control over violent actors reflects that, as in Colombia, events such as the fragmentation of organizations or the capture of criminal leaders are far from serving as a guarantee of the end of trafficking and illegal markets. At the beginning of Peña Nieto's administration the control of the Sinaloa DTO seemed to consolidate, and Guzmán's escape from prison reinforced perceptions that the government favored this organization. However, five years into Peña Nieto's term, other criminal groups kept operating and fragmenting, and as some new organizations consolidated—for example, the Cartel Jalisco Nueva Generación in central Mexico—the power of the Sinaloa cartel, which appeared to be fragmenting further, seemed far from determining the security situation throughout the entire country. There were too many interests and power centers for that to be possible.[153] Although some of the organizations perceived as the most dangerous—like the Zetas—seemed to have weakened with the capture of their leaders, violence remained very high, even if core centers of violence shifted and the visibility of violence decreased. This transformation seems to confirm that the power of an organization is not the sole determinant of the violence it creates—after all, the weakening and fragmentation of crime groups in Colombia has been linked to less, not more, violence. But, as in Colombia, criminal actors may adapt to enforcement policies aimed at eliminating the highest leaders of criminal groups by arresting or killing them— that is, *the so-called kingpin strategies*—by becoming less visible but remaining capable of inflicting significant damage.

Has State Enforcement Capacity Increased in Mexico?

The explosion of violence since 2006 illustrates the potential trade-off between state capacity to control violence and its autonomy from criminal influence. As the Mexican state has democratized, it has become less able to regulate violent actors; at the same time, it has become less able to establish centralized corrupt networks. Yet, as discussed at the beginning of the chapter, this does not mean that centralized authoritarian states are better for public security or that violence is the price to pay to reign over powerful, corrupt, and violent organizations and to build better institutions, as the Calderón government repeatedly stated. During the PRI's authoritarian rule, violence was not completely absent, but rather it was hidden and regulated. Similarly, in the new era, corruption has not disappeared but it has become more decentralized, and institutions are yet to become accountable, democratic, and efficient.

The difficulty of establishing a new *pax priista* where the PRI can rearrange peaceful relations with criminal groups, reflects that the electoral arena has indeed become open in Mexico, with two consequences in a context where enforcement capacities and justice are extremely limited. On the one hand, electoral violence has increased. According to Ley and Trejo, since between 2006 and 2012, more than three hundred subnational authorities and political leaders have been assassinated.[154] On the other hand, allegations of corruption of candidates for local office have proliferated, and while impunity is rampant, a more critical mass of citizen mobilization against corruption, violence, and impunity has increased. The conflicts and electoral fragmentation, and the government's subsequent inability to control violence, reflect that the older scheme of interaction, while inextricably linked to the PRI, was not solely attached to the party but intertwined with the bureaucratic and electoral power it held. With more competitive elections and with a radically changed bureaucracy, even when the PRI wins elections, the party does not hold the ability to control politics the way it did before. Here again, potential trade-offs between corruption and violence are not automatic, as they are shaped by underlying power structures.

Several institutional changes that have occurred since the mid-2000s could contribute to more efficient and accountable law enforcement in the long run. An attempt to clearly separate policing from legal prosecution by reducing the involvement of the Mexico Attorney General's Office in law enforcement could modernize the provision of justice and security. Increases in budget and technical and investigative capacities of the police and efforts to professionalize its ranks could help build modern police forces. Yet, by focusing on declaring war against traffickers as the only option available to confront extremely powerful and already violent drug-trafficking organizations, caught amid disputes for turf and territory in a context of extended corruption, the potential of these reforms has been undermined.

Despite record numbers of drug-related detentions at the federal level since 2006[155] and the capture of over 150 criminals labeled as priority targets (most of whom have been captured during Peña Nieto's term), prosecution and punishment for drug crimes remained extremely weak at the time of this writing: it is estimated that during the Calderón administration, 80 percent of organized crime detainees went free.[156] This may signal incompetence of the judicial system, irregularities during arrests, or the existence of many unfair detentions. Although the federal police grew significantly, and efforts to professionalize the ranks and eliminate corruption within them became more comprehensive, the mechanisms to train officers, evaluate police performance, and investigate and prosecute corruption have stayed weak. Peña Nieto's creation of yet another police force, the Gendarmería Nacional, while supposedly intended to focus on the protection of citizens, has assumed roles in the same type of militarized anti-drug operations, and its role is still unclear.[157]

Corruption cases at all levels of government and enforcement agencies are overwhelming and are generally followed by massive firings rather than by investigation and strategic planning. Human rights violations and state abuses have proliferated: there had been more than 28,000 victims of disappearance since 2006, according to data through 2017.[158] Human Rights Watch recorded that out of 249 cases of disappearance between 2007 and 2012, state forces participated actively in at least 149 cases,[159] and investigations are plagued by state inefficiency, anomalies, and impunity. While the decline in violence during the last year of Calderón's term and in the first years of Peña Nieto's created hopes that the strategies were working, as Peña Nieto's term was coming to an end it was clear that the security situation was still extremely delicate and unstable.

Considering these elements, it is impossible to claim that a death toll of more than 160,000 people between 2006 and 2015 is a sign of state consolidation and of the state's capacity to enforce the law. While I was conducting research in Mexico at the height of the violent escalation during Calderón's term, a high-level public official of the Secretariat of Public Security told me, "The state is improving and one has to evaluate tendencies. Homicides cannot be the only variable [to assess] a process of war occurring in tandem with institution building."[160] This idea is not only morally wrong but also untenable in the face of the pervasive corruption, violence, and injustice ten years after the initial declaration of war against criminals.

We may conclude, at this juncture, that the Mexican drug war illustrates the trade-off between state coercive capacity and state autonomy, between order and democratic checks and balances. The authoritarian state under PRI rule was more able to regulate criminal behavior than the recently democratizing state that is building up institutions. Yet the trade-off is not a zero-sum game. The problems of the justice system and of the increasingly powerful—but not necessarily professional—police forces suggest that democratic checks and balances have not been effectively introduced even though the one-party rule no longer exists. In the long run some steps taken since the mid-2000s (such as separating the prevention, investigation, and prosecution of crimes) may strengthen the state's ability to enforce the law. Criminal power, corruption, incapacity, and state abuse are still rampant, but a more vigilant civil society may be one of the signs of hope, and one of the paradoxical positive consequences of violence. Extreme violence has motivated civil society mobilization, advocacy, and organization, and in response to civilian demands, the government issued a law for the protection of victims for the first time in 2013. A more vigilant civil society has been crucial in exposing the government's corruption and incompetence in some of the most egregious acts of violence since 2006. This is one crucial reason why democracy is necessary even if it does not deliver all good things: it opens the space for civilians to influence politics.

Conclusion

The evolution of drug trafficking in Colombia and Mexico differs in some aspects, such as the lack of effective centralization of political power and the existence of an armed conflict in Colombia, the different composition of the illegal markets, and different interactions with the United States. Yet the two countries illustrate that state security apparatuses undergo progressive transformations responding both to political and bureaucratic changes. How states and criminals interact in particular junctures is a function of the respective power configurations at play. Colombia and Mexico also illustrate the paradox that institutional transformation and democratization can sometimes increase violence, and thus these countries illustrate the possibility that a state that is transforming its capacity to regulate interactions with citizens can also lose capacity to regulate interactions between citizens, as Daniel Brinks suggests.[161] In my theory's terms, a cohesive state that can assert its coercive capacity can also provide predictable protection to traffickers. The challenge for countries that are confronting criminal actors while still building professionalized, accountable, and democratic state security forces is as Ana Maria Bejarano and Eduardo Pizarro[162] put it, to rebuild authority without authoritarianism and corruption.

As illustrated in this chapter, a trade-off does not imply a zero-sum game. Institutional transformations can unleash violence but also improve states' crime-fighting capacities. As violence increases, efforts to combat crime can strengthen the state's enforcement ability over time. In other words, while confronting criminals, states do not have to choose only between corruption and violence; they have to reconstruct a cohesive state that is autonomous, accountable, and democratic. Eventually Mexico can emerge out from its public-security crisis with stronger police institutions, as occurred to some extent in Colombia—although even there, the state's ability to impose the rule of law is marked by militarized frameworks and still limited by impunity, corruption, and abuses of power, especially at the local level.

As this chapter outlined, and as developed in the following chapters, drug violence results from complex interactions between states and criminals. While absence of violence can reflect a state's improved capacity to control territories, it may also imply that the state is not autonomous from criminal actors. Moreover, relatively low violence does not imply absence of violent criminal activities, and frequent but not visible violence may exist even when the state is cohesive. These elements are particularly relevant to understand Medellín, the subject of next chapter.

4

Medellín: From Extreme Wars to Unstable Pacification

Medellín, capital of the northwestern department (state) of Antioquia, and Colombia's second-largest city, has been besieged by multiple armed and criminal actors since the 1980s and has witnessed stark transformations in the forms and perpetrators of violence. An initial period of extreme violence was followed by quieter wars; a subsequent phase of pacification started in 2003, when Medellín gained attention from observers and academics alike, as it experienced a historic decline in homicide rates that coincided with broad urban transformations and was labeled the Medellín "miracle."[1] Yet, a fourth phase characterized by a return of "quiet wars" started in 2008. Since 2012 the city experienced a new decline in homicide rates.

What explains this sharp variation? How can we explain that a city dubbed the most violent in the world in the 1990s experienced a sharp decrease in homicide rates in the 2000s? This chapter shows how interaction between state cohesion and competition within the illegal market shaped the four periods of violence and illustrates clearly how the type of criminal armed coercion and the relations between gangs and criminal organizations have important consequences for violence. Over these periods, when the state security apparatus has been cohesive, violence has been hidden, because the state is more credible in protecting (or, conversely, persecuting) criminals. Alternatively, violence has been visible when the state has been fragmented. Furthermore, frequent violence persisted in Medellín for a long time due to the competition between multiple trafficking actors, exacerbated by complex interactions between traffickers, guerrillas, and paramilitaries. The outsourcing of criminal coercion to youth gangs has characterized the most violent periods. Pacification occurred when there was a monopoly of criminality and criminals disciplined youth gangs. The comparison over time provides the most controlled test of this book's argument as it holds crucial variables constant, such as Medellín's economic importance, its history as a hub for early industrialization, and the characteristics of its urban landscape.

Each section in this chapter discusses the key variables in the argument and their impact on violence over the four periods. The first period (1984–1993) is known as the narcoterrorist war. During that confrontation, both the frequency and visibility of violence increased exponentially as the Medellín DTO and Pablo Escobar besieged the city. This period can be described as a "perfect storm" when variables combined to produce extreme violence: a very fragmented state, a competitive criminal market, and outsourcing of violence to youth gangs. The second period starts with Escobar's death in 1993 and continues until 2002, when drug trafficking generated a high homicide rate but confrontations were characterized by less visible violence than during the period of narcoterrorism. The third period (2003–2007) was marked by pacification, in which a cohesive state and a criminal monopoly created the conditions for a reduction in violence. The criminal leader of the time, Diego Fernando Murillo (aka Don Berna), strategically disciplined gangs to maintain "peace." The last period (2008–2011) saw "quiet wars," after Murillo was extradited to the United States and succession disputes ensued, yet as a tactical adaptation to a cohesive state that became more efficient in capturing criminals, criminals learned to be "less visible." These periods are summarized in Table 4.1.

Figure 4.1 illustrates how homicide rates increased during the first period, decreased during the second (although remaining high), and then dropped dramatically before increasing again in 2008. In the three periods of high frequency, homicide rates in Medellín grew to be at least three times higher than national rates as a result of outsourcing to gangs. Table 4.2 and Figure 4.2, based on the data set I constructed, illustrate the changes in the visibility of violence as operationalized in chapter 2, for a few selected years. In 1989, during the narcoterrorist period, criminals employed more methods to publicly display violence than in 1984 and 2009; likewise homicides involving public targets of violence, such as police officers, were far more common in 1989 than in the other years.

Such relentless violence, has, paradoxically, generated organized civil society and state responses that contributed to improvements in living conditions and urban governance in Medellín in the mid-2000s. Because this book is not about socioeconomic factors, I do not explore these transformations in detail, although they are important for understanding the steadier declines in violence after 2012. However, validating this book's central argument, such improvements alone cannot account for changes such as the pacification in 2003, because in 2008, despite improved social programs, violence spiked again following an increase in criminal competition.

Before discussing each period of violence, is it worth mentioning important characteristics of the city. Medellín was the center of an early industrialization and modernization process in Colombia, heavily promoted by local,

Table 4.1 **A Political-Economy Approach to Drug Violence in Medellín**

Period	Criminal Market	State Security Apparatus	Type of Armed Coercion: Relation between Criminal Actors and Gangs
1984–1993 HF-HV	Competitive: Medellín DTO dominated, but militias and guerrillas also operated.	Fragmented: Military deployments in urban antinarcotic operations generated conflicts; coordination between national and local government was lacking; local authority was fragmented; political competition increased.	Outsourcing: Gangs proliferated at the service of traffickers. Petty criminality became more violent as gangs acquired arms and money. There were some rules of behavior, but traffickers did not regulate gang behavior strictly.
1994–2002 HF-LV	Competitive: Militias, trafficking groups, *oficinas*, guerrillas and paramilitaries were all struggling for power.	Increased cohesion: Toward the end of the period the state successfully coordinated military-police action.	Transition to complete control over gangs: High-level actors in the drug trade and paramilitaries attempted to co-opt gangs but also to regulate their behavior.
2003–2007 LF-LV	Monopoly: Under the leadership of Don Berna, DTO had successful control of different criminal activities and eliminated or controlled criminal competitors.	Cohesion: Incentives created by peace process eliminated conflicts between national and local government; more coordination between enforcement agencies emerged.	Complete control of gangs.
2008–2011 HF-LV	Competitive: Successors of Don Berna strived for control; reconfigured paramilitary groups competed.	Cohesion: State remained relatively cohesive in enforcement agencies. Political alternation prevented consolidation of state protection rackets.	Outsourcing: Criminal actors used gangs as armed force but did not have enough power or willingness to discipline them.

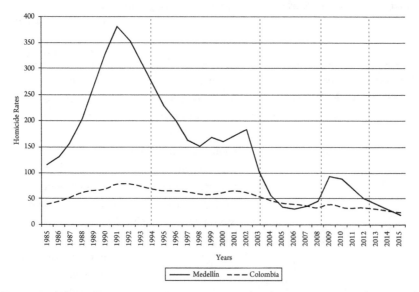

Figure 4.1 Homicide Rates in Medellín 1984–2015 (per 100,000 Inhabitants).
Source: Author's elaboration, based on data from Policia Nacional de Colombia, Secretaria de
Gobierno de Medellín. Dotted vertical lines indicate the periods of violence.

conservative elites.[2] As a result, beginning in the 1950s, the city attracted large
migratory flows[3] of people motivated by economic opportunities but also by
the need of rural populations to escape growing violence in other parts of the
country.[4] Economic incentives attracted young labor forces that in times of economic boom were ready to be employed, but in times of economic crisis they
suffered the consequences of poor infrastructure and social services. These
economic processes transformed social structures, and traditional conservative
values clashed with new consumer habits and ideas, older crime traditions, and
the advent of drug trafficking.[5] The history of illegal actors is inextricably linked
to Medellín's geostrategic importance in connecting key drug producing areas,
important transportation routes, infrastructure projects, and highly profitable
markets for both legal and illegal products.[6]

Medellín's deep social, cultural, and economic transformations, together with
the city's geostrategic importance, are essential for understanding its history of
violence, yet social and economic factors—which generally move slowly—
cannot explain sharp changes in violence.[7] A multitude of actors mixing criminal, political, and personal agendas created an extremely complex dynamic
where rivalries, alliances, and motivations for violence have been extremely
fluid.[8] Despite this complexity, however, it would be impossible to understand
Medellín without considering drug trafficking and its interconnection with the
armed conflict.

Table 4.2 **Methods of Violence in Medellín**

	1984	*1989*	*2009*	*Total*
Sexual Violence		2	1	3
Simple Use of Firearms	131	832	30	993
Strangulation		4	3	7
Simple Use of Knives	28	94	2	124
Drive-by Shooting (*sicariato*)	75	66	7	148
Forced Disappearance	2	17	1	20
Combat with Fire Guns	1	31	5	37
Car Bomb	3	4		7
Combat with Explosives		2		2
Corpse with Note		2		2
Fire		24		24
Grenade		4	3	7
Head in Cooler	1	1		2
Mutilation or Incineration	4	2	2	8
Simple Use of Explosives	9	48		57
Torture	4	21	1	26
Wrapped in Blanket		2		2
No Information	2	182	19	203
Total	260	1,338	74	1,672

Methods appear listed from low (top) to high (bottom) visibility, following the classification presented in Table 2.1.

The "Perfect Storm" of Violence (1984–1993)

This section explores how between 1984 and 1993, state fragmentation, disputes between the Medellín DTO and other armed actors, and the explosion in traffickers' use of gangs were at the core of a violence epidemic. The war waged by traffickers against extradition was enabled by a context of state fragmentation.

The Rise and Fall of the Medellín "Cartel"

The origins of drug trafficking in Medellín were tied to old smuggling traditions dating back to the nineteenth century. In the 1970s, crackdowns on

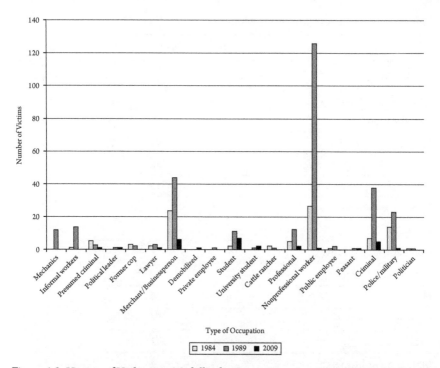

Figure 4.2 Victims of Violence in Medellín, by Occupation. Source: Author's data set on drug-related violence, information compiled from *El Colombiano* newspaper (Medellín). The data here covers only those cases where occupations were clearly identified.

emerging cocaine networks based in Chile and Cuba enabled the first successful Colombian drug traffickers, coming from very poor upbringings, to amass large fortunes. This decade also witnessed a boom of drug carriers known as *mulas,* or "mules,"[9] who, although not as financially successful as their bosses, helped extend trafficking networks. In 1976, Pablo Escobar appeared publicly when he was first arrested on drug-trafficking charges; by the 1980s, the organization known as the "Medellín Cartel" made the city infamous worldwide due to its extreme violence, its declaration of war against the state, and Escobar's megalomaniac personality, which transformed the world of drug trafficking.[10] The intense frequency of drug-related violence in Medellín resulted from disputes within a competitive market, and the extreme visibility of the violence resulted from a fragmented state security apparatus, which made protection unpredictable and complicated anticrime operations.

At first glance, it seems counterintuitive to argue that there was a competitive criminal market in Medellín, considering that Escobar's power and influence were enormous and probably only a few criminals fit the popular image of a *capo,* or drug lord, as he did.[11] The Medellín DTO, however, was far from having a complete monopoly or territorial control over the city even at the height of Escobar's power, to a large extent because of the presence of multiple armed actors associated with the Colombian armed conflict. Criminal and territorial competition explained the sustained increase in the frequency of violence reflected in an average homicide rate of 232 homicides per 100,000 inhabitants between 1984 and 1993, far above the average homicide rate of 63 for the entire country. A historic peak of 381 homicides per 100,000 population occurred in 1991 and constituted Medellín's most violent year ever (see Figure 4.1.).

By the mid-1980s, Escobar had consolidated a strong organization controlling previously fragmented trafficking groups. At the same time, urban guerrilla militias and self-defense militias also struggled for control in a city that was essential for their geostrategic interests. In 1984, demobilization camps were established in Medellín as part of peace processes between the national government and the M-19 guerrillas. These camps became a military training ground for young men who would later become militia or gang members.[12] Gangs proliferated due to the money provided by traffickers and to the combat expertise provided in guerrilla camps. As a result, extortion, robberies, drug dealing, and killings multiplied. Criminality in turn provided the motivation for self-defense militias and vigilante groups, which also became violent players in their alleged quest for "protecting" the community and "reducing" criminality.

Guerrillas and militias were not directly fighting for turf with traffickers, yet they challenged the Medellín DTO's power and complicated the alliances and confrontations among armed actors. Militias usually targeted lower-level gangs at the service of traffickers while tolerating the more powerful broker organizations in charge of hiring *sicarios* (hitmen, or contract killers). In some cases, militias stirred conflicts among gangs, so they would destroy each other.[13] In others, militias recruited members from the very same groups they were targeting (economically disadvantaged adolescents and young men). Traffickers did not curtail these violent dynamics, and gangs supported by traffickers fought gangs supported by militias. The confrontations snowballed into a war of all against all.[14]

Criminal competition worsened at the beginning of the 1990s, as Escobar faced growing opposition within his organization and from his biggest competitors, the Cali DTO, thus sustaining the upward trend in homicides. The Cali DTO repeatedly rejected Escobar's plans to confront the state,[15] and on January 11, 1988, members of the Cali DTO activated a car bomb against one of Escobar's properties and he in turn responded with terrorist attacks in Cali, creating an all-out war between the two groups. Furthermore, by the early 1990s some of Escobar's partners started to criticize terrorist actions (explained below) and the monetary quotas Escobar extracted from them to wage war against the state.[16]

In June 1991, Escobar handed himself over to government authorities under a policy known as *sometimiento a la justicia* ("surrender to justice"), whereby the state offered judicial benefits to traffickers who confessed all their crimes.[17] During the year Escobar spent in jail, he killed three of his closest allies— Gerardo Moncada, and the brothers Fernando and Mario Galeano—thus fracturing his organization irreparably. The killing apparently had to do with money not paid for a drug transaction, but it also reflected Escobar's fear that the armed enforcement wing of the DTO, known as the Oficina de Envigado (Envigado Office), was getting too strong while he was in prison.[18] The Oficina was a broker criminal organization created to hire assassins, but later it became the main contract enforcer for traffickers.

The Galeano killings unleashed ire among other members of the Medellín DTO, especially Diego Fernando Murillo, who was the Galeanos' chief of security. He became a founding member of the vigilante-paramilitary group Los Pepes (a name that stood for "persecuted by Pablo Escobar") in January 1993. Los Pepes were an eclectic group that provided the opportunity for Escobar's internal and external enemies—the Cali traffickers, paramilitary groups, and betrayed allies—to work together and with the police toward the objective of bringing Escobar down. Los Pepes thus reflected the internal fragmentation and the external competition the Medellín DTO, and especially Pablo Escobar, confronted in the early 1990s, which in turn diminished his ability to control criminality. Eventually the Cali DTO and Los Pepes, working alongside government and international enforcement, succeeded in eliminating Escobar in 1993.[19]

Besides a highly competitive criminal market, two other factors were equally crucial to explain the extreme spiral of violence: (1) the outsourcing of violence to youth gangs and (2) the fragmentation of the state security apparatus, which prevented traffickers from controlling the state and made it difficult for the state to confront them efficiently.

The Narcoterrorist War and State Fragmentation

In 1984, Pablo Escobar assassinated Justice Minister Rodrigo Lara Bonilla in retaliation for Lara's open criticism and his enforcement operations[20] against drug trafficking and Escobar personally. The state struck back by enforcing extradition treaties, which led the Medellín DTO to declare a war on the state that was aimed at eliminating extradition,[21] a conflict that came to be known as the narcoterrorist war. These events unleashed the most visible deadly period in Colombian history, one that claimed the lives of hundreds of civilians, more than two hundred judges, seven hundred police officers, and several prominent politicians. The violence in this period was characterized by the use of notes or communiqués to claim responsibility for violence, tactical innovations in killing methods, collective violence, attacks that took place in broad daylight or in the middle of public spaces, and the targeting of public officials.

Such visibility resulted from complex interactions taking place within a fragmented state that was facing growing domestic and international pressure to combat drug trafficking. The United States pressured the Colombian government to enforce extradition, and starting in the late 1980s, the US government injected significant resources into counterdrug operations. Yet, despite these measures, during the first years of the narcoterrorist war the Colombian government was unable to effectively confront criminals and enforce the law. State fragmentation also complicated traffickers' ability to secure credible state protection. This book's theory focuses less on the events that initiated this wave of violence and more on the power relationships that framed these events. In this sense, it matters less who moved first to create violence; more important is how state fragmentation shaped the effects of the policies the state implemented to combat narcoterrorism—because enforcement operations may have different consequences if they occur within a fragmented state than if they are carried out by a cohesive one. Initial antinarcotic operations against Escobar directly generated violence by unleashing retaliation from traffickers and also by fueling abuses by state actors attempting to weaken the Medellín DTO's support base. This violence was more visible than it would have been if a cohesive security apparatus had implemented the anticrime operations. In a counterfactual scenario, the narcoterrorist war in Medellín could have been shorter and less visible had the government had more initial capacity to dismantle the Medellín DTO or had Escobar found stable state protection.

As argued in chapter 1, state fragmentation increases when there are conflicts among levels of government, between enforcement agencies, and when events such as democratization or anticorruption purges reduce the time horizons of elected and public officials. National processes generated all the elements that took on a particularly fragmenting character in Medellín. An opening of electoral competition in the mid-1980s shook political life in a city accustomed to domination by a conservative political elite.[22] In response to increasing violence, the central government deployed military force to carry out urban antigang operations that generated bitter conflicts between the military and the police and complicated the atmosphere of violence even more. Medellín's geographic location, contiguous to nine municipalities,[23] made policing efforts extremely dependent on the actions of the other municipalities' mayors. Also, some municipalities at the time had created bodies known as Departamentos de Seguridad y Control (Security and Control Departments) that even though under the formal command of the national police were independent. Finally, early attempts to transform police forces drastically changed the rules of the game for traffickers.

As the presence, power, and violence of traffickers grew, their relations with the state became more intricate. The political and electoral liberalization that Colombia experienced in the early 1980s, after a long power-sharing agreement between two political parties,[24] affected the interactions between illegal actors and political forces and also the feasibility of coordinating enforcement operations. A cornerstone of electoral liberalization was the introduction of popular elections for mayors in 1986, which multiplied the actors involved in local public security. Antinarcotics policy was not officially within a mayor's realm of action, but its violent consequences were, thus multiplying the government agents with veto power over local security policy and the possible conflicts between them. Coordination was more difficult given the extent of violence and the need to deal with the other mayors in the metropolitan area.[25]

Another cornerstone of political liberalization in the 1980s was increased electoral competition,[26] which provided renewed opportunities for criminals to access the state but also made it increasingly difficult for them to maintain stable corrupt deals, as denouncing corruption became a powerful tool of electoral competition. Political liberalization was profoundly felt because Medellín was the stronghold of a conservative political elite that started to face growing electoral challenges in the late 1970s and early 1980s.[27] This elite, starting to see its power challenged, reacted strongly to Pablo Escobar's attempt to mobilize popular classes; Escobar in turn reacted to the "bourgeoisie" that blocked his intentions. In the words of former minister of defense Rafael Pardo, Escobar's violence was not only a reaction to extradition but "the most violent expression of a social class trying to be recognized and finding a place in the Colombian society."[28] This class struggle was more profound given Medellín's political and economic inequalities.

The most vocal opponent of drug traffickers and champion of morality in politics was the Nuevo Liberalismo, the party formed in 1980 by Luis Carlos Galán. Nuevo Liberalismo had its electoral stronghold in major cities like Bogotá and Medellín. In February 1982, Pablo Escobar appeared on the congressional election ballot as an alternate member for the Lower Chamber with Jairo Ortega, a liberal politician of Antioquia, who was seeking support from Nuevo Liberalismo. When Galán and the Nuevo Liberalismo's coordinator in Antioquia, Ivan Marulanda, learned about Escobar's intention, they requested his elimination from the list. Escobar and Ortega nonetheless ran through the political movement Renovación Liberal and were elected for the Lower Chamber of Congress. Renovación Liberal also elected three council members in the neighboring municipality of Envigado, legislators who became loyal servants of Escobar.[29] Nuevo Liberalismo continued its naming and shaming and championed Escobar's expulsion from Congress in 1983. Escobar's infamous attempt to become a politician was a manifestation of the doors that democratization opened for traffickers to access the state, but Nuevo Liberalismo's reaction also reflected that democratization could seriously undermine traffickers' protection.

State fragmentation created incentives for Medellín traffickers to expose violence as a tool to intimidate, punish, and reaffirm their power, as first indicated in December 1981 with the creation of the group Muerte a Secuestradores (Death to Kidnappers), or MAS, an early manifestation of an explosive combination between paramilitary groups and drug trafficking. Pablo Escobar and two hundred traffickers founded MAS as a reaction to the kidnapping by the guerrilla group M-19 of the sister of the Ochoa brothers, Escobar's trafficking partners. The group announced its creation by raining leaflets over the crowd attending a soccer match, stating its objective to publicly execute kidnappers, to offer rewards for information, and to hang, shoot, and mark the executed.[30] Over the next few years MAS perpetrated violence that blurred the lines between criminal vendettas and political violence.[31] Many copycat groups emerged, and in the end both the original MAS group and the copycats nurtured the paramilitary phenomenon and violence. Traffickers incrementally introduced new killing methods, many of which publicly displayed violence—for example, using drive-by shootings (*sicariato*)[32] and explosions (see Table 4.1). New methods were used to attack state targets, to eliminate competitors, and to discipline and punish members of the organization.

Visibility escalated with Escobar's quick reaction to his expulsion from Congress: as noted above, he assassinated Justice Minister Rodrigo Lara Bonilla, a member of Nuevo Liberalismo. In reaction President Belisario Betancur issued an extradition order for Escobar's trafficking partner Carlos Lehder. On November 6, 1986, Los Extraditables, the organization founded by Pablo Escobar and members of the Medellín DTO with the goal of impeding extraditions, made its official appearance before the Colombian public, releasing a document calling for the end of extradition "in the name of national sovereignty, family rights, and human rights."[33]

Los Extraditables claimed responsibility for their attacks, usually through communiqués explaining their crucial objective of preventing the enforcement of extradition through intimidation (later on complemented with the objective of opposing "human rights abuses" by police forces). They also demonstrated a lack of concern for the consequences of media or enforcement attention. In a threatening note sent to a judge they claimed "not to be afraid of press scandals and repressions."[34] Occasionally, Los Extraditables also claimed responsibility through notes on corpses, especially in their attacks against their Cali DTO rivals. Corpses appeared on highways pierced with hand drills, burned, and shot and their bodies were accompanied by notes with messages such as "Members of the Cali Cartel, for attacking people from Medellín."[35]

The Medellín DTO's violent response to extradition also led to the systematic assassination of local officials such as the Antioquia state governor Antonio Roldán Betancur (July 1989), the Medellín police chief Valdemar Franklyn Quintero (August 1989), and the local senator Federico Estrada Vélez (April 1990). In August 1989, the presidential candidate Luis Carlos Galán was assassinated. This event was a turning point, eliciting the government's strongest reaction thus far toward traffickers and marking the highest point of an all-out war against the state by traffickers. Violence escalated, and killing methods aimed at exposing attacks, such as massacres and car bombs, became commonplace. The bombs prompted the emergence of the term "narcoterrorism" to describe this particular brand of violence. Between 1988 and 1993, 719 acts of violence were classified as "terrorist attacks" in Medellín.[36]

After Galán's assassination, the government initiated military urban operations that further fragmented the security apparatus because the army was still wary of antinarcotics action. In 1984, the army established its first battalion with a counterinsurgency mandate based in Medellín, but it was not tasked with antinarcotics operations. In the words of Colonel Augusto Bahamon, who was in charge of first establishing the battalion:

> Back then, the army was not interested in waging a war that they knew in advance they were going to lose with a high toll in lives and prestige, because the mission of the army differs from that of the police, and this was very clear to all our superiors.[37]

Medellín became the epicenter of the state's military response to narcoterrorism, and the army's Fourth Brigade implemented Plan Genesis, which moved monitoring posts into the neighborhoods most affected by drug trafficking.[38] By 1989, the army was engaged in massive urban antinarcotics and antigang operations. The army's use of indiscriminate search techniques and illegal detentions undermined its relationship with the community,[39] while its parallel role in dismantling corrupt local police agencies created constant confrontations with the police and made the framework in which criminals interacted with the state even more unpredictable than before. According to Colonel Bahamon:

> In the fight against *sicarios* there was no way to copy a model from another country as has been done in antiguerrilla campaigns both urban and rural. There were no legal procedures that facilitated the troop's work. The executive branch tried to modify this situation creating

military commands in Bello, La Estrella, and Envigado. After operating with and without them, it can be said that they were a path that the military was not used to traveling. The government believed that creating legal attributions was enough to obtain the desired results. The reality was quite different because the military commands were institutions without means, which were born and died without leaving a trace.[40]

Bahamon's remarks capture the army's frustration as well as the deep conflicts that divided institutions in the antidrug trafficking campaign, reflecting how the militarization of antidrug operations, by adding enforcement agencies, could, and can, fragment the state. Such operations could also directly generate violence by unleashing violent responses among traffickers, who at the time lacked strong incentives to hide attacks. Benjamin Lessing contends that traffickers engaged in violence against the state to lobby against extradition because of key conditions existing at the time the narcoterrorist war was launched: first, the end of extradition was a viable issue to bargain for because it was popularly opposed and in a judicial limbo; second, DTOs were at relative peace; and third, traffickers believed they could force concessions from the state in a context where other armed actors were negotiating with the state.[41] While these factors are very important, one cannot completely explain the differing strategies of the Medellín DTO compared to the Cali DTO (explained in chapter 5), or the fact that Cali traffickers actively opposed the narcoterrorist tactics, without considering how protection networks were organized. The Medellín DTO had a strong but unpredictable network of protection they could lose, and at the time, the state capacity to repress was still weak and not seen as entirely threatening for criminals. So even though they believed they could force concessions through violence, they also believed those concessions could not be achieved by just using corruption, and they probably did not fear the state response sufficiently. The state structure and the unpredictability of protection and enforcement made Medellín criminals believe the state was vulnerable to violent pressure but also unreliable as a protector.

As military and police antinarcotics operations increased, and Escobar's protection within police agencies grew more unstable, he initiated a campaign to eliminate police officers. The Medellín DTO had enjoyed protection among the Security and Control Departments in the municipalities surrounding Medellín.[42] Evidence of corruption led the national government to eliminate these municipal police forces, and as the national police engaged more forcefully in operations against the DTO and gangs, state protection became increasingly unstable. Despite their ability to corrupt wide sectors of law enforcement, Pablo Escobar and the Medellín traffickers also faced many actors willing to attack them. The assassinations of municipal police reflected that it was difficult for

Escobar to find predictable protection in enforcement officials, even though he had ample corruption networks.[43]

The killing of police officers illustrates the multiple forms in which drug violence can be reproduced when both state and criminals are fragmented. Pablo Escobar set a price for every police officer killed in Medellín, a strategy that led to the death of 737 policemen: 420 in 1990 and 317 between 1992 and 1993.[44] Escobar's offer to pay about five hundred dollars per cop killed unleashed a "witch hunting" period when young sicarios killed cops to get the reward; police personnel in turn refrained from wearing uniforms, making targeting more difficult and increasing "mistaken" attacks. Dangerous alliances emerged among sectors of the police and nascent antigang militias and paramilitary groups[45] as they targeted young men they suspected to be sicarios.

The argument that extreme state fragmentation complicated both enforcement and protection, thus reducing criminal incentives to hide violence, challenges a narrative of violence as determined by traffickers' personalities and operation styles. Although Escobar's megalomaniac personality undoubtedly played a role in explaining the methods he used, it is only part of the story, because in a few occasions he hid violence: for example, during his brief stint in prison and before escaping in 1992. Furthermore, other actors used visible violence: Los Pepes exposed targeted killings of Escobar's associates, using notes on the corpses of victims who had been tortured before their murder. For example, on February 28, 1993, when the architect Guillermo Londoño White, accused of having links with Escobar, was found dead, his face had a dozen bullet holes, his hands were tied with duct tape, and a note on his body signed by Los Pepes read, "Luis Guillermo Londoño White, faithful figurehead and initiator to Pablo Escobar's kidnappers."[46] According to some estimates, Los Pepes alone killed about 125 people in Medellín during 1993[47] and were predecessors not only to the horror techniques[48] used by paramilitaries in Colombia[49] but also to the brutal methods used by Mexico's traffickers to publicize violence. Visible violence was thus not exclusive to Escobar.

Combos, Bandas, and Oficinas

The narcoterrorist war and the state response to it affected Colombia as a whole, but it was extreme in Medellín not only because that city was Escobar's home but also because of local political and criminal dynamics. The "perfect storm" of violence cannot be fully explained without considering the outsourcing of violence to youth gangs. Escobar used gangs to conduct violence, but he did not try to inhibit the common crimes they produced, as was later the case with Diego Fernando Murillo in the 2000s. As a result a culture emerged around drug trafficking, gangs, *sicariato*, and Pablo Escobar, which deeply affected an entire young generation in the 1980s, in what Alonso Salazar and Ana María Jaramillo labeled "the subculture of drug trafficking."[50]

The history of gangs did not start with Escobar, but their presence increased and became more sophisticated under his influence. Unlike the Cali DTO, which mainly recruited former security personnel (military and police) to provide for their security (as explored in chapter 5), Escobar made local gangs his main armed force, partially because his access to local police forces was not as extended as that of Cali traffickers. In the words of a military official closely involved in prosecuting the Cali DTO, "The Cali people, because of their style and because they wanted to be different, their sicarios were less preposterous, more sophisticated; they, unlike the sicarios of Medellín, were not paid by their crimes, they were part of the organization and in consequence the sicarios of the Rodríguez Orejuela [leaders of the Cali DTO] could not violate the organization's parameters; the Rodríguez Orejuela intercepted their sicarios' communications to keep them controlled."[51]

Not all youth gangs worked directly for Escobar, and it is likely that he directly hired a relatively small proportion of them. Yet the expectations of the money that could be made working for traffickers motivated gangs to proliferate.[52] As the supply of potential soldiers increased, so did the violent competition among them to obtain the best and more profitable jobs, as described by a gang member interviewed by Salazar in the first ethnography ever made about youth gangs in Medellín:

> There have been many gangs in the neighborhood: Los Nachos, Los Montañeros, la del Loco Uribe, Los Calos. And as the song goes, 'There is no bed that can hold so many people.' We need to remain active because if we lower defenses other gangs expel us and start screwing people . . . . We also fight with the police but things are easier with them because they come up shitting their pants while one knows the terrain.[53]

Outsourcing to youth gangs made discipline more difficult to maintain and violence more likely to spread. Escobar had symbolic power over criminality and there was a relatively hierarchical, even if diffuse and not completely regularized, structure of gangs. Yet high-level traffickers did not have direct contact with all gangs and especially with low-level sicarios—consequently, they were unable or unwilling to control gang behavior. Another interview with a gang member conducted by Salazar clearly reflects this dynamic where traffickers used gang services but did not control them vertically:

> What the Brigade [the army] says about sicarios is a televideo. It does not work like that, with a regular structure. They put together the gangs

that work directly for Escobar with others that have nothing to do with him. Everybody respects him, because he has been kind with the people and his people handle many threads, but there are also many independent *combos*. Around the area where I have been working, the thing works like this: there is a small group of strong ones who handle the contacts at the highest level, and you don't get to see them around anymore. They handle relationships with the *bandas'* bosses, and these bosses are the ones who handle the selection process when there is a *job* to be done . . . . But many of the kids [*pelados*] who benefited from the business were not as serious as the first ones. Many outlandish little bands emerged. They are abusing people, killing because you did or you did not look at me. That is the people who damage the business, the eccentric ones (*visajosos*).[54]

Outsourcing took place through a three-tiered model composed of *oficinas, bandas,* and *combos*.[55] The limits between these three levels were sometimes diffuse and complicated by the multiple armed actors operating in the city, yet a hierarchical organization could be ascertained. *Oficinas* were (and still are) broker organizations, in charge of hiring and controlling gangs' relationships with drug traffickers. *Bandas* are relatively sophisticated, usually older gangs, with territorial power, significant armed and economic resources, and direct relationships with traffickers and oficinas. *Combos* are territorially limited gangs (usually controlling blocks within neighborhoods) that sell their services to the *bandas*, who in turn sell them to *oficinas* and traffickers.[56] In this model of outsourced coercion, the socialization of gang members in violence and the use of firearms, coupled with the excess supply of force, also created incentives and capacities for gangs to engage in other criminal activities such as extortion, bank robberies, or kidnappings that provided income when they did not work for traffickers. The expansion of criminal activities and competition among gangs became additional sources of violence. These dynamics illustrate how, as explained in chapter 2, analyzing drug violence does not require assuming that every violent act is directly associated with a drug-trafficking dispute but rather understanding that the power dynamics of trafficking organizations may reproduce or inhibit other expressions of violence.

Outsourcing explained the upward spike of violence in Medellín because it multiplied the number of potentially violent actors in the city and exacerbated conflicts among them. In fact, besides the visible violence generated by the Medellín DTO, massacres also became commonplace during the narcoterrorist period. On July 1, 1984, seven heavily armed men opened fire on a group hanging out in a creamery after a funeral, killing five and leaving six wounded.[57] Massacres like this spread out all over as gangs became better armed and engaged in power struggles among themselves. Massacres initially affected depressed areas of the city, but eventually they also began occurring in elite neighborhoods, as on June 23, 1990, when seventeen young people inside a bar were forced to lie on the floor and were then executed. Notes were placed on the corpses announcing that four upper-class young people would die for every sicario killed. Some events of collective violence also reflected an identification problem.[58] As enemies became difficult to identify, mistakes or careless attacks became more common: for instance, men on motorcycles (or in cars) arrived at public places such as restaurants and opened fire into the crowd even if they were targeting just one person. Some massacres also reflected the action of vigilantes, militias, and police forces.

Outsourcing of violence by no means was a phenomenon that involved all young people and gangs as criminals. In fact, the percentage of youth directly involved in criminal activities was small relative to the size of the young population. According to Salazar, only 30 percent of gangs were related to drug traffickers.[59] Nonetheless, outsourcing reproduced violence to extreme levels and beyond trafficking disputes, claiming many civilian lives.

By way of a recap, the competition for control of territories and illegal markets between multiple armed actors, and the complexity of the relations between those criminal actors and youth gangs, was a driving force behind the extreme violence of the narcoterrorist period. Visible violence reflected the difficulties of a fragmented security apparatus in confronting criminals (despite the escalation of state antinarcotics operations), and the criminals' difficulty in obtaining credible protection within the state. Outsourcing explains how violence in the city spiraled out of control.

Two issues stand out in this period of narcoterrorism in Medellín. First, not all victims or perpetrators of drug-related violence were drug traffickers. Both victims and perpetrators included traffickers and criminals, but also civilians and state officials. The motivations for violence were diverse: traffickers' attacking the state and competitors, state officials illegally using force, criminals using copycat techniques, criminals revenging violence, and even regular citizens solving personal disputes. The mix was further complicated through the influence of guerrilla and paramilitary groups, which both allied with and confronted traffickers in their quest to gain territorial control. This complexity highlights the difficulty of defining drug violence as discussed in chapter 2. A broad definition would include events where motivations are complex and may transcend criminality, but it bears repeating that reducing drug violence strictly to events that include criminals or that pit criminals against the state ignores how drug trafficking spurs or mitigates other sources of violence. In Medellín, drug-trafficking organizations radically transformed violence. While waging war against rivals and the state, traffickers made arms more easily available, socialized youth gangs into violence and fueled competition among them, and complicated the armed conflict.

The second issue that stands out during Medellín's narcoterrorist wars is that even though the visibility of violence was significantly higher than in any other period, visible attacks did not cause most lethal victims. As shown in Table 4.2, most attacks entailed the simple use of firearms, when a single killer targets a single victim—but these events became relatively normalized by the public and the media. This process often appears in other locations and periods: acts producing the most victims may be less visible and therefore can come to be ignored as routine, whereas relatively fewer instances of visible attacks can gain wide attention, creating images of environments of extreme brutality. Nonetheless, because visible events do not emerge all the time or in all cities, when they do emerge they represent a crucial change—even if they produce less victims than routine, less visible violence.

A Market in Transition (1994–2002)

The second period of drug violence in Medellín was marked by greater state cohesion, which started to increase toward the end of the narcoterrorist period, leading to a clear decline in visible violence.[60] In 1993, the joint military-police command known as Bloque de Busqueda (Search Bloc), which facilitated coordination between enforcement agencies, succeeded in hunting down Escobar and killing him in 1993.[61] US government funding and support together with the collaboration of Los Pepes was also crucial in bringing down Escobar.[62] Throughout the narcoterrorist war, the state changed radically because the police gained technical expertise and became the center of growing cohesion in the security apparatus. Homicides decreased, but violence was still extreme because the criminal market remained competitive.

Militias, Paramilitaries, and Traffickers

Pablo Escobar's death contributed to a reduction in homicides but violence remained high in the 1990s. The criminal market was still competitive, directly and indirectly involving militias, guerrillas, paramilitary groups, and traffickers from the Medellín DTO who had not been eliminated and were reaccommodating. Competition among criminal groups drove the violence that continued to besiege the city. A great deal of violence during this period resulted from militia actions against rival militias and low-level criminals as well as from local wars between neighborhood gangs.[63] Militias had consolidated by the mid-1990s and were, in the most basic definition, neighborhood vigilante groups created to "defend" communities from petty criminals. Yet their roots and composition were complex, and mixed groups derived from guerrilla training camps, criminal bands defending turf, police forces, and economic elites.[64]

The militias' engagement in drug trafficking was indirect and contradictory. On the one hand, in their alleged attempt to control criminality, militias targeted and eliminated drug consumers and petty criminals. On the other hand, militias rarely targeted high-level traffickers or the oficinas and combos that worked for them. Sometimes traffickers supported militia "cleansing" activities that they saw as a way to control the "disorder" brought by petty criminals.[65] Yet unstable alliances and confrontation generated violence, because trafficking factions aligned with different militias and enemies sometimes allied to defeat common threats.[66] The average homicide rate in Medellín between 1994 and 2002, although lower than in the previous period, was still higher than the already high national average: 187 deaths per 100,000 inhabitants compared to a rate of 63 for Colombia as a whole.

The aftermath of the Medellín DTO has been described as a period of fragmentation between microcartelitos, the smaller trafficking organizations.[67] The illegal market indeed became more fragmented, but a far more complex process was taking place. In order to consolidate power, former members of the Medellín DTO and the Oficina de Envigado strengthened alliances with paramilitary groups, which in turn benefited financially and militarily from the alliance. A protagonist of this process was Diego Murillo, the man who had started as Escobar's hit man, founded Los Pepes, and eventually achieved a monopoly of power in Medellín. The microcartelitos were the surface of a complex reaccommodation. Murillo himself recognized 1994 as a crucial year in the consolidation of alliances with paramilitaries and in the expansion of the paramilitary project, which mixed political and criminal motivations intricately.

In 1994, some militias demobilized within a process promoted by the national government that ended up failing because many demobilized members were assassinated or remained criminally active, while others were not part of the process. Militias thus lowered their public profile but retained influence in the city's violent and criminal dynamics.[68] Meanwhile, paramilitaries were becoming stronger, partially through private security agencies known as *Convivir*, created by the governor of Antioquia, and later president of Colombia, Álvaro Uribe.[69] By 1997, paramilitary power had consolidated nationally,[70] with Medellín as an epicenter where a faction known as Bloque Metro (Metro Bloc) started to wipe out militias and guerrillas. This changing correlation of forces in the armed conflict had enormous consequences for local illegal markets.

The boundaries between criminal and political violence became increasingly blurred because paramilitaries consolidated control over drug-trafficking activities without abandoning their counterinsurgent motivations, and the money and armed power of criminal groups became vital for paramilitary expansion. This codependence between criminals and paramilitaries is illustrated by the story of La Terraza, a gang that emerged in the Manrique neighborhood, grew under Pablo Escobar's leadership, and was then used by Murillo to carry out paramilitary-sponsored assassinations of leftist intellectuals and leaders, in addition to other killings and robberies.[71] As La Terraza grew more powerful and its leaders became increasingly unhappy about their low profits, they carried out attacks against Murillo in 2000, hoping to replace him and gain greater involvement in drug trafficking.[72] Yet Murillo survived and assassinated La Terraza's leaders, a victory that reasserted his power. The Oficina de Envigado, a structure existing since Escobar's years and responsible for coordinating the taxing of traffickers and common crime, also commanded by Murillo, became the main criminal node in the city and established direct relations with the paramilitary Bloque Metro.

By 2002 the Oficina de Envigado and the remains of La Terraza mutated into a paramilitary faction known as Bloque Cacique Nutibara, commanded by Murillo, which, along with the Bloque Metro, successfully defeated militias and guerrillas. Soon after, a battle for Medellín's control ensued between these two factions, generating more violence.[73] Murillo eventually won this battle (as discussed below). The illegal market after 1993 was thus highly competitive and fluid, and this explained the persistence of violence, as armed actors struggled to eliminate each other and engaged in unstable alliances.

The State and Its Transformations

During this period, the state underwent institutional changes that reduced fragmentation and paved the way for more stable state-criminal collaboration while also increasing the state's capacity. These changes reduced criminal incentives to publicly display violence. Anticrime operations at the national level, still driven by militarized frameworks, grew and became more efficient. For instance, drug interdiction capacities and police intelligence led to faster arrests of criminal kingpins. This contributed to reducing the visibility of violence by transforming the criminal market while forcing Colombian traffickers to engage in risk-sharing agreements, which sometimes diminished their power—for example, vis-à-vis Mexican criminals. These outcomes underscore this book's emphasis on the importance of the power structure that underlies enforcement actions: drug policies that are carried out by fragmented states are likely to generate visible violence because criminals have not adjusted their incentives. In the Colombian case, during this new era of enforcement, the decapitation of criminal organizations or drug busts were not fiercelessly fought, as was seen during the Escobar years. Criminals started to learn that too much attention was detrimental for them and that it was better to adapt than to fight the state. Violence could still appear if market disputes emerged, but not as publicly as before.

Three factors were crucial in the growing policing capacity toward the late 1990s. First, increasingly blurred lines between antinarcotics and counterinsurgency agendas enabled the US government to channel more military aid to Colombia, allowing the Colombian government to deploy the military in antinarcotics. Second, coordination between the police and the army grew toward the late 1990s. And third, paramilitaries' corrupt networks became consolidated across large political sectors. In Medellín this environment created interlocking incentives for armed actors to hide violence. This meant, for one, that disappearances became more prevalent. Similarly, "social cleansing" proliferated at the hands of militias attempting to impose their own social order. The "cleansing" practices of militias, directed at anything they considered a threat—from drug consumers to bad neighbors[74]—were visible within Medellín's local communities but not necessarily visible at the state level and to the general public, as was the case during the period of narcoterrorism.

At the local level, state cohesion increased because in the late 1990s, despite increasing electoral competition, traditional political elites dominated elections[75] and promoted collaboration across levels of government.[76] The collaboration between enforcement agencies was essential for state cohesion and was solidified with joint military-police actions aimed at defeating guerrillas (FARC and the National Liberation Army or ELN) in their strongholds such as the Comuna 13.[77] In 2002 alone, there were eleven military operations in this part of the city,[78] and two of them—Operations Mariscal and Orión—were prominent because of their size, the type of arms deployed, and because the police and army operated along the Security Administration Department (DAS) and the Attorney General's Office. These operations, unlike those in the 1980s, were highly coordinated. In an interview, the army general who commanded these operations emphasized that teamwork had been key in antiguerrilla joint operations in Medellín,[79] something that did not happen in other cities like Cali.

Successful coordination among enforcement agencies also became the norm because the national government led by President Álvaro Uribe, and Medellín's mayor Luis Pérez Gutiérrez, jointly supported this type of military operation. These operations undermined guerrilla presence, thus weakening one competing armed actor in the city, but they generated serious human rights violations and, most importantly, were facilitated by, and were instrumental in, paramilitary consolidation.[80] In fact, the dark side of the cohesion that allowed effective enforcement in these large-scale operations was precisely that paramilitaries were receiving political protection from numerous state actors and consolidating their control, thus reducing state autonomy from criminal influence. Paradoxically, as Aldo Civico argues,[81] the state reasserted its presence through a complex intertwining with illegal actors.

The protection that paramilitaries received from sectors of the local political class motivated them to privilege hidden violence such as disappearances[82] and to use mass graves to hide the remains of people. Paramilitaries used mass graves to hide victims of disappearance in the Comuna 13[83] in a technique that extended into the following period of pacification.

By the end of this period, an interesting paradox emerged: a city wounded by extreme violence also became more active in confronting it.[84] As one community organizer expressed to me in an interview:

> In the nineties, one could see very strong levels of solidarity, of social organization. Grassroots efforts developed and a new spirit in the region was brought to life, that of working together. That process called to action a society that examined itself critically, through norms and state support. Many groups were created in Medellín, such as those promoting musical interests among young people.[85]

These community efforts are important for two reasons. First, organized civil responses seem more likely to emerge when cities experience extreme violence. As seen in chapter 5, civil society's efforts appear more limited when wars are quiet, as in Cali or Culiacán. Second, these community efforts are crucial for mitigating the impacts of violence, but they seem limited for explaining those dynamics because strong community efforts and programs existed both during the pacification and during the subsequent return of violence that will be explained below.

Youth Gangs in the Transition

During this second period, outsourcing and the complex links between small youth gangs (combos) and larger criminal groups continued, thus contributing to continued high homicide rates. Young people were the main victims of the militias' cleansing activities, and later of paramilitary groups, while at the same time they constituted attractive soldiers for guerrillas, paramilitaries, and militias. The complex relationships that linked gangs to different armed groups generated territorial and turf disputes between combos and bandas and created *fronteras* (frontiers), which marked the localized limits of power within neighborhoods and between gangs. These conflicts underscore the key difference between outsourcing and other sporadic forms of contracting services with gangs: in outsourcing, gangs can identify clearly who they work for—there are clear lines of alignment even if lines of authority are not totally clear. Interestingly, precisely because of these "local wars" the Medellín mayor's office promoted pacts aimed at reducing violence in neighborhoods. Many pacts succeeded in reducing violence temporarily, but they were often unstable and short-lived, precisely because they did not acknowledge the strong links between youth gangs, larger criminal groups, and broader conflict dynamics.[86]

The outsourcing relationship between gangs and criminals started to change toward the late 1990s. Rather than contracting out violence, militias, traffickers and especially paramilitaries attempted to discipline and co-opt youth gangs. Because paramilitary structures were relatively new and their knowledge of the urban space was limited, gangs' familiarity with Medellín's geography was key for the paramilitary project of urban consolidation[87] and it was necessary for paramilitaries to use gangs as an armed force. Paramilitaries tried to vertically integrate gangs into their structure, they strictly controlled youth behavior, and they recruited and sent gang members to military training camps.[88] Social cleansing of drug consumers and low-level criminals became more common, and paramilitaries imposed norms controlling the times of circulation, dress codes, and drug and alcohol consumption of young people. In the words of a community organizer, in the late 1990s "the bandas were crushed with blood; there were fliers distributed in convenience stores showing that there were *others* coming to exert social control."[89] The vertical integration, cooptation, and repression of gangs by paramilitaries did not reduce violence while the criminal world was competitive and militias and guerrillas remained strong, but it had a powerful violence-reducing effect when one criminal actor effectively dominated the city after 2002. In other words, when illegal market competition disappeared, dominating gangs was essential to achieve complete control over the city's violent actors.

Medellín's "Miracle" (2003–2007)

Beginning in 2003, Medellín experienced unprecedented social transformations and policy changes: an urban reform promoted by Sergio Fajardo, elected mayor in 2003; the demobilization of paramilitary groups; and a reduction in violence that seemed impossible in a city with such a complicated story of violence and sorrow. In 2003, homicide rates decreased by about 46 percent; the rate reached a historic low of 34 homicides per 100,000 inhabitants in 2007. Such a stark transformation bewildered observers and inhabitants, and it was happily attributed to the peace process and the urban transformation. Mayor Fajardo introduced a large-scale program of investment in marginalized areas based on the premise that inequality and violence were closely connected, and thus urban reform could "close the entrance door for youth into criminality."[90] Over time, and especially when violence returned a few years later, less flattering causes for the decrease became clear. Without denying the benefits of the urban transformation, the sudden reduction can be explained by the consolidation of a criminal monopoly under the control of Diego Fernando Murillo and by state cohesion that provided the incentives to hide violence.

The story of Diego Fernando Murillo, aka Don Berna, perfectly illustrates the evolution and complexity of Medellín's violence. As already explained, Murillo started as a member and then enemy of the Medellín DTO, but he successfully mutated into a paramilitary leader who consolidated power by co-opting some gangs, eliminating rivals, and finally winning over a rival paramilitary faction, the Bloque Metro.[91] His success stemmed from his ability to wage and win subsequent wars against criminal and political competitors. As one expert defined it, Murillo "was the winner of all the city's wars."[92] The successful monopolization of criminality entailed controlling different markets, from extortion to local drug distribution, but also imposing rules of conduct over civilians. Murillo's control over different types of criminality questions arguments linking growing violence to the diversification of criminal portfolios, because for him diversification served as a tool to accumulate more power, and in turn regulate violence.

Murillo commanded a tight criminal network with deep social roots, as manifested in May 2005, when his group ordered a bus stoppage that paralyzed the city, in reaction to an Attorney General's Office arrest warrant. This event made evident the intimidating power and criminal control over the extortion market of transportation routes. Bus drivers agreed to stop out of fear. In a similar episode in 2007, armed men tried to persuade the principal of a local school to fill two buses with people so they could attend a judicial public audience to support Murillo.[93] The paramilitary consolidation that started in the previous period, along with Murillo's social and criminal power, significantly reduced criminal competition. Given the role that gangs had played in violence, the radical reduction of homicides that started in 2003 would not have occurred without Murillo's ability to discipline gangs, regulate their violent behavior, and broker their conflicts.

Disciplining Gangs

Murillo's success in controlling violence depended on his ability to regulate the violent behavior of youth gangs and on strictly disciplining the young population in marginal areas of Medellín.[94] In words of an analyst from the mayor's office, "Nobody could move without Berna's permission; there was a subjugation of bandits."[95] In Don Berna's own words, "at some point we had total control over Medellín .... we coopted those groups [bandas and combos] and they became part of our organization."[96] Rather than prohibiting drug use, one of the markets Murillo dominated, criminals controlled where and how drugs could be used. In an interview with the NGO Instituto Popular de Capacitación (Popular Institute for Training), a young man asserted that "paramilitaries in many occasions warn young people not to drink alcoholic beverages or use psychoactive substances in certain places, but at the same time they indicate where they can do it; in other words, there is control not only based on immediate violence, but in a consolidated power that is well-known to the youth."[97] Interviews and human rights reports suggest that paramilitaries and criminals used punishments that made an example of those who did not follow their rules. For instance, they would force the young men to remain in the sewers for hours on end, forbidding families from seeing or getting close to them for the duration of their punishment[98] and forcibly displacing them to other neighborhoods within the city. Murillo and his organization expelled those who did not comply with the rule of using violence only when authorized by the high commands. A local police commander told me in an interview that "Don Berna ordered not to kill" while he was in prison, "and nobody killed. I met a kid who knew his mother's assassin but he did not do anything because he knew he could be killed as well" by don Berna's people.[99]

Sexual violence in Medellín increased from 843 reported cases in 2003 to 1142 in 2007,[100] perhaps reflecting its strategic use by gangs as a punishment and intimidation for those opposing their rules.[101] This type of violence, however, was less likely to generate massive reactions or to be publicly noticed, partially because, as Pilar Riaño contends, the population often displays contradictory attitudes toward sexual violence[102] and also because the relations between sexual violence, armed conflict, and criminality have not been systematically recognized in Colombia.[103] While multiple factors underlie sexual abuse, the increase parallel to the decrease in homicides could reflect the criminals' interest in hiding violence while maintaining social control.

Murillo's ability to regulate gang behavior highlights that the mere presence of gangs or the existence of large young populations does not determine the involvement of youth in violence and criminal activities. It also underscores that reduced gang criminality may sometimes hide dangerous dynamics of manipulation by powerful criminals. Notably, despite the tight grip that criminals exerted on social behavior, some communities preferred such control to all-out criminal wars, thus highlighting the complex interaction between criminal behavior and its social acceptance. For example, Murillo had a reputation for settling disputes between gangs, which led him to use the nickname of Adolfo Paz (Adolf Peace) during the negotiation that preceded paramilitary demobilization. Not surprisingly, as Brenda Carina Oude Breuil and Ralph Rozema note, community members regarded Murillo with a peculiar combination of fear and admiration for his ability to bring peace.[104] The overall reduction of violence (which is undeniable even when considering the hidden violence at work) brought enormous relief to the population of Medellín, but the criminal arrangements that sustained it became the basis of the return of violence.

Hiding Violence to Maintain Peace

Collaboration between national and city governments was crucial for solidifying the cohesion in Medellín's national security apparatus that started in the late 1990s and became consolidated by 2003. In 2002, the government of President Álvaro Uribe (2002–2010) started a demobilization process for paramilitary groups. The process benefited not only paramilitaries but also many drug traffickers disguised as paramilitaries, and Murillo, who became a paramilitary leader, entered the peace process. In November 2003, as commander of the Bloque Cacique Nutibara, he demobilized along with 873 men, many of whom were members of local gangs rather than paramilitary soldiers.[105]

For Álvaro Uribe, Medellín was a crucial test for the peace process, because it received the largest concentration of demobilized soldiers in the country: 3,270 by 2007.[106] Medellín mayor Sergio Fajardo, the first mayor from a party independent from traditional political parties elected in the city, was not officially part of the peace negotiation or a member of Uribe's political coalition, but he decided to support the process—which he defined as an opportunity to take advantage of "an exit door from delinquency"—even though he did not really know what had been negotiated.[107] This situation created a strategic concurrence of interests that eliminated conflicts between national and local governments: the local government did not question the negotiation, and the national government did not intervene in local security initiatives.[108] The success of the process depended on collaboration between elected authorities: the national government controlled the process politically, but the local government coordinated the reinsertion of the demobilized soldiers.[109]

As became evident later, while engaged in the peace process, Murillo continued controlling illegal markets, but he knew that, in principle, the state was not going after him if he did not use excessive violence, because both local and national authorities needed a successful peace process and thus initially condoned some of Murillo's behaviors. In the words of a local police commander: "The order was not to follow them [criminals], because there was a pact between the president and the mayor's office. There was political resistance to bother them . . . . because there was a peace process ongoing."[110]

On several occasions, the national government protected Murillo despite growing evidence of his criminal activity. In 2005, Murillo was accused of ordering the assassination of a local politician in the northern state of Córdoba, and the government ordered his arrest. As Murillo handed himself over to authorities, the demobilization continued. Later, in response to an extradition request on drug trafficking charges made by the United States in 2004, the Colombian government announced that Murillo would not be extradited if he continued collaborating with the peace process and abandoned his illegal activities, a decision that was not endorsed by the United States but that guaranteed the continuation of the demobilization. Murillo was transferred from the demobilization camp in northern Colombia to a prison near Medellín, and in 2007 after recurrent reports of criminal activity he was taken to another high- security prison. Finally, under pressure from the United States, the Colombian government finally extradited Murillo in May 2008. The government thus tried hard to maintain a process that was reducing violence by creating a credible promise of not prosecuting criminals. Violence reduction here derived from two interrelated processes: the monopolization of the criminal market and increasing state cohesion, which created a shared interest between state and criminals to reduce violence. In fact, some people have colloquially labeled this relation *donbernabilidad*, a play on the Spanish word *gobernabilidad* (governability), referring to Don Berna's power in setting the terms of governance.

Homicide rates declined significantly, yet if violence was necessary, it was carefully hidden. Events of collective violence in Medellín decreased by 69 percent between 2002 and 2003[111] while reports of forced disappearance, homicides with blunt objects or knives, and suffocation increased. According to community leaders, such methods reflected an interest in hiding the responsibility of those committing crimes because these methods tend to be quickly associated with common crime or interpersonal disputes.[112] Between 2003 and 2006, the proportion of total homicides committed with knives more than doubled, from 9.3 to 22 percent,[113] and many of them were committed by paramilitaries who wanted to divert attention and elude responsibility on violence.[114] Victims' testimonies and paramilitaries' confessions add up to suggest that in one location alone at least three hundred corpses of disappeared people were buried between 2002 and 2005 in Medellín.[115]

During the pacification, a crucial political paradox emerged: electoral competition was high but there was state cohesion. Independent political forces (represented by Mayor Fajardo) got stronger at the same time that some traditional and emerging politicians were co-opted by paramilitaries. In Murillo's own words, "We had in Medellín an enormous influence over communities. Many people who ran for mayor or senator during the emergence of the Bloc [Metro] had relationships with us in one way or another."[116] The large-scale alliance between paramilitaries and politicians known as *parapolitica*, carefully documented by the political analyst Claudia López,[117] became the basis of a judicial process that linked 139 congressmen nationally and 22 in Antioquia to paramilitary groups.[118]

The political paradox of this situation is that the security apparatus acted cohesively despite electoral competition between these two political sectors— the new civil movement and the colluded politicians. This occurred because both political sectors found incentives to make the peace process work. The coordination of enforcement agencies and levels of government was achieved despite the lack of political alignment between government and corrupt sectors. Even though the split between political sectors continued after the pacification years, state cohesion has remained to some extent because each of these political sectors has enough political resources to govern the city. Protection rackets can be established when the corruptible sector wins—because once in power, networks can work cohesively—but protection may be unstable because the other sector can gain power back. For example, in 2011, the independent network led by Fajardo regained its power back from another political network closely linked to the *parapolitica* scandal.[119]

Breakdown of the Monopoly (2008–2011)

Murillo's criminal monopoly started to face internal and external pressure after July 2006. On July 3, Gustavo Upegui, a sports entrepreneur and politician widely known as a leader of the Oficina de Envigado, was assassinated, and the disappearance of one of Murillo's closest collaborators followed his death, indicating power struggles within the criminal market. After Murillo's extradition in 2008, struggles evolved into disputes for control, which produced a notable— and for many leaders and observers, unexpected—increase of the city's homicide rates, which doubled from 45 in 2008 to 94 in 2009.

Quick reaccommodations followed the first few months after Murillo's extradition: some of his successors were arrested, killed, or handed themselves to authorities. By 2009, two former sicarios, Sebastián and Valenciano, filled the leadership vacancy and disputes between them drove the increase in violence between 2009 and 2011. Their power was significant, but not comparable to that of former criminal bosses; indeed, as one security expert noted, in 2010 delinquency could be described as "very violent and not very organized," whereas "before, it was very violent and very organized."[120]

When violence reemerged, national authorities quickly associated it with a struggle for controlling local drug markets (microtrafficking) and emphasized its criminal nature, thus trying to depoliticize violence and disconnect it from problems associated with the paramilitary demobilization or with the armed conflict—a discursive move criticized by many activists and experts.[121] While government depictions of violence in the 1990s tended to decriminalize violence, ignoring the paramilitaries' engagement in drug trafficking, depictions in the 2010s depoliticized it, ignoring the way that actors in dispute were closely linked to the evolution of the armed conflict. In fact, some actors fighting for control after 2008 belonged to the structures known as neoparamilitaries, or BACRIM (criminal gangs), which were formed by paramilitaries that never demobilized, some recidivate demobilized soldiers, and new recruits.[122] Two of these groups, the Urabeños and the Paisas, which emerged outside Medellín, entered the city and fought for control over its criminal markets.

Criminal markets besides drug trafficking, including drug retailing, extortion, stealing of gasoline, and control of gambling, became more consequential for criminal income even though they were not new. As many experts told me, with the breakdown of Murillo's monopoly, these illegal markets became highly contested among factions vying for criminal dominance. For instance, extortion in public transportation functioned as an effective protection racket under Murillo's criminal monopoly: transporters paid their quota and they were effectively protected from petty criminals. But after 2010, assassinations associated with this illegal activity became widespread.[123] According to observers from a reputed NGO, as the monopoly of criminality fragmented, no single "protector" could guarantee safety for transporters, and thus, a single bus line could be extorted and threatened by multiple actors.[124] This example illustrates, once again, that diversification of criminal markets alone may not cause violence; violence instead depends on the type of control exerted on criminal markets and on the connections established between different criminal activities. Furthermore, controlling local markets such as extortion can be a product rather than a source of violence, because markets that are tied to local territory, like retail drug sales or extortion,[125] can provide soldiers with monitoring posts for larger criminal enterprises. According to a local analyst, Sebastián and Valenciano competed on the basis of how many combos they controlled, which in turn determined their ability to control illegal commerce, territories, and access points to strategic drug-trafficking routes in the Urabá port and in the drug-producing area of the Bajo Cauca.[126]

"Quiet Wars"

The return of violence brought worry to both the government and the public, yet it was far from causing the concern that violence had caused in the 1990s. National authorities quickly explained it as resulting from disputes for local drug markets rather than as a threat to national security. This differing perception partially reflected that the violent disputes emerging in 2008 were considerably less visible than those of the 1990s. In the words of a local analyst, "There is a [criminal] attempt to regain leadership. The difference is in the method for applying violence."[127] Violence, although widespread and deadly, did not threaten the wider public. As another practitioner in violence prevention programs stated: "Deaths nowadays are more selective, more focused. Before we felt involved as possible victims, but there is more indifference today,"[128] and that statement was echoed in similar terms by a local councilwoman: "The situation today is not as bad, because of what was done back then [in the 1990s] the mafiosi changed their profile. One does not feel scared of going to Seventieth Street as before. The problem of the *narco* can even be worse now, but the fact is that the bombs made [the 1990s] a more aggressive period."[129]

In this fourth period, attacks against high-level public officials were uncommon, even while methods hiding violence—such as disappearances and the destruction of corpses—increased. Local authorities reported that corpses were increasingly found in the stream of the Medellín River: forty-eight bodies were recovered from the river in 2010 alone. According to an investigator from the Attorney General's Office, "Criminal organizations throw the bodies with the intention of disappearing them. Thus the evidence, and the possibility of getting to the perpetrators, disappears."[130] Different human rights organizations also reported the use of brutal methods to hide violence; one human right worker interviewed in 2011 reported that disappearances were increasing in the Comuna 8, with "terrible methods that eliminated all remains, such as incinerations and the use of machines to destroy the bodies."[131] Similar stories emerged in conversations with members of a human rights group in the Comuna 6; according to one of them, criminals "torture, murder, chop, burn. People leave because they have been intimidated; there is fear about denouncing because of the infiltration in the police."[132]

These "quiet wars" reflected a strategic adaptation of criminals to a state that remains cohesive especially through the coordinated action of enforcement agencies. As explained in chapter 3, in Colombia traffickers have learned that when they gain too much state attention, they can be quickly captured. In fact, Sebastián and Valenciano had long criminal careers that dated back to the Pablo Escobar years, but they survived with a relative low profile that attracted little police attention before they became the identifiable leaders of criminal factions. They were arrested soon after their role in the criminal disputes was established: Valenciano was captured in November 2011, and Sebastián in August 2012.

Revitalizing the Combos

Sebastián and Valenciano had a long experience with criminality but not the symbolic power or control over armed force that their predecessors had.

Outsourcing violence to combos was crucial for them to wage war and control criminality. As in previous periods, not all combos worked for larger criminal structures, but the association with warring criminal groups marked gangs' territorial disputes. According to a security expert, Valenciano, for instance, made combos accountable for every criminal enterprise in their area (microtrafficking, extortion) but without establishing total control over them, or without making them part of his "organization's payroll, because it's easier to contract a *pelado* [kid] for a job than having him in the payroll."[133] Members of combos often do not personally know who they work for because "today the narcos are not known. The kids do not know who Sebastián and Valenciano are, but in the oficina they are told who they work for."[134] These statements illustrate the contrast with Murillo's all-out control. Gangs are hired to carry out violence, and there is a hierarchy that associates them with larger criminal disputes, yet this hierarchy is not strong enough to discipline them.

Outsourcing coupled with competition in the criminal market revitalized disputes within the relatively small territories that mark the boundaries of combos' turf, similar to the "local wars" of the 1990s. These territorial disputes illustrate how outsourcing contributes to upward spikes in violence: gangs acquire better equipment and money and compete with each other, and those contracting the gangs' services do not have the ability or interest in controlling them. Localized wars have created what neighborhood residents and public policy experts call *fronteras invisibles* (invisible frontiers), lines that demarcate combos' areas of control and that severely limit mobility in local communities. Invisible frontiers heightened processes of intraurban forced displacement that by 2011 totaled 17,912 people:[135] many of those displaced left their neighborhoods in order to avoid threats and territorial conflicts between combos. According to a human rights activist in the Comuna 6, "One cannot move to another neighborhood, because one can be killed; those who say that criminals are only killing each other are lying. There are always 'stray bullets.' Many die by mistake. Overall, disputes between combos have victimized more civilians in the population."[136]

The violence after 2008 was less intense than the "perfect storm" but still very high when compared with the Colombian national average and with many cities in the world. Criminal groups were probably more fragmented and weaker than before, but they were not detached from national dynamics and from the international drug trade. They preferred to hide violence because they learned that once they became too noticeable for authorities, especially for national ones, they could quickly be captured. It is possible, however, that if criminals want to expand, they may start displaying violence to show their power. This might be the motivation behind some killings and massacres that occurred in 2012.

After 2013, homicide rates started to recede again, and by the time of this writing (2017) they had kept a downward trend, thus taking Medellín out of the list of the world's ten most violent cities. Such a radical decline in violence has been influenced by multiple long- and short-term factors. The process of urban transformation that has improved conditions in marginalized areas and connected those areas to the city may have helped lowering the threshold for violence,[137] even though it has not eliminated inequality and marginalization. As Eduardo Moncada argues, close collaboration between business and political actors and the integration of civil society in policymaking was also crucial for propelling many social reform projects in the city.[138] Medellín's long tradition of grass-roots initiatives against violence has also played an important role while supporting and providing alternatives for at-risk youth, but also while actively confronting the tactics of armed actors.[139] Despite crucial improvements, armed actors still operate in the city, remain powerful, and control local governance— sometimes even coopting community- and state-sponsored projects.[140] While the baseline for violence is lower than in the 1980s, threats to security abound. Therefore, to understand violence in the short run, attention to state dynamics and to power correlations among armed actors remains essential.

Conclusion

Medellín illustrates the complexities that surround drug violence, especially when it overlaps with political violence. Armed actors that mutate and change sides and political motivations that overlap with criminal ones are common-place. Violence linked to the evolution of actors in the armed conflict has been inextricably linked to the dynamics of control over illegal markets, to the interactions between criminals and the state, and to close relationships between gangs and criminals.

Medellín's criminal market has experienced periods of monopoly with low-frequency violence, as well as periods of competition with high levels of violence. Likewise, the state has shifted from fragmented to cohesive, shaping criminal incentives to display violence. When state protection was less predictable and enforcement operations less efficient, criminals engaged in a narcoterrorist war to display power to their rivals but also because they believed they could force the state to shift enforcement pressure, especially stopping the extradition treaty. The multiple armed actors existing alongside the Medellín DTO made the criminal market more competitive—and as drug traffickers outsourced violence to youth gangs, extreme violence ensued. This story challenges conventional understandings of criminal power. One such example is the idea that Pablo Escobar was an almighty criminal. While his symbolic power and his control over the illegal market was undoubtedly enormous, he did not have a monopoly of violence and illegality in Medellín as it is often assumed. Outsourcing, at different moments and rates, also contributes to understanding extreme violence.

The evolution of the armed conflict at the city, regional, and national levels has played a key role in the story told in this chapter. Medellín was first a scenario where all armed actors coincided, thus complicating the establishment of criminal monopolies. Then it became a bastion of the paramilitary expansion occurring nationally, which was instrumental to creating a criminal monopoly. At the same time, as the most violent city in Colombia for over three decades, Medellín also concentrated antinarcotic and counterinsurgency operations that transformed the drug market. Regional and national conflict dynamics and policies thus frame its violent history, but they cannot completely account for local dynamics. One notable example of the relevance of the local level is the difference between Medellín's conflict, criminality, and violent dynamics and that of its country counterpart, Cali, where the armed conflict and criminal groups followed a different path.

Several insights derive from analyzing such extremely fluid violence. First, trajectories of violence might be path dependent but not necessarily cumulative or self-enforcing. They may be path dependent because today's criminal actors are connected to former periods of violence and former criminal actors. In other words, it is impossible to understand violence today without understanding its history. Furthermore, violence can persist despite positive institutional transformations and strong civil society responses. Yet violence may also be non-cumulative or self-enforcing because trends can change rapidly and reverse, as illustrated by the quick erosion of the peaceful equilibrium of the Murillo years after his power faded-away. Rapid changes can also occur in the distribution of state power: for example, through reaccommodations in relations between enforcement agencies and levels of government. This is a crucial insight because we often think of state capacity as relatively static and separated from political dynamics.

A second insight is that relations between youth gangs and criminal organizations are central to understanding violence. Yet violence is not the automatic result of the existence of gangs or large populations of youth. Gangs can exist without being associated with violence and criminal groups; gangs can relate to criminal groups only sporadically; or they can be clearly associated with criminal groups while maintaining a separate organizational structure. In the latter case, criminals may either use gangs to outsource violence or they may attempt to strictly discipline them to regulate violent behavior, as occurred during Murillo's time. Unpacking how these diverse relations take place provides important insights for better understanding urban violence.

Finally, the example of Medellín suggests that extreme and especially visible violence can create a paradox, as the need of both civilians and state actors to respond to violence can strengthen civil society responses and force the state to find more creative solutions. It is undeniable, for instance, that in its long experience with violence, the city developed more government programs dealing with youth,[141] violence, and conflict resolution than any other city in Colombia, as well as more communal and civil organizations experienced in dealing with vulnerable and at-risk populations and victims. This positive side effect of violence is not as noticeable in other violent cities that have experienced hidden violence or quieter wars. Cali and Culiacán illustrate this situation and will be discussed in the next chapter.

Since the mid-2000s the increase in social investment and infrastructure connecting Medellín's poorest neighborhoods has played an important role in accounting for why violence in the 2010s is significantly lower than in the 1990s. This urban transformation has also radically altered perceptions about the city, as expressed by an official from the mayor's office: "The city is like the Phoenix. Today there is a transformed city that has been humanized. In the past you could die everywhere. Would you have ever imagined that tourists would come to Medellín? Nobody thought that people could believe in Medellín."[142] These transformations, while important, cannot completely account for short-term and often sudden variations as the interaction between state and criminal power can do.

Cali and Culiacán: Hidden Violence and State-Criminal Collusion

If an external observer were asked to identify the most violent city in Colombia or Mexico, the first response would probably not be Cali or Culiacán. These two cities, despite having long histories with violence and drug trafficking, have not been the center of concern for national or international actors;[1] despite having homicide rates often surpassing national averages, they have not witnessed the civil and institutional responses against violence—however imperfect—that their country counterparts like Medellín or Ciudad Juárez have generated. Furthermore, despite the persistence and deadliness of violence, sectors of the population perceive older drug traffickers as "gentlemen" who respect "honor codes." These responses and perceptions of violence and traffickers suggest the prevalence of *frequent* but *low-visibility* drug violence—the focus of this chapter. How can we explain these strikingly similar histories in two cities imbued in different national contexts, each with different political and social histories?

This book's core argument is that variation in drug violence results from interactions among and power relationships between the state security apparatus and the criminal market. Whether the security apparatus is cohesive or fragmented determines visibility and whether the drug market is monopolized or competitive determines the frequency of violence. In this framework, the prevalence of "quiet wars" in Cali and Culiacán can be explained by a cohesive state often symbiotic with criminal organizations, which could allow impunity in the perpetration of violence but also created incentives for criminals to hide, as visible violence could force an otherwise friendly state to attack them. Criminal markets were competitive most of the time, thus explaining the persistently high homicide rates, but those rates did not experience upward spikes because for the most part criminal organizations insourced the perpetration of violence; therefore, although violence was high it did not triple national rates (the definition of an upward spike).

The two cities are framed in different political and social contexts. Cali has been affected by the armed conflict, while political violence has not been widespread in Culiacán; likewise, the politics of the latter cannot be understood without considering the decades-long hegemony of the Institutional Revolutionary Party (PRI) in Mexico. The extent of urban transformation is also different. While Cali has been subject to intense immigration waves that shape dynamics of social inclusion and exclusion,[2] migration flows to Culiacán tend to be seasonal, responding to labor demand in agriculture, and population growth has not been as sharp as in Cali (see Table 5.1. for basic socioeconomic statistics). Yet, besides being home to powerful criminal actors, the two cities share a prevalence of strong landowning and agro-industrial elites, relatively weak civil societies, and, most strikingly, similar configurations of violence that contrast sharply with their country counterparts.

To analyze these cities, the chapter is divided into two sections. The first analyzes the history of violence in Cali, the capital of the Valle del Cauca department (state) on the Pacific coast of Colombia, a city first dominated by the Rodríguez Orejuela brothers, leaders of the Cali drug trafficking organization (DTO). It explores how the existence of a cohesive state security apparatus allowed the extensive network of corruption created by the Rodríguez Orejuela family and created incentives for them to hide violence. After the Cali DTO

Table 5.1 **Cali and Culiacán: Basic Statistics**

	Cali			Culiacán		
	1985	2000	2010	1985	2000	2010
Population	1,350,565	2,236,709	2,244,536	560,011	745,537	858,638
Pop. Growth		65%	0.34%		33%	15%
Pop. 10–29 Years of Age	43%	37%	35%		50%	36%
Unemployment Rate		21.3%	12% (2008)		2.6% (2002)	6.1%
Gini Coefficient		0.54 (1998)	0.517		0.43 (2005)	
Agriculture as % GDP		0.16	0.33			12.3*
Industry as % GDP		20	22			8.1*

* Calculated for state (Sinaloa) GDP.

Source: Compiled from DANE and INEGI data.

was dismantled, disputes emerged among its heirs, which made the criminal market more competitive. Homicides increased, but for the most part conflicts remained as "quiet wars" due to the pervasive protection criminals found in the local state apparatus.

The second section is devoted to Culiacán, the capital of Sinaloa on the Pacific coast of northern Mexico. As in Cali, a cohesive state facilitated the collusion between traffickers and state officials, thereby determining the prevalence of low-visibility violence. In turn, competitive tendencies among trafficking leaders in Sinaloa have maintained high homicide rates. In 2008, violence exploded and became more visible, and Culiacán ranked among Mexico's three most violent cities as trafficking organizations experienced the most serious split in its history. Also, urban military deployments by the federal government fragmented the security apparatus. Despite these notable changes, the Sinaloa DTO still managed to control the market in Culiacán, insourced violence, and operated within a less-fragmented security apparatus than Tijuana or Ciudad Juárez. Table 5.2 summarizes the periods of violence in Cali and Culiacán.

Historically, homicide rates in Cali and Culiacán have been very high, as illustrated in Figures 5.1 and 5.2. Table 5.3 illustrates how visible methods have not been prevalent in either city and also indicates the surge in visibility that occurred in Culiacán after 2008, as multiple new methods to display violence appeared. Figures 5.3 and 5.4 highlight another indicator of low visibility: the relative absence of public targets in violent attacks. They also show, interestingly, a high proportion of violence against presumed petty criminals. As shown later, traffickers may use social-cleansing violence to preserve their control and please state collaborators.

The Cali DTO's Era (1984–1994)

Cali is Colombia's third-largest city, and by 2011, its population was 2,294,643 inhabitants. In the early 1980s, mafias associated with drug trafficking consolidated a strong nucleus in Cali led by Miguel and Gilberto Rodríguez Orejuela. The criminal network also extended to and associated with other regional traffickers in the department of Valle.[3] Over time, the Cali nucleus came to be known as the "Cali cartel" and earned the reputation of being "businessmen" that preferred not to engage in violence. This reputation became stronger as the Medellín DTO and Pablo Escobar declared all-out war on the Colombian state and against extradition, whereas the Rodríguez Orejuela brothers repeatedly refused to engage in this war. But the brothers did not renounce violence altogether; when it was necessary, they simply deployed it differently, hiding it.[4]

Table 5.2 **A Political-Economy Approach to Drug Violence in Cali and Culiacán**

Period/City	Criminal Market	State Security Apparatus	Type of Armed Coercion
1984–1989 Cali LF-LV	Quasi Monopoly: Cali DTO consolidated control.	Cohesion: Local state apparatus coordinated through local elites. Police forces aligned with local elites.	Insourcing: Cali DTO established only sporadic connections to local gangs. Armed coercion was carried out by allied police forces.
1989–2004 Cali HF-LV	Increased Competition: Cali DTO engaged in fights with Medellín DTO, although no local invasion by Medellín DTO.	Cohesion: Corrupt elites maintained control over city politics despite growing electoral competition. Increasing cohesion at national level.	Insourcing: Local gangs provided sporadic services, but no direct relations between gangs and traffickers.
2004–2011 HF-LV	Competitive: Remnants of Cali DTO and factions of Norte del Valle DTO struggled for control.	Cohesion	Traffickers started creating alliances with guerrillas and paramilitaries in rural areas and organized armed branches.
2005–2006 HF-HV	Competitive	Moment of Fragmentation: Police-military confrontations in rural areas.	
1984–2008 Culiacán HF-LV	Controlled competition: Trafficking groups born in Sinaloa competed with each other in oligopolistic fashion.	Cohesion: PRI control and governor's power facilitated coordination.	Insourcing: Traffickers used older, local *pistoleros* (hitmen) but did not employ local gangs (cholos).
1992, 1996 HF-HV	Competition increased after 1989.	Momentary fragmentation. Anticorruption purges in local police.	
2008–2010 HF-HV	Competitive: All-out war between factions within Sinaloa DTO (Beltrán Leyva versus Chapo Guzmán)	Fragmentation: Military operations created conflicts between enforcement actors. Governors retained power.	Insourcing: Use of local gangs remained limited although organization of armed apparatuses increased.

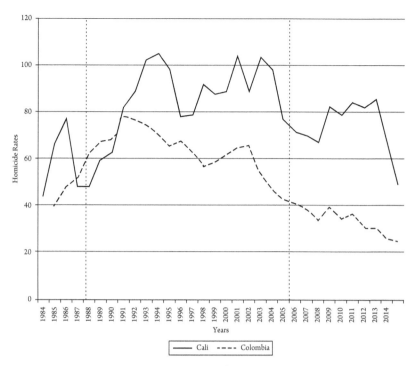

Figure 5.1 Homicide Rates in Cali 1984–2015 (per 100,000 Inhabitants).
Source: Author's elaboration, with data from DANE and Policia Nacional. Dotted vertical lines mark the violent periods and short periods of visibility.

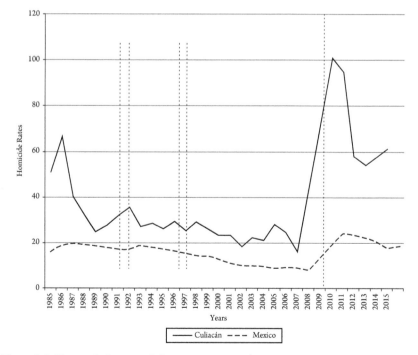

Figure 5.2 Homicide Rates in Culiacán 1985–2015 (per 100,000 Inhabitants). Source: Author's elaboration with data from INEGI and SINAIS. Dotted vertical lines mark the violent periods and short periods of visibility.

Table 5.3 **Methods of Violence in Cali and Culiacán**

	Cali			Culiacán						
	1984	*1989*	*2009*	*1984*	*1986*	*1992*	*1996*	*2002*	*2009*	*2010*
Sexual Violence		1			2			1		
Simple Use of Firearms	11	96	17	35	64	31	62	36	112	150
Strangulation			1			1			1	1
Simple Use of Knives		6	2	4	6	7	14	2	8	20
Combat with Firearms	4	4	3							
Drive-by Shootings (Sicariato)	21	64	10	17	29	18	16	25	118	171
Forced Disappearance (Paseo or Levantón)	1	2		2	10	4	4	13	26	59
Car Bomb	1	8	1			1				
Combat with Explosives		1								1
Combat with Firearms				5	11	5	8	5	5	7

Method									Total
Combat with Explosives and guns		1							1
Corpse with Note								34	27
Head in Cooler									2
Grenade	3	3							
Mutilation or Incineration without a Note	1	3						4	7
Mutilation or Incineration with a Note			1	4		2	3		5
Simple Use of Explosives	1	2							
Torture	2	7	1	7	11	12	8	6	17	67
Wrapped in Blanket		40	1		3		3	13	27
No Information	1	4	3		7	8	6	12	15
Total	42	200	81	72	140	86	121	99	353	559

Methods appear listed from low (top) to high (bottom) visibility, following the classification presented in Table 2.1.

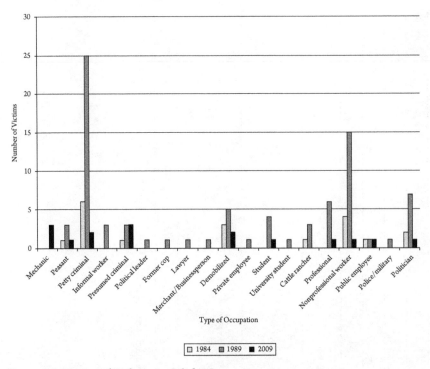

Figure 5.3 Victims of Violence in Cali, by Occupation. Source: Author's data set on drug-related violence, information compiled from *El País* newspaper (Cali). The data here only covers those cases where occupations were clearly identified.

As Figure 5.1 shows, during this period homicide rates were close to the national average—that is to say, not very high, but not too low, either—because the Cali DTO maintained a quasi-monopoly despite the presence of other non-state armed actors in the city including urban guerrillas, militias derived from guerrillas, and vigilante militias. The presence of these armed groups dates back to 1982, when demobilization camps were established in various cities as part of a peace negotiation between the guerrilla groups FARC, Popular Liberation Army or EPL, and M-19 and the government of President Belisario Betancur. Until the peace process broke down in 1985, the demobilization camps had become a training ground for gangs and militias, as occurred in Medellín (see chapter 4). Yet in Cali, militias and gangs were less numerous; thus their presence did not challenge the Cali DTO's control.

The characterization of the Cali DTO as a powerful cartel has been criticized as a misrepresentation of an organization that in practice was networked[5] and where leadership was dispersed among at least four main characters: Gilberto and Miguel Rodríguez Orejuela, Jose Santacruz, and Pacho Herrera. In fact, in an infamous interview with *Time* magazine in 1991, Gilberto Rodríguez called the Cali cartel "a poor invention of General Jaime Ruiz Barrera."[6] Yet if the organization

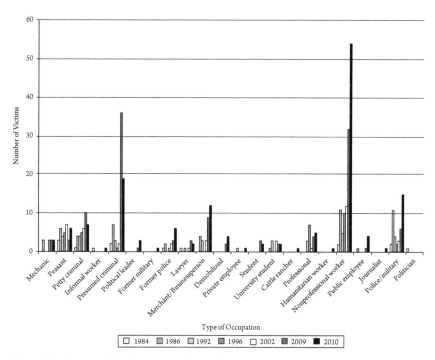

Figure 5.4 Victims of Violence in Culiacán, by Occupation. Source: Author's data set on drug-related violence, information compiled from *El Noroeste* newspaper (Culiacán). The data here only covers those cases where occupations were clearly identified.

was indeed an invention, then it would not be possible to explain its dense support network in Cali, which for a long time shielded its members from state action. In the words of a member of the Cali Search Bloc, the group created in the 1990s to dismantle the Cali DTO, "the cartel was a powerful and well-structured organization—they had neutralized the authorities. The technical part [of the operation against them] was very complicated; any movement we made, they knew it. There was an inability to combat the powerful groups."[7] Of course, just as criminals wanted to deny the existence of the organization, authorities were constantly creating images of a powerful organization. There is enough documentation, however, proving that the Cali DTO had power and a strong support network, which allowed it to keep illegal market disputes under control.

Toward the late 1980s, Pablo Escobar and the Medellín DTO openly confronted the Cali DTO, thus increasing market competition, and the frequency of violence, especially in 1991 when the conflict was at its height. Interestingly, Escobar did not threaten the Rodríguez Orejuela's control,[8] in part because he was unable to physically dominate the city,[9] and consequently Cali's criminal monopoly was not profoundly disjointed.

Although high, violence did not grow over the national rate as much as it did in Medellín because the Cali DTO *insourced* violence, using armed forces clearly controlled within the organization but not actively recruiting youth gangs. Such limited demand of gang recruits was the result of an organizational preference, facilitated by the extensive and successful enrollment of alternative sources of armed power, intelligence, protection, and security in networks that engaged taxi drivers and former or active military and police personnel. According to an army colonel who persecuted the Cali DTO, and to legal documents of the Proceso 8000, the large-scale judicial process initiated in 1995 that documented the links between the Cali DTO and state officials, about 60 percent of Cali's metropolitan police personnel appeared in the DTO's record of payments.[10] Another document of the Proceso 8000 listed two hundred police officials on the DTO's payroll in Cali. This penetration of the police guaranteed criminals not only nonenforcement of the law but also direct provision of security. The extensive recruitment of police and army personnel made outsourcing to youth gangs unnecessary[11] and facilitated the traffickers' regulation of the use of violence.

Limited outsourcing was also related to the relatively short supply of youth gangs. Compared to Medellín, where outsourcing was widespread,[12] Cali's gangs were weakly organized and armed, usually involving young people who gathered for drug consumption rather than for the commission of crimes and who sold services to criminals only sporadically.[13] The low supply of youth gangs did not simply reflect a smaller young population:[14] Cali and Medellín had similar population structures by age brackets, yet their youth-gang phenomenon was remarkably different.[15] Since traffickers did not deploy gangs systematically, gang organizational structures remained relatively simple and not very violent.

Proceso 8000: State Capture and Hidden Violence

The Cali DTO preferred to conceal violence rather than expose it. During the 1980s, the press reported mysterious crimes that involved, for example, the finding of bodies in the Cauca River[16] or the purposeful elimination of fingerprints on corpses so they could not be identified. As a military colonel who was part of the Search Bloc against the Cali DTO told me: "In Cali there were silent deaths, without noise, without paraphernalia."[17] An interview conducted by Darío Betancourt with a local woman in Cartago, a municipality close to Cali, summed up the hidden, and yet brutal, character of violence:

> Dead people started to show up, young people, some of them very humble, farm laborers, disfigured, burned, tortured; people said they were employees of the narcos who had snitched or robbed them; others were poor people, beggars, faggots, sluts, because it was necessary

to accommodate the city to the requirements of progress and such people were inconvenient . . . . A type of dead people that was not talked
about were women, young, girls, between sixteen and eighteen, pretty
and well dressed. The curious thing is that they hung out with mafiosi;
people said they were lovers who had cheated and so they were killed
[*muñequiar*]; others said that it was a punishment, because they did not
want to go out with narcos. The truth is that nobody wants to think
about it or remember it. There is a law of silence here, of suspicion;
every person who arrives is watched.[18]

Whereas the use of methods that concealed evidence was common, high-
profile victims, attacks against public and enforcement officials, or collective
attacks with more than three victims were uncommon in this period. Figure
5.3 shows that in 1984, most victims of violence were merchants and nonpub-
lic figures (street vendors, nonprofessional workers such as security guards or
mechanics, and presumed common criminals), and there were no attacks on
high-profile political or public figures. While they avoided prominent attacks,
the members of the Cali DTO promoted social cleansing—that is, the elimination of sectors of the population they considered as undesirable, such as petty
criminals, drug consumers, and prostitutes.[19] In the 1980s, social-cleansing
groups such as Cali Limpia (Neat Cali), Amor a Cali (Love for Cali), and
Palmira Eficiente (Efficient Palmira) proliferated, supported by various societal
sectors[20] especially drug traffickers, for whom this type of violence probably represented a source of legitimacy among both the population and the authorities,
who, given the profile of the victims, found social cleansing unimportant or even
acceptable.[21]

Traffickers' success in penetrating the state created incentives to maintain this
low-profile violence. Their corrupt network extended from local politicians to
national senators and was so extensive that it reached the coffers of the presidential campaign of Ernesto Samper, who became president of Colombia in 1994.
The Proceso 8000 revealed how the Cali DTO built a powerful protection network throughout the Colombian state and how the basis of such network was
carefully crafted in Cali. Local politicians indicted during the Proceso played
a variety of crucial roles: the mayor of Cali, Mauricio Guzmán (1992–1995)
created façade businesses to launder money for the criminal organization, and
Senator Gustavo Espinosa supported favorable legislation for traffickers. Other
indicted local politicians included a former secretary of government in Cali, a
former governor of Valle, and the general comptroller of the nation, as well as
local senators such as Álvaro Mejía López and Armando Pomarico.

The Rodríguez Orejuela brothers preferred bribing state officials rather
than killing them, but their success in obtaining state protection was not only a

personal choice—it was also allowed by a cohesive security apparatus. Cohesion provided secure state protection, lighter sentences, and cover-ups for money laundering. In exchange, state actors obtained less violent behavior, campaign funding, direct financial support and even collaboration in dismantling the Medellín DTO.[22] As explained in chapter 1, cohesion depends on the absence of intergovernmental conflicts, the absence of interagency conflicts, and the relative stability of time horizons for elected and enforcement officials. These characteristics were present during this period.

Cali was controlled by powerful, ingrained, and stable traditional political elites whose power was difficult to challenge.[23] At different times, political competition threatened the cohesion of the security apparatus (for example, with the first popular election of a mayor in 1988), but a powerful political and economic elite dominated politics,[24] blocking opposition and reformist efforts. At the same time, interagency conflicts were limited because the police force was the main antinarcotics actor in the city. The military carried out massive urban antiguerrilla operations in 1985 in Siloé, one of the poorest and marginalized neighborhoods of Cali, causing human rights violations.[25] These operations, however, caused little conflict between the army and the police because they were implemented as short-lived and well-coordinated joint operations.

In this context, accessing the state became easier for the Cali DTO. The following testimony of Miguel Rodríguez Orejuela before Colombian authorities encapsulates both his ideas about the use of violence and how these were linked to the collaboration established with the local security apparatus:

> Mr. Pablo Escobar . . . sent us a letter asking for our collaboration, physical and economic if you can say that, to start a war without barracks against the state and its institutions and representatives, including the justice sector. Our response, because of our beliefs and because of our respect not only toward institutions but also toward citizens, and because of our families' peace, was absolutely negative, and Mr. Escobar's reaction did not wait, sending people to Cali and Bogotá to spy on us . . . . Mr. Escobar became our enemy . . . . That led us to focus on protecting our families, the city of Cali, and ourselves, as many people can testify, especially the institution of the police, to which we always provided information and informants, with the results that happily, not only for us but also for all the country, the institution has.[26]

Eventually, the Proceso 8000 and the pressure it generated from the United States[27] forced the government to act against the Cali traffickers and to involve the military in urban antinarcotics operations. The national government created the joint military-police elite force known as the Cali Search Bloc, fashioned in the image of the elite force created to persecute the Medellín DTO and responsible for killing Pablo Escobar. In Cali, the Search Bloc relied on the army and focused on intelligence gathering rather than on direct military actions, because the Cali DTO's power resided in its penetration of the police and the political establishment: "The crucial difference between the Cali and Medellín Search Blocs," a former minister told me in an interview, "was that we understood the police had stronger links with the narcos in Cali. As a result, the Bloc relied on the army and the objective was to cut traffickers' communication networks in the city. We knew there were difficulties given the social acceptance these guys had."[28]

The Cali DTO's successful penetration of the state provided the organization with important benefits and protection, yet the emergence of the Proceso 8000 scandal illustrates how state protection rackets can be undone—in this case due to pressures from the United States and from a competitive electoral system at the national level. In fact, the first person accusing President Ernesto Samper of receiving drug money and then revealing evidence that led to the initiation of the Proceso 8000 was Andres Pastrana, the main competitor who lost the presidency to Samper.[29]

The Rodríguez Orejuela brothers were arrested in 1995. They operated from prison for a few years, but after their extradition to the United States in 2004 and 2005, the organization's structure crumbled. A reaccommodation in Cali's state security apparatus and in the illegal drug market followed. The population's perception about the traffickers who followed the Rodríguez Orejuela organization was that they were less respectable than their predecessors, as echoed in several interviews and conversations I had. A taxi driver told me, "Today's traffickers are not like their predecessors. Yesterday's were businessmen, respectable people. Today's are simply *matones*, mafiosos," while a woman who started conversation in a public bus told me, "In the past, mafiosi were not attacked by the government and there was employment for everybody. Today there is only unemployment." These statements illustrate that the Rodríguez Orejuelas' power was critically tied to their connections and acceptance within civil society, which, as Enrique Desmond Arias argues, are crucial sources of control for criminal networks.[30] The fact that social acceptance faded away for Cali DTO successors while their violent behavior remained similar, however, lends support to this book's argument that the interaction between state and illegal organizations, rather than traffickers' social connections, primarily determine the traffickers' violent behavior.

The massive corruption of police forces in Cali motivated major reforms in the Colombian police,[31] including the dismissal of all station commanders in Cali in 1995.[32] Despite these transformations, the security situation did not change radically in the following years.

Criminal Market Fragmentation (1995–2011)

With the dismantling of the Cali DTO, criminal groups in rural areas of the Valle department gained preeminence, turf battles between factions of the Norte del Valle DTO got more intense, and the market got more competitive. According to a local intelligence agent: "Since 1996–1998 the dynamic has always been the same, a fight for territorial control."[33] The city remained a center for criminal activity because it represented a hub for money laundering and a crucial connection from urban centers to smuggling routes in the Pacific coast of Colombia. Drug violence became more connected to dynamics in the northern rural areas of Valle, but it still had distinct dynamics in Cali, where it remained quiet because the security apparatus was still cohesive despite massive police firings. Criminals continued penetrating the state, and thus, with some exceptions, they preferred to reduce violence that could force state attention. In the words of a military member of the Cali Search Bloc: "The Norte del Valle Cartel assimilated the experience of the Cali DTO and focused on bribing at the municipal level."[34]

Disputes in the Post–Cali DTO Era

The disputes of the late 1990s involved high-level members of the Cali DTO who had not been captured and leaders of the Norte del Valle DTO such as Orlando Henao and Ivan Urdinola. More sophisticated enforcement operations that constantly targeted medium-level operatives and leaders contributed to heighten confrontations among traffickers. As leaders were imprisoned or assassinated, people who worked for them gained prominence. New criminals engaged in disputes for market control and also in retaliation against those who collaborated with US authorities, handing on information about their own associates, a practice that became common among Norte del Valle traffickers.[35]

Between 2002 and 2007, illegal market competition heightened as two prominent traffickers struggled to eliminate each other: Diego León Montoya, who became the leader of the Norte del Valle DTO, and Wilber Varela, who started as a bodyguard and ascended in the organization. This dispute increased violence, as reflected in an average homicide rate of 84 for those years. Both leaders created their own armies: Los Rastrojos worked for Varela and Los Yiyos and Machos worked for Montoya.

The war between Varela and Montoya subsided after a short truce between them in 2005.[36] The truce illustrated that reducing violence in a competitive illegal market through criminal arrangements is possible, but the aftermath also reflected their instability. After the army captured Montoya in 2007 and Varela was assassinated in 2008, their armies became more powerful. The Rastrojos and Machos further expanded operations on the Pacific coast of Colombia and entered more aggressively into urban areas. Beginning in 2008, the confrontations between these groups kept Cali's homicide rates high. The criminal market remained highly competitive; the names and protagonists of turf disputes varied when a leader was captured or killed, but constant confrontations and accommodations persisted.

Fuzzy Gang-Trafficker Connections

The protagonists of turf disputes in the 1990s and 2000s occasionally relied on sicarios (hitmen), with oficinas serving to broker transactions between the trafficking organizations and the sicarios.[37] Yet these traffickers did not engage in sustained outsourcing of violence to youth gangs, and for this reason, violence did not escalate too far above national rates. Sicarios were usually deployed to carry out single operations, often without knowing clearly who they worked for, yet traffickers relied on core groups of insourced force.

The relations between traffickers and gangs, although significant, were fuzzy and sporadic and therefore more difficult to identify and describe than in Medellín—where observers, gang members, and authorities could clearly name the connections between gangs and criminal organizations. In the words of a young man in Cali with a criminal record: "No one ever knows the boss; somebody looks for you and tells you 'Look, I have a *vueltica* [a job, killing or stealing],'... but one does not know who the boss is."[38] According to a government-run social research center in Cali, "[Gangs] sell and distribute hallucinogens and fire arms; they may have relations to *oficinas sicariales* and illegal groups, but as a whole, gangs do not devote themselves to committing homicides, although their members can oscillate on jobs like sicariato."[39]

During the 2000s, outsourcing occurred more often than during the Cali DTO period because youth gangs were more prevalent; by 2010 the metropolitan police of Cali and the mayor's office estimated the existence of 103 gangs.[40] Yet outsourcing was still limited because the availability of other sources of armed force that now included actors in the armed conflict limited the demand for gang soldiers. Traffickers such as Montoya and Varela established complex relationships with guerrillas and paramilitaries in rural areas, which supplied force and reduced the need to use youth gangs for killings. Varela initially recurred to a reliance on guerrillas,[41] and later on, various criminal factions established closer relationships with paramilitary groups that consolidated in northern Valle.[42] This process highlights how the evolution of Colombia's armed conflict dovetails with power dynamics in drug-trafficking organizations, yet the process plays out differently across locations. In Cali, unlike Medellín, traffickers and paramilitaries collaborated but did not merge successfully, thereby reducing the possibilities of creating an effective criminal monopoly.

By the time this book was going to press in 2017, gangs seemed to be playing a more direct role in the violence and illegal activities of the city. Yet, their connections to larger structures were still fuzzy, and an outsourcing dynamic where gangs know who they work for, or align clearly with a larger criminal organization, remained unclear.

Politics in the Aftermath of the "Big Cartels"

The criminal disputes following the demise of the Cali DTO were deadly, long, and destabilizing, but they did not cause the same public outrage as the trafficking disputes in the 1980s. Even the war between Montoya and Varela, which was particularly bloody, was, according to a local agent of the attorney's office, "not noticed; the society was indifferent because it did not touch us—the clubs [bars] were packed."[43] This situation reflected the persistent quiet wars. A press report declared that the war between Montoya and Varela left more than three thousand victims, yet most of them were reported as disappeared people.[44] This was the result of a local security apparatus that remained cohesive and prone to protecting criminals. In 2008, a regional development report produced by the UN Development Program identified the penetration of drug trafficking into public and political life, and the criminality of the political class, as key challenges to human development in the department of Valle.[45]

Powerful local political elites who successfully participated in national politics preempted conflicts among government levels and facilitated the protection of criminals. Some analysts argue that Cali's security problems resulted from the difficulty of creating governing coalitions because political competition brought in new players and independent leaders but no reformist coalition succeeded.[46] Although this difficulty can be interpreted as a sign of fragmentation, in practice it reflected the power of patrimonial political forces with strong illegal links that ended up penetrating even the campaigns of politicians seen as detached from corruption. "Clean" politicians lacked power to veto the dominant players in Cali's political life[47] and thus were unable to counteract the strong influence of illegal actors on city politics.

The 2011 imprisonment of Senator Juan Carlos Martínez Sinisterra for his alleged links with the Norte del Valle DTO and with paramilitary groups in Valle illustrates the persistent corruption in Cali. Martínez started his career[48] under the wing of the prominent politician Carlos Herney Abadía (investigated within Proceso 8000) and maintained close links with Abadía's son and then governor of Valle (2008–2010), Juan Carlos Abadía.[49] He experienced a meteoric rise in politics through links to criminals who provided him key assets for sustained electoral success: votes (obtained when necessary through paramilitary coercion on civilians) and money. In exchange, Martínez provided favorable public decisions (for example, assigning public contracts to illegal allies) and tolerated drug trafficking on the Pacific coast of Colombia.

Martínez's case illustrates how powerful corrupt political elites perpetuate themselves in power through the support of illegal actors. Martínez kept his influence even after he was imprisoned, as suggested by the continuous flow of prominent members of Cali's political class who courted him in prison and by his continuous electoral success. In 2010, his political party, the PIN (Party of National Integration), won twenty congressional seats, becoming the fourth-most-powerful political force in the country, despite the wariness that existed for its links with paramilitaries. In 2011, a new party called MIO (Movement for Inclusion and Opportunities), which included former PIN members and politicians linked to Martinez, consolidated as a political force in Cali's council and Valle's assembly despite some electoral defeats.[50] Martinez's story also shows that symbiotic relations between criminals and state cannot simply be reduced to a subordination of politicians to illegal forces. Politicians depend on illegal actors for their electoral success and power, but at the same time they provide illegal actors with privileged state access and incentives to hide violence.

As chapter 3 discussed, in this second stage of Cali's criminality, greater state cohesion at the national level also increased enforcement effectiveness and criminals learned that too much noise forced the state to confront them. Throughout the 1990s and 2000s reforms increased the technical, operational, and tactical capabilities of the Colombian National Police. Such police reform was guided by the increased militarization of police functions privileged by prohibitionist policies; despite the police's increased effectiveness, corruption, especially at the local level was still pervasive.[51] Yet reforms made enforcement more effective in targeting criminals. Consequently, hiding violence was an adaptation made by criminals as they tried to operate without attracting attention from national authorities that could arrest them more rapidly once they became a target of state action. This was particularly true for the Norte del Valle traffickers, who were the target of many antinarcotic operations in the 1990s and 2000s. According to authorities, the "life" of criminals in Colombia was shortened[52] because once identified, the time that elapsed before their detention was shorter than it had been in the 1980s. While such a statement ignores that criminals operate for a long time before they become high-priority targets, it illustrates that if a criminal becomes too public, he or she is under higher threat of being imprisoned. The low visibility of violence post–Cali DTO therefore resulted from criminals' interlocking incentives to maintain local state protection while avoiding national enforcement.

In line with the main argument, two short waves of visible violence emerged as a result of conflicts among enforcement agencies.[53] This was the case when the dispute between Varela and Montoya fractured corrupt networks, and local police members aligned with Varela while local military forces collaborated with Montoya.[54] According to intelligence analysts, mutual suspicions of corruption undermined the collaboration between police and military in enforcement operations.[55] The Montoya-Varela war therefore got very public in May 2006 after a military patrol killed ten members of an elite police force in Jamundí, a municipality located south of Cali. The judicial investigation revealed that Montoya hired an army colonel to eliminate a police group in search of a cocaine stash.[56] The incident not only complicated police-military relations—it also illustrated that illegal market competition may fragment state protection by permeating one agency more than other or by dividing protection from different agencies among criminal groups, thus producing more violence. Yet, although the Jamundí events reflected conflicts among enforcement agents, they did not completely fragment Cali's security apparatus, mostly because the army was not as involved in the urban struggle for security as it was in rural areas—like those where the incident occurred, where the army actively fought guerrillas and destroyed illegal crops.[57]

In sum, in the aftermath of the Cali DTO, local networks of collaboration between state and criminals persisted, debilitating state institutions and undermining democracy through corruption and the distortion of electoral competition as much as in previous periods. At the same time the Colombian state had acquired stronger enforcement abilities, which radically transformed criminal behavior. Not all allegations of corruption have been fully investigated, but it is clear that members of Cali's political class, with their large political, electoral, and power networks, have been associated with criminal and armed actors, and many remain powerful despite the scandals. Borrowing Peter Lupsha's definition of the relations between criminals and state in Mexico, "the players change but the game continues."[58] Even if protagonists change continuously, the process that connects criminals, state, and violence remains similar at the local level.

In Culiacán, similar processes have connected traffickers, state officials, and criminal sources of armed force, explaining the persistence of "quiet wars." Yet in 2008, the city experienced a far more extreme explosion of visible attacks, as the next section explains.

Culiacán: the Invisible "Chicago" of Mexico

The origins of drug trafficking in Mexico, as Luis Astorga[59] has carefully documented, date back to the late eighteenth century in the state of Sinaloa. Modern drug-trafficking organizations took shape in this region between the 1920s and the 1940s, as the focus of narcotics enforcement shifted from public health to public security.[60] Culiacán became the bridge between entirely rural areas, where most marijuana and poppy crops were located, an urbanized and commerce-oriented economy,[61] and the coastal area where drugs could be shipped. By the 1960s and 1970s, drug trafficking had become consolidated in the region and the first law enforcement responses emerged. During this period, confrontations among traffickers gave the city the reputation of "the Chicago of Mexico," as observers compared it to Mafia disputes in Chicago.[62]

In 1977, ten thousand soldiers of the Mexican military with US support and under the command of the Mexico Attorney General's Office carried out a large-scale illegal drug-crop eradication campaign known as Operación Cóndor. The operation led to massive displacement of poppy cultivators, known as *gomeros*, and of civilians in the rural areas of Sinaloa. It also entailed significant human rights violations and caused temporary but major shifts in trafficking organizations.[63] To avoid further state action, many traffickers relocated from Culiacán, moving southeast to the city of Guadalajara. These transformations demonstrate the way that state antinarcotic operations can shape violence by causing organizational fragmentation or by relocating trafficking groups. Yet, the potential violence generated by these operations can be more or less visible depending on the state structure. Operación Cóndor had profound impacts but did not generate visible violence because the Mexican state was still cohesive. Toward the beginning of the 1980s, many trafficking operations and traffickers had returned to Culiacán.

Political Protection and Criminal Power Struggles (1984–2008)

By 1986, Culiacán had a very high homicide rate of 66 per 100,000 inhabitants, which remained above national averages throughout the decade, as shown in Figure 5.2, reflecting the disputes that emerged as traffickers resettled in Culiacán.[64] This high-frequency violence contrasted with its low visibility, reflected both in the methods employed by criminals and in the population's perception that violence only affected criminals: In the words of a local journalist, "the disputes were between *them* [criminals], if you did not have problems with *them*, nothing happened."[65] According to many civilians, experts, and authorities I interviewed,[66] the historically high homicide rates tragically reflected in the multiple *cenotafios* (cenotaphs, or memorial crosses), which mark places where people have been shot,[67] were not threatening because they were thought to affect only criminals. People believed that if they did not get involved with traffickers, they were unlikely to be victims of violence.

Conflicts that surrounded a criminal market under constant threat of dispersion due to confrontations between Sinaloan criminal factions were the motor of Culiacán's high homicide rates. Most early drug traffickers were born in Sinaloa, and their common origin facilitated certain continuity in criminal leadership but at the same time generated strong disputes among leaders who operated in an oligopolistic fashion.[68] In the 1980s, Miguel Ángel Félix Gallardo, a prominent trafficker who started his career as bodyguard for a Sinaloan governor, managed to keep these oligopolistic tendencies in check. He engaged in disputes with other traffickers, such as Héctor Palma and Joaquín Guzmán,[69] but consolidated power through his pervasive political and economic connections. Even though Félix Gallardo resided in Guadalajara, he constantly traveled to Culiacán, where he maintained businesses and close relationships with politicians including Governor Antonio Toledo Corro. He also had a reputation as a "discreet" narco.[70]

On April 8, 1989, the Federal Judicial Police (PJF) captured Félix Gallardo because of his involvement in the assassination of the DEA agent Enrique Camarena in 1985 (described in chapter 3). While in jail, Félix Gallardo divided the major trafficking territories in Mexico, including the states of Baja California, Chihuahua, Tamaulipas, and Sinaloa, among the different criminal factions.[71] Such decision had a double effect: on the one hand, it decentralized disputes, moving some violence away from Culiacán (as occurred in Cali after the demise of the Cali DTO); on the other, it contributed to making the market more competitive. Homicide rates increased throughout the decade as disputes grew, especially between the *serranos* (rural-born traffickers from the mountains), such as Ismael "El Mayo" Zambada and Joaquín "El Chapo" Guzmán, and the urban Arellano Félix brothers, leaders of trafficking in Tijuana. These disputes always had a manifestation in Culiacán, because even the traffickers who relocated, like the Arellano Félix brothers, retained properties, businesses, power, and access to drug-producing areas in and around Culiacán.

Drug traffickers in Culiacán preferred to insource violence, and as a result homicide rates, although very high, never grew to be more than twice the national rate. Most Sinaloan traffickers were from rural origins[72] and gained the allegiance of older peasants who acted as their armed muscle.[73] Using older peasants as sicarios guaranteed discipline and allegiance. Furthermore, youth gangs never took off in Culiacán. In the 1980s youth gangs and *cholos*[74] became common but never reached the strength they had in border cities like Ciudad Juárez; furthermore, most cholos were not armed or violent.[75] The proportion of homicides by age group presented in Figure 5.5 is an observable implication of insourcing to old and loyal workers: compared to Ciudad Juárez and Tijuana, Culiacán had fewer homicides among the population aged twenty-four or younger in the period 1985–1996 but significantly more homicides

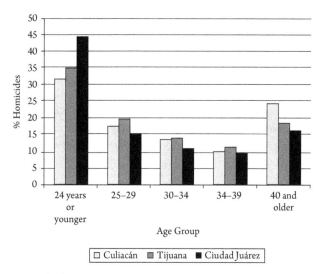

Figure 5.5 Homicides by Age Group in Culiacán, Tijuana, and Ciudad Juárez 1985–1997. Source: Author's elaboration, based on SINAIS data. The graph shows homicides in each group as a proportion of the total homicides in the city for the period.

among an older bracket of the population. This pattern persisted even after the "war" exploded in 2008.

Sinaloan Governors as Drivers of State Protection

From the 1980s through the 2000s violence in Culiacán was not very visible, as corroborated in my data set of drug violence. Events of collective violence were uncommon: before 2009 there were few events with more than two victims, and a high percentage of violent events (62 percent) did not produce fatalities but only left people wounded. As Table 5.3 and Figure 5.4. show, methods aimed at exposing violence were rare and most homicide victims were unlikely to attract significant public attention: peasants, nonprofessional workers, and petty criminals. Finally, a high proportion of violence occurred in rural areas: specifically, in Tierra Blanca, a poor neighborhood connecting the city with the mountains. A higher percentage of homicides and bodies were found in the rural areas of Culiacán (37 percent) than in the other cities compared in this book (the average from all other cities was 16 percent). A significant amount of violence was thus hidden from public attention. There were places in the city known as *botaderos* (dumps) for corpses: for example, the Cerro del Tute in the 1970s and 1980s and the La Costerita road in the 2000s.[76] Traffickers likely hid violence in these locations, usually connected to land they owned, because few people frequented these out-of-the-way places. In fact, while driving around one of these locations accompanied by a trusted informant, I had my first experience of being followed by a car, in a reminder that these areas are not normally transited by city dwellers.

Violence of course was noticeable and known to *culichis* (Culiacán locals), but traffickers were careful in keeping their confrontations under the radar so they would not endanger the stable protection provided by a cohesive state. Such cohesion was rooted in the PRI's stability in elections and in the historic power of Sinaloa's governors, which shadowed local mayors and reduced intergovernmental conflicts, thereby facilitating the stable relations between traffickers and authorities. Additionally, as the Camarena case had taught traffickers, visible violence could mobilize that same cohesive state security apparatus quickly and effectively against them.

Beginning in the 1980s, powerful governors such as Antonio Toledo Corro (1981–1986) were accused of protecting traffickers;[77] mayors in Sinaloa were seen as "submissive to the governor"[78] and considered irrelevant,[79] while governors were seen as "almighty." Many Sinaloan governors were part of presidential cabinets,[80] and their relations with the federal government were correspondingly collaborative. Such collaboration was reinforced by the PRI stability both in gubernatorial and mayoral elections. Sinaloa was a PRI stronghold, and even though in the early 1990s the opposition parties PAN and PRD gained space, the PRI remained unchallenged.[81]

Gubernatorial power and PRI dominance explain how, despite the undeniable reality of violence and the increasing accusations of corruption in Culiacán's political class, neither of these two issues became top priorities for authorities— there was no strong political opposition that could benefit electorally from corruption scandals. As Astorga documents, at different points in the 1980s and 1990s, authorities downplayed violence in the state and in the city.[82] A state's justice attorney, for example, declared that violence in Sinaloa was not very different from violence in any other part of the world, and Governor Renato Vega in 1993 declared that the existence of drug traffickers in the state was "pure hallucination"; Vega's position stood in sharp contrast to the position of his competitors for the gubernatorial election in 1992, who presented drug trafficking and violence as two priorities in their political platforms.[83]

At different moments, local state cohesion was challenged by the intervention of the military in antinarcotics policies and by occasional anticorruption efforts in state and municipal police. These interventions, as expected in my argument, led to temporary increases in the visibility of violence ("controlled signaling"). Public figures were assassinated in 1977 (Alfredo Reyes, the underchief of judicial police in Sinaloa, and Gustavo Samarco, a military advisor for Operación Cóndor), in 1983 (the municipal police commander Jaime Cota Félix and the chief of the Secretariat of Public Security Ceferino Ojeda), and in 1990 (the human rights defender Norma Corona, who publicly spoke out about the protection that security officials and Governor Toledo Corro provided for Félix Gallardo). Corona's killing, for example, followed a removal of commanders in the municipal Secretariat of Public Security in 1989; these removals could jeopardize the state protection given to criminals. Short of major political transformations, however, these temporary shake-ups were not enough to change the pattern of quiet wars in the city. The military had a long history of intervention in rural areas, especially in crop-eradication campaigns, and it was perceived to be a strong institution, the only one that "destroys plantations and confronts gunmen (*gavilleros*)."[84] Yet the army was not permanently engaged in public security in Culiacán, thereby mitigating the fragmenting impact of military operations. The nature of the quiet wars derived from criminal disputes and stable state protection changed radically in 2008, as the "war" exploded.

"The War Started on April 30, 2008"

On April 30, 2008, a battle erupted in the Colonia Guadalupe, an upper-middle-class neighborhood in Culiacán. Around the corner from the governor's house, a joint military-police group engaged in open fire with armed gunmen at a *casa de seguridad*, or safe house.[85] The operation resulted in the detention of twelve people and the seizure of an extensive arsenal including munitions, police uniforms, and US$379,980. (Enormous bullet holes in the house's façade were still observable three years later, when I conducted fieldwork in 2011.) As this battle ensued, two members of the state police, supposedly responding to a backup request made by the soldiers and federal police at the safe house, were intercepted and killed by sicarios. Soon after, two members of the state judicial police (ministeriales) were killed as they attempted to capture the sicarios who had attacked the state police.[86]

The official version of the events was that the battle started when federal police attended a call to search the safe house. Many other unofficial versions emerged in the following days; the most widespread was that the Beltrán Leyva organization was retaliating against its former partners in the Sinaloa DTO, El Chapo Guzmán and El Mayo Zambada, for a betrayal that led to the capture of Alfredo Beltrán Leyva, known as El Mochomo, on January 20, 2008.

Violence existed prior to April 30, but the visible events that occurred that day marked the initiation of the war in the public imagination. All my interviewees pointed to that day as signaling a radical transformation in the "honor codes" of violence. Visibility increased, as well as the sense that violence was more indiscriminate. In the words of a local journalist,

> We were used to death before; there was constant violence, but it was hidden; the victims appeared, but it was not high-impact violence . . . . After April 30th, 2008, a collective psychosis started. On May 5th, five

federal police were killed. We went from hidden violence to high-impact violence, with shootouts downtown. The drain finally overflowed.[87]

The words of a local transit police officer I interviewed also illustrate this perception that the "codes" of violence were fundamentally broken in 2008:

> When I started [as a police officer], there was a different mentality of the people dedicated to illicit jobs and they respected the cop, as they respected women and children. Of course there have always been limitations, like when they tell you not to go to that *colonia* [neighborhood]. Respect no longer exists; they kill women, children; the command that existed in those years has been lost and that's why violence has proliferated.[88]

On the one hand, perceptions like these ignored that innocent people could have been targeted in the past, or they minimized how the state, although powerful, protected trafficking interests and tolerated their violence. On the other hand, they highlight how previous, more hidden, violence seemed to be more acceptable. These perceptions became more deeply ingrained as the frequency of violence skyrocketed.

Between 2007 and 2008, homicides increased in Culiacán by about 180 percent and the methods deployed in violence multiplied rapidly, including those aimed at exposing violent attacks, as seen in Table 5.3. Within a few days of the events of April 30, *mantas,* banners carrying messages, covered the city, and their content provided some clues to explain the turmoil. Most of the mantas that appeared within the first week of the battle in Colonia Guadalupe were directed at Guzmán and Zambada and at members of police departments and the military. The Beltrán Leyva group signed many of these mantas, accusing Guzmán and Zambada of collaborating with state authorities in the capture of Alfredo Beltrán and promising to take revenge. In one of them the threat read, "This is the reverse for you Chapo, the UKA—the cock without wig—will fall on you . . . . hold on tight Mayos and Zambadas, you have awakened the monster of the skies."[89] Although some threatening mantas against army officials appeared back in 2006 and 2007, after April 2008 mantas and notes on corpses became daily routine: both frequency and visibility proliferated.

These changes resulted from an extreme rupture in the trafficking organizations. In the words of one of my informants, this dispute, unlike former disputes, was between "family members," one that generated more extreme retaliation. The five Beltrán Leyva brothers allegedly introduced Guzmán to the secrets of drug trafficking and later on, as he accumulated power, became his close associates.[90] The public displays of violence also reflected a rupture in the state protection racket; corruption did not decrease, but it became less predictable. The open threats of the Beltrán Leyva organization against the military and police reflected that they did not trust state protection, which had turned less predictable as the army was deployed for urban antinarcotic operations and as corrupt networks split between the two warring sides.

The War against Drug Traffickers and State Fragmentation

The army was deployed to Culiacán after President Felipe Calderón declared war against trafficking organizations in 2006. The changes that followed illustrate that the security apparatus can fragment rapidly—for example, when the military is suddenly deployed in large-scale urban operations. Visible violence, which was already increasing because protection networks were breaking apart, escalated. In September 2006, a corpse was tossed in front of the military compound with a threatening message for General Rolando Hidalgo Eddy, who had been commanding operations against Joaquín Guzmán.[91] Because protection was no longer guaranteed, exposing violence to demonstrate power and scare away the state and competitors acquired more value.

On January 21, 2007, President Calderón started Operation Triángulo Dorado (Golden Triangle), covering one of the major drug-producing areas in Mexico, a region comprising the states of Sinaloa, Durango, and Chihuahua. The operation, which mobilized nine thousand soldiers with the aim of reestablishing "conditions of peace and tranquility in the region," was the first step toward extending into urban areas the historic military presence in Sinaloa. In May 2008, the government implemented the joint military-police Operation Culiacán-Navolato in response to the April 2008 events, mobilizing 2,723 armed personnel including soldiers, federal police, marines, and the attorney general's police.[92] These operations fragmented enforcement, because the army saw and treated local law enforcement as corrupt and interagency conflicts ensued. The words of a local state police officer reflected the tension that permeated relations between security agencies: "Now the military are harsh, very strict with the cops."[93] State coordination was also compounded in 2010 when PAN's Mario López Valdez[94] was elected as Sinaloa's governor while a PRI mayor was in power in Culiacán.

As the security apparatus fragmented so did the protection rackets. And as the powerful trafficking organizations split, their networks of support within the police and the political class did, too. This was reflected in the messages sent by the Beltrán Leyva organization to state and federal police. Another indication of the fragmentation of state protection occurred on January 20, 2008, when after the capture of Alfredo Beltrán Leyva, national newspapers revealed a list found in his residence detailing local enforcement in Culiacán connected to him and to the Sinaloa DTO; soon after, most of the list members had been assassinated.[95]

Compared to the other cities that saw military deployments during Calderon's war, Culiacán retained some state cohesion based on the structure of its political power. The collaboration between levels of government (president, governor, and mayor), the PRI's still-strong electoral power, and the fact that the military had been present in the region at least since Operación Cóndor mitigated the disruptive effect of the army presence. The governors preceding and during the explosion of violence (Juan Millán, 1998–2004; Jesus Aguilar, 2004–2010; and Millán's protégé Mario López, 2010–2016) were mentioned in all of my interviews as powerful figures controlling the region's politics. Meanwhile, the mayor of Culiacán was not mentioned as a protagonist of security decisions. The political allegiances of mayors and governors remained aligned, as was traditionally the case.[96] It is possible that traffickers' commitments to the local political class led them to redirect visible violence, which attacked state officials and rivals in 2008 but seemed to change in 2009 and 2010, targeting victims that were a lesser public concern, such as petty criminals. The visible violence that persisted in 2009 and 2010 seemed to serve a different purpose: to discipline or eliminate local criminality instead of defying the state.

It is clear that national dynamics were inextricably linked to Culiacán's situation, as changes in the local state apparatus occurred in the context of a federal government decision (declaring war on traffickers), thus reflecting how overlapping jurisdictions and sovereignties can coincide in a city.[97] Yet the military mobilization created different dynamics across Mexican cities: Culiacán's increase in homicide rates was significantly lower than the increase in Ciudad Juárez (chapter 6), illustrating the relevance of local dynamics on which this book focuses. To further understand how local dynamics unfolded in Culiacán during Mexico's drug war, it is crucial to consider the role played by the continued insourcing of armed force by traffickers.

"Disciplining" of Trafficking Soldiers

In 2008, Culiacán's homicide rates grew to surpass national rates by four times, reflecting an increasing involvement of young people and some outsourcing. The scale of fighting required greater armies, and indeed the Beltrán Leyva DTO started to organize its own army known as the FEDA (*Fuerzas Especiales de Arturo*, or Special Forces of Arturo).[98] However, for the most part the armed apparatus of the Sinaloa DTO in Culiacán remained insourced, clearly controlled within the organization's hierarchy, and youth gangs did not proliferate.

As expressed by prominent local journalist Javier Váldez, who was cowardly murdered in May 2017,

> There are no gangs here; the last gangs existed in the eighties and were basically cholos. What we see here is cells within the organization, commanded by experienced killers at the service of capos . . . . These cells are identified by the name of the killer who commands them—for example, sicarios would say, "I am the Machoprieto's people" or "I am the Ondeado's people."

Váldez further explained,

> There is a monopoly of crime in the hands of the Sinaloa Cartel. If I work for the cartel and I kill without permission, they kill me, because you are heating up the *plaza*, you are too noisy. The bosses say, "I don't want to see you *pistiando* [drinking] or stealing," and in the sectors they control there are less robberies and assaults . . . . The strategy of the Sinaloa cartel is not to make noise; if there are robberies, they attract attention."[99]

Referring to the relations between hitmen and traffickers, an informant told me, "There is a pyramidal structure in the Sinaloa cartel; identity is constructed face to face, respect for the boss is huge, because they know closely who is who. Now the Ondeado is starting to bother El Chapo precisely because he is too crazy."[100] The traffickers' historic roots and control over the local population partially explain the choice for insourcing, but personal preferences do not tell the whole story, because (as seen in chapter 6) the same traffickers led by Guzmán outsourced violence to youth gangs when they did not have a local loyal armed force, as when they "invaded" Ciudad Juárez.

Insourcing can also explain why so much violence in 2009 and 2010 was directed to low-level criminality: once the Sinaloa DTO defeated its rivals, it was necessary to deescalate the war and reestablish "social control." In 2009, out of thirty-five notes that accompanied corpses, thirty were directed against common delinquents and car thieves (*robacarros*) the bodies were generally mutilated; and the remains publicly displayed with a note and a toy car placed on the body. The notes usually threatened others with the same treatment if they continued stealing. In 2010, the mantas and messages on corpses continued to reflect a pattern of visible violence that did not target police forces or criminal competitors as in 2008 but instead seemed aimed at "cleaning up" petty criminality. Out of thirty-nine messages on corpses found in 2010, seven were directed to "rats"; and twelve more to kidnappers, car thieves, and rapists; three to people who "messed with married people." Another seven made a direct reference to the criminal groups confronted in the region: Beltrán Leyva, Arellano Félix, or Zetas. All these aspects suggest that criminal leaders attempted to regulate common criminality and everything that they considered a social malady, as a way of gaining honor and keeping their legitimacy among elite sectors of the population but, above all, as a way of controlling their armed force.

Conclusion

Cali and Culiacán differ in many respects, yet they share a common pattern: the persistence of relatively "quiet wars." This situation results from criminal organizations that drive up violence as they compete for market control and from the successful collusion between criminals and state structures at the local level. The protagonists of violence have constantly changed in these two cities, reflecting that, as some authors put it,[101] in urban spaces, arrangements between the state and "informal sovereigns" such as criminal actors are periodically renegotiated. Yet the process and mechanisms that connect state and criminals have remained constant, thus explaining the low profile of violence.

I finished the formal analysis for this book in 2011 but the dynamics seen ever since suggest the persistent stability of the patterns described in Cali and Culiacán. In Culiacán, after reaching their peak levels in 2010 and 2011, homicides decreased by little less than half in 2012. Although homicides remained higher than in the period previous to the war, the criminal market seemed to have returned to the control of the Sinaloa DTO, with conflicts driven mostly by internal disputes, and short of major political shuffles, with similar dynamics of collaboration with security agents. However, due to the increase in federal operations and the rotation of federal agents,[102] arrangements of protection since 2011 have been less predictable, sometimes leading to visible attacks. The initial arrest of Joaquín Guzmán in 2014 did not seem to radically change criminal dynamics, and the effects of his recapture in January 2016 were still unclear by the time this book went to press. It is possible that the latest arrest really reduced Guzmán's control, and thereby perhaps opened the space for more struggles for control—or for a generational succession with Guzmán's sons, which according to some may be more prone to violence. Indeed, an army commander in Culiacán attributed an ambush that killed five soldiers in October 2016 to an attempt by Guzmán's sons to rescue a criminal arrested by the army.[103]

Similarly in Cali, violence is still very high. Since violence in the country as a whole has gone down, now Cali's situation is more evident for the national public, but it is still characterized by low visibility. There are two main criminal groups operating in the city: remnants of Los Rastrojos, and one of the so-called criminal gangs (BACRIM), self-proclaimed as the Gaitanista Self-Defense Forces of Colombia (Autodefensas Gaitanistas de Colombia), and known to the government as the Gulf Clan (Clan del Golfo). Allegedly, a criminal pact between these forces reduced homicides rates in 2015, but the homicide rate was still significantly higher than the homicide rate for the country (49 versus 25). This reflects that even though criminal groups contract out some services to youth gangs, they do not control them, and therefore, when they establish a pact, their ability to reduce violence as it happened in Medellín during Don Berna's years is limited.

The two cities thus illustrate that even when violence is not perceived as extreme or as a threat to national security, it is extremely damaging for societies. Civilians suffer even when people believe that violence affects only criminals, because in order to maintain turf, criminals not only eliminate their competitors but also whomever represents a threat to their power. Furthermore, low-level criminals are often marginalized people with little options. Even if violence were only limited to criminals, the legitimization of certain forms of violence further weakens the state's claim to the monopoly of force, because it deems some forms of nonstate violence acceptable.

Cali and Culiacán show that the mechanisms sustaining low-visibility violence can sometimes be more damaging for democratic institutions than those generating extreme violence, because they spread corruption across enforcement agencies and elected officials. Trafficking organizations, for instance, were weakened after the demise of the Cali DTO but the criminal-state nexus remained ingrained. The changing power of traffickers in the global commodity chain of drug distribution or the state-expanded abilities and resources to persecute criminals did not alter these nexus. This is because traffickers' choice to lower the profile of violence is not only driven by their changing position in the trade but also by their connections to the state and their ability to adapt to the state's greater enforcement capacity.

This chapter also highlights why anticrime and antinarcotic operations such as anticorruption purges or large-scale military operations can backfire and alter not only the quantity but also the quality of violence: they fragment the state and, at least in the short run, have low success possibilities and high risks and costs. This does not mean that states should abandon the possibility of combating corruption and violence but rather that the conditions of these operations need to be carefully considered before they are implemented. Furthermore, short of transformations in power structures, these changes may only create short-term reaccommodations: for a cohesive state to become a source of effective policing rather than a source of corruption, checks and balances, justice, and reduction of impunity need to be in place.

National contexts matter differently for the stories told in this chapter: homicide rates in Cali are significantly higher than in Culiacán because of Colombia's armed conflict; Culiacán's explosion of violence in 2008 cannot be separated from the federal decision to declare war against trafficking organizations; criminal-state links in Cali are more unstable partially because national institutions and media play a more active role in initiating high-level judicial processes. Impunity rates are similar in both countries, yet there have been more high-level judicial processes and indictments of politicians in Cali than in Culiacán, where no significant political figure has been officially investigated. These national dynamics, however, cannot explain why criminal violence in Cali is so different from Medellín, why Culiacán is so different from Ciudad Juárez or Tijuana, and why dynamics of violence are so similar in Cali and Culiacán.

Pervasive links between criminals and civil society have been crucial in both cities: the power of the Rodríguez Orejuela in Cali cannot be separated from their legitimacy among both businessmen and popular sectors; similarly, the power of Ismael Zambada and Joaquín Guzmán is clearly linked to their connections within Culiacán's society. Yet these links seem insufficient to explain changing violence: in Cali, the Norte del Valle traffickers seemed less popular among the population, yet their violent tactics resembled those of their predecessors; in Culiacán, criminal legitimacy among civil society seems to have decreased, but it appears to be more a result, than a cause, of violence.

Finally, weak state and civilian mobilization in these two cities suggest that visibility may affect responses to violence. Antiviolence programs have existed, especially in Cali, which was a precursor of citizen security programs in the early 1990s when Mayor Rodrigo Guerrero innovated citizen security programs through a public health perspective, and where multiple civil organizations exist. Yet they have been arguably weaker than those of its country counterpart Medellín. Studying how forms of violence shape civil society and state responses thus constitutes a direction for future research. Low-visibility violence may be less likely to motivate strong civil society or state responses because it may not generate a sense of victimization among the wider population. In Culiacán, for example, for over twenty years one woman, Mercedes Murillo, was pretty much the only public face of human rights and civilian antiviolence efforts.

6

Ciudad Juárez and Tijuana: Beyond a Border Tale of Violence

Ciudad Juárez and Tijuana have been marked by their location on the border of the United States. From the Mexican-American War in 1846, through the emergence of "vice districts" during the prohibition of alcohol and prostitution in the United States in the 1920s, to the expansion of drug markets fueled by the proximity to the largest market for illegal drugs in the world, the evolution of illegality in these cities has been shaped by border controls, transborder movements and exchanges, and US legislation and foreign policy. Yet the histories of drug violence in Ciudad Juárez and Tijuana have not been completely parallel, and their border status cannot completely account for the different trajectories of illegality and violence they have experienced over time.

How can cities within the same country, similarly shaped by their border status, by the powerful influences of economic globalization, and by diverse migrant populations, experience diverging patterns of drug violence? I explain these patterns as the result of interactions between the state security apparatus and competition in the illegal market and of different strategies of armed coercion used by drug traffickers. The cross-city comparison presented in this chapter challenges the rhetoric, especially widespread among US enforcement agencies, that border cities are inevitably dangerous and prone to violence and represent a national security threat to the United States.[1] It also highlights that national policies, such as the declaration of war against trafficking organizations by President Felipe Calderón in 2006, often frame radical changes in trafficker's violent strategies. Yet a local focus is necessary to fully explain fine-grained variation in drug violence. While the Mexican federal government's mobilization of the military deepened state fragmentation and violence in the two border cities, local security apparatuses and criminal strategies mediated the effect of national policies: insourcing and a more cohesive security apparatus led to more limited and short-lived increases in the frequency and visibility of violence in Tijuana than in Ciudad Juárez, where outsourcing and fragmentation became prevalent.

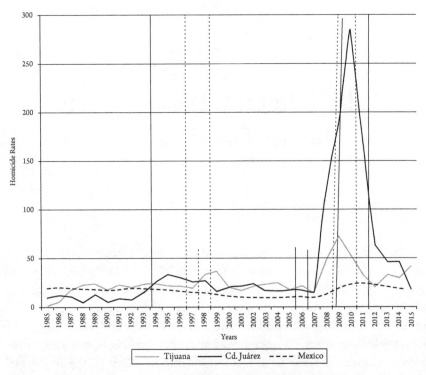

Figure 6.1 Homicide Rates in Ciudad Juárez and Tijuana 1985–2015 (per 100,000 Inhabitants). Source: Author's elaboration with data from SINAIS and INEGI. Dotted vertical lines represent periods of violence in Tijuana; solid vertical lines represent periods in Ciudad Juárez.

Differences in the timing of violent waves can be seen in Figure 6.1, which shows an earlier increase in homicides in Tijuana in the 1980s as well as a clear difference in the scale of the increase that occurred after 2008. Table 6.1 and Figures 6.2 and 6.3 illustrate how, after 2008, visible violence surged in both cities, with an increase in methods that displayed violence and an increase in high-profile victims. Among this book's cases, Ciudad Juárez, along with Medellín, experienced the most noticeable targeting of police and army personnel. The data also illustrates how extreme violence receded more quickly in Tijuana than in Ciudad Juárez.

The chapter first focuses on Tijuana. It describes how the Arellano Félix organization (AFO) established a criminal monopoly in the second half of the 1980s and wove networks of protection within the state, maintaining a situation of relative peace. As competition to the AFO grew in the 1990s, violence increased but remained relatively hidden because the security apparatus remained cohesive and criminals retained protection. This situation changed

Table 6.1 **Methods of Violence in Ciudad Juárez and Tijuana**

	Ciudad Juárez			Tijuana			
	1983	1984	2010	1984	1992	2002	2010
Combat with Knives		1					
Poisoning						1	
Sexual Violence		1				5	
Simple Use of Firearms	1	47	315	7	35	45	161
Strangulation		1		0	2	1	5
Simple Use of Knives		24	15	7	16	15	19
Combat with fire guns		8	15				
Drive-by Shooting (Sicariato)		8	160	5	12	27	97
Forced Disappearance			19	2	1	15	12
Combat with Firearms					3	3	8
Combat with Explosive			4				
Combat with Explosives and Guns			3				
Corpse with Note			4				6
Fire			2				
Frozen Corpse			1				
Head in Cooler			8				3
Mutilation or Incineration without a Note			12				9
Mutilation or Incineration with a Note			9			9	14
Torture		7	36	3	3	34	37
Wrapped in Blanket			7		2	9	24
No Information		34	89	12	54	27	14
Total	1	131	699	36	128	191	409

Methods appear listed from low (top) to high (bottom) visibility, following the classification presented in Table 2.1.

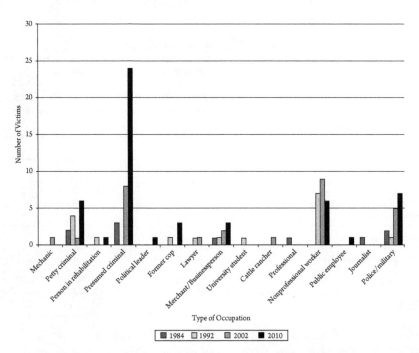

Figure 6.2 Victims of Violence in Tijuana, by Occupation. Source: Author's data set on drug-related violence, information compiled from *El Sol de Tijuana* newspaper (Tijuana). The data here only covers those cases where occupations were clearly identified.

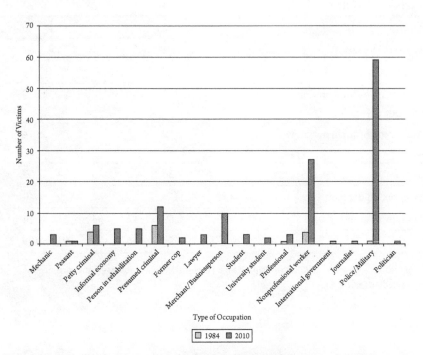

Figure 6.3 Victims of Violence in Ciudad Juárez, by Occupation. Source: Author's data set on drug-related violence, information compiled from *El Diario de Juárez* newspaper (Ciudad Juárez). The data here only covers those cases where occupations were clearly identified.

radically in 2008, when conflicts within the AFO became an all-out war and the state fragmented due to the deployment of military troops and massive changes in enforcement, thus leading to high-frequency and high-visibility violence. The situation in 2008 was less extreme than in Juárez because traffickers maintained their historic preference for insourcing violence by using elite young men rather than gangs composed of marginalized youth as part of their armed apparatus.

The second section focuses on Ciudad Juárez and shows how an illegal market controlled since the 1980s by the Juárez DTO[2] reduced the incidence of lethal violence. A cohesive state that provided stable protection reduced the incentives for the Juárez DTO to display violence. In 2008, the situation changed radically as the Sinaloa DTO invaded Juárez, and extreme conflicts among government levels and enforcement agencies exploded, leading to extreme violence that transformed Ciudad Juárez into the world's most violent city. I explain how even though youth gangs always existed, it was not until 2008 that they were actively deployed by trafficking organizations. Outsourcing is crucial to understanding why Ciudad Juárez experienced a more extreme and longer spike of violence than Tijuana. Table 6.2 summarizes the periods and the factors driving violence in the two cities.

The AFO Consolidates in Tijuana (1984–1996)

Tijuana is a relatively young city, located in the northwesternmost tip of Mexico, bordering the US city of San Diego, and founded in 1889. In the 1960s, Tijuana quickly grew and expanded through growing migration flows and the *maquiladora* industry,[3] which attracted even larger masses of migrants in search of economic opportunities. Currently, it is Mexico's fifth-largest city, with a population of 1,559,683, and is also the busiest border crossing in the world, with about 80,000 daily commuters. Its history of illegal markets dates back to the 1920s, when alcohol and drug prohibition in the United States created profitable opportunities for rum runners and drug traffickers. The modern era of drug trafficking, however, is tied to a family originally from Culiacán that arrived in Tijuana in the early 1980s, the Arellano Félix family.[4] Upon their arrival, they allied with Jesús Labra Avilés, a long-time trafficker in the region, and started to build up their power by carefully crafting connections with the state and with the society. Relative peace characterized the period after the arrival of the Arellano Félix until 1987. In 1985, the homicide rate in Tijuana was only 1.5 per 100,000 inhabitants (Figure 6.1).

In 1989, the power of the Arellano Félix organization increased when, as described in chapter 5, the judicial police captured trafficker Miguel Ángel Félix

Table 6.2 **A Political-Economy Approach to Drug Violence in Ciudad Juárez and Tijuana**

Period/City	Criminal Market	State Security Apparatus	Type of Armed Coercion
1984–1996 Tijuana LF-LV	Quasi-monopoly: Arellano Félix Organization consolidated power.	Cohesion: Coordination among enforcement actors through Attorney General's Office.	Insourcing: Narcojuniors (elite young men) worked for the Arellano Félix DTO. Use of US based gangs.
HF-LV	After 1987 some struggles for control with other regional organizations.	No conflicts between national and local government. Increased political competition did not radically transform power structure.	
1996–1997 Tijuana LF-HV	Quasi-monopoly: Arellano Félix organization remained in control.	Increased fragmentation: Enforcement operations of the Attorney General's Office and rotations and purges.	Insourcing: Narcojuniors deployed together with use of US-based gangs.
1998–2007 Tijuana HF-LV	Increased competition: Arellano Félix organization in competition with Sinaloa traffickers.	Cohesion: Coordination between state and federal actors and enforcement agencies.	Insourcing: Incidence of narcojuniors seemed to recede. Use of US-based gangs. No systematic use of local gangs.
2008–2009 HF-HV	Competitive: Arellano Félix organization split; splinter faction allied with Sinaloa DTO.	Fragmentation: Military operations created conflicts between enforcement actors.	Insourcing: No systematic use of youth gangs.
1984–1993 Ciudad Juárez LF-LV	Quasi-monopoly: Amado Carrillo and Juárez DTO in control.	Cohesion: Coordination among enforcement actors.	Insourcing: Availability of youth gangs but no demand of armed coercion.

Table 6.2 **Continued**

Period/City	Criminal Market	State Security Apparatus	Type of Armed Coercion
1994–2007 Ciudad Juárez HF-LV	Increased competition: Conflict within the Juárez DTO.	Cohesion: Coordination among enforcement actors and government levels, political competition grew but power remained stable.	Insourcing: No systematic deployment of youth gangs.
2005–2006		Increased fragmentation due to rotation and purges in municipal and state police.	
2008–2010 Ciudad Juárez HF-HV	Competition: Sinaloa DTO invaded Juárez and confronted Juárez DTO for control.	Fragmentation: Military deployments created conflicts between enforcement actors. Confrontations between mayor and governor, and then between mayor and federal police.	Outsourcing: Juárez and Sinaloa DTOs deployed youth gangs to wage war. Sinaloa deployed Artistas Asesinos, Mexicles, and Gente Nueva; Juárez DTO deployed Aztecas.

Gallardo, considered the leader of Mexican trafficking groups. Félix Gallardo divided trafficking territories along geographic lines in order to keep the trafficking business afloat, thereby giving more power to the Arellano Félix in Tijuana. In 1993, when Félix Gallardo was transferred into a high-security prison, thus losing control of the business, competition between regional leaders increased, especially between the Arellano Félix Organization and its competitors Joaquín Guzmán and Ismael Zambada in Culiacán. The control of territories became more consequential for the drug business because inland trafficking routes through Mexico had become crucial in the 1980s as the United States cracked down on the aerial routes that had been used by Colombian traffickers to move drugs through the Caribbean. Mexicans were increasingly important for Colombians, and the financial stakes of drug trafficking grew. Along with an interest in controlling territories, the struggles between these two sides were also fueled by personal differences: As Luis Astorga puts it, Guzmán and Zambada represented the rural mafioso, whereas the Arellano Félix, born in Culiacán's middle class and educated, represented the urban, businesslike trafficker.[5]

Between 1987 and 1996, such inter- and intraorganizational disputes caused an increase in violence, and Tijuana's homicide rates grew to be slightly above the national average (see Figure 6.1). As discussed in chapter 3, the fight between the Arellanos and Guzmán took on a visible character at the national level in 1993 with events such as the assassination of Cardinal Posadas Ocampo. Nonetheless, the local situation remained controlled, because such disputes did not imply the physical invasion of Tijuana or a breakdown of the Arellanos' local power. Violence had low visibility, and it remained relatively stable at around 20 homicides per 100,000 inhabitants.

Violence in this period was, consequently, used to protect the organization from growing threats posed by traffickers from other regions aiming to access Tijuana. The Arellano Félix also employed violence to discipline occasional traffickers who refused to pay *derecho de piso*—that is, the right to pass drugs through the territory of the larger organization. According to Jesus Blancornelas, a journalist from Tijuana who dedicated a good part of his life to documenting and denouncing the actions of narcotraffickers, the organization charged a fee for small-time traffickers who wanted to pass drugs through Tijuana and other neighboring municipalities in Baja California, but it did not tolerate attempts to move larger amounts of drugs.[6]

The Narcojuniors: An Uncommon Strategy of Armed Coercion

For the most part, the Arellano Félix insourced their armed force and employed a different strategy to recruit armed force, using young people from elite families rather than local youth gangs. They recruited young men from Tijuana's upper class as their hitmen and operators.[7] These young elites came to be known as the *narcojuniors*,[8] and according to journalistic accounts, by 1996 they were responsible for many killings. But why and how did traffickers recruit members of the elite to be their soldiers? Although there is no good information about how this process started, it is likely that the Arellano Félix's ability to penetrate the highest ranks of society allowed them to establish contacts with elite families.

The phenomenon of the narcojuniors became increasingly public as more elite youth were linked to homicides and to the Arellano Félix DTO in the mid-1990s.[9] Perhaps the most prominent case was that of Alfredo Hodoyan, who was captured in San Diego in 1996 and was linked to several murders. His declarations to Mexican and US authorities revealed the extent to which elite young men in Tijuana had become the most prominent killers for the Arellano Félix organization.[10] This case gained even more attention as Alfredo's brother, Alejandro, who was first detained in 1996 and made similar declarations, disappeared in 1997 after being captured by police officials.

The Arellano Félix contracted out youth gangs not in Tijuana but in San Diego. Specifically, traffickers sought out the services of the Barrio Logan gang,[11] whose origins date back to the 1940s in San Diego,[12] and also to the prison- based Mexican mafia, known as La Eme.[13] This collaboration was initially sporadic.[14] Later on, the AFO's relations with these US-based gangs became more permanent but still without engaging local gangs. As a member of the Secretariat of Public Security in Tijuana told me, "There [were] gangs, but they [were] not very involved in the business. That is because of the type of leaders, with the Arellano everything was managed through the *narcojuniors* . . . . The enforcers of the Arellano Félix were the Logan gang, while local gangs were only *grafiteros,* cholos, slackers [graffiti artists, gang members], but they were not a problem."[15] Lack of outsourcing to Tijuana's youth gangs resulted from the combination between a short supply of gangs and a short demand for outsourced violence.

The supply of youth gangs was limited despite the existence of a large youth population. In the 1980s and 1990s, there were few reports of violence or petty criminality associated with gangs. In 1984, while 23 out of 131 violent events in Juárez were attributed to youth gangs, in Tijuana there was no record of gangs linked to violent events.[16] In general, homicides in Tijuana tended to occur among older and better-educated sectors of the population than in Ciudad Juárez:[17] Between 1985 and 1997, 35 percent of homicides in Tijuana occurred among the population twenty-five years old or younger, whereas in Ciudad Juárez the proportion was 44 percent.[18] The lack of supply of gangs may also have resulted from the Arellano Félix's attempt to eliminate "social maladies" through social cleansing. As evidence of this, in 1997, the mother of two narcojuniors who had disappeared in Tijuana wrote a letter where she denounced Ramón Arellano Félix as a ruthless killer who asked the judicial police permission to "clean up" the city from the cholos that were killing each other in neighborhoods.[19]

Two factors limited the demand for outsourcing. First, the Arellano Félix organization strived to create the image of educated businessmen, just as the Rodríguez Orejuela brothers had in Cali in the 1980s (as documented in chapter 5). Perhaps this interest in posing as business elite led them to employ the uncommon strategy of armed coercion based on elite young men rather than lower-class operators. Furthermore, involving elite families in the organization provided crucial advantages. Authorities were likely to protect potential killers given their social status, and many narcojuniors had dual citizenship—thus they could easily cross the border into the United States to smuggle drugs or to escape. Second, demand for outsourcing was limited because, as explained below, the Arellano Félix DTO secured stable protection in enforcement agencies, which mitigated the need to recruit masses of young people.

Securing Protection in a Democratizing State

In the 1980s and early 1990s, a cohesive state security apparatus in Tijuana allowed the Arellano Félix organization to expand its connections with political and enforcement actors. Cohesion was possible because enforcement agencies were centralized around the Attorney General's Office, which allowed the establishment of stable protection even in the face of growing democratization pressures in the city and the state of Baja California. Additionally, cohesion provided the state with the ability to conduct quick enforcement when it was necessary to discipline traffickers' behavior. State protection motivated criminals to hide violence in exchange for the license to operate and smuggle drugs.

As seen in Table 6.1, during the early years of the Arellano Félix, there were few methods used to publicly display violence and no high-profile targets: the majority of victims whose occupation could be identified were either petty criminals, along with nonprofessional workers; violence rarely targeted public figures such as police officers or public officials. Low visibility was also manifested in that most violent acts did not cause fatalities, or they produced only one victim: in 1992, 53 percent of violent attacks produced no victims, while 43 percent left only one fatal victim.

An exception to this hidden violence privileged by the Arellano Félix DTO occurred on May 24, 1993, when the Catholic priest Cardinal Juan Jesús Posadas Ocampo was gunned down at the airport of the city of Guadalajara. Although the specifics and motivation of that attack were unclear, and remain so to this day, the official version is that the attack was carried out by the Arellano Félix to eliminate its rival Joaquín Guzmán, who was at the airport at the time—but the attack failed and the cardinal died accidentally in the crossfire.[20] According to other speculations, the cardinal was targeted because he was closely connected to the Arellanos or because he was strongly opposed to drug traffickers. Because, as emphasized in chapter 1 and 2, visible violence can attract enforcement attention, the cardinal's assassination increased enforcement pressure on the Arellano Félix organization and eventually led to the capture of Francisco Javier Arellano on December 4, 1993. Joaquín Guzmán was arrested on June 9, 1993.[21] The enforcement actions following the cardinal's death illustrate why it was costly for criminals to expose violence when they faced a cohesive state that could strike back quickly.[22] It is likely that this attack, and others occurring the same year that were attributed to the fight between Guzmán and the Arellanos, were manifestations of growing cracks within protection networks.[23] Yet the state could still manage criminal conflicts. This also illustrates my argument that state actions can directly affect the behavior of criminal groups, and thus violence, but state structure is key to determining the type of violence that emerges in response to state actions. Unlike the takedowns of criminal leaders that occurred in the late 2000s, those of the 1990s fragmented the organizations and created conflicts between them—but they were not received with multiple visible violent attacks, presumably because traffickers still feared state power and wanted to preserve the protection they received.

In sum, hiding violence, especially at the local level, was crucial for traffickers to benefit from the police protection that allowed them to move drugs relatively freely, to influence the appointment of security officials, and even to obtain credentials as security personnel.[24] The ample protection provided by state officials to the AFO was evident in episodes that linked members of the army, state, and federal police with the organization.[25] For example, Blancornelas recounted how in 1985 the army accused an agent of the state attorney's office of protecting a marijuana cargo and the situation was reported in the *Zeta* magazine. Soon afterward, the State Judicial Police bought the entire production of the magazine, thereby revealing the state's interest in maintaining the corruption case out of public sight.[26] The corruption cases that eventually became public showed that protection networks were not just sporadic interactions. For example, in November 1992, a major in the Mexican army, Juan José Sánchez Gutiérrez, was detained and accused of serving as liaison between Benjamín Arellano and army officials.

Centralization of state power gave stability to the protection networks crafted by the Arellano Félix brothers even though in 1989 a path-breaking political and electoral event threatened state cohesion—when, for the first time, an opposition party won a governorship in Mexico after seventy years of rule of the Institutional Revolutionary Party (PRI). Ernesto Ruffo Apel, from the National Action Party (PAN), won the governorship of Baja California, challenging the PRI's decades-old monopoly of power and marking a watershed in Mexico's democratization.[27] Ruffo's election represented the pinnacle of the growing competition between the PRI and the PAN that had unfolded in Tijuana between 1986 and 1992.[28] The election also initiated confrontations between the PAN-dominated state government and the PRI-dominated federal government. The Arellano Félix brothers, however, managed to keep their network of protection despite the political transition. In fact, there were allegations that Ruffo himself had established a pact with the Arellano Félix, whereby the state guaranteed that traffickers would be protected from prosecution in exchange for not using Baja California as a battlefield.[29] The allegations were never confirmed, but there is evidence that Ruffo at minimum avoided direct involvement in antitrafficking operations.

Why didn't growing electoral competition translate immediately into a more fragmented state security apparatus? First, the PAN had little experience governing and a limited membership base; thus, many members of Ruffo's cabinet were PRI officials—notably the first state attorney general[30] and the state director of transit and transportation;[31] for this reason, the electoral transition did not translate immediately into a bureaucratic makeover. Second, the new competitors at the subnational level were reluctant to take on drug-trafficking enforcement as a local responsibility. The power of the Arellano Félix was so ingrained when the PAN came to power that the party did not have the ability or the experience to confront them, and instead it focused on the administrative challenge of governing without having much prior experience.[32] While the political transition increased the independence of the state and local governments in social and economic policy (budgeting, public works, and urban policies such as trash collection and transportation)[33] it had a limited impact on public security.

A tension between Governor Ruffo and Mexico's attorney general Ignacio Morales Lechuga illustrated the reluctance of PAN-identified politicians to crack down on trafficking. In a letter addressed to the journalist Jesús Blancornelas in 1994, attorney Morales Lechuga highlighted that "Ernesto Ruffo Appel minimized or undervalued the grave problem of local insecurity and attempted to explain the complex local phenomenon of drug trafficking as a federal responsibility"; many years later, Ruffo responded to the letter alleging that he tried to coordinate actions with the federal government but "sadly, our federal government was extremely involved in the terrible problem of drug trafficking and its consequences."[34] This correspondence illustrates the growing tension that followed the political transition in Baja California, but it also shows why in the short run the tension did not fragment the state. The local government, at least initially, left enforcement actions in the hands of the federal government and the PRI, while PAN members such as Tijuana's mayor Carlos Montejo (1990–1992) avoided public actions against drug trafficking.

The distribution of power in the state continued to change incrementally throughout the mid-1990s without fragmenting it. During 1996 and 1997, however, a series of purges, rotations, and reforms in law enforcement led to momentary fragmentation in the security apparatus and to episodes of visible violence.

Controlled Signaling (1996–1997)

Between 1996 and 1997 Tijuana experienced an uncommon pattern of violence, in which visibility increases but frequency does not change. A series of high-profile attacks captured the attention of enforcement authorities, even though the city homicide rates remained relatively stable (20 in 1996, 21 in 1995, and 19 in 1997). The targets included at least eight high-ranking government officials, twelve police officers, and the journalist Jesús Blancornelas.[35] The Attorney General's Office was a prominent target, and eight members of that agency were killed, including two former delegates in Tijuana, two commanders of the Federal Judicial Police, and one former commander of the Federal Judicial Police.[36]

Most of these killings were retaliatory responses to anticorruption policies and enforcement actions that destabilized protection arrangements between the state and the Arellano Félix DTO. These anticorruption policies had started in March 1996 when the Attorney General's Office conducted two operations with military support (Operations Alacrán and Cancer) that led to large seizures of drugs and entailed an intensive search of the Arellano Félix and their associates' properties. Even though there were no arrests in these operations, high-profile attacks ensued.[37] Then, in July 1996, a member of the National Institute for Combating Drugs (INCD) made an unusual accusation denouncing extreme corruption in Mexican antinarcotics agencies. This accusation led to the appointment of a member of the opposition party PAN to the Attorney General's Office, who then purged about half of the members of the Tijuana delegation of the general attorney's office. The newly appointed director of the federal police in Tijuana echoed denunciations of corruption in September 1996, and not surprisingly he was assassinated a few days after being sworn in. These operations, rotations, and purges increased state fragmentation and temporarily reduced traffickers' incentives to hide violence.

Previous enforcement actions, like that leading to Francisco Arellano's arrest in 1993, did not cause retaliation because they were not part of a sustained enforcement campaign and because the state structure had not been changed through rotations and purges[38] as occurred in 1996, so the state could still provide traffickers with reliable protection. This case thus illustrates how in the context of a relatively noncompetitive illegal market, visible violence can emerge in retaliation for state actions that threaten the structure of criminal organizations, if criminals believe they can force the state to change its policies or reestablish protection arrangements. In other words, criminals have to be experiencing high losses because of state actions but still consider themselves powerful enough vis-à-vis enforcers to engage in frequent and visible violence. This is likely to be the case when the state is fragmented, as in this case, when some state actors clearly wanted to go after the Arellano Félix but many others still protected them.

Judicial investigations did not fully clarify whether the authorities killed had been targeted because they refused to collaborate with traffickers or

because they did not abide to previous arrangements made to protect traffickers from enforcement operations.[39] In any case, the strong market control
of the Arellano Félix organization guaranteed that, at least in the short run,
violence would not escalate. The visible acts of 1996 and 1997 were effective in reestablishing arrangements between traffickers and criminal actors in
subsequent years.

Reaccommodation and Quiet Wars (1998–2007)

After the high-profile attacks of 1996 and 1997, confrontations between factions
of the Arellano Félix DTO, and with outside competitors, continued to produce
violence. Partially in response to pressure from the United States, the AFO suffered some key blows: two main leaders of the organization were eliminated
in 2002, causing leadership instability and some internal competition: Ramón
Arellano died in February and the police captured Benjamín Arellano in March.
These leadership changes, along with the capture of other midlevel operational commanders of the AFO, weakened but did not challenge the DTO's
control. Because there was no outright territorial invasion by competing trafficking groups, control remained within the family, and leadership succession
was relatively peaceful when Fernando Sánchez Arellano, a.k.a. El Ingeniero
(The Engineer), nephew of the former leaders, became the new boss. When
the remaining Arellano Félix brothers, Francisco Javier (a.k.a. El Tigrillo) and
Eduardo, were later arrested in 2006 and 2008, respectively,[40] the organization
became more vulnerable to the internal and external competition that exploded
in 2008, as described below.

Homicides in Tijuana increased by 70 percent between 1997 and 1998, from
19 deaths per 100,000 inhabitants to 32. Up to 2007, the city's average homicide
rate remained similar to the levels seen between 1987 and 1995, at about 20 per
100,000, but did not escalate to reach more than twice the national rate because
insourcing remained the main strategy of armed coercion. Between 1998 and
2007, the narcojunior phenomenon became less prominent, and US gangs still
played important roles as enforcers for the AFO,[41] but local gangs remained disconnected from the DTO. Violence was high but relatively stable and without
major increases up to 2008. It was also hidden.

The Act of Disappearing Bodies

In the late 1990s and 2000s, the AFO deployed violence to control the market
but became even more careful in hiding it. Perhaps the most brutal example

of hiding violence was the use of acid to destroy corpses of people killed by traffickers. The remains of the bodies would then be dumped into sewage systems or buried in the outskirts of the city by employees of the criminal organizations. Such techniques to hide attacks only became public in 2009 when Mexican authorities captured the criminal Santiago Meza López, known as El Pozolero del Teo (Teo's Stewmaker).[42] Meza confessed that for over ten years he and other collaborators, including a criminal known as El Cris, had disintegrated more than three hundred bodies in the course of working for the Arellano Félix, and especially for the DTO's enforcers, El Efra and later El Teo.[43]

Meza's capture and his methods were quickly labeled as examples of the brutality of Mexico's drug violence since 2006, yet his testimony revealed a more intricate puzzle. For almost a decade, Meza's job had been to eliminate the evidence of violence; but in 2008, when disputes exploded inside the AFO, he was specifically instructed to change his method of disposing of bodies: instead of hiding bodies, he was to place them in the middle of a well-transited street, along with a note that read, "This is what happens to El Ingeniero's people. We are going to make *pozole* with you."[44] This example powerfully illustrates that brutality, seen as a marker of post-2006 violence, in fact has older roots, and differs from visibility: traffickers could be very brutal, yet, before 2008, they were careful in hiding it. Disappearing bodies was an old technique used to hide traffickers' responsibility, and it became known to the public only when traffickers changed their strategy and decided to display violence.

A few human rights organizations concerned by the tragedy of disappeared people thought to be victims of drug traffickers in Baja California denounced this hidden violence, but there is no reliable information about how many people disappeared throughout the late 1990s and 2000s. Existing information comes from relatives of the disappeared who individually, or in weakly organized groups, attempted to find their relatives. One such case is that of Cristina Palacios de Hodoyan, whose son was first detained in 1996 and then disappeared in 1997. Since 1997 she has been tracing his whereabouts, albeit unsuccessfully. In her quest, she met other victims of disappearance, and according to the information she collected, about 20 disappearances were recorded between 2002 and 2007 and about 132 between 2007 and 2011.[45] Yet according to another activist and victim, between 1989 and 2007 the official number of investigations initiated for disappearances was 430, and it is likely that some victims could have been disappeared by *pozoleros*.[46] According to him "The stuff of the pozoleros has a long history. The Arellano Félix in the 1980s brought a group from Israel to teach them how to disintegrate bodies."[47] The key point is that although disappearances became public in the late 2000s, they had been occurring for a long time and were clearly aimed at eliminating the evidence of traffickers' violence.

Press reports in my data set of drug violence also document traffickers' efforts to hide violence in this period of criminal reaccommodation. In 2002, newspapers reported the increasing finding of bodies with signs of torture, usually naked, and wrapped in plastic. Out of forty-five bodies found with signs of torture and attributed to criminal disputes in 2002, twenty-seven were found in the outskirts of the city, in abandoned lots, rivers, or private residencies, as opposed to public areas and streets. Brutality seemed to be increasing, but for the most part, criminals tried to hide it. For example on October 20, 2002, the press reported the finding of a corpse in the sewage system of a neighborhood in Tijuana. The corpse had been mutilated, and the body parts, with the exception of the head, were distributed in three plastic bags.[48] In a similar case, in November a woman found the remains of an incinerated body at the base of a hill[49] and the following day workers found another incinerated body in an abandoned lot.[50] In most cases, bodies were disposed of in private or abandoned spaces, as if the intention was that the bodies should not be found.

Such a time investment in hiding violence was aimed at keeping the protection networks of the AFO. A notable example of such protection involved a PRI politician and owner of Mexico's largest sports betting company, Jorge Hank Rhon, the son of Carlos Hank, a powerful stalwart of the old PRI elite. Jorge Hank became Tijuana's mayor between 2005 and 2007, but since the late 1990s he had allegedly appeared in DEA files as a money launderer for the AFO.[51] In 2009, the US consul in Tijuana expressed in a leaked cable to the US secretary of state that "Hank is widely believed to have been a corrupt mayor and to be still involved in narco-trafficking."[52] Between 1998 and 2007, the PAN consolidated its electoral power, winning local and state governments throughout the period. Even though part of the Arellanos' support network was linked to PRI politicians such as Hank Rhon, the PAN did not carry out any massive antitrafficking efforts in Tijuana. Perhaps the AFO avoided visible violence because it did not want to provoke an unfriendly government that had higher chances of going after them—especially after Mexicans elected Vicente Fox as the first non-PRI president, because Baja California and Tijuana as PAN strongholds were better positioned to mitigate the conflicts among government levels that followed the presidential transition. Or perhaps the AFO had been successful in securing protection among PAN politicians. At any rate, this situation changed radically in 2008 when both the state and the criminal organization fragmented profoundly; the breakdown of protection networks eliminated the incentives that maintained Tijuana's violence hidden. Hank Rhon's arrest on arms-trafficking charges in 2011 illustrated the vulnerability of protection, even though he was later released by the army due to lack of evidence.

Violent Explosion and Return to Relative Peace (2008–2010)

In 2008, Tijuana experienced a historic explosion of violence caused by the escalation of conflicts for illegal market control and by the state fragmentation accelerated by federal military deployments in January 2007. Homicide rates in the city increased by 245 percent going from 13 in 2007 to 42 in 2008 and to 72 in 2009.

Violence proliferated as conflicts within the Arellano Félix DTO finally split up the organization between two factions, one led by Teodoro García Simental (El Teo), a high-level killer, and the other led by Fernando Sánchez (El Ingeniero).[53] The split became even more consequential for violence as El Teo allied with Joaquín Guzmán and the Sinaloa DTO, which had initiated an aggressive strategy of territorial expansion.[54] Visibility also increased as methods exposing violent attacks proliferated (see Table 6.1) including shootouts in the middle of the street, the display in public spaces of mutilated bodies with notes, and the use of banners where criminals sent messages to their rivals and to the state. Public authorities became more frequently targeted, and in 2010, nine police officers and soldiers died in violent attacks.[55] In 2010, a newspaper made public the content of banners that had appeared throughout the city and revealed the nature of the confrontations:[56] most were directed against Aquiles, a former member of the AFO who had allied with El Teo and the Sinaloa DTO.

Visible violence ensued after military deployments fragmented the security forces. In January 2007, the federal government deployed 3,296 soldiers, marines, and federal police, for an enforcement effort labeled Operación Conjunta Tijuana (Joint Operation Tijuana).[57] At the operation's onset, there were confrontations between the Baja California governor, Eugenio Elorduy, and the commander of the military zone, Sergio Aponte Polito. Aponte Polito was publicly critical of corruption in state police, and in a few occasions he ran paid advertisements in newspapers to denounce state police corruption.[58] The military mobilization therefore generated tensions between elected authorities and also between enforcement agencies, complicating coordination and protection. These tensions, however, eased by 2010, thus making Tijuana's explosion of violence shorter than Ciudad Juárez's.

A Fragmented State Quickly Recovers

The state fragmentation that followed the federal decision to deploy troops in anticrime operations was shorter lived in Tijuana because a military leadership supported by all three government levels catalyzed a renewed state cohesion.

In 2008, José Osuna Millán was elected governor of Baja California. As he took office, he declared that General Aponte was in charge of public security and informally gave Aponte the power to coordinate enforcement. In turn, Mayor Jorge Ramos publicly supported this decision. These declarations signaled that political authorities were jointly granting military authorities the command of Tijuana's public security, and the political decision contributed to improving the relations between the governor, the mayor, the chiefs of public security, and the commander of the military zone.

General Aponte Polito appointed current and former military officials in key public security positions; the most notable appointment was that of Lieutenant Colonel Julián Leyzaola, who became Tijuana's chief of public security. Leyzaola had been the commander of the state preventive police, and this experience allowed him to garner trust within state police when he was appointed at the municipal level. In Leyzaola's words, "I had complete support from the state police, because I trained them myself."[59] Leyzaola became the most visible face of what would be known as the Tijuana Model, a label used to refer to the relative quick demise of violence in the city. Leyzaola also became infamous as a result of his controversial, but very public, discourse regarding criminals as "dirty ones" who did not deserve any consideration regarding individual rights.[60] An official of the municipal Secretariat of Public Security described the political and enforcement coordination as follows:

> In 2007, there was a substantial change in the municipal police because of the people who came to direct the agency, the military . . . . We removed security chiefs and placed commanders with military training . . . . Part of the success had to do with the ability of the municipal police to initiate actions through a strong command, which was that of Lieutenant Colonel Leyzaola. The mayor made a commitment because he let the chiefs [of public security] work, he looked for resources. Political will matters a lot. With General Aponte Polito everything started; he named Leyzaola and everything started there. The governor had no other choice but to ride along.[61]

When General Aponte Polito was relieved from his post in August 2008,[62] General Alfonso Duarte Múgica replaced him and became the de facto commander of all enforcement agencies. When Duarte arrived, Governor Osuna Millán again declared publicly that security was in the hands of the general, who also headed a group of interinstitutional coordination. Military influence continued, and in fact, most people grant Duarte, rather than Aponte Polito, the recognition for facilitating enforcement coordination. Military influence was crucial to induce coordination in enforcement agencies, creating a de facto single command. As one expert put it, the single command "has not been created constitutionally, but it exists de facto because there is a subordination of the civil government to General Duarte."[63]

Along with military influence, political coordination was also crucial to inducing state cohesion, because the mayor, governor, and president were all from the same party, the PAN. As a businessman put it, "There has been political will of the governor and the municipal presidents, the proof is that all of them accepted a former military in each Secretariat of Public Security at the municipal level."[64] Additionally, the limited role of the federal police in Tijuana as well as the reduced number of municipalities in the region (there are only five municipalities in Baja California Norte) facilitated the path to regaining cohesion after the military deployments and made it easier for politicians and commanders to coordinate. Under these circumstances, by 2010, homicide rates had decreased by 50 percent and visible violence had also decreased considerably.

Continued Insourcing

State cohesion facilitated the successful implementation of high-profile enforcement actions—for example, the capture of some of the most violent criminal leaders of DTOs. El Teo was captured on January 12, 2010, and his associates Raydel Lopez, a.k.a. El Muletas (The Crutches), and Manuel Garcia, a.k.a. El Chikilin (The Little One), were detained on February 8, 2010; Juan Francisco Sillas, the main enforcer for El Ingeniero, was captured in November 2011. These high-profile captures had an immediate and notable impact on violence because, to a great extent, even at the height of the violent peak, warring factions in Tijuana continued insourcing violence, and therefore the arrests of the organizations' main enforcers greatly reduced the violent behavior of those under their command.

Limited outsourcing, even in the context of a war, partially reflected a path-dependent effect, as the legacy of the Arellano Félix's use of narcojuniors prevented the reproduction of gangs in the city,[65] and those gangs that existed were not directly linked to drug-trafficking organizations;[66] this situation remained true after the explosion of violence in 2008. There were reports linking the US-based gang Mexican Mafia (La Eme) and the gang Los Sureños, based in San Diego, to trafficking organizations in Baja California. El Teo, reportedly used indigent local youth to carry out violence.[67] Yet, local gangs and trafficking organizations were not clearly aligned, and the US-based gangs had weak connections to Tijuana gangs. In 2009, and in line with tendencies seen in other years, the proportion of homicide victims between the ages of fifteen and twenty-four was lower in Tijuana than in Ciudad Juárez, whereas the proportion of homicide victims ages thirty-five to forty-four was far higher in Tijuana.[68]

Lieutenant Colonel Leyzaola described the lack of outsourcing to youth gangs as follows, "In Tijuana crime was organized, specialized . . . . There were gangs, but not linked to crime; they [the traffickers] had their own killers and gangs were used only sporadically."[69] The capture and elimination of violent lieutenants thus had an immediate impact on violence because killers were under direct control of traffickers. As expressed by a human rights worker: "We have gangs in the periphery, but they have not been used by organized crime; there has not been a need for an army like in Juárez where they [gangs] are linked as labor force. Here we have fifty thousand unemployed and a cell of the Familia Michoacana [a trafficking group], but once the cell of El Teo was captured, they calmed down."[70] Insourcing was crucial as an explanation for why Tijuana experienced a less-pronounced spike of violence than Ciudad Juárez and why enforcement actions disintegrated criminal's armed coercion more rapidly. This underscores why the type of armed coercion criminals employ is crucial for explaining drug violence.

The Return of Low-Visibility Violence

The homicide reduction experienced in 2010, dubbed the Tijuana Model, did in fact reflect important successes in law enforcement, which were largely facilitated by local state cohesion. Other factors also played a key role, however, such as an involvement of the business sector in monitoring violence trends, in shaping the image of city as a safe place for business and tourism, and in shaping public representations of violence. In line with this book's argument, the decline of violence also followed a reduction in criminal competition that ensued as the Sinaloa DTO gained control and the most violent faction of the Arellano Félix DTO was dismantled. Such reduction was reinforced by a criminal pact between warring factions. The remaining leaders of the AFO, renamed as the Tijuana (or the Sánchez Arellano) DTO, conscious of their weakness, preferred to strike a pact that allowed them to remain active. They chose to return to the old system in which they charged other criminal organizations, such as the Familia Michoana, for the right to pass drugs through their territory. Because criminal pacts tend to be unstable and the new criminal leadership in Tijuana seems to lack clear hierarchies,[71] conflicts among traffickers may generate increases in homicides as occurred in 2012. Indeed after a 60 percent decline in homicides between 2009 and 2011, homicide rates increased again in 2013, and after another decline, they increased by 40 percent in 2015. Yet, this violence remains low profile, as criminals have learned that there is a high price to pay for displaying violent behavior.

The violence that persisted after 2010, even during the recent peaks, has been mostly hidden. According to human rights workers, the apparent success of authorities in reducing violence in 2010 was no more than a change in the nature of attacks, which are not as brutal and visible as they were in 2008. Violence now occurs in the outskirts of the city and involves low-level drug dealers rather than high-ranking criminals. Killings are usually carried out with simple gunshots rather than methods that make a display of violence, such as beheadings or notes and banners on dead bodies.[72] In the words of a photojournalist:

> There has always been violence . . . there will always be assassinations, but the high-impact crimes changed. The twelve-person convoys that you used to see became three guys in a sedan that shoot three times. It became more discreet. And you no longer see the violence; it's difficult to see it on the street. I was very surprised by the amount of sirens you could hear before. The high-impact crime, which is the one that worries society, has decreased a lot, and we, the society, believe that calm feeling.[73]

An official of the state attorney's office echoed this statement: "Currently we have no homicides in broad daylight, but clandestine homicides. The weapons also change. They use strangulation but not high-power weapons."[74] These statements underscore the importance of assessing visibility. Although positive, Tijuana's pacification masks a reality of less-visible violence, of militarization of public security, and of a public relations campaign that creates a positive image of the city but that may ignore persistent low-profile violence.

To recap, Tijuana's pacification resulted from the ability of authorities, especially military ones, to reduce state fragmentation. This led to more successful enforcement operations driven by militarized frameworks. It was also a result of traffickers adapting to the new conditions. Many traffickers suffered crucial blows and therefore preferred to return to a more peaceful arrangement that allowed them to keep operating without forcing the state to act, but which required them to hide violence. Finally, the lack of connections between traffickers and youth gangs facilitated both the effectiveness of state actions and the strategic adaptation of criminals. These three elements—reduced state fragmentation, strategic adaptation of criminals, and insourcing—did not exist when violence skyrocketed in Juárez in 2008.

In 2010, Ciudad Juárez became the world's most violent city. The meteoric rise in violence starting in 2008 was unexpected but not unpredictable. The next section describes how during most of the 1980s and 1990s one major organization—the Juárez, or Carrillo Fuentes, DTO—dominated the city's illegal market and maintained stable networks of protection. Such a combination created a relatively stable pattern of low-visibility and low-frequency violence. Toward the late 1990s, however, competition in the illegal market started to increase, and violence rose as well. In 2008, three sharp changes combined to create a "perfect storm" of violence: a war exploded between the Juárez DTO and the Sinaloa DTO, both groups outsourced violence to the gangs that had for years existed in the city independently from trafficking groups, and militarization, along with confrontations between government authorities, immersed Ciudad Juárez in its worst period of violence.

Consolidation of the Juárez DTO: 1984–1994

Ciudad Juárez is located in the northern Mexican state of Chihuahua, bordering El Paso, Texas. It is also strategically close to the tristate intersection between Chihuahua, Texas, and New Mexico. Since the 1960s, life in Ciudad Juárez has been marked by the proliferation of the export maquiladora industry that attracted large immigration flows from other parts of Mexico and employed women almost exclusively, thus radically transforming family dynamics and creating social clashes and transformations.[75] The jobs that for decades created a city of "full employment" did not improve the quality of life for maquiladora workers, as most employment was low skilled and labor conditions were precarious.[76] Along with the city's lack of infrastructure, ingrained corruption in the political system and government abandonment made Juárez the poster child of globalized production processes and their negative consequences.[77]

These political and social factors are essential for understanding the extreme public security crisis that plagued Juárez since 2008, yet they are not enough to account for the timing of that crisis. The spike of violence in 2008 coincided with an increase in estimated unemployment numbers from 2.5 percent in 2005 to 3.2 in 2007, 4.9 in 2008, and 8.4 in 2009.[78] Yet, previous employment crises were not matched by increases in violence (for example between 2000 and 2002, when unemployment grew from 2.0 percent to 3.7 percent).[79] For this reason, even though profound socioeconomic problems are breeding grounds for violence, the timing and short-term causes of violence in Juárez after 2008 can be better understood by looking at the changing interaction between the state security apparatus and the structure of the drug market. The story thus should start with the consolidation of the Juárez DTO in the early 1980s.

Ciudad Juárez has a long history of smuggling and a trafficking tradition that seems to be older, more ingrained, and more territorialized than in Tijuana.[80]

This tradition can be traced all the way back to the 1920s, with traffickers like Ignacia Jasso, a.k.a. La Nacha, and later, in the 1970s and 1980s, with Pablo Acosta Villarreal, a.k.a. El Zorro de Ojinaga (the Ojinaga Fox), and Héctor González, a.k.a. El Árabe (The Arab). In the early 1980s, a commander of the Federal Security Directorate (DFS), Rafael Aguilar Guajardo, and Rafael Muñoz, organized previously dispersed drug-smuggling groups in what came to be known as the Juárez DTO.[81]

In 1985, Ernesto Fonseca Carrillo, a.k.a. Don Neto, an old-time trafficker, sent his nephew Amado Carrillo, from Sinaloa, to take control of the *plaza*, or drug turf, of Ojinaga, another municipality in the state of Chihuahua.[82] Carrillo allied with the drug traffickers Rafael Aguilar, Rafael Muñoz, and El Greñas to establish an almost monopolistic control of illegal markets in Ciudad Juárez,[83] an arrangement that generated only sporadic violence between 1984 and 1993. In this period, homicide rates were lower than national rates, at an average of 8.63 homicides per 100,000 inhabitants (Figure 6.1.).

Amado Carrillo consolidated a network of aircraft, aerial routes, and landing strips that gave him the nickname El Señor de los Cielos (The Lord of the Skies). Carrillo also mastered relationships with Colombian trafficking organizations. In the words of the former commissioner of the National Institute for Combatting Drugs (INCD) for Ciudad Juárez, the control Carrillo achieved was comparable to a tyranny, as he did not let anyone "smuggle a gram that [was] not his."[84] A former official of the Federal Security Directorate (DFS) who arrived in Ciudad Juárez in the late 1980s described the control as follows: "When I arrived in Juárez everything was peaceful; it is the most important frontier and everything was coordinated—there was only one [trafficking] group there."[85]

Gangs Proliferate but Outsourcing Remains Limited

During these early years, armed coercion by the Juárez DTO remained within the organization, even though there was a significant supply of nonviolent youth gangs. In the 1980s, gangs spread throughout Juárez, providing young men who adopted similar dress styles and shared cultural norms with a source of socialization and identification. These young men, known as cholos, were rarely violent, according to José Manuel Valenzuela, but the public, and especially the media, often stigmatized them as perpetrators of crimes; crime suspects were usually described as "males with cholo appearance."[86] Contrary to what these stigmas suggest, in this period there was no systematic connection between gangs and traffickers. An analysis of newspaper reports in 1984 shows, for instance, that street gangs— also known as *barrios*—were mostly involved in minor offenses such as street fights and robberies, but rarely in violent homicides. Deaths emerged more often as a result of social antipathy toward cholos than as a result of the gangs' own vio-lence. Young gang members occasionally worked for traffickers, but they were usually lookouts or carriers of drugs (*mulas*)[87] rather than assassins.

The lack of outsourcing therefore resulted mostly from a lack of demand, rather than a lack of supply, as youth gangs existed but were disconnected from trafficking organizations. Traffickers in Ciudad Juárez, unlike their Tijuana peers, did not try to eliminate gangs through social cleansing, but they did not demand their labor, either. Because the relative monopoly of the Juárez DTO made vio-lent disputes with competitors sporadic, it was unnecessary for the DTO to garner massive numbers of soldiers for war. Additionally, as shown below, the protection that the Juárez DTO secured in enforcement agencies also reduced demand for outsourced violence. These networks of protection also explained why violence, if employed, was not visible.

State-Sponsored Protection in Ciudad Juárez

Amado Carrillo and the Juárez DTO gained protection from broad sectors of a cohesive state. The Juárez DTO established a thick network of support among police forces and enforcement officials; the best example of this collaboration involves the army general Jesús Gutiérrez Rebollo, head of the INCD, convicted for protecting Carrillo and for selectively enforcing the law against Carrillo's Tijuana rivals. Gutierrez Rebollo was detained in February 1997 soon after he had been named head of the INCD, and eight days after a US White House drug policy chief, General Barry R. McCaffrey, had described him as "an honest man and a no-nonsense field commander."[88] The Mexican defense secretary declared that for seven years the general had protected cocaine shipments for Amado Carrillo in exchange for vehicles, real estate, and cash.[89]

In the 1980s, state cohesion in Ciudad Juárez depended on the power of the Mexico Attorney General's Office and its police branch, the Federal Security Directorate (DFS). These offices were able to reduce conflicts among enforce-ment agencies and created incentives for criminals to hide violence. In the words of a former member of the DFS who worked in Ciudad Juárez: "The Attorney General's Office coordinated everything, sometimes even the army. There was order even in the relation with the state's attorney. There were executions, but the *bodies disappeared, they were not thrown out in the streets.*"[90] The state and munic-ipal police also provided protection, controlling and sometimes even extorting criminals; according to a human rights worker, "The weight of the judicial police was enormous, they controlled criminality."[91]

Limited political competition and PRI control expressed in high win mar-gins and party coordination among government levels, which as in other cities in

Mexico allowed extraordinary political coordination, also facilitated cohesion. In 1983, the PRI experienced one of its earliest electoral defeats when Francisco Barrio from the PAN won elections and became the mayor of Ciudad Juárez.[92] As in the case of the first PAN government in Baja California, over time Barrio's election became consequential for the democratic transition, but in the short run, it posed only a minor challenge to PRI control at the state and federal levels.[93] In fact, after this PAN victory, the PRI returned to power in 1986.

The early PAN victory had a limited effect on challenging the cohesive power structure, but it contributed to create a pattern of active intervention by the mayor that was uncommon in other localities where the PAN or the opposition did not have early victories. An opposing mayor was more likely to challenge the governor, and consequently clashes between PAN mayors and PRI governors became commonplace.[94] Just as the electoral success of the opposition in the presidential election of 2000 created a new relationship between presidents and governors, providing more power to the latter,[95] in Juárez the early electoral transition transformed the relationship between mayors and the governor. Power within the state, however, remained relatively centralized until the mid-2000s.

Criminal Competition (1994–2007)

In 1993, Amado Carrillo assassinated one of his associates, Rafael Aguilar, clearing a path to become the sole leader of the Juárez DTO. The killing, however, generated grievances and competition within the organization. Competition with rivals from Tijuana and the Gulf DTO also escalated.[96] Homicide rates almost doubled, from 14 to 25 per 100,000 between 1993 and 1994. Between 1994 and 2007 homicide rates remained high, at an average of 21 per 100,000 inhabitants (Figure 6.1.).

In 1997, Amado Carrillo died in mysterious circumstances while undergoing facial plastic surgery. After his death, his brother Vicente Carrillo took over the organization, and although he managed to maintain the dominance of the Juárez DTO, he dealt with opposition from leaders like Rafael Muñoz, who fought for control until his death in 1998.[97] On September 10, 2004, in Culiacán, Joaquín Guzmán, leader of the Sinaloa DTO, allegedly oversaw the assassination of Rodolfo Carrillo, another member of the Juárez DTO, because Guzmán was vying for controlling border trafficking routes.[98] This episode generated confrontations between traffickers that used to operate as business partners, and in consequence, violence increased. The confrontation, however, did not become an all-out war until late 2007, when the Sinaloa DTO physically moved forces into Ciudad Juárez, as explained below.

Violence was frequent, but it did not escalate too far above national rates because, as in the former period, there was no outsourcing of armed coercion to youth gangs. During the late 1990s and early 2000s, the municipal Secretariat of Public Security reported that there were three hundred gangs with more than fifteen thousand members.[99] Some of them participated in local drug dealing, but for the most part there was no evidence of systematic connections between traffickers and gangs, especially regarding the outsourcing of criminal coercion. Violence also remained strategically hidden as the networks of state protection and control persisted.

Persistent State Control

After the election of PAN's Francisco Barrio as Chihuahua's governor in 1992 political challenges to PRI rule grew,[100] but networks of protection for criminals remained strong. The political change fell short of a real challenge to the old power structure, and in fact Governor Barrio was criticized for maintaining cozy relations with the PRI federal government.[101] Although Barrio carried out massive firings that disjointed the judicial police, the new police forces quickly reinstalled relations with criminal forces. In fact, during the tenure of Mayor Gustavo Elizondo (1998–2001) the Juárez DTO formed an enforcement branch comprising former and current transit police, municipal and state police, and some federal police, known as La Línea (The Line).[102] Over the years, La Línea recruited mainly from among the ranks of former and current police and established tight support networks that combined judicial officials, cops, taxi drivers, and contract killers.[103]

State cohesion also persisted because the Attorney General's Office still mitigated conflicts between enforcement agencies, which could derive, for example, from military presence in enforcement operations. Military presence was usually covert and did not employ the massive numbers, the street operations, and the raids that became routine years later, in 2008. For example, in 1995 the Attorney General's Office carried out an antinarcotics operation against the Juárez DTO, which deployed seventy-two people operating as temporary agents.[104] According to a former official of the Attorney General's Office, the operation "was coordinated with the commander of the military zone and with the Attorney General's Office."[105] The operation lasted about four months and although initially it forced the Juárez DTO to reduce smuggling and hide, eventually it failed because the soldiers ended up involved in corruption scandals.[106]

In this operation, the leading role of the Attorney General's Office prevented conflicts of operation that could derive from the simultaneous presence of military and judicial police and it also allowed them to quickly cover up the operation's failure, which was not very publicized. This case reflected, however, that although state cohesion gave state officials the upper hand in regulating drug trafficking, as Astorga has intelligently put it,[107] the Juárez DTO also had power to push the state to withdraw when enforcement operations became too costly for them. Of course, the organization's fear of losing state protection limited the pushback, and thus the criminal's reaction to this operation was not nearly as violent as that caused by military operations after 2008.

This operation illustrates that even though anticrime actions that fragment organizations can directly lead traffickers to compete with each other, not all enforcement operations cause similar responses. Reactions may not be as publicly displayed if criminals fear the retaliation of a cohesive state or if they highly value the protection they receive. A cohesive state can organize and control enforcement operations more easily (in this case, troops were quickly withdrawn after problems emerged), thereby motivating criminals to be more cautious in their violent reactions. Had the Juárez DTO's reaction been too violent, it could have forced the state to crack down on the organization. State cohesion thus made enforcement more threatening while at the same time still provided the possibility of credible protection. This bounded the criminals' violent reaction and created incentives for them to hide violence—for example, through disappearances.

Disappearances in Ciudad Juárez

Between 1994 and 2007 disappearances became a prevalent tool to hide violence. In 1997, Sam Dillon, a journalist from the *New York Times*, wrote an article revealing crucial aspects of disappearances in Ciudad Juárez. He described how in many cases victims appeared to have been detained by police or soldiers, who were likely contracted by traffickers to eliminate their rivals and debtors.[108] The participation of federal police in disappearances was even acknowledged by Governor Francisco Barrio (1993–1998) and by a special envoy of the attorney general who declared that municipal police had told him "the desert surrounding Juárez is a vast cemetery, a huge mausoleum full of corpses."[109] Police participation in disappearances revealed the systemic links between state and criminals.

Available information suggests that victims of disappearance were killed and buried in mass graves; therefore both the evidence and the perpetrators were almost impossible to track. A relative of a victim interviewed by Dillon stated, "They [perpetrators of disappearance] use a large oven to cremate the disappeared."[110] In fact, in November 1999, a protected witness helped the FBI locate two mass graves. The FBI and the Mexico Attorney General's Office initiated a joint enforcement operation on the site but recovered the remains of only nine bodies. In subsequent years, sporadic discoveries of mass graves kept revealing a silent violence that could be uncovered only when members of criminal groups became informants of enforcement agencies. One of the most notorious was the

discovery in 2003 of eleven buried bodies in a house that belonged to a leader of
the Juárez DTO. This case was memorable as some of the killings carried out in
this house had been witnessed by a DEA undercover agent.

It is unclear how many people disappeared during the late 1990s and early
2000s in Ciudad Juárez. Jaime Hervella, an accountant and a resident of El Paso,
started to track cases of disappearance when he created an association to search
for his friend's son and daughter-in-law who had disappeared at the hands of
traffickers. In 1997, Hervella published an advertisement inviting victims' relatives to report cases, and in the course of a few days he received more than
fifty reports. By 2003 he had identified 196 cases, of which authorities officially
acknowledged 181.[111] Hervella's efforts and the efforts of other victims forced the
attorney general to send special envoys to investigate disappearances, yet there
was never an official resolution to any case. Rumors abounded, but as Charles
Bowden put it, for the most part, "The entire matter would exist outside the talk
of governments."[112] Violence thus remained hidden, because evidence was only
occasionally recovered and because the victims' status as possibly involved in
criminal activities led authorities, and even families, to pursue these cases less
resolutely. According to Hervella, the documentation of cases became more difficult over time because people would "bring information but then would tell
us that they did not want anything published . . . . The families did not want to
get involved because they feared retaliation, but also because they had doubts
[about their relatives] and preferred not to get involved."[113]

Many disappearances lost preeminence vis-à-vis the killing and torture of
women known as feminicides, which took center stage and made the city sadly
infamous beginning in 1993. Some feminicides were characterized by the deliberate use of sexual violence and atrocity aimed at exposing the gender-related
dimension of the attacks.[114] The investigation of feminicides was also characterized by impunity and corruption, yet it encouraged civil society to demand
justice to a greater extent than the disappearances supposedly associated to
drug trafficking. The discursive construction of victims of disappearance as possible criminals therefore contributed to keeping trafficking violence unknown.
Hidden violence also allowed traffickers to maintain networks of protection,
which despite political changes remained ingrained in political and enforcement
agencies, although more vulnerable than before. Such vulnerability explained
sporadic events of visible violence in the 2000s.

Visible Attacks in the 2000s

Toward the end of the 1994–2007 period, political and enforcement changes
reduced the power of the Attorney General's Office at the federal level, which

generated moments of state fragmentation and short episodes of visible violence in Juárez. Incidents of feminicide in 2001 that seemed to be deliberately publicized could be interpreted precisely as a traffickers' reaction to the state's withdrawal of protection through anticorruption purges.

Feminicides constitute an extremely complex phenomenon, and more than twenty years after the first cases became public, their causes remain unclear and justice elusive—any detailed interpretation of the motivations and perpetrators of feminicides transcends this book's focus. The crucial point here is that existing evidence suggests that some of the killings in that category could have been perpetrated directly by, or with the protection of, drug traffickers and corrupt policemen, and it is especially likely that the cases in 2001 were deliberately made public to retaliate and even publicize the local government's incapacity.

In 2001, eight bodies of young women were found in an empty property known as the Cotton Field, located near a busy intersection of Ciudad Juárez. Forensic evidence suggested that not all the women dumped in the lot had been killed at the same time, as if the perpetrators had deliberately stored victims at different moments until they decided to display the corpses en masse.[115] Some analysts have interpreted this case as a strategy to hurt then-governor of Chihuahua Patricio Martínez by drawing attention to the persistent impunity and lack of effective investigation in the feminicide cases.[116] According to a prominent human rights defender, some feminicides could have been carried out by former police officers in reaction to massive firings and the rotation of municipal and state police officers that took place during the administration of Martínez, who was a vocal critique of narco-corruption in the state.[117] That is: exposing feminicides publicly, precisely when the government was under heightened scrutiny for the lack of results in feminicide investigations, was a deliberate attempt to publicize the government's incapacity vis-á-vis powerful criminal actors, and thereby, perhaps, persuade the government not to be so vocal against drug traffickers. Other events in 2001, prominently a murder attempt against Governor Martínez, added to the general sense that criminals were concerned with the governor's public stance rejecting drug trafficking.

In 2005, similar instances of visible violence occurred when a number of prominent public figures—including the chief of the state investigation agency, José Antonio Torres, and at least thirteen federal, municipal, and state police—were assassinated in Ciudad Juárez and in the capital city of Chihuahua.[118] A member of a now-defunct state Judicial Police agency, Ignacio Sánchez, was kidnapped and later found dead, blindfolded, with barbwire around his neck, and accompanied by a note. In January 2006, a Ciudad Juárez lawyer, Sergio Dante Almaraz, who had publicly denounced the involvement of trafficking organizations and state complicity in feminicides, was also assassinated. Visible killings also included another commander of the state judicial police, Arturo Nassar Contreras.

This visible violence occurred even as the frequency of violence remained relatively unchanged, at about 16 homicides per 100,000, suggesting that it was not the result of heightened criminal disputes. Rather, the events occurred after members of the state police, including the chief, were arrested on charges of collaborating with the Juárez DTO, forcing Governor José Reyes Baeza to create a new state Secretariat of Public Security in 2004 and to rotate directors of the Secretariat of Public Security.[119] These reforms were unsuccessful in the long run, as the new agencies ended up being equally permeated by corruption,[120] but in the short run they unsettled the interactions between criminals and state actors.

In the period between 1994 and 2007 violence thus increased due to growing disputes between the Juárez DTO and outside challengers. The visibility, however, remained relatively low because persistent cohesion of the security apparatus allowed stable and predictable state protection as well as better coordination in enforcement actions, which discouraged traffickers from confronting the state. Yet growing political competition increased the use of scandals as a tool for electoral competition, and mayors and governors were frequently accused of protecting drug traffickers—as was the case with governors Francisco Barrios (1992–1998) and José Reyes Baeza (2004–2010). Scandals forced political authorities to conduct high-profile purges and rotations in enforcement agencies, creating sporadic changes in the interaction between criminals, cops, and politicians that generated instances of visible violence. These changes, nonetheless, fell short of reducing corruption; accusations of wrongdoing never became full-fledged judicial processes,[121] law enforcement remained corrupt, and the state security apparatus still generated incentives for criminals to prefer the concealment of violence. Despite their attempts to clean up police forces, governors and mayors remained reluctant to acknowledge publicly the existence of either violence or drug trafficking. In 2004, for example, Governor Reyes Baeza criticized the international attention to the situation of violence because it damaged Ciudad Juárez's image.[122] Despite cosmetic police reforms, corruption remained ingrained and state power did not change radically until 2008 when confrontations between political and enforcement authorities proliferated.

The Perfect Storm of Violence (2008–2010)

Since 2006, Mexico has experienced the worst period of drug violence in its history, and by 2015 there had been more than 180,000 homicides, with victims including more than 75 mayors,[123] 132 journalists,[124] and hundreds of military and police personnel. In Ciudad Juárez violence took on an even more extreme dynamic: the average homicide rate between 2007 and 2010 was 140 compared to a national average of 13, and a peak homicide rate of 250 occurred in 2010.

Homicides increased by 713 percent over the course of only one year (2007–2008) (see Figure 6.1).

The explosion of the conflict between the Juárez DTO and the Sinaloa DTO led to a radical change in the criminal market and to an extreme increase in violence. By late 2007 members of the Sinaloa DTO decided to "invade" Ciudad Juárez. Until then, confrontations between the two DTOs generated killings in each other's territory but not an actual mobilization of forces. A criminal arrested by the federal police, Noel Salgueiro,[125] confessed that in 2007 he was commissioned by the Sinaloa DTO to invade Juárez with five hundred gunmen, entering the city from the south with the aim of displacing the Juárez DTO. After the Sinaloa gunmen entered in January 2008, violence ensued, federal forces moved in, and the city ended the year transformed by unprecedented death tolls, fear, brutality, and activities (such as extortion) that were relatively unheard of up to that point.

After Amado Carrillo's death, important changes had occurred inside the Juárez DTO that made it more vulnerable to the Sinaloans' invasion. These changes included the relaxation of the organization's hierarchy, a process that strengthened splinter sectors, which then allied with Sinaloa, and a heavy investment in armed power[126] that was deployed to its fullest capacity during the war. La Línea, the enforcement branch formed in 2004 by former police members, became the most violent branch of the Juárez DTO. The invasion of Sinaloa traffickers radically transformed criminality from a quasi-monopolistic into a competitive criminal market in dispute.

Visible Violence and Extreme State Fragmentation

The deployment of soldiers and federal police in 2008, as part of the declaration of war against drug trafficking organizations by President Felipe Calderón, unleashed a rapid and profound fragmentation of the state: extreme conflicts between municipal, state, and federal authorities undermined the protection that criminals previously obtained; tensions between security agencies became more acute; and constant rotation and purges of enforcement officials deepened the distrust between enforcement agencies and between criminals and the state. In this context, earlier corrupt arrangements between criminals and state officials became unpredictable; if a security agency protected a criminal organization, another agency could persecute it. Furthermore, networks of protection split up, and criminal actors targeted security agencies in a pattern that pitted not only criminal organizations against each other but also against different enforcement actors. Traffickers from both sides accused and targeted enforcement officials whom they saw as supporting their rivals. Such fragmentation also complicated state operations and consequently, even though traffickers were increasingly vulnerable to enforcement, at least in the short run it seemed that they could gain more from using the most violent techniques to eliminate unfriendly state officials and rivals.

Visibility represented a key tool for intimidation and retaliation against both competitors and state officials, and thus violence became a semantic system where, as Howard Campbell notes, traffickers used violence to signal "who is either in charge or attempting to take charge of a particular plaza and to explain why specific individuals have been or will be slaughtered."[127] The protagonist of the 2011 documentary *El Sicario*, which describes the life of a paid killer in Juárez, explained that each method of killing or displaying a corpse signaled a different message: "Throw it face up, that's one message, face down, it's another message, cut a finger and put it in the mouth, another message, cut a finger and introduce it in the anus, message, take out the eyes, take out the tongue."[128]

Extreme fragmentation in the security apparatus ensued in March 2008 when the federal government initiated Operación Conjunta Chihuahua (Joint Operation Chihuahua), deploying five thousand military troops and twenty-seven hundred federal police to Ciudad Juárez as part of a strategy to dismantle trafficking organizations. Unlike in the past, the Attorney General's Office had no power to control and coordinate the multiple enforcement actors. The military troops under deployment clashed with the municipal police, because the federal government and the military saw municipal police as particularly corrupt, in light of the force's well-known connections with La Línea. Human rights complaints of military abuse multiplied. Furthermore, sectors of the military resented being deployed for operations they were not prepared to handle and that could undermine their prestige, even though they would not say this publicly.[129]

The army conducted anticorruption operations within the municipal police and consequently transformed police schemes of operation as well as the traditional channels for criminals to deal with police officers. In the words of a human rights defender: "The army's logic is to defeat and disarm every citizen in the city, and the first to be disarmed were local cops."[130] In this context, municipal police officers were reluctant to work with the army, and mutual distrust grew as traffickers declared a war against police officers who refused to collaborate with them or whom they considered as protectors of their rivals.

In February 2009, the municipal police chief quit after several officers were slain and traffickers threatened to kill a police officer every forty-eight hours. The attack against municipal police motivated local authorities to bring in Lieutenant Colonel Julián Leyzaola as the chief of the municipal Secretariat of Public Security, due to his record in Tijuana. Even after Leyzaola's arrival, confrontations persisted. In 2010, a total of seventy-seven law enforcement officials from municipal, state, and federal agencies were killed, often appearing with notes carrying messages such as "I'm a cop at the service of ____,"[131] in a pattern of accusations and rumors that linked the federal police with the Sinaloa DTO, and the municipal police with La Línea and the Juárez DTO. The messages found near victims of violence reflected a more systematic targeting of state officials than in the other Mexican cities discussed in this book, and more specifically of federal and municipal police. In 2010, 8 percent of events in Ciudad Juárez identified police officers or soldiers as homicide victims (fifty-five events) while in Culiacán the proportion for the same year was 2.8 percent (sixteen events) and in Tijuana 1.9 percent (nine events).[132]

Confrontations between government levels further fragmented the state. Initially, both the governor of Chihuahua, José Reyes Baeza, and the mayor of Ciudad Juárez, José Reyes Ferriz, supported military deployments. Soon, however, confrontations between them escalated. The governor did not fully support the mayor's security policies and seemed to do little to improve the situation,[133] and the mayor was perceived to be weak and detached from reality. In fact, he was widely criticized for taking residence in El Paso after receiving death threats. When Reyes Ferriz's term ended in 2010, he denounced the lack of collaboration of the state government, especially in prosecuting criminals whom municipal authorities had arrested.[134] Such confrontation reflected the empowerment of local mayors mentioned earlier, which became evident when violence skyrocketed, federal operations started, and the mayor actively confronted other authorities. However, the mayor's actual power to do something was limited.[135] The confrontation also illustrated how state fragmentation complicated not only the protection provided to criminals but also effective law enforcement, even though enforcement operations had multiplied.

Confrontations between mayors and governors were not common to all cities in Mexico where the federal government deployed the military to combat drug crime. The impact of the federal government's decision to militarize was mediated by local power and political conditions. An official of the Federal Secretariat of Public Security explained why military deployments had different dynamics in Culiacán (described in chapter 5) and Ciudad Juárez in this way:

> Sinaloa is an entity formed by eighteen municipalities . . . and in that sense the relationship between mayors [*presidentes municipales*] and the governor is easier than in Chihuahua where there are sixty-seven municipalities. Distances are also shorter in Sinaloa than in Chihuahua; therefore the conditions for the operation of authority are different. Until last year in Sinaloa, all local governments were *PRIistas*. Chihuahua, by contrast, was one of the states that first experienced political alternation, and although there have been a few *PRIista*

governments, the mayor of Chihuahua and Ciudad Juárez have usually been on *PANista* hands.

Militarization therefore generated state fragmentation across cities, but local histories were crucial in determining how the process unfolded.

In this context of fragmentation, the methods used to display violence proliferated, as illustrated in Table 6.2, which contrasts the variety of methods used in 2010 with the few used in 1984. These methods were used to intimidate criminals and state officials. In July 2010, a car bomb killed three people, including a federal police officer; even though the bomb did not kill many civilians, it was a clear message for authorities. According to the testimony of El Diego, a killer for La Línea who confessed to organizing the explosion, the attack was in retaliation for the capture of another member of the criminal group.[136] This particular event illustrates that visible violence is not necessarily indiscriminate: methods that could be quickly labeled as indiscriminate (like bombs) may not be aimed at targeting many people but aimed instead at sending a message.

Messages in crime scenes usually indicated who the victims were or what criminal dispute they were linked to. On July 28, 2010, for example, two beheaded bodies appeared along with explicit notes: "I'm a kidnapper and extortionist. I'm an Azteca" and "I do carjacking and work for La Línea and the Aztecas [armed branches of the Juárez Cartel]." In another case, in August 2010, the body of a federal policeman was found scattered in pieces behind a mall and in a sign painted on a wall the group La Línea assumed responsibility for the attack.[137]

The assassinations of public figures such as two journalists from the local newspaper *El Diario* and five human rights activists[138] represent further episodes of visibility. In September 2010, after the murder of a photographer, *El Diario* published a highly controversial editorial addressed to "members of the different organizations who are fighting for turf in Juárez" in which the newspaper asked the traffickers "to explain what is it that you want from us, what is it that you expect us to publish or to refrain from publishing? So we know what to expect."[139] The editorial reflected how the terms of criminal interaction, which even civilians perceived to be predictable, had become uncertain. This uncertainty, along with the lack of proper investigation of homicides, made it even more difficult to determine whether traffickers, state forces, or common criminals were responsible for a particular attack. As discussed in chapter 2, the difficulty in identifying victims and perpetrators reflects how a definition of drug violence limited only to cases where traffickers confront each other, or the state, fails to recognize how violence is reproduced more broadly. It also fails to recognize how civilian casualties, even when not directly the result of a trafficker eliminating a rival or attacking the state, can be defined as drug related.

Visible violence persisted even after the 2010 elections brought a new governor, César Duarte, to Chihuahua, and a new mayor, Hector Murguía, to Ciudad Juárez. The new governor seemed more forcefully committed to investigating crimes and collaborating with other authorities,[140] but at the same time, the relationship between the federal government and the mayor became highly contentious. In 2009 the US consul in Ciudad Juárez had expressed concerns about the lack of trust between government levels and enforcement agencies in a confidential cable that was leaked in 2010.[141] Such concerns were echoed in February 2010, in a declaration by the National Human Rights Commission that stated that Juárez's climate of violence resulted from the lack of coordination among different enforcement agencies.[142]

The municipal-federal confrontation heightened due to clashing responsibilities and goals between the federal and the municipal police. Criticisms and multiple complaints about human rights violations by the army had forced the federal government to replace soldiers with federal police. After April 2010, the federal police assumed incremental control over security, not only carrying out antinarcotics raids but even assuming roles of municipal police, such as traffic control, thus generating a confrontation with municipal forces, which in turn felt empowered under Chief Leyzaola's command. Leyzaola described the tension between the federal and municipal police as follows:

> There is no coordination in the operational part. I do have communication with the commissioner of the federal police, but that's it. For example, one day, here at the Chihuahua District we detained ten people and seized arms, the federals were there and seized two arms. When the time to imprison the detainees arrived I told the federals, let's make a joint arrest, and the commander said, "That is not possible—the central command ordered me to send everything to them," and I said, "No, you don't take my stuff—he is your commissioner, not mine." Before I arrived, the municipal police was subordinated to the federals.[143]

This municipal-federal confrontation was extremely public and involved Mayor Murguía himself. On May 5, 2011, in front of television cameras, Murguía engaged in a vivid discussion with federal police who held his bodyguards at gunpoint while crossing a security checkpoint. During the discussion Murguía yelled that such behavior explained why the local population did not like the federal police. The incident was the third episode that directly involved Murguía and the federal police[144] and illustrated both the excesses committed by the federal police but also the pattern of mayor-federal government confrontation described earlier.

In sum, the rapid increase in violence in 2008 resulted from heightened criminal competition, which continued escalating as enforcement actions generated leadership turnovers, increased intercartel fighting, and broke up chains of command.[145] Yet, unlike previous enforcement operations that changed criminal structures (such as those conducted in the mid-1990s), these operations were met with visible violence, explained by the incentives created by a fragmented security apparatus. State fragmentation also reproduced frequency, because enforcement agencies confronted each other, confronted different trafficking organizations, and abused force against civilians in the name of confronting traffickers. These factors were also present when violence exploded in Culiacán and Tijuana, yet the outsourcing of coercion to youth gangs in Ciudad Juárez made violence surpass the growing national average by a high margin, as each warring trafficking faction garnered additional force to dominate the city.

Cholos, Crews, and Barrios in Ciudad Juárez

In 2008, when the Sinaloa DTO entered Ciudad Juárez, the turf war required extreme firepower if territorial control was to be achieved, and outsourcing was necessary because the organization did not have strong organizational roots in the city. On its part, the Juárez DTO, despite its historic strength and despite having La Línea, began outsourcing violence to youth gangs to match and overpower its competitor. The Sinaloa DTO employed large gangs (crews) known as Los Mexicles and Los Artistas Asesinos (Assassin Artists), brought killers from other areas of the country, and supported splinter groups from the Juárez DTO such as Gente Nueva. For its part, the Juárez DTO employed the already-existing crew Los Aztecas and Barrio Azteca, through the intermediation of its enforcement branch La Línea.[146] These large gangs had, according to some calculations, at least three thousand members,[147] and some of them, like the Barrio Azteca, also operated across the border in the United States.

The large gangs recruited young men from the smaller, usually noncriminal gangs, or barrios, of which according to the police there were at least 460. It would be difficult to claim that all small gangs worked for traffickers, but without a doubt their dynamics and incentives changed radically as traffickers recruited them. In November 2010, a state attorney from Chihuahua declared that there were at least 250 gangs dedicated to kidnapping and extortion in Ciudad Juárez,[148] and even though not all of them were related to drug-trafficking organizations, they were using copycat techniques.

The control over street gangs allowed crews and their respective employers to access micro–criminal markets such as drug distribution, but most importantly, it provided armed muscle and tangible territorial control, crucial to displace rivals and keeping them out. A community organizer (former gang member) considered that "the narco has always been present, but now there is more need to have soldiers; in the past anybody could make a business out of selling drugs, now they have to sell for a specific group."[149] This statement casts doubt on the hypothesis, advanced especially by Mexican authorities, that violence increased as criminals diversified their portfolios into local drug dealing. If anything, the testimonies of gang members suggest that local drug dealing existed for years in Ciudad Juárez, but it became violent as powerful criminals attempted to control it.[150]

Outsourcing radically altered the interactions between formerly nonviolent gangs. Traffickers sometimes asked gang members not to "heat up" the plaza and to quiet down their small territorial disputes for the control of a few blocks, but for the most part they used them to violently defend territory from gangs that worked for rival crews and traffickers. In the words of a community organizer who worked with gangs in Juárez:

> The "kids" [*chavos*] know if they are *doblados* [from the AA, or Artistas Asesinos] or if they are "buddies" [from La Línea]. Violence even receded when the narcos arrived: now they tell them, "be careful about kicking up a fuss"; now they do fight for being part of one or the other crew, but they do not fight between them. Formerly, a barrio controlled a territory with its identity; conflicts emerged when boundaries were crossed. Formerly they fought with stones—the issue is when they start to articulate with the narco, there are no longer stones because it is no longer about identity but about defending turf. If they belong to similar godfathers violence is reduced.[151]

Former gang members and community organizers echoed similar sentiments:

> Drug trafficking has changed gang violence a lot. In the past violence was a personal matter, now it is a business matter . . . . Violence of the barrio does not exist anymore, because when there are points [of drug sales] the cholos cannot do things they did before, such as painting graffitis [narcos tell them, you cannot heat up the damn [drug dealing] point]. Years ago the disputes of the barrios killed two or three in two years, now they kill three or four in two or three hours.[152]

Violence spiked upward because gangs became better armed and more willing to fight violently. Even though traffickers sometimes attempted to discipline youth gangs, the traffickers' need to employ gangs as assassins or guards surpassed their ability and interest for controlling the gangs' nontrafficking related disputes. A local drug dealer interviewed by Campbell described how microconflicts for territoriality between street gangs persisted even when they worked for the same crew:

> The Juárez downtown area is divided into zones, territories or areas in which different groups operate by means of pushers. Since the god-fathers are all—or mostly all—members of the Aztecas prison gang, there's no problem when these zones are invaded or when they overlap. The problems are all with—and between—the smaller, zealously terri-torial street gangs. Close to my zone of operation there's two of these street gangs: *Los Jodidos* (the fucked up ones) and the *Teipiados* [the Taped ones, a reference to drug murder victims who are often wrapped in tape by their killers]. (Jorge, drug dealer in Juárez).[153]

The relationship between drug cartels and street gangs was hierarchical and tiered, but such hierarchy did not facilitate disciplining or controlling the smaller gangs because connections were loose, and competition between larger criminal organizations professionalized gangs in using violence. The same gang member interviewed by Campbell described such hierarchy as one in which

> Theirs is a tiered, hierarchical society, where every godfather has a pro-tector, until you reach the very top of the hierarchy, where there's a guy, the leader who is currently in jail and will probably remain there for a very long time, if not for the rest of his life.[154]

The largest gangs mediated between trafficking bosses and gang bases,[155] but there was no direct link between trafficking kingpins and armed force. Outsourcing therefore radically changed the behavior and structure of gangs and made it more difficult for authorities to disintegrate trafficking organizations. According to Colonel Leyzaola, "In Tijuana, from one detention, we were able to get five more. Here [in Juárez] from one detention we only get one detainee, because they don't know each other."[156]

The large-scale involvement of youth gangs multiplied the instances of col-lective violence with three or more victims because criminal soldiers tried to eliminate cells of opponents. Ciudad Juárez experienced more collective mur-ders and massacres than its country counterparts, 103 in 2010 compared to 19 collective attacks in Culiacán and Tijuana.[157] Some of these events had a crucial impact on the government's responses, as was the case with the Villas del Salvárcar massacre on January 2010, which forced the federal government to mobilize a vast social program known as Todos Somos Juárez (We Are All Juárez). In this massacre, eighteen young students were assassinated at a party in the Villas de Salvárcar neighborhood. President Felipe Calderón's first reaction was to label the victims as members of a "criminal gang," but as criticism to his quick labeling mounted, he retracted the statement. In July 2010, the confession of the criminal El Diego confirmed that the students were killed in a case of mistaken identity, as members of the Aztecas gang thought members of the rival Artistas Asesinos gang were at the party.[158] Other acts of collective violence included the Colonia Horizontes massacre (with fourteen dead and fifteen wounded) on October 2010, and massacres within rehabilitation centers for drug addiction. El Diego also claimed that he ordered massacres in rehabilitation centers that he thought to be safe houses for Sinaloa rivals. These examples illustrate that massacres were not simply a reflection of indiscriminate or random attacks but could also be the result of misidentification or mistaken efforts, and sometimes were the outcome of poorly prepared operations to eliminate rivals.

The money provided by criminal organizations attracted impoverished young men with no professional or educational opportunities or young people who simply could not risk the violent retaliation of traffickers if they refused to work for them. The provision of arms and sophisticated "jobs" for street gangs created opportunities for reproducing violence among larger sectors of the population. As another gang member expressed while referring to local drug dealing: "Now the Aztecas are in control. Before, everybody worked independently. Now, if you don't work for them, they don't let you work [at all]."[159] The outsourcing of violence spread out the abilities to use violence among a larger pool of people. Before the explosion of the trafficking disputes, male youth were recognized within their barrio for their particular skills and only a handful were recognized as the brave or violent ones, but this situation changed with outsourcing. In the words of the community organizer:

> This is how I see things. In the barrios there has been a similar transformation to the one that occurred in the *maquila* [factory]. In the maquila there is a universal operator, who can operate any machine. There is something like that in the barrio. In the past there were specialized jobs: you were the dealer and you did not have anything else to do, or you were the post [watchman], or you were the rapper, or you were the assassin and you went and fucked somebody and that was it—you didn't have to do anything else. If you were an observer, you only had to be *wachando* [looking]; the falcons only watched. Each one had a role. As the situation started to get fired up, or the risks became greater, the universal *narquito* was born, the one that is a falcon and at the same time is fucking you; it stopped being Fordist to become Toyotist for the sake of adapting to a market where there are

more risks. In the past you entered the barrio, you worked, and you left. Now it is not so easy to leave because while being there you get to know the structure.[160]

The articulation between gangs and traffickers that fully developed in 2008 was unprecedented but not unpredictable. The outbreak of the confrontations between the Juárez and Sinaloa DTOs and the fragmentation of protection networks increased the demand for outsourced armed coercion. Such demand met the large supply of gangs and marginalized youth. The supply of gangs was also nurtured by the binational character of gangs such as Los Aztecas, which had guns, soldiers, and money in El Paso. Additionally, the dreadful conditions within the Juárez prison system facilitated the reproduction of crews within prisons, and massive deportations created an additional supply of poor youth in border cities without social, economic, or family roots.[161] Even if not all members of gangs and barrios engaged with crews, their modes of interaction changed radically after 2008.

Return to Normality?

By the end of 2011 homicide rates had significantly decreased in Ciudad Juárez. Although the reasons remain controversial, in line with this book's political-economy framework, the pacification seemed to reflect a reduction in state fragmentation and in illegal market competition. The security apparatus became more cohesive as federal forces reduced their presence after October 2011, and the collaboration between state authorities improved. Many residents of Ciudad Juárez contend that extortion decreased as the federal police left.[162] At the same time, confrontations in the drug market receded as the Sinaloa DTO gained control[163] and allegedly established a pact with the weakened Juárez DTO and La Línea. The government also claims violence reduction as a success derived from the federal police strategy of targeting midlevel operational members of criminal organizations, from the security strategies of Julián Leyzaola (inspired by the "broken windows" theory, which takes an iron-fist approach and calls for the concentration of forces in hotspots attacking even the most minor crimes); and from the social interventions of the Todos Somos Juárez program.

The city's changing situation, after years of extreme violence and suffering, without a doubt brought relief to the population. In the long run, however, the sustainability of the process could be endangered: if criminal reaccommodations played a role in reducing violence, the reduction can be unstable and vulnerable. Furthermore, the indication that violence decreased when federal forces left the city casts serious doubts about federal police behavior in enforcing the rule of law. Even though the municipal police force has taken the lead in public security in a way that did not occur before, its tactics seem extremely militarized and human rights complaints about its actions and its constant targeting of marginalized populations have increased. Marginalized youth report that the municipal police forces have stigmatized them even more than the federal forces did.[164] As in Tijuana, reasons for improvement seem to have less to do with improvements in socioeconomic conditions, or the elimination of trafficking activities, and more with changes in interactions between states and criminal actors. It is possible, however, that if violence erupts again in Ciudad Juárez it will not be very visible, partially because traffickers learned that the cost of waging war is too high and also because the government and civil society have indeed gained more professional, even if still limited, law enforcement and social promotion capacities.

Conclusion

The realities of drug trafficking and violence in Ciudad Juárez and Tijuana are interconnected. Both cities have been affected by international pressures such as those against the Arellano Félix organization in the 2000s and by national events like the institutional transformations in federal enforcement, the declaration of war on trafficking organizations by President Felipe Calderón, or the interconnection of trafficker's strategies such as the attempt of the Sinaloa DTO to invade northern territories in the late 2000s. Furthermore, similar strategies have characterized traffickers' actions, such as the use of disappearances in the late 1990s. The timing and evolution of violence, however, has differed, affected by the micropolitics of criminal competition, democratic alternation, and institutional transformation. The difference was notable after the federal government's decision to militarize the war on drugs in 2006 that fragmented the security apparatus more pronouncedly and led to more violence in Juárez than in Tijuana. The trajectories of violence in the two cities show that even though their border status makes them prime locations for drug trafficking, it does not make them inevitable candidates for violence.

This chapter's comparison also highlights the importance of disaggregating the type of armed coercion criminals employ. In Tijuana, traffickers always preferred alternate sources of force, such as elite young men, thus slowing down the reproduction and criminal engagement of local youth gangs. By contrast, in Ciudad Juárez, traffickers did not block the reproduction of gangs, and in the late 2000s they actively outsourced armed coercion to gangs, thereby contributing to the extreme spike of violence.

Consistent with the book's argument, this chapter illustrates how state cohesion provides incentives for traffickers to hide violence. Credible state-sponsored protection helped regulate state-criminal interactions and maintain criminals' relatively hidden violence. State cohesion also created a powerful deterrent for traffickers to display violence, as state officials had the power to enforce the law more effectively if necessary (as occurred after the assassination of Cardinal Posadas Ocampo) but only did it selectively. This highlights that a state's power to control violence does not equate with professional or unbiased law enforcement, because of the potential tradeoff between state capacity and state autonomy discussed in chapter 3. The contrast seen in reactions generated by enforcement actions in the 1990s compared to the late 2000s further illustrates that even though state anticrime operations can increase violence by, for example, fragmenting organizations, whether that violence is displayed or not is a function of state cohesion. This explains why instances of visible violence emerged sporadically when rotations and purges disrupted the interaction between state and criminals as occurred in Tijuana in 1996 and in Juárez in 2005. Whether these sporadic displays are followed by peace or evolve into more violence depends on whether other components of the security apparatus change and further fragment the state, and also on whether criminal organizations have enough power to regulate violence.

The evolution of state power in the border cities also highlights why the definition of state cohesion I advance—combining electoral competition, intergovernmental relations, and interagency interactions—is relevant. An early electoral opening in the northern states of Baja California Norte and Chihuahua was crucial in setting the stage for democratization in Mexico, yet it had a limited immediate effect on the interactions between states and criminals. Although important, formal electoral dynamics were only one factor of state cohesion and were often surpassed by informal dynamics that impeded real attacks on corrupt elites or on trafficking groups (as illustrated after the election of Ernesto Ruffo Appel as the first non-PRI governor). Assessing state cohesion thus requires an analysis not only of electoral competition but also of informal dynamics of political cooperation and a careful consideration of power relations between law enforcement agencies. For example, while in Tijuana in the late 2000s the coincidence of PAN affiliations among president, governor, and mayor facilitated coordination, in Ciudad Juárez the most notable confrontations occurred between a mayor and a governor who shared PRI affiliation.

The relatively quick abatement of violence in Ciudad Juárez and Tijuana after the explosion in 2008, compared with the ingrained violence that took years to recede in Medellín, suggests that not all extreme violent situations become protracted and that relatively quick changes can be attainable if the state can recompose its forces and criminal organizations adapt to less-violent strategies.

Quick reductions of violence are undoubtedly positive, yet if the recomposition of state forces is an ad hoc process (facilitated by military leadership in Tijuana, for example) without long-term reforms or the creation of checks and balances that can instill cooperation while preventing the formation of protection rackets, such changes may be prone to insecurity relapses. Additionally, since the reduction of violence can be partially attributed to a reorganization of criminal forces and to pacts between trafficking groups that reduce competition and violence temporarily but tend to be fragile, the situation of these cities can be unstable and needs to be constantly monitored. This further underscores this book's emphasis on the importance of analyzing not only cases of extreme violence but also those of relative peace.

The disappearances in Ciudad Juárez and Tijuana since the 1990s reveal crucial aspects of the relation between visible and hidden violence. In the 1990s, disappearances proliferated, but a mix between fear, corruption, stereotypes, and rumors about the involvement of victims in criminal activity bred impunity and apathy. Families feared retaliation or the revictimization of their loved ones, as they knew that they were often, in fact, related to drug traffickers. Rumors about the fate of victims abounded—for example, that they had struck deals with Mexican or US authorities and were in fact simply hiding. This situation delegitimized the voice of the few relatives who dared to push the government for answers.

When violence exploded in 2008, disappearances multiplied, thus suggesting that in cases of all-out war, all forms of violence, including less visible ones, intermix. As attacks became more visible and affected civilians considered to be innocent and unrelated to traffickers, the stigma on victims decreased, and thus relatives' efforts to find their loved ones became more legitimate and public, even if still doomed by impunity. People had less fear of the stigmatization, and therefore the method of disappearing people has become, paradoxically, more noticed (although still effective to avoid justice). But as the cases of the 1990s show, disappearing can be an effective way to hide violence, especially when victims are perceived to be only those "who deserve it."

Finally, Ciudad Juárez and Tijuana, as the other cities analyzed in this book, illustrate that the lines between state and criminals can be strongly blurred. Police officers and politicians sometimes not only allow drug trafficking but become direct perpetrators of violence and criminality, as illustrated by multiple reports of enforcement agents being directly involved in disappearances and other human rights violations. In this context, separating a state from a criminal actor may seem meaningless. Nonetheless, as the political-economy framework for explaining drug violence stresses, even when boundaries between state and criminals seem blurry they remain distinct realms; it is possible to understand, systematically, their interactions and the varied impacts of such interactions on political and social order and, more specifically, on drug violence. Furthermore, despite the key role of corruption, states do more than simply regulate criminals, and they enforce the law against them for multiple reasons that range from international pressures, as occurred when the government captured key members of the AFO in the early 2000s, or from electoral pressures, as was partially the case in President Calderón's decision to declare a war against traffickers in 2006 to boost his legitimacy.

Conclusion

Drug violence constitutes a severe problem for countries around the world, especially in Latin America, where the growing violence during an era of (potentially limited) democratic governance has puzzled scholars and become a crucial concern for policy makers. Many factors contribute to making Latin America the region with the world's highest homicide rates—however, organized crime and drug trafficking are key contributors. Yet, what is often absent from common depictions of violence as resulting from a new era dominated by a new breed of drug traffickers prone to become "criminal insurgents" is that criminals' violent strategies as well as their interactions with the state change constantly. Sometimes these changes are very rapid and vary not only across but also within countries. Explaining such variation has been this book's central goal.

Violence is not an inherent attribute of the drug trade but rather is the result of complex interactions between states and criminal actors. I have explored how variation in drug violence results from interactions between cohesion in the state security apparatus and competition in the illegal market, and it is also affected by criminals' strategies of armed coercion. In this sense, this book challenges the notion that violence in drug markets is an automatic result of the illegality of the market or is solely dependent on the economic aspects of the trade such as the size and profitability of markets. These factors, as well as national and international drug and crime policies, constitute necessary but not sufficient conditions to explain the localized variation in violence seen across drug-trafficking hot spots. Building on the idea that government enforcement actions can generate violence, I have shown that the power dynamics within the state underlying those actions are essential for understanding the diverse impact of enforcement on criminal violent behavior. Thus, this argument also challenges the idea that crime and illegality simply reflect state absence, and it highlights the importance of unpacking power relations within the state when analyzing illegal markets.

There is wide variation in the manifestations of lethal violence that can emerge within drug markets, and one of this book's central contributions has been to unveil violent patterns beyond headline-grabbing events like those that appeared all over Mexico after 2006. Criminals can sometimes display violence in horrific ways, but even the most ruthless criminals can also sometimes deescalate violence.[1] Pablo Escobar and Los Extraditables declared a bloody war against the Colombian state, but they announced the dismantlement of their military machinery when a new Constitutional Assembly declared extradition unconstitutional in 1991.[2] Even Los Zetas, considered pioneers of trafficking brutality in Mexico, sometimes instructed their operatives not to instigate armed confrontations with authorities or with other people, to avoid "heating up the turf" (*calentar la plaza*).[3]

This book advanced a multidimensional understanding that considers not only the frequency of violence but also its visibility—that is, the instances where criminals display, or claim responsibility for, the attacks they carry out. By assessing visibility systematically, I have uncovered strategic uses of violence that would not be apparent by simply looking at isolated numbers. Criminals not only decide whether they should or should not use violence; they also decide whether they should or should not expose violence to an audience beyond the direct targets of the violent action. This approach also provides a strong theory about drug violence, because it highlights the importance of analyzing not only extreme cases of violence, which tend to garner the most attention from scholars and the media, but also hidden and less-frequent forms of violence.

By assessing two interrelated but opposite puzzles—if violence is unavoidable for regulating transactions in illegal markets, how can criminals regulate its use? and if visible violence can attract attention that is detrimental for the criminal business, why do criminals decide to expose violence?—I found that cohesion in the state security apparatus affects the visibility of violence. Criminals are more likely to hide violence when they receive credible state protection or when they fear the retaliation of an effective state, and this occurs when the security apparatus is cohesive. By contrast, when criminals do not receive predictable protection, or do not fear effective law enforcement, they lose incentives to avoid state attention and may decide either to expose violence or to abandon the extra steps necessary to hide it. This occurs when power within the state is fragmented.

While the structure of the security apparatus affects visibility, competition within the illegal market determines the frequency of violence, and competitive markets are therefore more likely to generate violence than monopolistic markets. While certain markets where two or more organizations coexist can sometimes be peaceful, this is usually a result of pacts or different arrangements of collaboration between illegal actors, which tend to be unstable and short-lived. The theory I developed also unpacks the importance of analyzing the different ways in which criminals organize their armed apparatuses and specifically whether they outsource violence to youth gangs. By including this variable, the book challenges simplistic connections between youth gangs, drug trade, and violence and shows that there are multiple ways in which organized traffickers and youth gangs can relate to each other: gangs can exist without generating violence and without being related to criminals, they can be a violent actor relatively independent from organized crime, they can work for criminals and thus become a more violent actor, or they can sometimes be disciplined or eliminated by more powerful criminals.

This book exploited the enormous variation in violence that the cities of Cali, Ciudad Juárez, Culiacán, Medellín, and Tijuana have experienced over time to validate the theory in a wide range of cases, but of course further testing of the theory's generalizability requires both detailed analysis of different cases and large-N quantitative comparisons (to the extent that limited data on this topic allows). Yet a cursory look into other cases is consistent with my argument. One example is the increase in criminal violence in Central America since the early 2000s, which many observers have been quick to attribute to an expansion of criminal actors from Mexico and to an increase in drug trafficking. Yet several facts suggest that the situation is more complex because in fact it precedes Mexico's wave of violence and is closely tied to domestic political conditions.[4] Homicide rates were rising in countries such as Guatemala long before violence skyrocketed in Mexico (and even declined between 2009 and 2015, at the height of Mexico's drug violence) and drug-trafficking networks have a long tradition in the region. It is possible, then, that the increasing perception of an extensive violence problem is related to increases in visibility linked to changes in state cohesion or to localized subnational variation. Furthermore, increases in violence have not been homogenous within Central America; for instance, while Honduras has seen rising violence, historically violent countries like El Salvador saw a temporary decline in violence in 2012, without drastic changes in the profitability or volume of illegal markets.

A modest analysis of El Salvador seems particularly consistent with this book's theory, especially as a way of showing that illegal actors often seen as inherently violent can strategically change their use of violence. Since March 2012, the two major gangs in El Salvador, Mara Salvatrucha and Barrio 18, struck a truce that reduced homicide rates by 50 percent in one year.[5] The reduction was first possible because of the truce that relieved the competition between the two groups. But such a reduction would not have occurred if the state had not been able to credibly commit to enforce the pact by providing judicial concessions to the gangs. This in turn was achievable because the state gained cohesion by coordinating the actions of the president, the security minister, and local authorities. Further illustrating the importance of the visibility of violence, there is evidence suggesting that although El Salvador experienced a real decrease in homicides, gang members still deployed violence during the truce but kept it underground.[6]

The truce crumbled as the state lost its cohesion when one of the truce's key architects stepped down and the new president reinstated "iron fist" policies against gangs, partially in response to pressures derived from a fragmented electoral camp. Massacres occurring in 2015 suggest that absent the incentives to hide violence through judicial concessions, gangs have been displaying violence to reemphasize their power and to pressure the state.

Outside Latin America, drug-trafficking markets in Southeast Asia are particularly interesting to test this book's theory, because they have been associated with lower violence.[7] Myanmar's case seems to lend further support for this theory, because the cohesion associated with the military regime has been crucial for the state in regulating the behavior of drug-trafficking markets. Myanmar is the world's second-largest opium producer, and drugs have played a crucial role in funding insurgent groups in one of the world's longest-standing conflicts. Yet, the state has been able to cut deals with insurgents by allowing them to produce and trade drugs in specific areas, thus reducing the potential violence associated with disputes over illegal markets, especially after the 1990s.[8] Violence appears to be deployed by the military and by government-supported militias to repress the population, ethnic resistance groups, or community leaders trying to shy users and petty dealers away from drugs,[9] but given state control and the collusion between state and traffickers, visible violence for market control or against state enforcement seems uncommon. In Thailand and Vietnam, the power of centralized and authoritarian states facilitated the suppression of opium production, although at a very high cost in terms of human rights.[10] In-depth analyses of these cases within the frame I propose could greatly expand our understanding of the relations between drug trafficking and violence.

My argument has emphasized that cohesion shapes both the state's ability to corruptly deal with criminals and to enforce the law against them. However, the case of El Salvador suggests an additional possibility: that cohesion can affect the state's ability to legally—even if not publicly—negotiate with criminals. In light of the possibility that short of complete legalization the incentives to engage in drug trafficking are unlikely to disappear, it is important to consider that negotiating with—not corruptly tolerating—criminals is a plausible avenue for mitigating violence. Yet just as with corrupt deals or with enforcement actions, the balance of power within the state may shape the outcome of such negotiation attempts. Furthermore, and because criminals may also manipulate violence strategically to elicit responses from state officials, such negotiations need to consider that criminals may not simply reduce violence but rather they may hide it, or decide to become "traffickers in silence," to minimize state attention. For example, in Medellín, Diego Murillo (Don Berna) responded to the incentives created through the peace process, but he also manipulated the visibility of violence to continue extracting judicial benefits from the state.

The remainder of this conclusion examines some theoretical implications of the argument beyond the realm of drug violence, explores directions for future research, and ends by briefly reflecting on the implications for policies aimed at addressing violence and drug trafficking as well as the implications for discussions about the need to reform the current drug-prohibition regime.

The State in the Analysis of Violence

One crucial finding of this book is that understanding drug violence requires unpacking power dynamics within the state. In other words, the state should not be conceptualized as one unitary actor that simply struggles against, or collaborates with, criminal actors. Power struggles *within* the state shape the ways in which it confronts or collaborates with criminal and nonstate actors. While differentiating between cohesive and fragmented states, we can see how state actions, either to confront or to protect criminals, vary depending on power struggles within the security apparatus.

This emphasis on the centrality of power within the state not only contributes to understanding criminal violence, but can also expand the already vibrant and ever-growing research on political violence and civil wars. Of course interesting debates derive from discussing how criminal violence is different from, and sometimes even more lethal than, traditional forms of civil war and political violence[11] and therefore from discussing how distinct theoretical frameworks are required to understand criminal violence. There are, however, crucial overlaps and conceptual advantages in bridging the analysis of civil wars and the analysis of criminal violence. For the most part, research on civil wars has analyzed states as unitary actors that oppose and confront armed opponents. Understanding how different actors *within* the state behave, collude, and bargain for security policies can also greatly expand how we understand conflict dynamics. The complexity of relations between state and armed actors has been addressed in analyses of elections and violence and of the resilience of insurgent organizations,[12] yet the complexity of state power is still underexplored in civil war and illegal markets research. Bridging the analysis of criminal and insurgent actors is also essential to continue developing theoretically the connections between illegal markets and civil wars beyond the simplistic greed-and-grievance debate that reduces insurgents to criminals and directly connects illegal markets and violence.

Institutional Change and Violence

Chapters 1 and 3 discussed how processes of institutional change such as democratization, decentralization, and anticorruption reforms affect state cohesion. Consequently, these processes can affect interactions between states and criminals and shape criminals' incentives to expose violence. My argument thus connects to long-standing debates about institutional change. Traditional approaches emphasize the persistence of institutions and the difficulty of changing them in the short run.[13] More recent approaches have emphasized how institutional change can occur in the margins of state institutions and can be cumulative.[14] Following this latter conceptualization of institutional change, my analysis of state security shows that institutions can indeed change significantly in the short term.

Some changes can be cumulative, as occurred in Mexico beginning in the mid-1990s when increasing political competition and reforms in security agencies started to transform power relations within the state. There can be, however, abrupt changes, such as the institutional changes that arose during the presidency of Felipe Calderón in Mexico, which accelerated the slow transformations that had been occurring over the previous two decades. The case studies in this book show that institutional transformation can also be nonlinear and regressive. In Medellín, despite positive evolutions in the security apparatus—such as greater coordination between enforcement agencies— along with the emergence of independent political actors and their ability to advance progressive social reform agendas,[15] the city returned to violence after a period of apparent pacification. Of course, the violent situation after 2008 was much better than it had been in the 1980s and suggests a positive path (deepened with homicide decreases after 2013). The idea to underscore here is that the outcomes derived from institutions—in this case those associated with the provision of security—are not necessarily linear, cumulative, or progressive.

An analysis of the state at the local level also highlights the importance of thinking about institutions and regimes at the subnational level. There is a well-established but also increasingly expanding body of literature analyzing regimes at the subnational scale.[16] The present study contributes to this area of research by showing how local institutions shape the behavior of criminal actors who often transcend local spaces and connect to both national and transnational arenas. My analysis does not isolate criminal actors from the national and transnational forces that shape them but rather shows how these forces are reshaped at the local level. Furthermore, the variation and rapid changes that often characterize drug violence show that although structural factors—drug prohibition, neoliberal reforms that marginalize sectors of the population in vast areas of Latin America, and socioeconomic conditions—are necessary conditions to understand violence, they are insufficient to fully account for the variation this book illustrated.

Directions for future Research

One natural direction for future research is to expand and test this theory in other cases. In this book, I decided to sacrifice parsimony—that is, theoretical simplicity—for the purposes of developing strong theoretical bases for a topic that has recently started to be explored systematically. In this sense, further research would benefit from disaggregating and testing different components within the variables I explored, such as the interactions between electoral and bureaucratic dynamics or the sources of organizational fragmentation in illegal markets. Analyses by other authors of the logic of criminal attacks against the state, of the temporal reproduction of violence in response to enforcement, or of the possibilities of alliances between criminal groups illustrate the benefits of such disaggregation.[17] My theoretical framework also emphasized the primary effect of (1) state cohesion on the visibility and (2) competition on the frequency of violence. This distinction has been crucial for highlighting the different reactions that state enforcement generates among criminals depending on the state structure that underlies those actions and the different manifestations that criminal disputes take depending on the state structure in which they take place. However, further theorizing about how, in certain cases, state fragmentation helps push the frequency of violence to extreme levels—as occurred in Mexico—is also an important addition to this theory. Besides these additions to the framework I propose, there are also three additional directions for research that derive from this book's theory, covered in the three sections that follow.

The Links between Gangs and Criminal Actors

I explored how the type of armed coercion that criminals employ, specifically the insourcing or outsourcing of violence to youth gangs, can determine whether drug violence grows to extreme levels. Outsourcing is not an automatic result of the existence of youth gangs or of marginalized young populations. For outsourcing to emerge, there needs to be a concurrence between the supply of youth gangs and the demand for armed coercion. It is crucial to better specify how such concurrence takes place. Do the preferences of youth gangs about whether they want to engage in criminal activities and violence matter? Or rather, is outsourcing mostly a top-down process, determined by the preferences of higher echelons of organized crime? How do the relations between street gangs and organized crime evolve over time, creating path-dependent dynamics that, for example, may strengthen a gang as an independent armed actor? Analyzing this link is crucial not only to better understand how young populations engage in

crime and violence but also to design policy interventions to prevent these connections between criminals and gangs from occurring.

State Cohesion, the Paradoxes of Democratization, and International Influences

In the previous chapters I advanced a broad definition of "state security apparatus" that encompasses three complex dimensions: collaboration between government levels, collaboration between enforcement agencies, and time horizons
of public officials—the latter being crucially determined by democratization
and anticorruption reforms. As such, "state security apparatus" was presented
as a broad concept that was necessary to advance the theory on an underresearched topic but that could be disaggregated into multiple and interesting
research questions—of which I would like to highlight three.

First, the book discussed how processes of democratization often play an
essential role in state fragmentation and in changing state-criminal relations.
However, because the three dimensions of the security apparatus do not necessarily vary together, a crucial question is this: when does electoral competition
translate into greater state fragmentation? Recent research shows that electoral
competition is related to growing criminal violence in Mexico,[18] and there is also
vibrant literature on links between political competition and violence in civil
wars.[19] For the most part, higher competition can fragment the state and create
more violence by affecting the other two dimensions of the security apparatus.
Yet, state fragmentation can also occur as a result of bureaucratic changes not
necessarily attached to electoral dynamics. Furthermore, in some cases, electoral
competition may not fragment the state, or may not lead to further transformations in enforcement agencies, if political elites remain ingrained—as occurred
in the first years of electoral alternation in the northern states of Mexico. The
fragmenting impact of electoral competition on enforcement can also be mitigated and contribute to democratic law enforcement when political actors create
strong political coalitions or collaborate across party lines, as has partially been
the case in Medellín since the late 2000s.

Taking into consideration the discussion presented in chapter 3, in order to analyze the conditions under which electoral competition affects relations between
government levels and the organization and capacities of enforcement agencies,
we need to further examine the possible trade-off between the state capacity to
control violence and the state's autonomy from criminal influences. This, in turn,
can shed light on the situations in which increased electoral competition may
reduce the state capacity to control violence and the situations in which, over
time, the state can regain such capacity through democratic law enforcement.

The second area for further research regarding state transformations involves analyzing two related questions: (1) how and when can fragmented states become effective in enforcing the law? and (2) how can cohesive states become accountable and independent from criminal influence? There are cases of fragmented security apparatuses, such as that of the United States, that are effective in enforcing the law. This can be a result of incentives that generate cooperation between multiple layers of government and between different enforcement agencies. This possibility, however, suggests that there is room to better conceptualize what, exactly, law enforcement entails (coordination, efficient use of resources, control of violence, respect for individual rights)—as a way of understanding when and how enforcement structures can become not only more efficient but also more accountable and independent from criminal influences.

The third area for further research is to explore other sources of state fragmentation that do not relate to political or bureaucratic changes. As mentioned in chapter 3, states can fragment when economic crises or international influences break down the channels through which state authorities deal with societal groups and elites. Given the focus of this book on drug trafficking, one area that can be further developed is the connection between international antinarcotics agendas and state cohesion. The possibilities suggested in chapter 3 can be further explored, for example, by systematically testing whether state fragmentation increases when international antinarcotics aid is given to one state agency to the detriment of other, less-trusted agencies or whether state protection rackets are strengthened when narcotics aid is given to more cohesive—but not necessarily democratic—states. By the same token, an area that can still be explored is the way in which domestic state structures shape the specific form, pace, and manifestations of foreign-imposed policies.

The State as a Performer of Visible Violence

This book focused on analyzing when and how criminals change their violent strategies, but as became evident in the case studies, in its interactions with criminal organization—both to confront them or to collude with them—the state itself is a crucial perpetrator of both lawful and unlawful violence.

One can, then, apply the concept of visible violence to state actions and analyze when, in the process of law enforcement, state actors would display their coercive actions and when they would hide them. States may need to hide violence in their interactions with criminal actors when they resort to dubious human rights practices in the process of identifying or incarcerating suspects. Forced disappearance by state agents is a prominent illustration of state forces hiding violence. Yet state actors sometimes also publicize their use of violence as a way of bolstering their popularity and legitimacy and reinforcing the idea that the state holds a monopoly on the use of force. Highly publicized military deployments to confront criminals in urban areas are perhaps the clearest illustration of a state carrying out visible violence to confront criminals. Such operations have not only emerged in Mexico and Colombia but have also been common in places including Brazil and Central America.

The Consequences of Violence

Analyzing the causes of drug violence becomes inevitably intertwined with considering the question of its consequences. In the cases presented in this book, there have been different reactions toward criminal violence, especially in terms of organized responses through civil society organizations. Medellín and Ciudad Juárez display an extensive network of civil society organizations that advocate against violence and for justice, monitor violence trends, and implement creative solutions that attempt to address the root causes of violence and its consequences for local communities. By contrast, Cali and Culiacán display seemingly weaker civil society efforts to confront criminality, despite their long histories with drug violence. An interesting line of research thus would derive from comparing these diverse responses to drug violence and to criminal violence in general and analyzing how they can influence patterns of violence.

Analyzing the consequences of drug violence requires bridging bodies of research that make opposing assessments about citizens' reactions to violence. On the one hand, research on the institutional and social consequences of civil war has found that "victimized people have been found to be more politically active and to display greater trust toward citizens as compared to non-victimized people,"[20] and this participatory effect can even extend to the perpetrators of violence and to peacetime.[21] On the other hand, research on the fear of crime shows that crime nurtures vigilantism, segregation, and the privatization of security[22] and hinders collective responses to violence. The seeming variation in how citizens react suggests that specific types of violence can both hinder and promote civil society organization. Interesting research on diverse individual and communal responses to violence in crime-ridden areas is already growing and points to the importance of political and social networks in shaping responses to violence. The framework I presented suggests that the type of violence and especially its visibility can also shape differential citizen responses among both victims and nonvictims. For instance, in Culiacán weaker civil responses coincide with the prevalence of low-visibility violence.

Policy Implications

The objective of this book was not to evaluate the effectiveness of policies to prevent and confront violence and criminality, but nonetheless some clear policy implications may be derived from the analysis.

First, a decline in violence does not necessarily imply the disappearance of violent trafficking organizations or the elimination of the most powerful ones. Low violence in criminal markets can be associated either with an organization's ability to establish a monopoly or with the establishment of temporary nonviolent arrangements between a few organizations. The best illustration of the first option is the large reduction of violence in Medellín between 2003 and 2007. An illustration of the second option is the reduction of violence in Tijuana between 2010 and 2012. A crucial implication of understanding that criminal groups can mitigate their use of violence is understanding that situations of relative peace need to be monitored constantly because monopolies and criminal arrangements that bring about peace are prone to instability and, consequently, to the return of violence.

Second, acknowledging that lethal violence can be hidden reminds us that sometimes situations labeled as relatively peaceful may actually be situations where criminals hide violence. Thus, interventions to mitigate violence cannot stop when the most visible violence has decreased. For example, in 2008, the increase that followed the historic reduction of violence in Medellín did not cause the same national and international outcry that it did in the 1980s. Yet this violence was not less harmful for the local population. In this light, all programs aimed at tackling violence should adopt metrics that allow for a broader assessment of violence.

Third, even though drug trafficking is a transnational phenomenon, the violent consequences of trafficking are most strongly felt at the local level. Furthermore, local conditions matter in determining violent outcomes, as illustrated by the fact that the same organization can exhibit quite different violent behavior across locations. A case in point is the Sinaloa DTO, which uses varied violent methods across Mexico. Policies aimed at reducing violence or targeting certain organizations (or both) should thus consider the power dynamics among local enforcement agencies and political actors. Furthermore, well-intended policies aimed at reducing corruption can have the effect of generating violence while fragmenting the state in the short term, and enforcement actions undertaken when states are undergoing radical processes of institutional change (such as democratization) are likely to backfire when state actors cannot coordinate well. This is especially the case with massive purges of security forces, which not only can generate violent reactions by criminals but can also push many of the purged elements into criminal organizations. This is also the case with large-scale military deployments, which can further fragment the state and generate human rights violations. This does not mean that anticorruption policies or enforcement actions should not be carried out, but rather that they should always be thoroughly planned, paying special attention to national and local enforcement conditions.

Finally, the impact of outsourcing on drug violence highlights the importance of creating programs that prevent the engagement of nonviolent youth gangs in criminal activities. It is crucial to understand that direct connections between gangs and organized criminals are not automatic, and consequently, if youth involvement in crime is to be minimized it is essential to avoid the stigmatization and criminalization of marginalized youth and of gangs as violent actors. If the connection emerges, then the emphasis should be on breaking it up. This implies targeting the brokers who connect the (not necessarily violent) youth gangs with criminal organizations and controlling the mechanisms that allow connections, such as recruitment within prisons facilitated by lax prison controls and inappropriate prison conditions. It also implies providing marginalized youth with viable alternatives outside criminal activities. This is, however, a long-term process, and thus the success of broad social reforms cannot be assessed just through short-term evaluations of security conditions. It is important to note, in this context, that gangs can also be engaged in low-level criminality and have sporadic or nonsystematic interactions with criminals, but these connections are often mistaken by authorities as a form of outsourcing. Therefore, carefully considering the varied relations that exist among different nonstate actors, gangs, and organized traffickers, and avoiding quick or simplistic generalizations, is essential for better drug and crime control policies.

The Future of Drug Policies and Violence

Chapter 1 emphasized how the complex variations of drug violence could not be simply explained by the illegality of drug markets. Other factors such as power dynamics within states, relations among and within criminal groups, and social conditions that determine the existence of gangs and the engagement of criminal actors with young populations are all essential for understanding why, within the same prohibition regime, criminals can behave in so many different ways. Yet this does neglect the reality that prohibition creates an environment that favors violence and that constrains policies toward militarized, reactive, and repression-oriented responses.

The global drug-prohibition regime that emerged at the beginning of the twentieth century and that consolidated between the 1940s and 1970s has not succeeded in its intended outcomes of reducing the consumption and production of drugs or eliminating criminal organizations. Drug markets keep growing and expanding geographically, and criminal organizations keep finding incentives to engage in activities that are highly profitable. Therefore, drug policies that are deemed successful in one location are often associated with the displacement of trafficking actors to other locations.[23] In 2014, according to the UN Office on Drugs and Crime (UNODC), an estimated 247 million people, or 5.2 percent of the world's population, had used illicit drugs at least once during that year.[24] While criminalizing consumers, the prohibition regime has also curtailed the exploration of alternatives to deal with drug consumption. Criminalization has generated prison overcrowding and contributed to high costs in criminal justice systems that often deal with nonproblematic consumers or low-level operatives rather than with highly dangerous drug lords.

In this context, and in the midst of a historic change in the terms of debate about drug regulation that has opened the space to discuss the limitations of traditional drug policy, two crucial questions emerge: Is it possible to foresee a change in the current prohibition regime? And if so, how could that change affect current levels of violence? While answering these questions clearly requires an effort that supersedes what I can say over the next few paragraphs, and is a task that is in fact being undertaken by academics and many civil society groups, I would like to offer a few thoughts.

In his analysis of the global drug-prohibition regime and its workings within the United Nations system, David Bewley-Taylor[25] describes insightfully how, since the late 2000s, the prohibition regime has experienced a substantial weakening derived from the "soft defection" of countries that have implemented harm-reduction approaches toward drugs and alternative regulations on cannabis. He also shows that, paradoxically, this soft defection has contributed to maintaining the regime—for example, when the UNODC claims that everything done under UN drug conventions fits the idea of harm reduction.[26] In this context, Bewley-Taylor argues, major overhauls of the regime do not seem plausible in the short run; considering that the regime is closely tied to the global distribution of power, change is unlikely to happen unless major powers, chiefly the United States, agree on it.

Since 2012, however, a crucial change has indicated an alternative path toward better drug policies that does not engage powerful players in the international system. For the first time, incumbent presidents, including those of Colombia, Guatemala, and Mexico, declared publicly their willingness to discuss the pertinence of current drug policies. The declarations of these presidents, all of them from Latin America and thus at the center of the "war on drugs," marked a sea-level change in discussions about the need to redefine the war on drugs. Since the 1950s, any public figure who questioned the drug-prohibition regime was demonized, and no sitting president even dared to question the need of "the fight" against drugs. The open involvement of presidents in the discussion, followed by the legalization of marijuana in eight states (plus the District of Columbia) in the United States (starting with Washington and Colorado in November 2012) and in Uruguay in 2013, suggests that substantial change on narcotics enforcement is becoming politically feasible. That being said, the major consensus seems to be around the need to legalize or depenalize marijuana, on the need to focus on harm reduction, and on the need to advance a health approach to drug use. It is likely that legal changes, even if uneven, can occur over the 2020s in these policy areas even if still implausible at the UN conventions level. Regulatory changes on other drugs such as cocaine, heroin, and methamphetamines seem unlikely in the near future.

If legal changes regarding the possession of drugs and the status of marijuana occur, the question then becomes, how would they impact drug-related violence? The answer is not simple. First, there is considerable debate about how much income drug-trafficking organizations derive from marijuana production and therefore about how much legalization would affect the income of trafficking groups.[27] Regardless of the amount that criminal groups derive from marijuana, it is clear that legalization can reduce profits associated with an illegal commodity and thus the incentives to protect turf violently. Legalization could indeed reduce the income of trafficking groups, although there is uncertainly about how big the effect could be.

Many of the potential effects of legalization or depenalization of drug use on the size of the market will depend on the taxing schemes in the newly legalized market. They will also depend on dynamics of policing and enforcement, because it is likely that even if the marijuana legalization trend expands more evenly across and within countries, there still will be different regulation schemes in place (for example, from full legalization to depenalization only, and from active state intervention to more privatized schemes). The persistent illegality of other drugs could keep incentives for criminals to violently protect their trafficking turf and the high profits that can derive from it. And even if other drugs were legalized, it is possible that criminals could diversify portfolios into other criminal activities such as extortion to compensate for their lost income. We still need substantial research to understand when and how criminals diversify their portfolios and migrate into other illegal activities that can be violent. But even if diversification is possible, many criminal organizations may not migrate into other illegal activities; they may instead migrate into the legal sector and this could, in the long run, eliminate incentives for people to engage in criminal organizations.

Legalization or decriminalization of marijuana may not have an immediate impact on dismantling powerful criminal groups and on reducing violence—mainly because most of these groups combine income from different drugs—but it could have a positive impact in separating the market for cannabis from that of other drugs, reducing consumers' contact with dangerous settings. The depenalization of drug use, and the legalization of one market that has been demonized for decades, could also have other consequences that indirectly could reduce violence in the short and medium run. First, it could reduce prisoner populations and, correspondingly, the pool of people who get trapped into circles of recidivism and criminal behavior when entering prisons. Second, it could save expenses in criminal justice that have been directed to nonviolent offenses, and these savings could be directed into violence- and drug use–prevention programs. Third, by simply changing the public discourse, legal changes regarding drug use and marijuana could open the space to think about alternate ways to deal with drug production and with harder and more problematic drugs. Fourth, and as the Global Commission on Drugs and Democracy has recognized, by undermining the taboo that links drugs and drug consumers with crime, and by focusing on reducing the harm produced by the illegal narcotics trade, depenalization of drug users could help in focusing enforcement on the most violent organizations that generate more instability and insecurity.

The last point brings me full circle, to conclude by connecting these possibilities with my own analysis of violence. Changes in the global drug prohibition regime—at least those that seem plausible in the short to medium term—may generate slow changes in the dismantling of criminal organizations and in eliminating violence. Yet changing a global drug-prohibition regime that has clearly failed opens up an essential avenue for policy innovation, by treating drug trafficking, drug use, and violence as interrelated but different policy priorities. This could reduce the militarization that has characterized drug policies around the world, but especially in Latin America, and that has fed corruption, human rights violations, and forms of policing that deepen marginalization and exclusion of the most vulnerable people in society. Reforms over current drug policies can also promote better and more targeted enforcement, something that seems to have been successful in the UPPs, Unidades de Polícia Pacificadora or Pacification Police Units, implemented since 2010 in Rio de Janeiro. The UPPs represent, in very broad terms, a scheme of highly targeted and publicized military interventions in crime-ridden favelas.[28] In the initial years these units were partially effective in reducing homicide rates by combining both a highly selective enforcement approach and a combination of military and social policies.

Yet if targeted enforcement policies like the UPP are applied elsewhere, it is essential to recognize, as I have shown, that the link between drugs, criminal organizations, and violence is not automatic. Relatively peaceful scenarios may sometimes be the result of highly powerful criminal organizations combined with extended networks of state corruption and protection that may hide situations of less-visible violence. In the case of the UPPs, the homicide reductions in some favelas have been offset by the displacement of violence or criminal groups into other locations of the state of Rio de Janeiro or of the country or by the incidence of some less-visible forms of violence such as disappearances perpetrated as criminals attempt to lower their profile. Also, the success of enforcement operations is highly dependent on the state cohesion and enforcement efficiency. In the case of the UPPs, state cohesion, in the form of collaboration between all levels of government (city, state, and federation) seems to have been essential in the success of the approach. In other words, a selective enforcement approach is not efficient in a vacuum, but rather it depends on the structure of enforcement institutions.

In sum, all policy redefinitions that can become plausible in a more flexible regulatory framework for psychoactive drugs need to recognize the possible trade-offs and unintended consequences that can emerge as enforcement is redirected toward reducing or targeting the most violent trafficking organizations. For example, such targeting can leave powerful organizations untouched, ignore certain forms of violence, or motivate criminals not to reduce violence altogether but instead to make it less visible. No policy framework is free of possible trade-offs, and this will certainly be the case with any new regulatory alternative on psychoactive drugs. It is necessary to be aware of all the possible scenarios and not to expect immediate results in the elimination of drugs, violence, or organized criminality. But it is clear that the current regime is exhausted, that the human costs are too high, and that there is an unprecedented window of political opportunity to finally rethink a failed regime.

Appendix

CODING PROTOCOL
FOR DRUG-VIOLENCE EVENTS

This protocol explains the criteria used to classify information about drug-violence events in Cali, Ciudad Juárez, Culiacán, Medellín, and Tijuana using the main local newspapers in each city. These newspapers were *El País* (Cali), *El Diario* and *El Mexicano* (Ciudad Juárez), *El Noroeste* (Culiacán), *El Colombiano* (Medellín), and *El Sol* (Tijuana). This protocol partially draws on the protocol created by Benjamin Lessing for his project "Observatory of Drug-Related Violence." It was adapted for the specific needs of this data set, identifying categories that indicate high- and low-visibility violence.

The database also includes information on metropolitan areas and surrounding municipalities for each city.

An event of violence was considered drug related if (1) the police, observers, or journalists attributed the action to drug trafficking; (2) the perpetrators acknowledged their responsibility; (3) the method suggested that the event was drug related (for instance, use of heavy weaponry or cases involving torture; see chapter 2 for an extended discussion about the definition of drug-related violence).

For each event the following information was coded:

1. ID: consecutive identification number for each event preceded by a letter that corresponds to the newspaper source (thus, C1 is the first event coded in *El Colombiano*).

2. DATE AND PLACE OF OCCURRENCE
    a. Date: Date on which the event took place. The date was inferred if there was no clear information (e.g., an event occurred "ten days ago"). If there was no date or reference to time frame, it was assumed that the event occurred the day before the publication of the newspaper.

b. Location:
  - Municipality and neighborhood: If the event occurred on an intermunicipal highway, the closest municipality was coded.
  - Place of occurrence: Name of the place (if available) and type of place according to the following categories: bar, restaurant, highway (connects municipalities), street (urban roads), mall, rehabilitation center, field, commercial building, public building (including prisons), creamery, park, private residence (including country houses), river (including ocean), cemetery, abandoned lot. If the victims died at a clinic after the attack, the original location of the attack was coded. If an attack occurred in front of a residence or restaurant, on the street, the location was coded as street.
  - Urban: Determines if the event occurred in places of low population density and where agricultural activities prevail (rural) or in areas of high population density and with primacy of commercial activities (urban). The cell contains a 1 if the area was urban and 0 if rural.
  - Public: Public space was defined as any place where the land is public and access is unrestricted, such as parks, streets, highways, public buildings, and other places that become public because of the service they provide such as bus stations, libraries, schools, hospitals, malls. Private spaces are private residences, commercial buildings. Bars and restaurants were classified as private because access can be restricted. If an attack occurred in front of a private residence in the street, the location was classified as public. The cell contains a 1 if the place was public and 0 if private.

3. TYPE OF EVENT
  a. Unilateral action: An event that did not imply a reaction of the victims or did not lead to combat. If an attack caused a retaliation that shortly followed the attack but was not immediate, the two events were coded separately. If a combat followed the arrival of police to a crime scene, the two events were also coded separately. The cell contains a 1 for a unilateral action and 0 otherwise.
  b. Combat: An armed confrontation or exchange of fire, implies a reaction from the target of the attack. If an attack generated a reaction by bodyguards it was coded as combat. The cell contains a 1 for combat and 0 otherwise.
  c. Common grave finding: In this cell 1 refers to the finding of three or more bodies in the same place. A common grave is created with the purpose of hiding bodies; therefore, the finding of bodies in the middle of a street was not classified as common grave.

d. Corpse finding: In this cell 1 refers to the finding of one or two bodies, when the bodies were found after the violent attack took place and there were no witnesses to determine the circumstances of the event. For example, if it could be determined that there were paid killers on the scene, a 0 appears in this cell.

4. SPECIFIC TYPE OF ACTION
   - Threat
   - Publicity action
   - Murder
   - Attempt: When there was an attempt on the life of a person but the person did not die, or when an explosive was deactivated. When the objective was achieved, the action was not classified as an attempt.
   - Explosion
   - Forced disappearance: When there was no information on the victims' whereabouts.
   - Kidnapping: When there was a ransom or the captors were known. If the victim returned alive or paid the ransom, no method was classified. If captors were not known and the victim was murdered, the specific type of action was classified murder, and the method as disappearance.
   - Massacre
   - Combat
   - Enforcement operation: If there were no casualties in an enforcement operation, no method was classified. If there was a response from criminals then the action was classified as enforcement operation and the method was confrontation. If the operation was in response to a criminal action then the type of action was combat (if the reaction was immediate).
   - Social cleansing: Murder of unprotected sectors of the population such as drug abusers, prostitutes, petty criminals, or homeless people.

5. NAMES OF GROUPS THAT PARTICIPATED IN THE ACTION
   Up to three groups were coded. If no specific group was mentioned, the following categories were used:
   - Armed command: Three or more people, armed. If the information did not clarify the number of people participating, but a group action could be inferred, it was classified as armed command.
   - Common delinquent: If the perpetrators were identified as common criminals.
   - Armed group: Armed collective with a political agenda.
   - Organized crime: If the note clearly identified the responsibility. Drug distributors were included in this category.

- Gang: Included terms like cholos, bandas, barrios. If a group of young people was armed with knives it was classified as gang rather than armed command.

If there were only one or two individual perpetrators without clear membership in a group, this category was left blank.

In a few cases, if the clipping provided information that allowed the coder to infer the group, then the group was inferred. For example, a note from the *Noroeste* referred to a group of former military operating in Tamaulipas, and the coder inferred the group to be the Zetas, a criminal organization formed by former military and originally from Tamaulipas.

If there was a combat, group 1 is the group that initiated the action

6. ATTRIBUTION OF RESPONSIBILITY
   a. Origin of attribution of responsibility: For each group the database determines the origin of the information that led to identification in the following categories.
      - Divergence: The cell contains a 1 if there was divergence about the groups involved, 0 otherwise.
      - Accusation: The cell contains a 1 if the report explicitly accused one group, 0 otherwise.
      - Suspicion: The cell contains a 1 if the group was only mentioned as a potential perpetrator.
      - Responsibility: The cell contains a 1 if the group itself claimed responsibility, 0 otherwise.
   b. Source: When there was suspicion or accusation, the origin of the information was included in this column. The possible sources of information are: civilian, state, armed group, journalistic, police or military.
   c. Method to claim responsibility: This cell is filled when the cell responsibility contains a 1. The possible methods are as follows: public statement, note in the location of events, note on corpses, direct communication with a person, direct communication (of the perpetrator) with a person such as a public authority or journalist, propaganda action (if the perpetrators claim their responsibility publicly). If there was a corpse with a note, but the note did not claim responsibility, this cell was left blank, except when the note threatened a specific group and it could be assumed that the source was another organized crime group. In such case the origin of attribution was classified as suspicion, the method was a note, and the source was journalistic.

7. METHOD OF CARRYING OUT THE VIOLENT ACTION
   This column codes the methods used to perpetrate lethal actions. When one action combined different methods, the cell coded the most visible one.

a. List of methods:
  - Head in cooler: When a head was found in a cooler, separated from the rest of the body.
  - Car bomb
  - Wrapped in blanket: When the corpse was wrapped in a blanket. If the corpse had signs of torture, then the method was torture, but if the body had signs of shots, then the method that prevailed was "wrapped in blanket." Includes corpses found in plastic bags, bed sheets.
  - Combat with explosives
  - Combat with firearms
  - Combat with knives
  - Frozen corpse
  - Use of explosives and firearms (without combat). When more than three people perpetrated an attack, the method classified was sicariato, and the type of arm was explosives.
  - Execution
  - Grenade: When a grenade was used in the attack.
  - Fire (of a place)
  - Mutilation or incineration with a note
  - Simple mutilation or incineration (without note)
  - Forced disappearance: When the person disappeared. Includes methods identified as *paseo* ("trip") or *levantones* ("lift"). If a person disappeared but then was found alive, the type of action was kidnapping and there was no method classified. If a disappeared person was found with signs of torture, disappearance prevailed in the classification. If a body was not recovered, both the type of action and method were forced disappearance. There are three possible combinations of type of action-method in this case. If the person disappeared and the body was found, the type of action was murder and the method disappearance. If the person appeared alive, the type of action was kidnapping and the method disappearance. If the person never appeared, both type of action and method were classified as forced disappearance.
  - Sicariato: The use of paid assassins. Given the difficulty of determining if the perpetrator was a paid assassin, sicariato was coded depending on whether the event suggested planning and previous identification of the target. The criteria used to determine this was if the action involved more than three people, a moving vehicle, or attacks from one moving vehicle to another. In Colombia, an action that included two people on a motorcycle was coded as sicariato.

- Torture: If the note referred to mutilation, then the method classified was mutilation, and if there was mutilation and a note on the body, then the latter method prevailed. Torture usually involves the finding of naked bodies, with hands tied, and signs of heavy beating.
- Simple use of knives
- Simple use of firearms: Generally when just one or two individuals attacked, using few shots, generally in private locations.
- Explosives
- Sexual violence: In any instance in which a murder was accompanied by signs of sexual violence, the method was classified as sexual violence
- Strangulation and asphyxiation
- Simple use of blunt objects
- Corpse with a note (when there were no mutilations)
- Poisoning

b. Type of arm used: This cell contains the arms used to cause the death. Unlike the method, the arm coded was the one that caused the death, not the most visible.

- Knives
- Firearms
- Fire elements (gasoline)
- Explosives
- Assault weapons
- Blunt objects
- Rope, duct tape
- Plastic bags

8. TARGET

The presumed target of the violent attack. Except in cases where the event was clearly a result of interpersonal violence, the classification assumed the target using the occupation of the victim—that is, a murder of a cop was interpreted as police or military target. Considering the discussion in chapter 2, the information about target was mostly speculative and therefore the analysis uses the category type of victim, explained below. The categories included are as follows: civilians, rival organizations, petty criminal, civil servant, public infrastructure, private infrastructure, members of the same organization, criminal organization (when it was not clear whether the target involved rivals or members of the same organization), police, or military. Street-level drug distributors were categorized as criminal organization.

a. Source of attribution: As in the group variable, this cell contains information about whether the target was identified through suspicion, accusation, or direct responsibility of the perpetrators, or if there was divergence among sources.

b. Source: Origin of the attribution (as in the Group variable, no. 4).

9. VICTIMS

These cells contain information on the number and type of victims. The number in each cell corresponds to the number of victims in each of the following categories:

- Dead
- Wounded
- Detained (when law enforcement detained people)
- Retained (when an illegal organization retained people)
- Disappeared (when a person was taken and there was no information about captors or whereabouts)
- Not wounded (as when people escaped from an attack without wounds)

The dead and wounded categories in turn contain subcategories that include the number of victims per subcategory:

- Member of criminal organization
- Relative of member of criminal organization
- Law enforcement (police and military)
- Public authority (politicians or civil servants)
- Petty criminal
- Female and males over twenty-five years old
- Children (male and female under twenty-five years old)

10. OCCUPATION

Profession, occupation, or job of the victim (only for fatal victims; if an action only wounded people there was no classification of occupation). If there was more than one victim and more than one occupation identified, each different occupation was determined in a second or third column. When a clipping identified the occupation of the victim and a presumption of criminal engagement, the occupation was classified in this column, and the presumed criminal status in the subcategories of victim. The possible categories were:

- lawyer
- attorney's agent
- peasant
- merchant or businessperson
- social leader
- high school student, university student
- civil servant
- mechanic
- member of criminal organization
- journalist
- police or military
- politician

- presumed criminal
- professional
- nonprofessional worker (e.g., driver, general services employee, guard, construction worker, employee of a store)
- human rights worker
- informal economy worker (e.g., street vendor)

11. SOURCE OF INFORMATION
    a. Name of newspaper
    b. Section
    c. Page
    d. Date of publication (month, day, year)

12. OBSERVATIONS
    Contains a summary of the press clipping for coding reliability.

GLOSSARY

barrio Literally, "neighborhood," but in Mexico this term is also used as a synonym for a youth gang or for a strong identity connection with those in the neighborhood.

bonanza barimbera Used to refer to a marijuana boom in Colombia that took place during the 1970s.

botaderos Dumping places for corpses.

casa de seguridad Literally, "safe house." A place used to hide cash or drugs, to conduct killings, or to hide victims of kidnapping.

cenotafios Cenotaphs; crosses used to mark places where people have died, often in violent circumstances, particularly in Culiacán, Sinaloa.

cholos A slang term that has multiple connotations in different Latin American countries. In Mexico, it is often used to refer to a youth cultural expression (especially in cities bordering the United States) associated with particular dress codes such as wearing baggie pants and bandanas. Cholos are often associated with criminality in the public imagination, although in most cases cholos are not actually criminals or members of a street gang.

colonia Neighborhood (Mexico).

combos Term used particularly in the city of Medellín to refer to street gangs associated with the control of specific areas within neighborhoods. While combos are not inherently violent or criminal, they may be associated in complex ways with higher levels of criminality.

derecho de piso A fee paid by occasional drug dealers, or drug traffickers, when moving or selling drugs in a territory controlled by a more powerful group.

Frente Nacional A pact between the Liberal and Conservative parties in Colombia confirming agreement to evenly share all public posts in government and to rotate the presidency between the two parties. The pact was aimed at ending the interparty violence that besieged the country beginning in 1949. It lasted from 1958 to 1970.

gavilleros Members of old, rural gangs (particularly in Sinaloa).

gomeros Opium gum collectors (Mexico).

Kaibiles Guatemalan elite military force specializing in rural warfare and counterinsurgency, created at the height of the Guatemalan civil war. They have been associated with multiple human rights violations and participated in the training of the Zetas in Mexico.

levantón A form of kidnapping or disappearance, term particularly used in Mexico to refer to cases when someone was taken away by unknown people.

mantas (or narcomantas) Banners used by drug-trafficking groups to send messages to each other or to the police, to claim responsibility for attacks, or simply to serve as threatening notes. They became common in Mexico after 2006—they were sometimes left with corpses and sometimes stood on their own.

maquiladoras   Assembly or manufacturing plants in Mexico run by foreign companies that export the production to their country of origin.

mulas   Literally, "mules." Individuals who transport drugs, often within their bodies. They are often female.

narcos   Drug traffickers.

narcojuniors   The children of older drug traffickers—the second generation. In Tijuana the word also refers to elite young men who came to be associated with drug traffickers, often as hitmen, particularly with the Arellano Felix organization.

oficinas   A term used in Colombia to refer to criminal groups who act as intermediaries among different drug traffickers, or between traffickers and lower-level groups such as gangs. They often collect debts and payments and serve and contract enforcers, but they may also play roles such as hiring assassins, and they sometimes act as their own criminal enterprise.

paseo   kidnapping or disappearance. Similar to *levantón*. Term particularly used in Colombia in the 1980s to refer to cases when someone was taken away, and often driven around in cars. Some of the kidnapped people would be returned; others disappeared permanently.

pelado   Colombian slang for "young person."

pistiar   Slang for "drinking" (Mexico).

pistoleros   Armed people, mostly rural, who hire out as hitmen (Mexico).

plaza   Refers to the concession given by corrupt Mexican police to run a drug business in a particular locale; also loosely used to refer to a trafficking group's turf, or particular area of control.

pozole   A traditional thick Mexican soup.

pozolero   A person who makes pozole, a "stewmaker." In the context of drug violence in Mexico, used to refer to someone in charge of destroying corpses in acid.

Santa Muerte   Holy Death. A female deity in Mexican folk religion who personifies death. While its followers have grown in number since the 2000s, the cult of Death has a long tradition in Mexico. It has come to be associated with drug traffickers, as many petty traffickers and gang members follow it; however, the cult is most widespread among the poor and working-class.

serranos   Rural-born drug traffickers from the mountains (Mexico).

sexenio   The six-year term of a Mexican president.

sicariato/sicarios   Sicarios (hitmen) carry out sicariato (murder for hire). In Colombia, sicariato came to be associated with particular methods, such as shooting a victim from a moving motorcycle.

traqueto   Slang used in Colombia to refer to someone who traffics in drugs or who kills for drug traffickers.

ventanilla siniestra   Literally, "sinister window." Refers to an informal process through which the Colombian government unofficially allowed the proceeds from the marijuana boom to enter the formal economy, through lax regulations in currency-exchange houses.

NOTES

Chapter 1

1. Paley, *Drug War*.
2. This calculation of drug homicides in Mexico is based on government and media estimates of homicides associated with drug trafficking. The definition of a "drug-related homicide" is controversial, and thus this number presents a conservative estimate of the death toll in Mexico. Overall, homicide statistics add up to 150,000 deaths between 2006 and 2015. For detailed analysis of this issue, see Heinle et al., "Drug Violence."
3. Andreas and Wallman, "Illicit"; Friman, "Drug Markets"; Reuter, "Systemic."
4. For a discussion of this in other illegal markets, see Reuter, *Disorganized*.
5. Visible violence is more likely to attract enforcement and media attention, but attracting such attention does not define visibility. Violence is not always rational, but the emphasis of this book is on explaining criminals' purposeful use of visible violence.
6. BACRIM, for *bandas criminales* (criminal gangs) is an acronym used by the government of Colombia to refer to criminal structures devoted to drug trafficking. The term BACRIM is controversial, as these groups are linked to old paramilitary structures; many analysts consider "neoparamilitaries" (that is, new paramilitary groups) to be a better label.
7. Author's interview conducted with intelligence official of the Attorney General's Office, Criminal Investigation Unit, Bogotá, September 13, 2010. The key in this statement is not the official's assumption that there is no message in violence but that criminals try to hide its use. (All author's interviews were originally conducted in Spanish, and then translated into English by the author, unless noted otherwise)
8. Expression used by intelligence official in author's interview, Bogotá, September 20, 2010.
9. Medellín's average homicide rate was 228 per 100,000 inhabitants between 1984 and 1993 and fell to an average of 154 between 1994 and 2005, with a low point of 34 in 2005. By contrast, in the same periods Cali's average was 68 and increased to 91, with a high peak of 104 in 1994.
10. Davis, "Irregular"; Koonings and Kruijt, *Societies*; Moser, *Reducing*.
11. Trejo and Ley, "Federalismo."
12. Moncada, *Cities*.
13. Naim, *Illicit*. Andreas ("Illicit") criticizes the misconceptions attached to the idea of transnational or globalized organized crime, one of which is the idea that as the power of global organized crime increases, so does the violence associated with it.
14. Fearon, "Why Do Some"; Ross, "What Do We Know."
15. Kaldor, *New and Old Wars*.
16. The relationship between illegal markets, natural resources, and civil war is an ongoing debate in the literature on civil wars. Many scholars acknowledge that the effect of drugs (as a distinctive type of commodity) on war is still far from being clarified and that the mechanisms

explaining the connection are complex and not automatic. See Cornell, "The Interaction," and Ross, "What Do We Know." Few of these debates explore the noninstances of the relationship—for example, when rebel groups have not recurred to drug trafficking as a funding source or when drug markets generate less violence.

17. Andreas and Wallman, "Illicit Markets"; Astorga and Shirk, "Drug Trafficking"; Garzón, *Mafia & Co*; Lessing, "The Logic of Violence"; Osorio, "Hobbes"; Rios, "How Government"; Rios and Shirk, "Drug Violence"; Snyder and Durán-Martínez, "Does Illegality."

18. Reuter, *Disorganized*; Reuter and Haaga, "The Organization"; Schelling, *The Strategy*.

19. Castillo et al., "Illegal Drug Markets."

20. Reuter, "Systemic Violence."

21. Goldstein, "The Relationship."

22. Gambetta, *Sicilian Mafia*; Skaperdas, "Political Economy."

23. Guerrero, "La Raíz."

24. Latin American Commission on Drugs and Democracy (LACDD), *Drugs and Democracy*; Youngers and Rosin, *Drugs and Democracy*.

25. Gootenberg, "Cocaine's Long March."

26. Serrano, "Narcotráfico."

27. LACDD, *Drugs and Democracy*; Transform Drug Policy Foundation, *Alternative World Drug Report*.

28. Davis, "Irregular Armed Forces"; Koonings and Kruijt, *Societies*; Moser, *Reducing*; Moser and Rodgers, *Change*.

29. Thomas et al., "Securing the City."

30. Paley, *Drug War*.

31. Scholars of urban violence recognize the complex and changing character of violence and relate it to rapid socioeconomic transformations; see Moser and Rodgers, *Change*. Yet while focusing on highly violent situations, they tend to overlook the socioeconomic changes that do not produce criminal violence or the contexts where the criminality produced by these changes is not openly violent.

32. I follow the analytical traditions of looking at the state as an autonomous entity that impacts political and social processes through its policies and its patterned relationships with social groups and through the creation of political opportunity structures. See Skocpol, "Bringing the State Back In"; Tarrow, *Power in Movement*. I expand on this view by looking at the impact that the state security apparatus has on violence and its interaction not with *legal* but with *illegal* actors. Studies in anthropology of the state have pointed out that one limitation of the state-society framework is that it conceptualizes two completely separate arenas when in fact state and society often overlap and are not unified actors; see Hansen and Stepputat, *States of Imagination*. This is especially important in the case of state-illegal actor relations, because corruption may completely blur the limits between state and society. I acknowledge this evanescent boundary but assert the validity of analyzing state and illegal actors as two separate fields.

33. Arjona, *Rebelocracy*; Kalyvas, *Logic*; Kalyvas, "Wanton and Senseless."

34. Arias, *Drugs and Democracy in Rio De Janeiro*; Arias, "The Impacts"; Moncada, "The Politics of Urban Violence"; Schelling, *The Strategy*. Marten and Staniland analyze how even rebels sometimes collaborate with states; see Marten, *Warlords*; Staniland, "Cities on Fire," "Militias."

35. Analyses of ethnic violence and social mobilization provide insights into the importance of unpacking power within the state to understand violent outcomes, as discussed in chapter 3.

36. Lessing, "Logics of Violence."

37. Andreas, "Illicit"; Friman, "Forging."

38. Caulkins et al., "What Supply"; Friman, "Forging"; Goldstein et al., "Crack"; Rios, "How Government."

39. Lessing, "Logics."

40. Osorio, "The Contagion."

41. Lessing analyzes the conditionality of crackdowns on crime ("Logics"). Calderón et al. analyze leadership decapitation ("Beheading").

42. Gambetta, *Codes*.

43. Criminals can display violence to scare away enforcers or to retaliate when they have been attacked. Yet, if criminals' fear of state action is greater than their belief in their ability to pressure state actors, they may refrain from retaliation through visible violence.

44. Snyder and Durán-Martínez, "Does Illegality."

45. Although rational, displaying violence is often detrimental in the long run. That is, criminals may gain power or extract state concessions through visible violence, but they can end up forcing security agencies to focus resources on destroying them.

46. I define law enforcement as the agencies that engage in patrolling, surveillance, investigation, and apprehension. See Hess, *Introduction to Law Enforcement.*

47. Sometimes fragmented enforcement apparatuses can be effective, as in the United States, if overlapping jurisdictions increase checks and balances and if law enforcers are able to coordinate their actions.

48. The emphasis of this book is on drug trafficking, yet illegal markets are complex, and one criminal organization can engage in several activities at the same time. A case in point is Medellín, where criminal organizations fight not only for drugs but also for controlling extortion and gambling. This was the case even during Pablo Escobar's time. See El Espectador, "Cerrojo a la oficina."

49. Christia, *Alliance Formation.*

50. Friman, "Drug Markets"; Skaperdas, "Political Economy," 187; Skaperdas and Konrad, "The Market."

51. Idler, "Exploring Agreements"; Rios, "How Government"; Williams, "Cooperation." In Mexico, such an arrangement can take the form of *derecho de piso,* or the right to pass through a territory in exchange for a monetary payment. In Colombia, criminal actors and armed actors coexist in a variety of arrangements with implications for the level of violence. There are indications that coexistence arrangements leading to peaceful interactions may have reduced violence in Cali in the mid-2000s, in Tijuana after 2010, and in Ciudad Juárez in 2011.

52. Christia, *Alliance.*

53. Lessing, "Logic."

54. In a competitive market, a cohesive state can protect one organization and attack its rivals, and rivals in turn may use visible violence against the state. However, a cohesive state can effectively enforce the law, and thus rivals may refrain from exposing violence because they know the state will enforce the law effectively against them. The situation changes if the state security apparatus is fragmented, because it may be less effective and different sectors may protect different organizations.

55. Criminals can outsource to other actors such as corrupt enforcement officials or mercenaries; however, access to such people is prohibitive and usually more complicated. Access to gangs is less prohibitive and more readily available.

56. Williams, "The Terrorism Debate."

57. Venkatesh, "The Social Organization."

58. Fujii, "The Puzzle."

59. Ceballos and Cronshaw, "The Evolution"; Salazar, *No nacimos.*

60. Arlacchi, *Mafia Business,* 221.

61. Grillo, *El Narco.*

62. Hagedorn, *A World of Gangs.*

63. Dowdney, *Children*; Misse and Vargas, "Drug Use."

64. Dowdney, *Children.*

65. The term "cartel" emerged mainly in journalistic and policy circles and is highly controversial in the academic literature on drug trafficking because it portrays a level of coordination that does not often exist in criminal organizations and networks. It is also criticized because the term "cartel" implies collusion to set prices, something that criminal organizations do not achieve often. Yet, organizations may be able to set prices and coordinate a broad range of actions, even if they operate in a decentralized manner. For example, in the 1980s the Cali and Medellín DTOs met to discuss the price of cocaine, and in 2004 several Mexican organizations met to try to set prices. Furthermore, as Molzahn et al. show ("Drug Violence"), the term "cartel" has a broader connotation in economics that includes formal and informal arrangements that affect production, competition, and prices, and trafficking

organizations do often engage in such agreements. To avoid the sometimes exaggerated connotation entailed in the term "cartel," I use the terms "drug-trafficking organizations" (DTOs) and "criminal organizations" to refer to organizations devoted to drug trafficking. The terms *DTOs* and *criminal organizations* can also be problematic especially when criminals engage in a variety of illegal activities, but I use it to emphasize the book's focus on drug trafficking. Sometimes I use the word "cartel" when an organization has been often known in this way and approaches some characteristics of the concept, as occurs with the Medellín cartel. For further discussion about the term "cartel," see Astorga, *El siglo de las drogas*; Dorn et al., *Traffickers*, x; Kenney, *From Pablo to Osama*; Naylor, "Mafias"; Paoli, "The Paradoxes"; and Reuter, *Disorganized*.

66. Dorn et al., "Drugs Importation"; Malm and Bichler, "Networks."
67. Idler, "Exploring."
68. Camacho and Lopez, "From Smugglers"; Eilstrup-Sangiovanni and Jones, "Assessing."
69. Guerrero, "La Raíz."
70. Bueno de Mesquita, "The Political Economy"; Gambetta, *Making Sense*; Ganor, "Terrorist Organization."
71. Shapiro, *Terrorist's Dilemma*.
72. Bailey and Dammert, *Public*; Fruhling, "Policia comunitaria"; Fruhling et al., *Crime and Violence*.
73. Davis, "Undermining"; Marenin, "Review."
74. Changes in the time horizons of public officials affect the predictability of power relations rather than fragmentation itself, yet uncertainty—or the possibility that power can be lost—implies that somebody can challenge power and, thus, that power is not concentrated in a single actor. In the minimalist definition of democracy, the uncertainty of electoral outcomes is possible because no single political force can determine them unilaterally (see Przeworski, *Democracy and the Market*, 12). Likewise, power within the security apparatus becomes more contested and fragmented when it is uncertain to achieve.
75. Moncada, "The Politics."
76. Putnam, "Diplomacy and Domestic Politics."
77. Gibson, "Boundary Control."
78. Kenny and Serrano, "Introduction."
79. Astorga, *El siglo*; Astorga and Shirk, "Drug Trafficking"; Flores, "El estado en crisis"; Serrano, "Narcotráfico."
80. Faletti, "A Sequential Theory."
81. Youngers and Rosin, *Drugs*.
82. Palacios and Serrano, "Colombia y México"; Ramírez, "Maintaining Democracy."
83. On scandals for electoral purposes, see Grzymala-Busse, "Beyond Clientelism," 658; Murillo and Martínez-Gallardo, "Political Competition," 124.
84. Colombia only experienced a brief dictatorship in 1957. Yet, for sixteen years (1958–1974) political competition was limited to two political parties in the framework of a power-sharing agreement known as Frente Nacional (National Front). On the effects of this political liberalization, see Gutiérrez, *Lo que el viento*; Romero, *Paramilitares*.
85. Astorga and Shirk "Drug Trafficking"; Snyder and Durán-Martínez, "Does Illegality."
86. Dell, "Trafficking Networks"; Osorio, "Hobbes"; Trejo and Ley, "Federalismo."
87. Shirk and Wallman, "Understanding."
88. Calderón et al., "Beheading"; Dorn et al., *Traffickers*, 35; Friman, "Forging"; Osorio, "The Contagion."
89. Lieberman, "Nested Analysis."
90. Snyder, "Scaling."
91. Lankina, "Sisyphean"; Moncada and Snyder, "Subnational."
92. Given the detailed coding involved and resource constraints, the data set includes only one year for most city-periods. Interviews and secondary data helped define these periods; this information then guided decisions about what years to collect information from in the data set, as the objective was to have detailed data for at least one year in each period. The process was dynamic and as fieldwork evolved I made new decisions about the need to collect information for a particular year.

93. I also assess frequency, comparing the national homicide rate and the evolution of violence in a city. Using homicide rates to measure frequency is not without problems but is the best estimate available for all city-years.
94. Andreas and Greenhill, *Sex, Drugs, and Body Counts.*
95. Finnegan, "The Kingpins."

Chapter 2

1. El Tiempo, "El Fin."
2. Parts of this chapter were originally published in *Violence and Crime in Latin America: Representations and Politics,* edited by Gema Santamaría and David Carey (Norman: University of Oklahoma Press, 2017).
3. *Pozole* is a traditional Mexican soup.
4. Procuraduría General de la República, Declaración.
5. Author's interview with the relative of a victim of disappearance in the mid-1990s, Tijuana, October 21, 2011.
6. Sartori, "Concept."
7. Kalyvas, *Logic*; Kalyvas, "Wanton and Senseless"; Tilly, *Regimes.*
8. Andreas and Wallman, "Illicit"; Astorga and Shirk, "Drug Trafficking"; Garzón, *Mafia*; Lessing, "The Logic"; Osorio, "Hobbes"; Rios, "How Government"; Rios and Shirk, "Drug Violence"; Snyder and Durán-Martínez, "Does Illegality." For a discussion about strategic uses of drug violence, see Williams, "The Terrorism Debate."
9. Lessing, "The Logic."
10. McCormick and Giordano, "Things," 312.
11. Hoffman and McCormick, "Terrorism"; Kydd and Walter, "The Strategies."
12. Tilly, *Regimes.*
13. Arias, *Drugs*; Dowdney, *Children.*
14. Staniland, "States."
15. Hoffman and McCormick, "Terrorism."
16. Kenney, *From Pablo.*
17. Attracting media and enforcement attention may not be the intended objective of using visible violence—the main intention may be to get the attention of rivals. But when criminals use visible violence, they are more likely to attract attention from law enforcement and media.
18. Eaton, "The State of the State."
19. Author's interview with former Colombian defense minister, Bogotá, January 13, 2011.
20. Author's interview with official from the Secretariat of Public Security, Mexico City, September 27, 2011.
21. Villagran, "The Victims."
22. Kalyvas, *Logic*, 59; Osorio, "Hobbes."
23. Author's interview with intelligence official from the Colombia Attorney General's Office, Bogotá, September 20, 2010.
24. Conrad and Greene, "Competition."
25. Paramilitary groups in Colombia lie in the blurry line between political and criminal violence, as they had a political agenda and they also consolidated control over international drug trafficking from the late 1990s on. Their actions could thus be both motivated politically and by the need to advance the trafficking business. Their reference here does not assume a criminal or a political motivation in their actions but rather shows that the concept of visibility captures fundamental changes in the strategic use of violence, especially when state complicity is present.
26. Confession hearings of commanders Jorge Laverde (El Iguano) and Ever Veloza (HH) taken from footage (and translation) in the 2011 documentary *Impunity*, by Juan José Lozano and Hollman Morris. Emphasis in the text is mine.
27. Moodie, "El Salvador," 60.
28. Goldstein, "The Drugs."
29. Goldstein, "The Relationship."
30. Kalyvas, *Logic.*

31. Kalyvas notes that the effectiveness of selective violence hinges on the perception that a process of selection is taking place (*Logic*, 192). Along these lines one could characterize violence in Mexico since 2006 as indiscriminate because the population perceives that the "honor code" of criminals has been broken and they kill randomly and nonselectively. Yet such perception is created more by the visibility of acts than by a technology of nondiscrimination.

32. Reuter, "Systemic."

33. Kalyvas, *Logic*, 23–25.

34. Arlacchi, *Mafia*, 28.

35. Author's data set on drug-related violence.

36. Weinstein, *Inside*.

37. Denyer Willis, *Killing*; Idler, "Arrangements.".

38. Blok, "Mafia"; Gambetta, *Codes*; Uribe, "Dismembering"; Uribe, *Matar*. Concepts like symbolic and performative violence could also appear useful but they are used to characterize nonlethal violence, such as protests or gendered violence, and not to parse out manifestations of lethal violence; see Bourdieu and Wacquant, "Symbolic"; Juris, "Violence."

39. Uribe, *Matar*.

40. Uribe and Medina, *Enterrar*.

41. Lomnitz, *Death*.

42. Bunker and Sullivan, "Extreme Barbarism."

43. Slone, "Responses."

44. Author's interview with a businessman, Tijuana, October 18, 2011.

45. According to the Committee to Protect Journalists (CPJ), forty-one journalists were assassinated in Mexico between 1992 and 2017 because of their profession, with most cases occurring since 2006. See CPJ's website: https://cpj.org/killed/americas/mexico/. Violence related to drugs and organized crime have made the country one of the most dangerous for journalism. Other sources that include cases where the motive has not been confirmed put the tally of journalists killed since 2006 over 130; see Heinle et al., "Drug Violence."

46. It is also plausible to think that if criminals have the power to manipulate journalists and they allow reports of their attacks, it is because they indeed have an interest in exposing violence. Not all manipulation is direct: given the enormous risks journalists face in Mexico, many of them have resorted to self-censorship.

47. For a discussion on a related concept, extralethal violence, see Fujii, "The Puzzle."

48. Arlacchi, *Mafia*, 14; Blok, "Mafia," 28.

49. El Espectador, "El Rio."

50. In this sense visibility is different from acts of violence that become scandals. Attacks that are not classified as visible in this book may end up generating scandals—often due to ad hoc circumstances. The trends that this book characterizes as visible go beyond single events that become scandals.

51. Observers in Ciudad Juárez in fact claim that federal forces were complicit or carried out extortion themselves. Author's interviews, Ciudad Juárez, July 2011 and March 2012.

52. For example, on May 1, 2010, a report from *El Diario* of Juárez read, "The employee identified as Moises Hernandez Martinez, 17 years old, was assassinated by several men that shot him with two firearms. According to the witnesses, the owner of the business had received several threats when he refused to pay 'the protection quota.'" (Author's translation from Spanish original).

53. The Stratfor Worldview report, "Polarization and Sustained Violence in Mexico's Cartel War," published on January 24, 2012 (now located on the Mafia&Co. website), describes, for example, how Los Zetas prefer brutality while the Sinaloa cartel prefers bribery.

54. Bailey, "What Do the Zetas."

55. Author's interview with official from the Secretariat of Public Security, Mexico City, October 27, 2011.

56. Los Zetas was created in 1996 as the enforcement branch of the Gulf DTO and was formed by a group of deserters from an airborne special forces unit in the Mexican military called the GAFES (Grupos Aeromóviles de Fuerzas Especiales). Los Zetas remained dormant for a few years, but beginning in 2003, they grew in size and power, becoming one of Mexico's most powerful criminal organizations, engaged not only in drug trafficking but also in a wide range

of criminal activities such as extortion and human trafficking. But even this mighty organization seemed to have weakened by 2013.

57. Duncan, *Del campo*, 30.
58. In Colombia both paramilitary groups and the guerrilla group known as FARC (Revolutionary Armed Forces of Colombia) made drug trafficking their main source of income complicating the armed conflict. The FARC's control focused for a long time on the cultivation and selling of coca paste while paramilitaries engaged more in commercialization and distribution; see Tickner, Garcia and Arreaza, "Actores," 421.
59. Trafficking organizations in Mexico do not have explicit political aims, with the probable exception of La Familia Michoacana and other smaller groups that publicized ideological platforms; see Finnegan, "Silver or Lead"; Grayson, "Mexico."
60. Laitin and Fearon define a civil conflict as one that involves "fighting between agents of (or claimants to) a state, and organized, nonstate groups who seek either to take control of a government, to take power in a region, or to use violence to change government policies"; see "Ethnicity," 76.
61. Bunker, "Introduction"; Grillo, *El Narco.*
62. Lessing, "The Logic"; Osorio, "Hobbes."
63. For a discussion of the controversies about counting drug-related killings in Mexico, see Ley, "El desafío"; Karlin, "Fueled by War"; Mendoza and Mossa, "El presidente"; Molloy, "Mexican Undead"; Molzahn et al., "Drug Violence"; and Steller, "Years of Killing."
64. The impunity rate (that is, the proportion of homicides that do not lead to a sentence, or that are never investigated) in Mexico was 84 percent in 2011 and for Colombia it was calculated at 97 percent in 2008; see Barreto and Rivera, "Una mirada"; Seguridad, Justicia, y Paz, "Impunidad."
65. Poire, "Los homicidios." Full coding details about the government's data set on drug related violence are available at http://www.presidencia.gob.mx/?DNA=119.
66. Restrepo et al., "El conflicto."
67. Comisión de Estudios, "Colombia."
68. Arocha et al., *Las violencias*; Guzmán, *Diagnóstico.*
69. Drug trafficking can generate other nonlethal forms of violence such as displacement. This book only focuses on lethal forms.
70. Pinheiro et al., "Homicídios"; Soares and Naritomi, "Understanding."
71. I thank Mundo Ramírez, Rocio Durán, and Ernesto Cañas for their valuable assistance in constructing this data set. Without their patient willingness to go through piles of dusty newspapers and, in a few cases, digital records, this database would have been impossible to construct.
72. Author's interview with security expert, Mexico City, August 20, 2008.
73. There might be cases of murder of public officials that do not capture much attention, as when there are isolated murders of street-level cops or when officers are killed off duty; see Denyer-Willis' study of the police in Sao Paulo (*Killing*) for an excellent discussion of this. Yet when police are systematically targeted, violence is visible, as in Medellín in the 1980s or in Ciudad Juárez since 2008.
74. Kalyvas, *Logic*, 89.
75. Grupo Interdisciplinario, *Informe.*
76. Most homicides take place in public spaces and thus the category does not present enough variation to be considered a separate dimension of visibility, especially because public spaces, as defined by property ownership, are not necessarily places that are constantly transited by the public, as occurs in rivers or roads. A further disaggregation of location in the database has been used to complement this characterization. Cities with more homicides in rivers are also cities where low visibility and high frequency have prevailed (Cali and Culiacán). The location of attacks has to be considered in tandem with the other variables, because an attack at a private space like a house can be very visible if it involves a shooting or an explosion.
77. Finnegan, "Silver."
78. Herman and Chomsky, *Manufacturing.*
79. Kleiman, "Surgical."

Chapter 3

1. Debates about the stability and quality of democracies in Latin America are active and ongoing. Many problems plague democracies with stable elections—for example, power concentration in the executive office. These problems have led scholars to advance more fine-grained concepts that capture the problems and paradoxes of democratic regimes; see, for example, Levitsky and Way, "Competitive Authoritarianism"; O'Donnell, "Delegative Democracy."

2. The paradoxical coexistence of violence and democracy in Colombia predates the democratizing wave of the 1990s. Colombia has long been one of the oldest democracies in the region and at the same time home to one of the longest-standing armed conflicts in the world; see Gutiérrez and Sánchez, Nuestra guerra. As Bejarano and Pizarro point out, however, the nature of such coexistence changed radically with the democratizing reforms of the mid-1980s; see "From 'Restricted' to 'Besieged.'"

3. Evans, Embedded; Skocpol, "Bringing."

4. Tilly, Regimes.

5. Beissinger, "Nationalist"; Brancati and Snyder, "Rushing"; Brass, Theft; Brubaker, Nationalism; Snyder, From Voting.

6. See Balcells, "Continuation"; Dunning, "Fighting"; Steele, "Electing."

7. Flores and Nooruddin, "The Effect."

8. For a discussion of this process in civil war, see Acemoglu et al., "The Monopoly"; in the case of criminal war, see Trejo and Ley, "Federalismo"; for a discussion of the toleration of riots, see Auyero, Routine; Wilkinson, Votes.

9. Arias and Goldstein, Violent Democracies, 21.

10. North et al., Violence.

11. Olson, "Dictatorship."

12. Pansters, Violence; Reno, "Congo."

13. Reno, "Congo."

14. Eaton, "The State"

15. Alexander, New Jim Crow.

16. Andreas and Durán-Martínez, "The International."

17. Kenney and Serrano, "Introduction."

18. Crandall, Driven.

19. Sáenz Rovner, La conexión, 146.

20. Meyer and Parssinen, Webs of Smoke.

21. Yongming, Anti-Drug.

22. Meyer and Parsinnen, Webs of Smoke.

23. Duncan, "Drug Trafficking."

24. Brinks, "A Tale."

25. Arias and Goldstein, Violent Democracies.

26. Sáenz Rovner, "Las redes."

27. Britto, "A Trafficker's"; Britto, "The Marihuana."

28. Gootenberg (Andean) traces the origins of cocaine as a legal global commodity to mid-nineteenth-century Peru. He describes how a small legal economy transformed into a large illegal commodity chain from the late 1940s onward. One key trend highlighted by Gootenberg, but still underresearched, is how regime and political transformations, such as the 1952 revolution in Bolivia, the 1959 Cuban Revolution, or the 1973 Chilean coup, transformed relations between states and drug-trafficking networks and shaped the specific routes, flows, and behavior of criminal actors.

29. Betancourt and García, Contrabandistas; Britto, "The Marihuana"; Sáenz Rovner, "Las redes."

30. Kenney, From Pablo to Osama.

31. Faletti, "A Sequential."

32. Thoumi, Political Economy, 213.

33. Procurator's intervention before the Senate, in Anales del Congreso, August 30, 1983 (translated from Spanish by the author).

34. In the 1970s, the army participated in marijuana crop eradication and it did not necessarily welcome these early antinarcotics roles, but as these operations were mostly rural, they were

not as contentious as the first attempts to deploy the army in urban antinarcotics operations. See Palacios and Serrano, "Colombia," 120.

35. An event that remains particularly controversial regarding the collaboration between traffickers and guerrillas is the seizing of the Palace of Justice by thirty-four members of the M-19 on November 6, 1985. According to a truth commission appointed to clarify the events, drug traffickers and Pablo Escobar may have supported this operation because it favored their opposition to extradition policies. However, it was concluded that not all the leaders of M-19 had knowledge of this alliance. See Gómez et al., *Informe final*.

36. Gutiérrez and Barón, "Estado"; Romero, *Paramilitares*.

37. Author's interview with former defense minister, Bogotá, January 13, 2011.

38. Pablo Escobar surrendered to authorities in June 1991, one month before the proclamation of the Constitution. After his brief stint in prison, violence in Colombia went to a new and even more extreme level. See Pardo, *De primera*, for a firsthand account of the events.

39. Pardo, *De primera*, 448.

40. Bowden, *Killing Pablo*.

41. Author's interview with former minister of defense, Bogotá, January 13, 2011.

42. El Tiempo, "Detenido el senador."

43. Freeman and Sierra, "Mexico," 285.

44. Crandall, *Driven*.

45. Ramírez, "Maintaining," 92.

46. Casas Dupuy, "Reformas."

47. Camacho, "La reforma"; Casas Dupuy, "Reformas"; Llorente, "Desmilitarización."

48. Even though after their capture the Rodriguez Orejuela continued operating in jail until 2000, when they were extradited.

49. Palacios and Serrano, "Colombia."

50. Crandall, *Driven*.

51. Gibson, "Boundary."

52. Thoumi, *Political Economy*.

53. Bagley, "Drug Trafficking"; Gootenberg, "Cocaine's Long March"; López, "Narcotráfico."

54. Felbab-Brown, *Shooting Up*; Gutiérrez, "Criminal."

55. Author's interview with former army colonel and former commander of the Search Bloc against the Cali DTO, Bogotá, September 1, 2011.

56. Mejía, "Evaluating."

57. There was also a social development component but it was small compared with the resources and political prominence given to the military component.

58. Mejía et al., "On the Effectiveness."

59. Mejía et al., "On the Effectiveness."

60. Tate, *Drugs*.

61. Dube and Naidu, "Bases."

62. Castillo et al., "Illegal."

63. Rico, "Las dimensiones."

64. Castillo et al., "Illegal"; Osorio, "The Contagion."

65. Even after the creation of the Autodefensas Unidas de Colombia (AUC, the United Self-Defense Forces of Colombia) in 1996, an umbrella paramilitary group that joined previously regionalized and fragmented groups throughout the country, the paramilitaries remained as a relatively decentralized organization; see Gutiérrez and Barón, "Estado." In this sense, international drug trafficking was not in the hands of a completely centralized and monopolistic group. But it was not in the hands of completely uncoordinated *cartelitos*, either.

66. Author's interview with former army colonel and former commander of the Search Bloc against the Cali DTO, Bogotá, September 1, 2011.

67. For a detailed discussion of the Democratic Security Polity, see Granada et al., "El agotamiento."

68. Granada et al., "El agotamiento," 51.

69. Duncan, *Los señores*; Snyder and Durán-Martínez, "Drugs."

70. Verdad Abierta, "Cinco años."

71. Comisión Nacional, *Disidentes*.

72. Romero, *Parapolítica*; Office of the High Commissioner, *Informe*.
73. Office of the High Commissioner, *Informe*; Uprimny and Saffon, "La ley."
74. Although limited by the above-mentioned problems, one positive consequence of the process was the creation of a Memory Group (Grupo de Memoria Histórica) that has produced excellent reports about armed actors in Colombia. Some reports are especially useful for clarifying the links between drug trafficking and paramilitarism.
75. Garzón, "La violencia."
76. Ávila and Velasco, *Democracias*; Office of the High Commissioner, *Report*.
77. International Crisis Group, *Desmantelar*.
78. Economic diversification sometimes extended to investment in legal activities such as oil exploitation or palm cultivation. For discussion of the diverse illegal activities of these groups, see Idler, "Exploring"; Indepaz, *Séptimo reporte*; International Crisis Group, *Desmantelar*.
79. Comisión Nacional, *Disidentes*; International Crisis Group, *Desmantelar*.
80. This is the case of a structure known as the ERPAC (Popular Revolutionary Anti-Insurgent Army of Colombia), which, rather than directly controlling production or international distribution, provided security and oversaw cocaine processing facilities; see International Crisis Group, *Desmantelar*.
81. Controversies about cultivation numbers are commonplace. In 2012, for instance, while the UN Office for Drugs and Crime reported a slight increase in hectares of coca cultivated in Colombia from 62,000 to 64,000 and a minor decrease in coca production of about 1 percent from 350 to 345 tons, the United States reported a decrease in cocaine production in Colombia of 25 percent from 270 to 195 metric tons of cocaine, falling behind Bolivia and Peru. See UNODC, *Colombia Coca Cultivation*; White House, "Survey Shows." Besides the wild divergences between the two sources, the US report was criticized because it was not clear how Colombia produced less cocaine than Bolivia even though it still had more hectares of coca cultivated. For an analysis of these numbers, see WOLA, "UN and US Cocaine"; Fox, "US Report."
82. Interview with intelligence official of the Colombia Attorney General's Office, September 13, 2010. Intelligence officials of the national police may be less likely to recognize the destabilizing power of criminal structures in the new era of drug trafficking.
83. Amat, "Debe permitirse" (author's translation).
84. Author's interview with police commander, Bogotá, August 30 and September 5, 2011.
85. Brinks, "A Tale."
86. A case in point is Lorena Henao, a member of the Norte del Valle DTO, who was captured in 2004 and released shortly afterward in 2011 after completing her sentence; see El Tiempo, "Asesinada."
87. In the United States the practice of reducing sentences in exchange for information has led many extradited criminals to get light sentences, as occurred with former members of the Cali DTO William Rodríguez, Phanor Arizabaleta, or Victor Patiño Fómeque, who obtained four years, nine months, and eight years in prison, respectively; see Revista Semana, "Fracasó."
88. Seguridad, Justicia, y Paz, "Metodología."
89. Focus group conducted in Medellín with Arturo Alvarado, Alberto Concha-Eastman, and the author in the framework of a comparative project titled "Juvenile Violence and Access to Justice in Latin America," coordinated by Arturo Alvarado at the Colegio de Mexico, funded by the International Development Research Centre (IDRC), and carried out between 2011 and 2013.
90. El Tiempo, "Son 903."
91. Molano, "Buenaventura." Interestingly, Victor Patiño, an old-time trafficker from the Norte del Valle DTO, commands the dominant group Los Rastrojos, reflecting the complex links between old and new traffickers.
92. Astorga, *El siglo*.
93. Astorga, *El siglo*.
94. Gootenberg, *Andean*, 273–275.
95. Astorga, *El siglo*, 101; Enciso, *Nuestra*.
96. Andreas, *Border Games*, 45–53.
97. Chabat, "Drug Trafficking."

98. Kenney and Serrano, "Introduction."

99. Astorga, *El siglo*, 169.

100. Lupsha, "Drug Lords"; Snyder and Durán-Martínez, "Drugs."

101. Paradoxically, military personnel of the garrison of the small town of Jiménez protected the plantation. See Arzt, *Democracia*.

102. Astorga, *El siglo*, 134.

103. In an illustration of the corruption of the DFS, Caro Quintero carried a DFS badge.

104. Arzt, *Democracia*.

105. *Sexenio* refers to the six-year term of Mexican presidents.

106. The pattern of PRI leadership resumed after the PAN attorney Antonio Lozano left in 1996, but it was broken again with the election of a PAN president in 2000. Another significant change in the Mexico Attorney General's Office was that since 1995 the attorney general's appointment by the president has been ratified by the Senate.

107. Artz, *Democracia*.

108. Author's interview with former high-level official of the Mexico Attorney General's Office, Mexico City, September 26, 2011.

109. Snyder and Durán-Martínez, "Does Illegality."

110. Snyder and Durán-Martínez, "Does Illegality."

111. Serrano and Kenny, "Introduction."

112. Artz, *Democracia*.

113. Kenny and Serrano, "Introduction."

114. Astorga, *El siglo*.

115. Raúl Salinas was also accused of being the intellectual author of the assassination of his brother-in-law José Francisco Ruiz Massieu.

116. Between 2000 and 2004, approximately 61,000 members of the GAFES and GANFES (the Amphibian Special Forces Group) deserted the military for their "lack of adaptation to the military environment." See La Crónica de Hoy, "Los Zetas."

117. El Universal, "Desertan"; Padgett, "Guatemala's Kaibiles."

118. Benítez Manaut, "México."

119. Kenny and Serrano, "Introduction."

120. Tokatlián, "The War," 72.

121. Bailey and Chabat, *Transnational*.

122. Calderón et al., "Beheading"; Osorio, "The Contagion."

123. Trejo and Ley, "Federalismo."

124. Arzt, *Democracia*.

125. Schatz et al., "The Mexican."

126. Author's interview with former high-ranking officer of the Mexico Attorney General's Office, Mexico City, September 26, 2011.

127. Molzahn et al., "Drug Violence"; Osorio, "Hobbes"; Rios, "How Government."

128. Escalante, *El homicidio*.

129. Durán-Martínez, "Drugs Around."

130. See National Drug Intelligence Center, *National Drug*. These statistics can be interpreted in different ways. An increase in seizures can reflect both heightened enforcement and growing markets. Yet decreased seizures are usually interpreted as a reduction in markets rather than as a sign of lenient policing.

131. Presidencia de la República, "Boletín."

132. Osorio, "Hobbes."

133. Calderón et al., "Beheading"; Osorio, "The Contagion."

134. Trejo and Ley, "Federalismo."

135. Guerrero, "La raíz"; Lessing, "The Logic."

136. Trejo and Ley, "Federalismo."

137. Shirk, "Drug Violence."

138. Durán-Martínez et al., "Drug Violence."

139. Molzahn et al., "Drug Violence."

140. México Evalúa, *Índice*; Osorio, "Hobbes."

141. Merino, "Los operativos."

142. Rodríguez, "La Iniciativa Mérida."

143. See Priest, "US Role."

144. See, for example, Barry McCaffrey's remarks in 2008, characterizing Calderón's policy as courageous and heroic ("After Action Report").

145. Calderón et al., "Beheading."

146. See Guerrero, "La raiz" and "La dispersión" for detailed analysis of the fragmentation of criminal organizations during Calderón's period.

147. Grayson, *The Evolution*.

148. In the first case, the migrants were killed for not paying an extortion fee (and probably also in a failed attempt at forced recruitment). In the second case, the casino was burned because the owners had not paid their protection quota.

149. Hernández Navarro, "Peña Nieto's."

150. See Heinle et al., "Drug Violence"; INEGI, "Datos."

151. Comisión Nacional, *Resumen*; Lohmuller, "No Solution."

152. Interamerican Commission, *Human Rights*.

153. For a discussion of the trends of criminal groups during Peña Nieto's term, see Corcoran, "Mexico Government."

154. Between 2006 and 2016, seventy-five mayors had been murdered. See La Jornada," Asesinaron"; Trejo and Ley, "High Profile."

155. There were 188,244 such detentions between January 1, 2007, and June 30, 2012, according to the Sixth Report of Activities of the Mexico Attorney General's Office, August 2012.

156. Stone, "Under Calderón."

157. Heinle et al., "Drug Violence."

158. According to data from the Registro Nacional de Datos de Personas Extraviadas o Desaparecidas, https://www.gob.mx/sesnsp/acciones-y-programas/registro-nacional-de-datos-de-personas-extraviadas-o-desaparecidas-rnped; see also Interamerican Commission, *Human Rights*.

159. Human Rights Watch, *Los desaparecidos*.

160. Author's interview with high-level official of the Secretariat of Public Security, Mexico City, September 27, 2011.

161. Brinks, "A Tale."

162. Bejarano and Pizarro, "From Restricted."

Chapter 4

1. See, for example, Faiola, "Sustaining"; Fukuyama and Colby, "Half a Miracle."

2. Franco, "Prácticas"; Safford, "Foreign"; Salazar and Jaramillo, *Medellín*; Walton, *Elites*.

3. In Medellín by 2005 the population more than doubled its 1973 size; see Lamb, "Microdynamics."

4. This period is known as La Violencia (with capital letters) and refers to the interparty violence initiated in 1948 that constituted the seed of modern armed conflict in Colombia; see Palacios and Safford, *Colombia*.

5. Roldán, "Wounded"; Salazar and Jaramillo, *Medellín*.

6. Comisión, *La huella*.

7. Escalante, *El Homicidio*; Kalyvas, *Logic*.

8. Gutiérrez and Jaramillo, *Medellín*, 197.

9. Riaño, *Dwellers*; Salazar, *La parábola*.

10. Bowden, *Killing*.

11. Some studies have questioned the idea of Escobar's organization as highly centralized and organized, see Kenney, *From Pablo*. Yet his leadership and power were far more centralized than the leadership that exists nowadays in Colombian trafficking organizations.

12. Lamb, "Microdynamics"; Salazar, *No nacimos*.

13. Medina Franco, *Historia*.

14. Salazar and Jaramillo, *Medellín*, 92.

15. The relationships between the Cali and Medellín DTOs were tense at least as early as 1984, when the Cali DTO leader Gilberto Rodríguez Orejuela was arrested in Spain and Escobar allegedly tried to take advantage of this situation to gain market share.

16. Communiqué of Los Extradibles to the Colombian people, April 1, 1990. Author's archives.

17. Escobar escaped from prison in July 1992 after a scandal made his luxurious living conditions in prison public and forced the government to announce Escobar's prison transfer. See Pardo, *De primera.*

18. Serrano, *La multinacional,* 85.

19. Bowden, *Killing;* Chaparro, *Historia,* 212–230; Clawson and Lee, *The Andean,* 176.

20. Such as the dismantling of the "Tranquilandia" drug-processing facility described in chapter 3.

21. Camacho and López, "From Smugglers."

22. Jaramillo and Salazar, *Medellín.*

23. Medellín and nine other municipalities make up the region known as the Metropolitan Area of the Valle de Aburrá. Administratively, each municipality is independent, but in practice they are extremely interconnected. In fact, Medellín's subway system runs from the municipality of Bello in the north to Itagüí in the south.

24. The Frente Nacional, described in chapter 3.

25. Sergio Fajardo, the mayor of Medellín in the period 2003–2007, who is credited with a reduction of violence in the city, told me in an interview that during his term there was no collaboration with any other mayor in the metropolitan area: "I could not count on the nearby government—for example, think about councilman [Gustavo] Upegui in Envigado, who was murdered because of his links with drug trafficking and yet was mourned in the city's council." Author's interview, Bogotá, November 6, 2010.

26. Gutiérrez, *Lo que el viento.*

27. The effective number of parties (a measure of political competition) for Senate elections in Medellín for the period 1970–1982 was 2.42 and it increased to 2.6 for the period 1982–1994. Similarly, the same indicator for the Lower Chamber was 2.40 in 1970–1982 and increased to 3.88 in 1982–1994, and in the local council the effective number of parties went from 2.54 in 1970–1982 to 3.30 in 1982–1994. (Author's analysis of data provided by Congreso Visible, Universidad de los Andes.)

28. Pardo, *De primera,* 193.

29. Arrázola, "Todo empezó."

30. Lamb, "Microdynamics," 55.

31. Salazar, *No nacimos.*

32. Lamb, "Microdynamics," 52.

33. El Tiempo, "Extraditables."

34. These communiqués belong to the author's personal archive.

35. Salazar, *La parábola,* 183.

36. According to statistics from the Directorate of Criminal Investigation and Interpol (DIJIN) in Colombia. In the same period Cali experienced fewer (270) terrorist acts.

37. Bahamon, *Mi guerra,* 14–15. Author's translation from Spanish original text.

38. Bahamon, *Mi guerra,* 27. Author's translation from Spanish original text.

39. After the assassination of presidential candidate Luis Carlos Galán, President César Gaviria issued a series of public order decrees. One of the measures that was adopted authorized the detention of suspects for seven days.

40. Bahamon, *Mi guerra,* 34. Author's translation from Spanish original text.

41. Lessing, *Logics.*

42. Author's interview with former minister Rafael Pardo, Bogotá, January 13, 2011; author's interview with Sergio Fajardo, Bogotá, November 6, 2010. See El Tiempo, "En Libertad."

43. At the beginning of 1990, Los Extradibles denounced that the police had massacred thirteen people with criminal antecedents at a farmhouse in the outskirts of Medellín. This was another of Los Extradibles' alleged motivations to declare a war against police officers.

44. Pardo, *De primera,* 344.

45. Medina Franco, *Historia.*

46. Serrano, *The Multinational,* 66.

47. Lamb, "Microdynamics," 67.

48. For extensive descriptions and accounts of paramilitary violence, see the websites www.verdadabierta.com and http://www.centrodememoriahistorica.gov.co/.

49. In fact, the Castaño brothers, paramilitaries who were part of Los Pepes, eventually became leaders of the main paramilitary force in Colombia, the Autodefensas Unidas de Colombia (AUC).

50. Jaramillo and Salazar, *Medellín*. Such influence even extends to current young generations engaged in violence. Referring to a twenty-year-old sicario captured in 2010, an intelligence official I interviewed remarked, "For Caliche [the sicario], Pablo Escobar is a guardian angel . . . They [sicarios] adore him and consider him a saint. You can see that Escobar's influence continues for an entire generation" (author's interview, Bogotá, September 13, 2010).

51. Author's interview with military intelligence official, Bogotá, January 31, 2011.

52. Ceballos and Cronshaw, "The Evolution," 118.

53. Quoted in Salazar, *No nacimos*, 32, author's translation from Spanish original text.

54. Quoted in Salazar, *No nacimos*, 68, author's translation from Spanish original text.

55. Ramírez, "Medellín"; Riaño, *Dwellers*.

56. Ramírez, "Medellín."

57. El Colombiano, July 1, 1984, 14b. Author's data set on drug-related violence.

58. Kalyvas, *Logic*.

59. Salazar, *No nacimos*.

60. Author's interview with former minister of defense Rafael Pardo, Bogotá, January 13, 2011.

61. Pardo, *De primera*, 448.

62. Bowden, *Killing*.

63. Riaño, *Dwellers*.

64. Ceballos and Cronshaw, "The Evolution"; Jaramillo, *Milicias*; Medina Franco, *Historia*.

65. Riaño, *Dwellers*, 33.

66. Jaramillo et al., *En la encrucijada*.

67. Bagley, "Drug Trafficking."

68. Ceballos and Cronshaw, "The Evolution," 125.

69. Roldán, "Wounded"; Valencia, "Los Caminos."

70. Romero, *Paramilitaries*.

71. These assassinations involved two academics-activists from a prominent Jesuit NGO (the Center for Research and Popular Education, or CINEP), an academic from the University of Antioquia, and the famous political comedian Jaime Garzón. See Semana, "La Entrega." This book's emphasis on criminal violence does not negate the complex motivations behind violence, which in these cases was purely political. Yet it is clear that without commanding both political and criminal groups, it was difficult for any armed actor to use criminality in the way the paramilitaries did.

72. Revista Semana, "El fin del terror."

73. Interview with former peace and security advisor of the Medellín mayor's office, Medellín, October 26, 2010.

74. Comisión Nacional, *La huella*.

75. Arenas and Escobar, "Discursos."

76. Moncada, *Cities*, documents how earlier in the decade Medellín's mayors opposed programs advanced by the national government to address violence. That situation changed in the late 1990s when mayor and president coincided in a militaristic approach to security.

77. A *comuna* is a numbered subdivision within the city, comprising several neighborhoods. There are sixteen comunas in Medellín.

78. Comisión Nacional, *La huella*, 76.

79. El Colombiano, "Desarticulada."

80. Angarita, *Dinámicas*; Comisión Nacional, *La huella*.

81. Civico, "We Are."

82. Oude and Rozema, "Fatal."

83. Evidence about these forms of violence became public as part of the demobilization process of paramilitary groups initiated in 2002. El Colombiano, "Don Berna reconoció."

84. Baird, "Héroes"; Riaño, *Dwellers*.

85. Author's interview with community organizer, Medellín, October 27, 2010.
86. Alonso et al., "Medellín"; Cruz and Durán-Martínez, "Hiding"; Riaño, *Dwellers*; Velez, "Conflicto."
87. Comisión Nacional, *La huella*, 60.
88. Riaño, *Dwellers*, 202.
89. Author's interview with community organizer, Medellín, October 27, 2010.
90. Author's interview with Sergio Fajardo, Bogotá, November 6, 2010.
91. Alonso et al., "Medellín"; Comisión Nacional, *La huella*.
92. Author's interview with former peace and security advisor of the mayor's office, Medellín, October 26, 2010.
93. Revista Semana, "Los secretos."
94. Instituto Popular de Capacitación, "En deuda," 162, 170; Instituto Popular de Capacitación, "Un poco," 223; Ramírez, "Medellín."
95. Author's interview with security analyst and social worker of the mayor's office, Robledo neighborhood, Medellín, October 28, 2010.
96. El Espectador, "Queríamos."
97. Instituto Popular de Capacitación, "En deuda," 170.
98. Personeria, *Informe*.
99. Author's interview with commander of police station, Medellín, October 23, 2010.
100. Insuasty, "Delitos."
101. Wood has analyzed the enormous variation that exists in forms of wartime sexual violence. Strategic sexual violence may be one of such forms that "appears to occur when an armed group believes it to be an effective form of terror against or punishment of a targeted group"; "Variation," 331.
102. Riaño, *Dwellers*.
103. Corporación Humanas, "Situación."
104. Oude Breuil and Rozema, "Fatal."
105. The demobilized men were concentrated for three weeks in La Ceja, a municipality near Medellín, and then they returned to their neighborhoods of origin. See Balbín, *Violencias*; Human Rights Watch, *Paramilitaries*; Vivanco, "Discurso."
106. Alonso and Valencia, "Balance."
107. Author's interview with former mayor Sergio Fajardo, Bogotá, November 6, 2010.
108. By contrast to Fajardo's decision, Luis Eduardo Garzón, Bogotá's mayor at the time, decided not to engage in the demobilization and to leave the responsibility in the hands of the national government. His relationship with the national government was conflicted on this issue. Author's interview with former peace and security advisor of the mayor's office, Medellín, October 26, 2010.
109. Alonso and Valencia, "Balance."
110. Author's interview with police commander, Medellín, October 25, 2010.
111. Instituto Popular de Capacitación, "En deuda."
112. Instituto Popular de Capacitación, "Un poco," 144.
113. Personal calculations based on statistics from DANE (National Statistics Department of Colombia).
114. Comisión Nacional, *La huella*.
115. Pressly, "The Dump."
116. El Espectador, "Las Confesiones," author's translation from Spanish original text.
117. See López, *Y refundaron*.
118. In total, 943 politicians were involved in the *parapolitica* scandal between 2007 and 2012, including 41 former mayors and 20 governors. Verdad Abierta, "Cinco años."
119. Ávila and Velasco, *Democracias*.
120. Author's interview with former peace and security advisor of the mayor's office, Medellín, October 26, 2010.
121. It is beyond the scope of this work to discuss the nature of the groups operating in Medellín after 2011, but several reports show that the political dimensions of their behavior, such as killing social leaders, were still present several years later. See Human Rights Watch, *Paramilitaries*.

122. Human Rights Watch, *Paramilitaries*; Misión de Apoyo, *Séptimo.*
123. Instituto Popular de Capacitación, "Transporte."
124. Interview conducted by Arturo Alvarado, Alberto Concha, and the author with NGO focused on violence and conflict issues, conducted for the project Juvenile Violence, Policing, and Access to Justice in Latin America, directed by Arturo Alvarado at the Colegio de México, Medellín, August 24, 2011.
125. Reuter, "Systemic."
126. Author's interview with security analyst and social worker from the mayor's office, Medellín, October 29, 2010.
127. Author's interview with local expert, Medellín, October 25, 2010.
128. Author's interview with violence prevention practitioner, Medellín, October 26, 2010.
129. Author's interview with local councilwoman, Medellín, October 28, 2010.
130. El Espectador, "El Rio."
131. Interview conducted by Arturo Alvarado, Alberto Concha, and the author with NGO, conducted for the project Juvenile Violence, Policing, and Access to Justice in Latin America, directed by Arturo Alvarado at the Colegio de México, Medellín, August 22, 2011.
132. Author's conversation with members of the Human Rights Association, Comuna 6, Medellín, October 29, 2010.
133. Interview conducted by Arturo Alvarado, Alberto Concha, and the author with NGO, conducted for the project Juvenile Violence, Policing, and Access to Justice in Latin America, directed by Arturo Alvarado at the Colegio de México, Medellín, August 22, 2011
134. Author's interview with security analyst and social worker of the mayor's office in the Robledo neighborhood, Medellín, October 28, 2010.
135. Personeria de Medellín, *Informe 2011.*
136. Author's interview with local human rights NGO, Medellín, October 29, 2010.
137. Cerdá et al., "Reducing."
138. Moncada, *Cities.*
139. Baird, "Héroes"; Samper, "Urban."
140. Abello-Colak and Guarneros-Meza, "The Role."
141. As of 2011, there were more than one hundred local programs for attention to youth in Medellín. The city budget for youth programs was about $3.7 million and the city office for youth programs (Metrojuventud) had a larger budget than that of the national office for youth (Colombia Joven).
142. Author's interview with analyst and social worker from the mayor's office, Medellín, October 27, 2010.

Chapter 5

1. In the early 1990s, and thanks to the leadership of Cali's mayor, the physician Rodrigo Guerrero, the city became internationally known for applying an epidemiological approach to violence and a preventive framework for citizen security, which was then promoted through the Interamerican Development Bank and other international institutions. The program was abandoned when Guerrero left office. (Guerrero was reelected as mayor in 2011). For a detailed discussion of these preventive security frameworks, see Concha Eastman et al., "La epidemiología"; Moncada, "Toward" and *Cities.*
2. Since the 1950s Cali has been subject to intense and diverse migration flows that derive from the city's midcentury industrial expansion but also from forced displacement caused by the armed conflict. The migration of black populations is particularly prominent, and Cali is the urban center with the largest population of African descent in Colombia, which is concentrated in the city's poorest areas. See Moncada, "Toward"; Barbary, "Afrocolombianos."
3. Betancourt, *Mediadores*, 132.
4. Chepesiuk, *The Bullet*, 63.
5. Kenney, *From Pablo.*
6. Quinn, "A Day." Rodriguez went to say, "[Ruiz Barrera] was commander of the Fourth Brigade from 1986 to 1988, if I'm not wrong. He chased Mr. [Pablo] Escobar and his partners persistently, and yet he failed in all his attempts. He didn't succeed with the Medellín cartel.

Thus the Cali cartel was invented, and with it the war over the New York market. Of course, this tale about the Cali cartel has been helped along by my differences with Mr. Escobar."

7. Author's interview with army brigadier, Bogotá, September 1, 2011.

8. Even though Escobar sent sicarios to Cali, there was never a massive move of force that could threaten the Cali DTO's local power. By contrast, the situation of Ciudad Juárez, described in chapter 6, shows how the power of the Juárez DTO was challenged by the physical move of force carried out by the Sinaloa DTO.

9. Vicepresidencia de la República, *Caracterización*.

10. Guillermo Pallomari, accountant for the Rodríguez Orejuela brothers, described in his judicial testimony that there was a person in the organization's security area whose role was to contact police officers and military to work for Miguel Rodríguez. (Fiscalía General de la Nación, Diligencia).

11. Chaparro, *Historia*, 127.

12. Guzmán, *Diagnóstico*, 24, 42; Universidad del Valle, *Construir*.

13. Vanegas, *Cali*; Vicepresidencia de la República, *Dinámica*.

14. Reuter suggests that the decrease of violence in drug markets in the United States might be related to a generational change and a shrinking young population. This book's cases show, however, that there is variation among cities with similar population structures. See Reuter, "Systemic."

15. Between 1973 and 2001, the population aged ten to twenty-nine years represented 41 percent of the total population in Cali and 40 percent in Medellín.

16. The Cauca River borders the eastern part of Cali.

17. Author's interview with army colonel, Bogotá, January 31, 2011.

18. Betancourt, *Mediadores*, 165, author's translation from original Spanish text.

19. The United Nations defines social cleansing as the elimination of impoverished and marginalized sectors of the population; see Stannow, "Social."

20. Guzmán, *Diagnóstico*; Guzmán and Camacho, *Violencia*; and Vanegas, *Cali* describe the complex dynamics and multiple actors involved in social cleansing in Cali, including state authorities, businesspeople, militias, neighborhood groups. They also describe how social cleansing was related to political violence and, especially in 1985, with an effort to eliminate the M-19, a major guerrilla group that started to expand its presence in the city beginning in 1984.

21. Stannow, "Social."

22. Betancourt, *Mediadores*, 136; Bowden, *Killing*.

23. According to Rodrigo Guerrero, the first mayor elected outside traditional parties in 1990, Cali's main problem is the control of a strong political class that blocks every reform effort. Author's interview, Cali, November 11, 2010.

24. Camacho and Guzmán, *Colombia*, 185.

25. Camacho and Guzmán, *Colombia* 139.

26. Rodríguez and Rodríguez, *Las confesiones*, 58, author's translation from original text in Spanish.

27. In 1994, the US government approved the use of a certification process to condition aid to Colombia on the progress on the war on drugs. In 1996, Colombia was for the first time decertified, and in the same year, the visa of the Colombian president Ernesto Samper was revoked.

28. Author's interview with former defense minister, Bogotá, January 13, 2011.

29. Vargas et al., *El presidente*.

30. Informal conversations between the author and residents during fieldwork conducted in Cali in July 2008; Arias, *Drugs*.

31. As seen in chapter 3, according to Casas Dupuy (*Reformas*), the operational changes that took place in the police between 1995 and 1998 reversed a reform process initiated in 1993 aimed at decentralizing the structure of police forces, strengthening their civilian nature and community oversight, and professionalizing them. By contrast, the process occurring between 1995 and 1999 recentralized police forces (for example, by giving the national director of the police discretionary authority over firings and dismissals) and gave more autonomy to the institution.

32. El Tiempo, "Bajo la presión."

33. Author's interview with local intelligence agent of the Attorney General's office, Cali, November 12, 2010.

34. Author's interview with military colonel of the Search Bloc, Bogotá, January 31, 2011.

35. This dynamic of dilation is narrated in the book *El Cartel de los Sapos* (The Snitches' Cartel) authored by Andrés López a former member of the Cartel del Norte del Valle, which has become the basis of numerous soap operas in Colombia.

36. A paramilitary leader who considered that the war was starting to be noisy and detrimental for illegal business and armed action in the region apparently mediated the truce. See El Pais, "El ocaso"; Revista Semana, "La jugada."

37. Duncan, *Del campo*, 45.

38. Interviews conducted by Alberto Concha-Eastman for the project Juvenile Violence, Policing, and Access to Justice in Latin America, directed by Arturo Alvarado at the Colegio de México.

39. Observatorio Social, *Homicidios*, 3, author's translation from original text in Spanish.

40. See Observatorio Social, *Homicidios*. This calculation includes organizations devoted to large-scale crime and connected to drug trafficking, oficinas, and "corner groups" usually dedicated to drug use and occasional petty robbery.

41. Author's interview with police commander, Bogotá, August 30, 2011.

42. Multiple reports document how Varela and Montoya attempted to ally with paramilitaries to be able to demobilize within the peace process that the government started in 2003. They did not succeed in posing as paramilitaries, partially because their trafficking past was too evident. Their failure contrasted with the success of the long-time criminal Diego Fernando Murillo in becoming a paramilitary leader in Medellín, which allowed him to demobilize and monopolize all sectors of criminality (chapter 4).

43. Author's interview with a local intelligence agent of the Attorney General's office, Cali, November 12, 2010.

44. Revista Semana, "Don Diego."

45. Programa de Naciones Unidas, *Hacia*.

46. Gutiérrez et al., "Politics."

47. A UN Development Program report (Programa de Naciones Unidas, *Hacia*, 291) explains that local governments in Cali have been poorly viewed in the public opinion, and in one case a mayor was impeached. Scandals, however, usually emerge out of civil society or media efforts but not out of exposure by political opponents.

48. Martínez was born in a small municipality of the Pacific department (state) of Cauca, and his power extended to the departments of Cauca, Choco, and Valle.

49. Revista Cambio, "El hombre"; El Tiempo, "Senador."

50. See Ávila and Velasco, *Democracias*; Corporación Nuevo Arco Iris, *Mafias*.

51. De Francisco, "El doble"; Llorente, "Desmilitarización."

52. Revista Semana, "La vida útil."

53. On October 13 and December 12, 2003, there were two massacres in Cali: one in a dance club and the other in a mall, both related to the confrontation between Varela and Montoya.

54. Revista Semana, "Corrupción."

55. Author's interview in Cali, November 12, 2010.

56. Revista Semana, "Un año."

57. Author's interview with local intelligence official from the Attorney General's Office, Cali, November 12, 2010.

58. Lupsha, "Drug Lords."

59. Astorga, *El siglo*.

60. Astorga, *El siglo*; Flores, "El Estado"; Serrano, "Narcotráfico."

61. According to data from the INEGI website, compared to other major cities and to the national average in Mexico, in Culiacán the share of agricultural activities to the GDP is very high (about 12 percent compared to 3.7 percent nationwide), and Culiacán is one of Mexico's leading producers of corn, tomatoes, peppers, and livestock. Yet commerce and service also represent a big proportion of the city's GDP (21 percent compared to 15 percent nationwide), and Culiacán is the headquarters for companies of national importance including Coppel, Casa Ley, and Comex.

62. Craig, "Operation"
63. Astorga, *El siglo*, 118; Smith, "Drug Trafficking."
64. The average homicide rate for Cali in the period 1984–2010 was 79.6, considerably higher than the Culiacán average of 34.1 for that period. This difference reflects the impact of long-standing armed conflict in Colombia. Yet these two cities are comparable because in their national context both were considerably more violent than the rest of the country.
65. Author's interview with journalist Javier Valdez (RIP), Culiacán, March 18, 2011. The same statement appeared in most of my interviews in Culiacán.
66. Interviews conducted between March 18 and March 26, 2011, in Culiacán.
67. There are so many of these cenotaphs that in 2008 the mayor's office discussed the possibility of removing all of them.
68. Astorga, *El siglo*, 166.
69. Astorga, *El siglo*, 145.
70. Órtiz Pinchetti, "El hombre."
71. Astorga, *El siglo*, 167; Blancornelas, *El cartel*, 54.
72. With the exception of the Arellano Félix brothers, who were born in Culiacán's middle class and were more educated and urban.
73. Astorga, *El siglo*, 178.
74. *Cholos* is a term used to characterize a youth cultural expression that emerged in the 1960s mixing American and Mexican identities, especially in border areas, and is associated with particular dress codes such as wearing baggie pants and bandanas. In the public imagination cholos are often associated with criminality, although in most cases cholos are not actually criminals or members of a street gang. See Valenzuela, *El futuro*.
75. Author's interview with academic, Culiacán, March 19, 2011; author's interviews with journalist Javier Valdez, Culiacán, March 18 and 19, 2011.
76. Author's interviews with an academic and local expert, Culiacán, March 19 and July 1, 2011.
77. Lazcano y Ochoa, *Una vida*.
78. Author's interview with state deputy for Sinaloa, Culiacán, March 23, 2011.
79. Author's interview with official from the Sinaloa governor's office, Culiacán, June 28, 2011.
80. Alvarado, "Las elecciones."
81. Alvarado, "Las elecciones."
82. Astorga, *El siglo*.
83. Alvarado, "Las elecciones," 285–289.
84. Lazcano y Ochoa, *Una vida*, 250, author's translation from original text in Spanish.
85. A safe house is a place used to hide arms, drugs, or hostages; safe houses are also often locations for conducting violent acts such as torture or hiding corpses.
86. For journalistic accounts of the violent events that day, see El Noroeste, "Arroja" and "Son doce."
87. Author's interview with local journalist, Culiacán, March 18, 2011.
88. Author's interview with transit police, Culiacán, March 13, 2011.
89. The translation of these messages is challenging given their extensive use of slang and grammar mistakes. The original message in this case read *Ay te va la reversa Chapo, te va a caer la Uka (la verga sin peluka) agarrense Chapos y Zambadas, despertaron al mostro de los cielos.* Another message read, *Dinastía Zambada, toda llena de cagada cuando no traicionan, matan a su misma gente como hicieron con Mario Quijote Deda Niño* (Zambada dynasty, all full of shit when you don't betray, you kill your own people, as you did with Mario Quijote Deda Niño). See El Noroeste, "Más narcomantas."
90. Author's interview with journalist Javier Valdez, Culiacán, March 18, 2011; Ravelo, "Historias."
91. Rio Doce, "El otro."
92. Franco, "Patrullan."
93. Author's interview with state police officers, Culiacán, March 25, 2011.
94. Although López Valdez had been a PRI politician and won with the support of the PRI machinery.
95. El Noroeste, "Vuelve."
96. Except in 1996 when Sadol Osorio from PAN was elected as mayor of Culiacán.

97. Davis, "Theoretical"; Davis and Libertun de Duran, *Cities*.
98. Grillo, *El Narco*, 106.
99. Author's interview with journalist Javier Valdez, Culiacán, March 18, 2011.
100. Author's interview with informant, Culiacán, July 1, 2011.
101. Hansen and Stepputat, *States*; Weinstein, "Mumbai's."
102. Tuckman, "Life after."
103. Associated Press, "Sons."

Chapter 6

1. For a discussion of the imageries constructed in the United States about security on the border, see Payan, *The Three*.
2. Also known as the Carrillo Fuentes organization.
3. *Maquiladoras* are the assembly plants of transnational companies that have located their production sites in Mexico to take advantage of low labor costs.
4. Comprising ten siblings (seven men and three women) and their mother, Alicia Félix, all of whom, to different degrees, became crucial protagonists of drug trafficking in Tijuana. See Blancornelas, *El cartel*.
5. Astorga, *El siglo*.
6. Blancornelas, *El cartel*, 187.
7. Astorga, *El siglo*, 178.
8. In other places, such as Sinaloa, people use the label *narcojuniors* to refer to the children of drug traffickers, the second generation.
9. Blancornelas and González, "Amigo"; Blancornelas and González, "Juniors."
10. Blancornelas, "Descobijaron."
11. Author's interviews with academic from Tijuana, September 13, 2011, and human rights worker, Tijuana, September 14, 2011.
12. Weisel, "The Evolution."
13. Jones, "Explaining."
14. Members of Barrio Logan participated in an attempt on the life of the journalist Jesús Blancornelas in November 1997. See Blancornelas, *El cartel*, 305.
15. Author's interview with official from the Secretariat of Public Security, Tijuana, September 13, 2011.
16. Author's data set on drug-related violence.
17. Martínez and Howard, "Mortalidad."
18. Author's calculation based on SINAIS data.
19. Blancornelas, *El cartel*, 301.
20. Aguirre et al., "Quiénes mataron."
21. Guzmán later escaped prison (in an infamous cinematographic episode), in January 2001.
22. Some reports suggest that Benjamin Arellano (the oldest and at the time most powerful Arellano Félix brother) in a good-will gesture to the authorities after the killing of Cardenal Posadas, arranged for safe houses to be sacrificed and that he turned the Logan gang members engaged in the shooting in to the police, to help the state give the appearance of a strong crackdown. See Jones, "The State Reaction."
23. Kenney and Serrano, "Introduction."
24. Ravelo, "Estructura."
25. Blancornelas, "Dicho."
26. Blancornelas, *El cartel*, 330.
27. Magaloni, *Voting*.
28. Rodríguez and Ward, "Political," 41.
29. Astorga, *El siglo*, 175.
30. The attorney general was then replaced by a member of PAN, Juan Francisco Franco, who was also later accused of (but not investigated for) providing official identification cards of the state attorney's office to hitmen of the Arellano Félix—who had been involved in a shootout at a club in Puerto Vallarta—and of otherwise supporting the Arellano Félix organization. Author's interview with journalist, Tijuana, September 15, 2011.

31. Rodríguez and Ward, "Political," 58–61.

32. Author's interviews with journalists, Tijuana, September 15 and 16, 2011.

33. Hernández and Negrete, *La experiencia*; Rodriguez and Ward, "Politics."

34. Blancornelas, *El cartel*, 83–86, author's translation from original text in Spanish.

35. Moore, "Drug Traffickers."

36. González and Ortíz, "Tijuana."

37. Blancornelas et al., "La mafia."

38. Blancornelas and González, "Juniors."

39. Blancornelas et al., "La mafia."

40. Ramírez Sánchez, "Inseguridad," 376.

41. For example, on November 5, 2002, alleged members of a US-based gang assassinated a local lawyer in Tijuana.

42. *Pozole* is a traditional thick Mexican soup, and *pozolero* can be translated as "stewmaker."

43. Procuraduría General de la República, Declaración.

44. La Jornada, "Hallan."

45. Author's interview with relative of a victim of disappearance, Tijuana, October 21, 2011.

46. Author's interview with relative of a victim of disappearance, Tijuana, October 21, 2011.

47. Author's interview with activist and relative of a victim of disappearance, Tijuana, October 21, 2011. Similar information appears in Blancornelas, "Entrenado."

48. Author's data set on drug violence, reported in *El Sol de Tijuana*, October 20 and 21, 2002.

49. Author's data set, *El Sol de Tijuana*, November 4, 2002.

50. Author's data set, *El Sol de Tijuana*, November 12, 2002.

51. Bowden, *Down*, 258.

52. Petrich, "Librarse."

53. Allegedly, one of the drivers of the split was El Teo's view that kidnappings were an appropriate funding strategy, something El Ingeniero opposed. See Jones, "Explaining"; Ramírez Sánchez, "Inseguridad."

54. Some versions identify April 20, 2007, as the day when the war exploded because El Teo refused to account for his actions to the AFO; see Ramírez Sánchez, "Inseguridad." This date, however, is not a clear marker of violence. In Culiacán, by contrast, April 30, 2008, clearly marks the initiation of violence.

55. Author's data set on drug-related violence.

56. *El Sol de Tijuana* only revealed the content of nine out of ten messages in 2010.

57. La Jornada, "Operativos."

58. Author's interview with journalist, Tijuana, September 15, 2011. See Valenzuela, *Impecable*, 317.

59. Author's interview with Lieutenant Colonel Julian Leyzola, chief of public security in Ciudad Juárez and former chief of public security in Tijuana, Ciudad Juárez, July 20, 2011.

60. Cave, "A Crime."

61. Author's interview with official from the municipal Secretariat of Public Security, Tijuana, September 13, 2011.

62. Marosi, "Antidrug."

63. Author's interview with public security expert, Tijuana, September 12, 2011.

64. Author's interview with businessman, Tijuana, October 19, 2011.

65. The feedback effect of outsourcing on the proliferation of gangs can be seen in the case of Medellín in the 1980s, described in chapter 4.

66. Zeta, "Pandillas."

67. Author's interview with DEA agent, El Paso, Texas, March 28, 2012. Jones, "Explaining"; Organization of American States, *Pandillas*.

68. This difference cannot be readily attributed to the proportion of youth population in each city. In fact, according to 2010 census statistics, the proportion of the total population twenty-four years or younger was 47 percent in Juárez and Culiacán and 57 percent in Tijuana.

69. Author's interview with Lieutenant Colonel Julian Leyzola, chief of public security in Ciudad Juárez, and former chief of public security in Tijuana, Ciudad Juárez, July 20, 2011.

70. Author's interview with human rights activist in Tijuana, September 14, 2011.

71. Jones, "Explaining."

72. Author's interview with human rights activists in Tijuana, September 14, 2011, and Mexicali, October 20, 2012.

73. Author's interview with photojournalist, Tijuana, September 12, 2011.

74. Author's interview with official of the state attorney's office, Tijuana, October 17, 2011.

75. Ampudia Rueda, "Empleo"; Swanger, "Feminist."

76. Ampudia Rueda, "Empleo."

77. Barraza, *Diagnóstico*; Bowden, *Murder*; Herrera, *El desgobierno*; Jusidman, *La realidad*.

78. Unemployment figures at the city level are not available; these numbers correspond to state figures, but experts consider the trends to be similar at the city level. See Ampudia Rueda, "Empleo"; Quintana, "Informe."

79. Quintana, "Informe."

80. Campbell, *Drug War*; Grayson, *Mexico*, 23; Poppa, *Drug Lord*.

81. Pérez-Espino and Páez, "Los Carrillo."

82. Gutiérrez, "Hombre inteligente."

83. See Campbell, *Drug War*, 97.

84. Gutiérrez and Ramírez, "El escurridizo."

85. Author's interview with former member of the DFS in Ciudad Juárez, Mexico City, June 13, 2011.

86. Valenzuela, *El futuro*.

87. Rodríguez, "Truncaron."

88. Golden, "Misreading Mexico."

89. Reed, "Certifiable,"

90. Author's interview with former member of the DFS in Ciudad Juárez, Mexico City, June 13, 2011. Emphasis is mine.

91. Author's interview with human rights worker, Ciudad Juárez, May 17, 2011.

92. In the same year the PAN also won the mayorship of Chihuahua City, the state capital.

93. Rodríguez and Ward, *Policymaking*, 60.

94. Rodríguez and Ward, *Policymaking*, 74.

95. Ochoa-Reza, "Multiple."

96. Lupsha and Pimentel, "The Nexus."

97. Dillon, "Mexican."

98. Ravelo, "La hora."

99. Pineda and Herrera, "Alternancia."

100. Alba Vega, "Chihuahua."

101. Rodríguez and Ward, *Policymaking*, 123.

102. Author's interview with human rights activist, Ciudad Juárez, May 17, 2011.

103. Sullivan and Logan. "La línea."

104. Arzt, *Democracia*.

105. Author's interviews with former high-level official at the Mexico Attorney General's Office, Mexico City, September 9 and 26, 2011.

106. The same official from the Mexico Attorney General's Office described that "the cartel tried to co-opt our soldiers; then they threatened; and then they started to execute people."

107. Astorga, *El siglo*.

108. Dillon, "A Toll"; Hervella, *Ciudad Juárez*. In some cases military or police could use disappearances to hide their excessive use of force in interrogating suspects of criminal activity.

109. Dillon, "A Toll"; Hervella, *Ciudad Juárez*.

110. Dillon, "A Toll."

111. Dillon, "A Toll"; Hervella, *Ciudad Juárez*.

112. Bowden, *Down*, 259.

113. Author's interview, El Paso, Texas, March 27, 2012.

114. The nature, perpetrators, and reasons for this horrendous violence are still subject to debate. Investigations are plagued by impunity, and the cases solved were perceived to rely on highly biased investigations. Existing analyses suggest that feminicides were perpetrated with varied motivations by a multiplicity of actors including state officials, drug traffickers, serial killers, and relatives of the victims, and they were permitted by the government's complicity

or lack of commitment to stop the tragedy. See Monárrez Fragoso, *Trama*; United Nations Committee, Report; Washington Valdez, *The Killing*.

115. The extreme cruelty and clear sexual connotations in feminicides could be defined as visible violence. The bodies found in the most-publicized cases were usually mutilated, stabbed, strangled, had signs of sexual violence and sometimes had signs carved on the back of the victim's bodies. Yet, the case in 2001 was different because it deliberately exposed the attacks.
116. Washington Valdez, *The Killing*, 40.
117. LaFranchi, "Mexico."
118. La Jornada, "Cuatro."
119. Pineda and Herrera, "Alternancia," 117.
120. Zavaleta et al., "El consenso."
121. Zepeda Bustos, "Violencia."
122. Amnesty International, *Mexico*.
123. See La Jornada,"Asesinaron."
124. These numbers vary widely depending on the source. This number includes all murders of journalists and media support workers, regardless of whether the motive was confirmed as organized-crime related. See Heinle et al., "Drug Violence 2015."
125. See Sedena, Procuraduría General de la República, "Comunicado Conjunto"; Moore, "The Legacy."
126. Ravelo, "Los Carrillo."
127. Campbell, *Drug War*, 28.
128. Rosi, *El sicario*. This documentary is based on an article of the same name by Charles Bowden that appeared in *Harper's* magazine in 2009.
129. Author's interview, high-level official of an international organization, Mexico City, February 21, 2011. For an analysis of the military's perception about being deployed in public security operations before the Calderón government, see Arzt, *Democracy*.
130. Author's interview with human rights activist, Ciudad Juárez, May 17, 2011.
131. This information is based on a review of the local newspaper *El Diario* in 2010, although the numbers were higher than what could be found in newspapers. The example mentioned here occurred on August 13, 2010, and the press clip omitted the name of the organization signing the note (Author's translation from original text in Spanish).
132. This analysis is based on the author's data set on drug violence. It is important to emphasize that newspapers identify only a small number of victims' occupations. Yet it is reasonable to think that a police officer or a soldier is more likely to be identified by occupation than is a civilian. These numbers correspond to 2010, but the situation was different in 2009 in Tijuana, when trafficking conflicts were far more visible
133. Author's interviews conducted with two business leaders and a human rights activist, Ciudad Juárez, May 16 and 17, 2011.
134. El Mundo, "Confesiones."
135. Author's interview with high-level official of the Federal Secretariat of Public Security, Mexico City, September 8, 2011.
136. YouTube video, interview with El Diego, no longer accessible on the website.
137. El Diario, "Dejan."
138. El Universal, "Balean."
139. El Diario, "Qué quieren."
140. Author's interviews in Ciudad Juárez, March 2012.
141. Vanguardia, "En Juárez."
142. Vanguardia, "Violencia."
143. Author's interview with Liutenant Colonel Julián Leyzaola, municipal secretary of public security, Ciudad Juárez, July 20, 2011.
144. In January, a federal police officer killed a member of Murguía's personal security, and later in the year his bodyguards were also held at gunpoint as the mayor's convoy patrolled the city. See Borunda, "Juárez"; El Diario, "Pos sí."
145. Calderón et al., "Beheading."
146. US District Court, Indictment.

147. Castillo, "Social," 309.
148. El Siglo de Torreón, "Operan."
149. Author's interview with community organizer and former gang member, Ciudad Juárez, July 19, 2011.
150. Durán-Martínez, "Drugs."
151. Author's interview with worker from youth NGO and former gang member, Ciudad Juárez, July 19, 2011.
152. Focus group conducted by Arturo Alvarado, for the project Juvenile Violence, Policing, and Access to Justice in Latin America, directed by Arturo Alvarado at the Colegio de México, Ciudad Juárez, March 2012.
153. Campbell, *Drug War,* 106.
154. Campbell, *Drug War,* 105.
155. Author's interview with human rights activist, Ciudad Juárez, May 17, 2011.
156. Author's interview with Lieutenant Colonel Julián Leyzaola, chief of public security in Ciudad Juárez and former chief of public security in Tijuana, Ciudad Juárez, July 20, 2011.
157. Based on analysis of the author's data set on drug-related violence
158. In November 2010, Arturo Gallegos Castrellón, a member of the Aztecas gang, confessed that he ordered the massacre because the Aztecas believed members of a rival gang were at the party. See El Paso Times, "Expert."
159. Author's interview with worker from youth NGO and former gang member, Ciudad Juárez, July 19, 2011.
160. Author's interview with worker from youth NGO, Ciudad Juárez, July 18, 2011.
161. Organization, *Pandillas.*
162. Interviews and focus groups conducted by the author, Ursula Alanís, and Arturo Alvarado for the project Juvenile Violence, Policing, and Access to Justice in Latin America, directed by Arturo Alvarado at the Colegio de México, Ciudad Juárez, March 2012.
163. Author's interviews in Ciudad Juárez and El Paso, March 2012.
164. Alanis and Durán-Martínez, "Jóvenes."

Conclusion

1. Violence can also sometimes be irrational, but such violence was not the object of this book.
2. Los Extraditables communiqué, Medellín, July 4, 1991. Author's personal archive.
3. See, for example, the declaration of an operative of Los Zetas in the city of Ciudad del Carmén. Procuraduría General de Justicia del Estado de Campeche.
4. For a good discussion of violent trends in Central America, see Cruz et al., "Political Transition."
5. Dudley, "5 Things."
6. I owe this observation to José Miguel Cruz and thank him for becoming a coauthor on a piece on this topic. See Cruz and Durán-Martínez, "Hiding."
7. Felbab-Brown and Trinkunas, "UNGASS."
8. Chin, *The Golden*; Kramer, "The Current State"; Snyder and Durán-Martínez, "Does Illegality."
9. Kachin, "Silent."
10. Windle, "Drugs and Drug Policy" and "A Slow March."
11. Lessing, "The Logic."
12. See, for example, Acemoglu et al., "The Monopoly"; Staniland, "Cities," *Networks,* and "Militias"; Wilkinson, *Votes.*
13. North, *Institutions*; Pierson, "Increasing."
14. Streeck and Thelen, *Beyond.*
15. Moncada, *Cities.*
16. Moncada and Snyder, "Subnational"
17. Idler, "Arrangements"; Lessing, "Logics"; Osorio, "The Contagion."
18. Ley and Trejo, "Federalismo"; Osorio, "Hobbes."
19. For example, Brancati and Snyder, "Rushing"; Brass, *Theft*; Flores and Nooruddin, "The Effect"; Snyder, *From Voting.*

20. Balcells, "The Consequences," 312.
21. Bateson, "From Violence"; Blattman, "Crime."
22. Caldeira, *City*; Malone, "The Verdict"; McIllwaine and Moser, *Encounters*.
23. Andreas and Durán-Martínez, "The International."
24. See UNODC *World Drug Report 2016*. According to the United Nations International Drug Control Programme (UNODCP), the predecessor to the UNODC, in the 1990s an estimated 192.7 million people had used drugs within the last year, an annual prevalence of about 3.34 percent of the world's population.
25. Bewley Taylor, *International*.
26. A clear example of this is the preface to the UNODC *World Drug Report 2012*, page iv, where the UNODC's director asserts, "We need to be equally clear about the importance of the international conventions on drugs, organized crime and corruption. Indeed, almost everything mentioned in this preface—focusing on drug demand, rehabilitation and reintegration, alternative development, shared responsibility, and fundamental human rights—are underscored in the conventions."
27. See Hope and Clark, "Si los vecinos"; Kilmer et al., "Reducing." These studies have estimated the income that Mexican organizations can derive from the marijuana trade and the potential impact that legalization of marijuana in US states can have on the income of Mexican organizations. Both studies highlight the uncertainty of the estimates, yet the first study highlights that with legalization some Mexican DTOs could lose up to 50 percent of their income, while the second suggests that the income may be significantly lower than assumed (between 15 and 26 percent).
28. Lessing, "When Business."

BIBLIOGRAPHY

Abello-Colak, Alexandra, and Valeria Guarneros-Meza. "The Role of Criminal Actors in Local Governance." *Urban Studies* 51, no. 15 (2014): 3268–3289.

Acemoglu, Daron, James A. Robinson, and Rafael J. Santos. "The Monopoly of Violence: Evidence from Colombia." *Journal of the European Economic Association* 11, no. 1 (2013): 5–44.

Aguirre, Alberto, Felipe Cobián, and Guillermo Correa. "¿Quiénes mataron al Cardenal? Testimonios sobre la matanza de Guadalajara" (Who Killed the Cardinal?). *Proceso*, no. 867, June 14, 1993. Reprint, special edition no. 32, May 2011, 43–46.

Alanis, Ursula, and Angélica Durán-Martínez. "Jóvenes en Ciudad Juárez, Chihuahua: Entre la falta de oportunidades y el miedo a la violencia" (Youth in Ciudad Juárez: Between Lack of Opportunities and Fear of Violence). In *Violencia juvenil y acceso a la justicia en América Latina*, vol. 2, edited by Arturo Alvarado, 63–112. Mexico City: El Colegio de México, 2014.

Alba Vega, Carlos. "Chihuahua: ¿Una alternativa sin alternativa?" (Chihuahua: An Alternative without an Alternative?). In *La Disputa del Reino*, edited by Rafael Loyola, 347–410. Mexico City: FLACSO, Universidad Autonoma de México, 1997.

Alexander, Michelle. *The New Jim Crow: Mass Incarceration in the Age of Color Blindness.* New York: The New Press, 2012.

Alonso, Manuel, and Germán Valencia. "Balance del proceso de desmovilización, desarme y reinserción (DDR) de los Bloques Cacique Nutibara y Héroes de Granada en la Ciudad de Medellín" (Assessment of the DDR process of the Bloques Cacique Nutibara and Héroes de Granada in Medellín). *Estudios Políticos* 33 (2008): 11–34.

Alonso, Manuel, Jorge Giraldo, and Diego Sierra. "Medellín: El complejo camino de la competencia armada" (Medellin: The Complex Road of Armed Competition). In *La parapolítica. La ruta de la expansión paramilitar y los acuerdos politicos*, edited by Mauricio Romero, 109–145. Bogotá: Corporación Nuevo Arco Iris, 2007.

Alvarado, Arturo. "Las elecciones para gobernador de Sinaloa en 1992" (The Elections for Governor in Sinaloa in 1992). In *La disputa del reino: Elecciones para gobernador en México en 1992*, edited by Rafael Loyola Diaz, 278–306. Mexico City: FLACSO, 1997.

Amat, Yamid. "'Debe permitirse el consumo controlado de marihuana': General Naranjo" (Controlled Consumption of Marijuana Should Be Allowed). El Tiempo, April 21, 2012. http://www.eltiempo.com/archivo/documento/MAM-5369021.

Amnesty International. *Mexico: Justice Fails in Ciudad Juárez and the City of Chihuahua.* Amnesty International, February 2005. https://www.amnestyusa.org/reports/mexico-justice-fails-in-ciudad-juarez-and-the-city-of-chihuahua/.

Ampudia Rueda, Lourdes. "Empleo y estructura económica en el contexto de la crisis en Ciudad Juárez: Las amenazas de la pobreza y la violencia" (Employment and Economic Structure in the Context of a Crisis in Juárez). In *Diagnóstico sobre la realidad social, económica, y cultural de los entornos locales para el diseño de intervenciones en materia de prevención y erradicación de la violencia en la Región Norte: El caso de Ciudad Juárez, Chihuahua*. Edited by Laurencio Barraza. México: Comisión Nacional para Prevenir y Erradicar La Violencia Contra Las Mujeres, Secretaria de Gobernación, Gobierno Federal, 2009.

Andreas, Peter. *Border Games: Policing the US-Mexico Divide*. Ithaca, NY: Cornell University Press, 2000.

Andreas, Peter. "Illicit Globalization: Myths, Misconceptions, and Historical Lessons." *Political Science Quarterly* 126, no. 3 (2011): 1–23.

Andreas, Peter, and Angélica Durán-Martínez. "The International Politics of Drugs and Illicit Trade in the Americas." In *Routledge Handbook of Latin America in the World*, edited by Jorge I. Domínguez and Ana Covarrubias, 376–390. New York: Routledge, 2014.

Andreas, Peter, and Kelly Greenhill, eds. *Sex, Drugs, and Body Counts: The Politics of Numbers in Global Crime and Conflict*. Ithaca, NY: Cornell University Press, 2010.

Andreas, Peter, and Joel Wallman. "Illicit Markets and Violence: What Is the Relationship?" *Crime, Law, and Social Change* 52, no. 3 (2009): 225–229.

Angarita, Pablo Emilio, Héctor Gallo, and Blanca Jiménez. *Dinámicas de guerra y construcción de Paz: Estudio interdisciplinario del conflicto armado en la Comuna 13 de Medellín* (War Dynamics and Peace Building: Interdisciplinary Study of Medellín's Comuna 13). Medellín: Iner, Universidad de Medellín, Corporación Región, Instituto Popular de Capacitación, 2008.

Arenas Gómez, Juan Carlos, and Juan Carlos Escobar. "Discursos políticos y resultados electorales en Medellín durante los años noventas" (Political Discourse and Electoral Results in Medellín in the Nineties). *Revista de Estudios Politicos* 16, (2000), 73–99.

Arias, Enrique Desmond. *Drugs and Democracy in Rio de Janeiro: Trafficking, Social Networks and Public Security*. Chapel Hill: University of North Carolina Press, 2006.

Arias, Enrique Desmond. "The Impacts of Differential Armed Dominance of Politics in Rio de Janeiro, Brazil." *Studies in Comparative International Development* 48, no. 3 (2013): 263–284.

Arias, Enrique Desmond, and Daniel Goldstein. *Violent Democracies in Latin America*. Durham, NC: Duke University Press, 2010.

Arjona, Ana. *Rebelocracy: Social Order in the Colombian Civil War*. Cambridge University Press, 2016.

Arlacchi, Pino. *Mafia Business: The Mafia Ethic and the Spirit of Capitalism*. New York: Verso, 1986.

Arocha, Jaime, Fernando Cubides, and Myriam Jimeno. *Las violencias: Inclusión creciente* (Violence: Growing Inclusion). Bogotá: Facultad de Ciencias Humanas, Universidad Nacional, CES, 1998.

Arrázola, Maria del Rosario. "Todo empezó en Envigado" (It All Began in Envigado). *Espectador*, February 12, 2011.

Arzt, Sigrid. *Democracia, seguridad, y militares en México* (Democracy, Security, and the Military in Mexico). Paper 544, Open Access Books, 2011. http://scholarlyrepository.miami.edu/oa_dissertations/544/.

Associated Press. "Sons of El Chapo Suspected of Mexican Convoy Ambush That Killed Five Soldiers." *Guardian*, October 1, 2016. https://www.theguardian.com/world/2016/sep/30/mexican-soldiers-killed-military-convoy-ambushed-sinaloa.

Astorga, Luis. *Mitología del narcotraficante en México*. Mexico City: Plaza y Valdes, 1995.

Astorga, Luis. *El siglo de las drogas*. Mexico City: Plaza & Janes, 2005.

Astorga, Luis, and David Shirk. "Drug-Trafficking Organizations and Counter-Drug Strategies in the US-Mexican Context." Working Paper Series on US-Mexico Security Cooperation, Woodrow Wilson International Center for Scholars, Mexico Project and Transborder Institute, University of San Diego, 2010.

Auyero, Javier. *Routine Politics and Violence in Argentina: The Gray Zone of State Power*. New York: Cambridge University Press, 2007.

Ávila, Ariel, and Juan David Velasco. *Democracias en venta: Partidos, corrupción electoral, violencia, y crimen en Colombia (2007–2011)* (Democracies for Sale: Parties, Electoral Corruption, Violence, and Crime in Colombia). Bogotá: Corporación Nuevo Arco Iris, 2012.

Bagley, Bruce. "Drug Trafficking and Organized Crime in the Americas: Major Trends in the Twenty-First Century." Washington, DC: Woodrow Wilson International Center For Scholars, Latin American Program, 2012.

Bahamon, Augusto. *Mi guerra en Medellín* (My War in Medellín). Bogotá: Intermedio Editores, 1991.

Bailey, John. "What Do the Zetas and Mc Donalds Have in Common?" *Insight Crime* December 5, 2011. http://www.insightcrime.org/news-analysis/what-do-the-zetas-and-mcdonalds-have-in-common

Baird, Adam. "¿Héroes olvidados? Activismo desde la sociedad civil y políticas de juventud en Medellín" (Forgotten Heroes: Civil Society Activism and Youth Policies in Medellín). In *Paz paso a paso: Una mirada desde los estudios de paz a los conflictos colombianos*, edited by Adam Baird and José Fernando Serrano, 29–48. Bogotá: Pontificia Universidad Javeriana, 2012.

Bakke, Kristin, Kathleen Gallagher, and Lee Seymour. "A Plague of Initials: Fragmentation, Cohesion, and Infighting in Civil Wars." *Perspectives on Politics* 10, no. 2 (2012): 265–283.

Balbín, Jesus, ed. *Violencias y conflictos urbanos: Un reto para las políticas públicas* (Violence and Urban Conflicts: A Challenge for Public Policies). Medellín: Instituto Popular de Capacitación, 2004.

Balcells, Laia. "The Consequences of Victimization on Political Identities: Evidence from Spain." *Politics and Society* 40, no. 3 (2012): 311–347.

Balcells, Laia. "Continuation of Politics by Two Means: Direct and Indirect Violence in Civil Wars." *Journal of Conflict Resolution* 55, no. 3 (2011): 397–422.

Barbary, Olivier. "Afrocolombianos en Cali: ¿Cuántos son, dónde viven, de dónde vienen?" (Afrocolombians in Cali: How Many Are There, Where Do They Live, Where Do They Come From?) In *Afrocolombianos en el área metropolitana de Cali: Estudios sociodemográficos*, edited by Olivier Barbary, Stephanie Bruyneel, Hector Fabio Ramírez, and Fernando Urrea. Documento de Trabajo No. 38, 31–52. Cali: Universidad del Valle, Facultad de Ciencias Sociales y Económicas, 1999.

Barraza, Laurencio, ed. *Diagnóstico sobre la realidad social, económica, y cultural de los entornos locales para el diseño de intervenciones en materia de prevención y erradicación de la violencia en la región norte: El caso de Ciudad Juárez, Chihuahua* (Diagnosis of the Economic, Social and Cultural Reality for the Design of Crime Prevention and Erradication Projects in the Northern Region, the Case of Ciudad Juárez). México: Comisión Nacional para Prevenir y Erradicar La Violencia Contra Las Mujeres, Secretaria de Gobernación, Gobierno Federal, 2009.

Barreto Nieto, Luis, and Sneider Rivera. *Una mirada a la impunidad en el marco del sistema penal acusatorio en Colombia* (A Cursory Look of Impunity in the Framework of Colombia's Accusatory Penal System). Bogotá: Ministerio del Interior y Justicia, 2009.

Bateson, Regina. "Crime Victimization and Political Participation." *American Political Science Review* 106, no. 3 (2012): 570–587.

Bailey, John, and Jorge Chabat. *Transnational Crime and Public Security: Challenges to Mexico and the United States.* San Diego: Center for US-Mexican Studies, University of California San Diego, 2002.

Bailey, John, and Lucia Dammert, eds. *Public Security and Police Reform in the Americas.* Pittsburgh, PA: University of Pittsburgh Press, 2005.

BBC News. "Mexico's Drug War: Lessons and Challenges." BBC News, December 31, 2011. http://www.bbc.com/news/world-latin-america-16337488.

Beissinger, Mark. "Nationalist Violence and the State: Political Authority and Contentious Repertoires in the Former USSR." *Comparative Politics* 30, no. 4 (1998): 401–422

Bejarano, Ana María, and Eduardo Pizarro. "From 'Restricted' to 'Besieged': The Changing Nature of the Limits to Democracy in Colombia." In *The Third Wave of Democratization in Latin*

America: Advances and Setbacks, edited by Frances Hagopian and Scott Mainwaring, 235–260. New York: Cambridge University Press.

Benítez-Manaut, Raúl. "Seguridad nacional y gobernabilidad en México: Criminalidad y fronteras" (National Security and Governance in Mexico: Criminality and Borders). *Revista Criminologia y Sociedad* 1, no. 1 (2008): 165–184.

Benítez-Manaut, Raúl. "México 2010: Crimen organizado, seguridad nacional, y geopolítica" (Mexico 2010: Organized Crime, National Security, and Geopolitics). In *Crimen organizado e Iniciativa Mérida en las relaciones México-Estados Unidos*, edited by Raul Benitez Manaut, 9–30. Mexico City: Colectivo de Análisis de la Seguridad con Democracia, 2010.

Betancourt, Darío. *Mediadores, rebuscadores, traquetos, y narcos: Las organizaciones mafiosas del Valle del Cauca entre la historia, la memoria, y el relato 1890–1997* (Intermediaries, Foragers, Traquetos, and Narcos: Mafiosi organizations in Valle del Cauca between History, Memory, and Tale 1890–1997). Bogotá: Ediciones Anthropos, 1998.

Betancourt, Darío, and Martha Luz García. *Contrabandistas, marimberos, y mafiosos: Historia social de la mafia colombiana, 1965–1992* (Smugglers, Marimberos, and Mafiosi: Social History of Colombian Mafia). Bogotá: Tercer Mundo, 1994.

Bewley-Taylor, David. *International Drug Control: Consensus Fractured.* New York: Cambridge University Press, 2012.

Blancornelas, Jesús. *El cartel: Los Arellano Félix, la mafia más poderosa en la historia de América Latina* (The Cartel: The Arellano Felix, the Most Powerful Mafia in Latin America's History). Mexico City: DeBolsillo, 2002.

Blancornelas, Jesús. "Descobijaron a los narcojuniors" (The Juniors Have Been Left Unprotected). *Zeta*, November 14–20, 1997, p. 12A–15A.

Blancornelas, Jesús. "Entrenado en Israel: Comando narco mató y remató a Federales" (Trained in Israel: Drug-Trafficking Liutenant Killed Federals). *Zeta*, November 21–27, 1997, p. 34A–38A.

Blancornelas, Jesús, and Héctor González. "Amigo de Xico Jr. posible víctima del 'Lobo' Hodoyán y Fabián 'El Tiburón'" (Xico Jr.'s Friend Is a Possible Victim of the "Wolf" Hodoyán and Fabián "The Shark"). *Zeta*, October 11–17, 1997, p. 26A.

Blancornelas, Jesús, and Hernán González. "Dicho por el propio Procurador Anaya: Policias corruptos, no tontos" (State Attorney Anaya Said: Corrupt, Not Silly, Cops). *Zeta*, August 15–21, 1997, p. 28A.

Blancornelas, Jesús, Francisco Órtiz, and Hernán González. "La mafia sigue adentro de la PGR" (The Mafia Is Still within the Attorney General's Office). *Zeta*, November 20–26, 1996, p. 26A

Blatmann, Christopher. "From Violence to Voting: War and Political Participation in Uganda." *American Political Science Review* 103, no. 2 (2008): 231–247.

Blok, Anton. "Mafia and Blood Symbolism." In *Risky Transactions: Trust, Kinship, and Ethnicity*, edited by Frank Salter, 109–129. New York: Berghahn Books, 2002.

Borunda, Daniel. "Juárez Mayor Confronts Feds: 'You Don't Rule City.'" *El Paso Times*, May 5, 2011. Article no longer available online.

Bourdieu, Pierre, and Löic Wacquant. "Symbolic Violence." In *Violence in War and Peace*, edited by Nancy Scheper-Hughes and Philippe Bourgois, 272–274. Blackwell, 2004.

Bowden, Charles. *Down by the River: Drugs, Money, Murder, and Family*. New York: Simon and Schuster, 2004.

Bowden, Charles. *Murder City: Ciudad Juárez and the Global Economy's New Killing Fields.* New York: Nation Books, 2010.

Bowden, Mark. *Killing Pablo: The Hunt for the World's Greatest Outlaw.* New York: Atlantic Books, 2002.

Brancati, Dawn, and Jack Snyder. "Rushing to the Polls: The Causes of Premature Postconflict Elections." *Journal of Conflict Resolution* 55, no. 3 (2011): 469–492.

Brass, Paul. *Theft of an Idol*. Princeton, NJ: Princeton University Press, 1997.

Brinks, Daniel. "A Tale of Two Cities: The Judiciary and the Rule of Law in Latin America." In *Handbook of Latin American Politics*, edited by Peter Kingstone and Deborah Yashar, 61–75. New York: Routledge, 2012.

Britto, Lina. "The Marihuana Axis: A Regional History of Colombia's First Narcotics Boom, 1935–1985." PhD diss., New York University, 2012.

Britto, Lina. "A Trafficker's Paradise: The 'War on Drugs' and the New Cold War in Colombia." *Contemporánea* 1, no. 1 (2010): 159–177.

Brubaker, Roger. *Nationalism Reframed. Nationhood and the National Question in the New Europe.* Cambridge, UK: Cambridge University Press, 1996.

Bruinsma, Gerben, and Win Bernasco. "Criminal Groups and Transnational Illegal Markets: A More Detailed Examination on the Basis of Social Network Theory." *Crime Law and Social Change* 41, no 1 (2004): 79–94.

Bueno de Mesquita, Ethan. "The Political Economy of Terrorism: An Overview of Recent Work." *Political Economist* 10, no. 1 (2008): 1–12.

Bunker, Robert. "Introduction: the Mexican Cartels: Organized Crime vs. Criminal Insurgency," *Trends in Organized Crime* 16, no. 2 (2013): 129.

Bunker, Robert, and John Sullivan. "Extreme Barbarism, a Death Cult, and Holy Warriors in Mexico: Societal Warfare South of the Border?" *Small Wars Journal*, May 22, 2011. http://smallwarsjournal.com/jrnl/art/societal-warfare-south-of-the-border.

Caldeira, Teresa. *City of Walls: Crime, Segregation, and Citizenship in Sao Paulo.* Berkeley: University of California Press, 2000.

Calderón, Gabriela, Gustavo Robles, Alberto Díaz-Cayeros, and Beatriz Magaloni. "The Beheading of Criminal Organizations and the Dynamics of Violence in Mexico." *Journal of Conflict Resolution* 59, no. 8 (2015): 1455–1485.

Camacho, Álvaro. "La reforma de la policía colombiana ¿Esperanzas o frustraciones?" (The Reform of the Colombian Police: Hope or Frustration?). *Nueva Sociedad* 129 (January–February 1994): 27–40.

Camacho, Álvaro, and Andrés López. "From Smugglers to Drug Lords to 'Traquetos': Changes in the Colombian Illicit Drugs Organizations." In *Peace, Democracy, and Human Rights in Colombia*, edited by Christopher Welna and Gustavo Gallón, 60–89. Notre Dame, IN: University of Notre Dame Press, 2001.

Campbell, Howard. *Drug War Zone: Frontline Dispatches from the Streets of El Paso and Juárez.* Austin: University of Texas Press, 2009.

Casas Dupuy, Pablo. *Reformas y contrarreformas en la policía colombiana* (Reforms and Counterreforms in the Colombian Police). Bogotá: Fundación Seguridad y Democracia, 2005.

Castillo, Juan Camilo, Daniel Mejía, and Pascual Restrepo. "Illegal Drug Markets and Violence in Mexico: The Causes beyond Calderón." Working Paper. Bogotá: Universidad de los Andes. http://fsi.stanford.edu/sites/default/files/143.illegaldrug.pdf.

Castillo, Nemesio. "Capital social y nivel de cohesión en Ciudad Juárez" (Social Capital and Level of Cohesion in Ciudad Juárez). In *Diagnóstico sobre la realidad social, económica y cultural de los entornos locales para el diseño de intervenciones en materia de prevención y erradicación de la violencia en la región norte: El caso de Ciudad Juárez, Chihuahua.* Edited by Laurencio Barraza. México: Comisión Nacional para Prevenir y Erradicar La Violencia Contra Las Mujeres, Secretaria de Gobernación, Gobierno Federal, 2009.

Caulkins, Jonathan, and Peter Reuter. "What Price Data Tell Us about Drug Markets." *Journal of Drug Issues* 28, no. 3 (1998): 593–613.

Caulkins, Jonathan, Peter Reuter, and Lowell J. Taylor. "Can Supply Restrictions Lower Price? Violence, Drug Dealing, and Positional Advantage." *BE Journal of Economic Analysis and Policy* 5, no. 1 (2006): 1935–1682.

Cave, Damion. "A Crime Fighter Draws Plaudits, and Scrutiny." *New York Times*, December 23, 2011. https://mobile.nytimes.com/2011/12/24/world/americas/mexican-police-chief-produces-results-and-scrutiny.html?mcubz=0.

Ceballos, Ramiro, and Francine Cronshaw. "The Evolution of Armed Conflict in Medellín: An Analysis of the Major Actors." *Latin American Perspectives* 28, no. 1, special issue: *Colombia: The Forgotten War* (January 2001): 110–131.

Cerdá, Magdalena, Jeffrey Morenoff, Ben Hansen, Kimberly Tessari Hicks, Luis Fernando Duque, and Ana Diez-Roux. "Reducing Violence by Transforming Neighborhoods: A Natural Experiment in Medellín, Colombia." *American Journal of Epidemiology* 175, no. 10 (2012): 1045–1053.

Chabat, Jorge. "Drug Trafficking and the United States–Mexico Relations: Causes of Conflict." In *Mexico's Security Failure: Collapse into Criminal Violence*, edited by Paul Kenny, Mónica Serrano, and Arturo Sotomayor, 143–161. New York: Routledge, 2012.

Chaparro, Camilo. *Historia del cartel de Cali* (The Cali Cartel's History). Bogotá: Intermedio, 2005

Chepesiuk, Ron. *The Bullet or the Bribe: Taking Down Colombia's Cali Drug Cartel*. Westport, Conn.: Praeger, 2003.

Chin, Ko-Lin. *The Golden Triangle: Inside Southeast Asia's Drug Trade*. Ithaca, NY: Cornell University Press, 2009.

Christia, Fotini. *Alliance Formation in Civil Wars*. New York: Cambridge University Press, 2012.

Civico, Aldo. "We Are Illegal, but Not Illegitimate. Modes of Policing in Medellín, Colombia." *Polar: Political and Legal Anthropology Review* 35, no. 1 (2012): 77–93.

Clawson, Patrick and Rensselaer Lee. *The Andean Cocaine Industry*. New York: Palgrave Macmillan, 1998.

El Colombiano. "Desarticulada en Medellín red logística de las FARC: Trabajo conjunto ha sido clave: Entrevista con General Leonardo Gallego" (The Logistic Network of the FARC Has Been Dismantled: Joint Efforts Have Been the Key, Interview with General Leonardo Gallego). Colombiano, September 13, 2003. Article no longer available online.

El Colombiano. "Don Berna reconoció las desapariciones en La Comuna 13" (Don Berna Recognized Disappearances in Comuna 13). Colombiano, October 6, 2006. Article no longer available online.

Comisión de Estudios Sobre la Violencia. *Colombia: Violencia y democracia: Informe Presentado al Ministerio de Gobierno* (Colombia: Violence and Democracy, Report Presented to the Government Ministry). Bogotá: Universidad Nacional de Colombia, 1987.

Comisión Nacional de Derechos Humanos. *Resumén ejecutivo informe especial sobre los grupos de autodefensa en el estado de Michoacán y las violaciones a los derechos humanos relacionadas con el conflicto* (Executive Summary of the Special Report about Self-Defense Forces in Michoacán and Human Rights Violations Related to Conflict). November 12, 2015. http://www.cndh. org.mx/sites/all/doc/OtrosDocumentos/Doc_2015_006.pdf

Comisión Nacional de Reparación y Reconciliación, Colombia. *Disidentes, rearmados, y emergentes ¿Bandas criminales o tercera generación paramilitar?* (Dissidents, Rearmed and Emerging: Criminal Gangs or Third Paramilitary Generation?) Informe 1 de La Comisión Nacional de Reparación y Reconciliación (Report 1 of the National Commission for Reparation and Reconciliation). Bogotá, 2007.

Comisión Nacional de Reparación y Reconciliación, Colombia. *La huella invisible de la guerra: Desplazamiento forzado en la Comuna 13* (The Invisible Imprint of War: Forced Displacement in Comuna 13). Informe del Grupo de Memoria Histórica de La Comisión Nacional de Reparación y Reconciliación (Report of the Historic Memory Group of the National Commission for Reparation and Reconciliation). Bogotá: Ediciones Semana, 2011.

Sedena and Procuraduría General de la República. Comunicado Conjunto "El Ejército Mexicano detiene a Noel Salgueiro Nevarez (A) "El Flaco Salgueiro," Fundador y líder de "Gente Nueva," Grupo delictivo de la organización criminal "Guzmán Loera." (Joint Press Release of the Defense Secretariat and the Attorney General's Office: The Army Arrests Noel Salgueiro Nevarez). Mexico City, October 5, 2011.

Concha-Eastman, Alberto, Victoria Espitia, Rafael Espinosa, and Rodrigo Guerrero. "La epidemiología de los homicidios en Cali, 1993–1998: Seis años de un modelo poblacional"

(The Epidemiology of Homicides in Cali). *Revista Panamericana Salud Pública* 12, no. 4 (2002): 230–239.

Conrad, Justing, and Kevin Greene. "Competition, Differentiation, and the Severity of Terrorist Attacks." *Journal of Politics* 77, no. 2 (2015): 546–561.

Corcoran, Patrick. "Mexico Government Report Points to Ongoing Criminal Fragmentation." *InSight Crime*, April 14, 2015. http://www.insightcrime.com/news-analysis/mexico-government-report-points-to-ongoing-criminal-fragmentation

Cornell, Svante E. "The Interaction of Narcotics and Conflict." *Journal of Peace Research* 42, no. 6 (2005): 751–760.

Corporación Humanas, Centro Regional de Derechos Humanos y Justicia de Género. *Situación en Colombia de la violencia sexual contra las mujeres* (Situation of Sexual Violence Against Women in Colombia). Bogotá: Ediciones Anthropos, 2009.

Corporación Nuevo Arco Iris. *Mafias y agentes ilegales buscan rentas y el poder local* (Mafias and Illegal Agents Seek Rents and Local Power). Bogotá: Nuevo Arco Iris, 2011.

Craig, Richard. "Operation Condor: Mexico's Antidrug Campaign Enters a New Era." *Journal of Interamerican Studies and World Affairs* 22, no. 3 (August 1980): 345–363.

Crandall, Russell. *Driven by Drugs: US Policy toward Colombia*. Boulder, CO: Lynne Rienner, 2002.

Crenshaw, Martha. "Explaining Suicide Terrorism: A Review Essay." *Security Studies* 16, no. 1 (2007): 133–162.

La Crónica de Hoy. "Los Zetas fueron capacitados por los Kaibiles antes de desertar del ejército mexicano" (Zetas Were Trained by Kaibiles before Deserting Mexican Army). *Crónica de Hoy*, October 3, 2005. http://www.cronica.com.mx/notas/2005/205304.html.

Cruz, José Miguel, and Angélica Durán-Martínez. "Hiding Violence to Deal with the State: Criminal Pacts in El Salvador and Medellín." *Journal of Peace Research* 53, no. 2 (2016): 197–210.

Cruz, José Miguel, Rafael Fernández de Castro, and Gema Santamaría. "Political Transition, Social Violence, and Gangs: Cases in Central America and Mexico." In *In the Wake of War: Democratization and Internal Armed Conflict in Latin America*, edited by Cinthya Arnson. Stanford, CA: Woodrow Wilson Center Press and Stanford University Press, 2012.

Davis, Diane. "Irregular Armed Forces, Shifting Patterns of Commitment, and Fragmented Sovereignty in the Developing World." *Theory and Society* 39, no. 3–4 (2010): 397–413.

Davis, Diane. "Theoretical and Empirical Reflections on Cities, Sovereignty, Identity, and Conflict." In *Cities and Sovereignty: Identity Politics in Urban Spaces*, edited by Diane Davis and Nora Libertun de Duren, 226–256. Bloomington: Indiana University Press, 2011.

Davis, Diane. "Undermining the Rule of Law: Democratization and the Dark Side of Police Reform in Mexico." *Latin American Politics and Society* 48, no. 1 (2006): 55–86.

De Francisco, Gonzalo. "El doble reto del conflicto armado y la seguridad pública: La evolución de la policía nacional de Colombia" (The Dual Challenge of Armed Conflict and Public Security: The Evolution of Colombia's National Police). In *Seguridad y reforma policial en las Americas: Tendencias y desafíos*, edited by Lucía Dammert and John Bailey, 171–191. Mexico City: Siglo XXI, 2005.

Dell, Melissa. "Trafficking Networks and the Mexican Drug War." *American Economic Review* 105, no. 6 (2015): 1738–1779.

Denyer-Willis, Graham. *Killing Consensus: Police, Organized Crime, and the Regulation of Life and Death in Urban Brazil*. Oakland: University of California Press, 2015.

El Diario. "Dejan 2 Decapitados en Hacienda de Las Torres" (Two Beheaded Bodies Left at the Torres Ranch). *Diario*, July 28, 2010. Article no longer available online.

El Diario. " 'Pos sí, pero no tiré': Federal que encañonó a los escoltas de 'Teto' " (Yes, But I Did Not Shoot: Federal Cop Who Aimed Gun at Teto's Bodyguards). *Diario*, May 5, 2011. Article no longer available online.

El Diario. "¿Qué quieren de nosotros?" (What Do You Want from Us?) *Diario*, September 19, 2010. http://diario.mx/Local/2010-09-19_cfaade06/_que-quieren-de-nosotros/?/.

Dillon, Sam. "A Toll of Disappearances in Mexico's War on Drugs." *New York Times*, October 7, 1997. http://www.nytimes.com/1997/10/07/world/a-toll-of-disappearances-in-mexicos-war-on-drugs.html?mcubz=0.

Dorn, Nicholas, Karim Murji, and Nigel South. *Traffickers, Drug Markets, and Law Enforcement.* New York: Routledge, 1992.

Dorn, Nicholas, Lutz Oette, and Simone White. "Drugs Importation and the Bifurcation of Risk: Capitalization, Cut Outs, and Organized Crime." *British Journal of Criminology* 38, no. 4 (1998): 537–560.

Dowdney, Luke. *Children of the Drug Trade: A Case Study of Children in Organised Armed Violence in Rio de Janeiro.* Rio de Janeiro: 7Letras, 2003.

Dube, Oeindrila, and Suresh Naidu. "Bases, Bullets, and Ballots: The Effect of US Military Aid on Political Conflict in Colombia." *The Journal of Politics* 77, no. 1 (2015): 249–267.

Dudley, Steven. "5 Things the El Salvador Gang Truce Has Taught Us." *Insight Crime.* http://www.insightcrime.org/news-analysis/5-things-el-salvador-gang-truce-taught-us.

Duncan, Gustavo. *Del campo a la ciudad en Colombia: La infiltración urbana de los señores de la guerra* (From the Countryside to the City in Colombia: Urban Entrance of Drug Lords). Bogotá: Universidad de los Andes, 2005.

Duncan, Gustavo. "Drug Trafficking and Political Power Oligopolies of Coercion in Colombia and Mexico." *Latin American Perspectives* 41, no. 2 (2014): 18–42.

Duncan, Gustavo. *Los señores de la guerra: De paramilitares, mafiosos, y autodefensas en Colombia.* Bogotá: Planeta, 2006.

Dunning, Thad. "Fighting and Voting: Violent Conflict and Electoral Politics." *Journal of Conflict Resolution* 55, no. 3 (2011): 327–339.

Durán-Martínez, Angélica. "Drugs around the Corner: Domestic Drug Markets and Violence in Colombia and Mexico." *Latin American Politics and Society* 57, no. 3 (2015):122–146.

Durán-Martínez, Angélica, Gayle Hazard, and Viridiana Rios. *2010 Mid-Year Report on Drug Violence in Mexico.* San Diego, CA: Transborder Institute, University of San Diego, 2010.

Eaton, Kent. "The State of the State in Latin America: Challenges, Challengers, Responses, and Deficits." *Revista de Ciencia Política* 32 (3): 643–657.

Eilstrup-Sangiovanni, Mette, and Calvert Jones. "Assessing the Dangers of Illicit Networks: Why Al-Qaida May Be Less Threatening Than Many Think." *International Security* 33, no. 2 (2008): 7–44.

El Espectador. "Cerrojo a la Oficina de Envigado" (Lock on the Envigado's Office). *Espectador,* July 27, 2008. http://www.elespectador.com/impreso/extradicion/articuloimpreso-cerrojo-oficina-de-envigado.

El Espectador. "Las Confesiones de Don Berna" (Don Berna's Confessions). *Espectador,* October 1, 2013. http://www.elespectador.com/noticias/judicial/confesiones-de-don-berna-articulo-584537.

El Espectador. "Queríamos que Castaño llegara a la presidencia" (We Wanted Castaño to Become President). *Espectador,* September 28, 2013. http://www.elespectador.com/noticias/judicial/queriamos-castano-llegara-presidencia-articulo-449263.

El Espectador."El Rio la fosa más grande de Medellín" (The River Is Medellín's Biggest Grave). *Espectador,* February 8, 2011. http://www.elespectador.com/noticias/nacional/el-rio-fosa-mas-grande-de-medellin-articulo-249770.

El Paso Times. "Expert: Azteca Leader's Arrest Won't End Violence." *El Paso Times*, December 1, 2010. Article no longer available online.

Enciso, Froylán. *Nuestra historia narcótica: Pasajes para (re)legalizar las drogas en México* (Our Narcotic History: Passages to Relegalize Drugs in Mexico). Mexico City: Debate, 2015.

Escalante, Fernando. *El homicidio en México entre 1990 y 2007* (Homicide in Mexico between 1990 and 2007). Mexico City: El Colegio de México, 2009.

Escalante, Fernando. "La Muerte tiene permiso" (Death Has Permission). *Nexos* January 3, 2011. http://www.nexos.com.Mx/?P=Leerarticulo&Article=1943189.

Evans, Peter. *Embedded Autonomy: States and Industrial Transformation.* Princeton, NJ: Princeton University Press, 1995.

Faiola, Anthony. "Sustaining the Medellín Miracle: Colombia Struggles to Hold On to Gains from Globalization." *Washington Post,* July 11, 2011. http://www.washingtonpost.com/wp-dyn/content/article/2008/07/10/AR2008071002746.html.

Faletti, Tulia. "A Sequential Theory of Decentralization: Latin American Cases in Comparative Perspective." *American Political Science Review* 99, no. 3 (2005): 327–346.

Fearon, James. "Primary Commodity Exports and Civil War." *Journal of Conflict Resolution* 49, no. 4. Special issue, Paradigm in Distress? Primary Commodities and Civil War (2005): 483–507.

Fearon, James. "Why Do Some Civil Wars Last So Much Longer Than Others?" *Journal of Peace Research* 41, no. 3 (2004): 275–301.

Fearon, James, and David Laitin. "Ethnicity, Insurgency, and Civil War," *American Political Science Review* 97, no. 1 (2003): 75–90.

Felbab-Brown, Vanda. "Human Security and Crime in Latin America: The Political Capital and Political Impact of Criminal Groups and Belligerents Involved in Illicit Economies." Miami: Applied Research Center, Florida International University, 2011.

Felbab-Brown, Vanda. *Shooting Up: Counterinsurgency and the War on Drugs.* Washington, DC: Brookings Institution, 2010.

Felbab-Brown, Vanda, and Harold Trinkunas. "UNGASS 2016 in Comparative Perspective: Improving the Prospects for Success." Foreign policy paper, Brookings Institution, Washington, DC, 2015.

Finnegan, William. "The Kingpins: The Fight for Guadalajara," *New Yorker,* July 2, 2012. http://www.newyorker.com/magazine/2012/07/02/the-kingpins.

Finnegan, William. "Silver or Lead." *New Yorker,* May 31, 2010. http://www.newyorker.com/magazine/2010/05/31/silver-or-lead.

Fiscalía General de la Nación (Attorney General's Office). Diligencia de indagatoria que rinde el señor Guillermo Alejandro Pallomari González (Testimony by Mr. Guillermo Alejandro Pallomari González during Preliminary Inquiries). Charlotte, NC: November 13, 1995.

Flores, Carlos. "El estado en crisis: crimen organizado y política: desafíos para la consolidación democrática" (The State in Crisis: Organized Crime and Politics: Challenges for Democratic Consolidation). PhD diss., Universidad Nacional Autónoma de México, 2005.

Flores, Thomas Edward, and Irfan Nooruddin. "The Effect of Elections on Postconflict Peace and Reconstruction." *Journal of Politics* 74, no. 2 (2012): 558–570.

Fox, Edward. "US Report on Colombia Cocaine Raises More Questions Than Answers." *Insight Crime,* August 1, 2012. http://www.insightcrime.org/news-analysis/us-report-on-colombia-cocaine-production-raises-more-questions-than-answers.

Franco, Luciano. "Patrullan Culiacán 2 mil 723 soldados y agentes" (Culiacán Patrolled by 2,723 soldiers and agents). *Crónica de México,* May 14, 2008. http://www.cronica.com.mx/notas/2008/361811.html.

Franco, Vilma. "Prácticas hegemónicas de la coalición políticamente dominante en Medellín y su entorno Urbano-Regional" (Prevailing Practices of the Dominant Political Coalition in Medellín). *Estudios Políticos* 26 (January–June 2005): 151–182.

Freeman, Laurie, and Jose Luis Sierra. "Mexico: The Militarization Plan." In *Drugs and Democracy in Latin America,* edited by Coletta Youngers and Eileen Rosin. London: Lynne Rienner, 2005.

Friman, Richard. "Drug Markets and the Selective Use of Violence." *Crime, Law, and Social Change* 52, no. 3 (2009): 285–295.

Friman, Richard. "Forging the Vacancy Chain: Law Enforcement Efforts and Mobility in Criminal Economies." *Crime, Law, and Social Change* 41 (2004): 53–77.

Fruhling, Hugo. "Policia comunitaria y reforma policial en América Latina ¿Cuál es el impacto?" (Community Policing and Police Reform in Latin America: What Is the Impact). Santiago de Chile: Centro de Estudios en Seguridad Ciudadana, Serie Documentos, 2003.

Fruhling, Hugo, Joseph Tulchin, and Heather Golding. *Crime and Violence in Latin America: Citizen Security, Democracy, and the State*. Baltimore: Johns Hopkins University Press, 2003.

Fujii, Lee Ann. "The Puzzle of Extra-Lethal Violence," *Perspectives on Politics* 11, no. 2 (2013): 410–426.

Fukuyama, Francis, and Seth Colby. "Half a Miracle." *Foreign Policy*, May–June 2011. http://foreignpolicy.com/2011/04/25/half-a-miracle/.

Gambetta, Diego. *Codes of the Underworld: How Criminals Communicate*. Princeton, NJ: Princeton University Press, 2009.

Gambetta, Diego. *The Sicilian Mafia: The Business of Private Protection*. Cambridge, MA: Harvard University Press, 1996.

Gambetta, Diego, ed. *Making Sense of Suicide Missions*. New York: Oxford University Press, 2005.

Ganor, Boaz. "Terrorist Organization Typologies and the Probability of a Boomerang Effect." *Studies in Conflict and Terrorism* 31, no. 4 (2008): 269–283.

Garzón, Juan Carlos. *Mafia & Co.: Las redes Criminales en México, Brasil, y Colombia* (Mafia & Co: Criminal Networks in Mexico, Brazil, and Colombia). Bogotá: Planeta, 2008.

Garzón, Juan Carlos. "La violencia que seremos" (The Violence We Will Be). *Razón Pública*, February 10, 2013. Http://Www.Razonpublica.Com/Index.Php/Conflicto-Drogas-Y-Paz-Temas-30/3556-La-Violencia-Que-Seremos.Html,

Gibson, Edward. "Boundary Control: Subnational Authoritarianism in Democratic Countries." *World Politics* 58, no. 1 (2005): 101–132.

Golden, Tim. "Misreading Mexico: How Washington Stumbled." *New York Times*, July 11, 1997. http://www.nytimes.com/1997/07/11/world/mexico-and-drugs-was-us-napping.html?mcubz=0.

Goldstein, Paul. "The Drugs-Violence Nexus: A Tripartite Conceptual Framework." *Journal of Drug Issues* 15, no. 4 (1985): 493–506.

Goldstein, Paul. "The Relationship between Drugs and Violence in the United States of America." In *World Drug Report 1997*. Vienna: UNODC, 1997.

Goldstein, Paul J., Henry H. Brownstein, Patrick J. Ryan, and Patricia A. Bellucci. "Crack and Homicide in New York City, 1988: A Conceptually Based Event Analysis." *Contemporary Drug Problems* 16 (1989): 651.

Gómez, Jorge Aníbal, Jose Roberto Herrera, and Nilson Pinilla. *Informe final de la Comisión de Verdad sobre los hechos del Palacio de Justicia* (Final Report of the Truth Commission about the Events of the Justice Palace). Bogotá: Universidad del Rosario, Comisión de la Verdad Palacio de Justicia, 2010.

González, Guadalupe, and Marta Tienda. "The Drug Connection in US-Mexican Relations." In *Papers Presented for the Bilateral Commission on the Future of United States–Mexican Relations. Dimensions of US-Mexican Relations*. Vol. 4. San Diego: Center for US-Mexican Studies, University of California, San Diego, 1989.

González, Hector. "Amigo de Xico Jr posible víctima del 'Lobo' Hodoyán y Fabián 'El Tiburón' (Xico Jr's Friend Possible Victim of "Wolf" Hodoyan and "The Shark" Fabian). *Zeta*, October 11–17, 1997, p. 26A.

González, Héctor, and Francisco Ortiz. "Tijuana: Las ejecuciones alrededor de la PGR" (Tijuana: The Assassinations Surrounding the Attorney Genera's Office). *Zeta*, May 24–April 3, 1996, p. 28A.

Gootenberg, Paul. *Andean Cocaine: The Making of a Global Drug*. Chapel Hill: University of North Carolina Press, 2009.

Gootenberg, Paul. "Cocaine's Long March North, 1900–2010." *Latin American Politics and Society* 54, no. 1 (2012): 159–179.

Granada, Soledad, Jorge Restrepo, and Andrés Vargas. "El agotamiento de la política de seguridad: Evolución y transformaciones recientes en el conflicto armado colombiano" (The Exhaustion of the Democratic Security Policy). In *Guerra y violencia en Colombia: Herramientas e interpretaciones*, edited by Jorge Restrepo and David Aponte, 27–124. Bogotá: Universidad Javeriana, CERAC, GTZ, 2009.

Grayson, George. *The Evolution of Los Zetas in Mexico and Central America: Sadism as an Instrument of Cartel Warfare*. Carlisle, PA: United States Army War College Press, 2015.

Grayson, George. *Mexico: Narco Violence and a Failed State?* New Brunswick, NJ: Transaction, 2010.

Grillo, Ioan. *El Narco: Inside Mexico's Criminal Insurgency*. Dexter, MI: Bloomsbury, 2012.

Grupo Interdisciplinario de Expertos Independientes. *Informe Ayotzinapa II, 2016* (Report on Ayotzinapa). México: Grupo Interdisciplinario de Expertos Independientes, 2016. http://centroprodh.org.mx/GIEI/.

Grzymala-Busse, Anna. "Beyond Clientelism: Incumbent Capture and State Building." *Comparative Political Studies* 41, no. 4–5 (2008): 638–673.

Guerrero, Eduardo. "La dispersión de la violencia" (The Dispersion of Violence). *Nexos*, February 1, 2012. http://www.nexos.com.Mx/?P=Leerarticulo&Article=2102543.

Guerrero, Eduardo. "La raíz de la violencia" (The Root of Violence). *Nexos* June 1, 2011. http://www.nexos.com.mx/?p=14318.

Gutiérrez, Alejandro. "Hombre inteligente, respetado, y querido según la DEA y el FBI es ahora el principal narcotraficante de México" (An Intelligent, Respected, and Loved Man Is Now the Most Important Trafficker in Mexico According to DEA and FBI). *Proceso*, no. 1003, January 22, 1996. Reprint, special edition no. 32, May 2011, 64–65.

Gutiérrez, Alejandro, and I. Ramírez. "El escurridizo" (The Slippery One). *Proceso*, no. 1054, January 13, 1997. Reprint, special edition no. 32, May 2011, 62–64.

Gutiérrez, Francisco. "Criminal Rebels: A Discussion of Civil War and Criminality from the Colombian Experience." *Politics and Society* 32, no. 2 (2004): 257–285.

Gutiérrez, Francisco. *¿Lo que el viento se llevó? Los partidos politicos y la democracia en Colombia (1958–2002)* (Gone With the Wind? Political Parties and Democracy in Colombia). Bogotá: Editorial Norma, 2007.

Gutiérrez, Francisco, and Mauricio Barón. "Estado, control territorial paramilitar y orden político en Colombia: Notas para una economía política del paramilitarismo 1978–2004" (State, Paramilitary Territorial Control and Political Order in Colombia: Notes for a Political Economy of Paramilitarism). In *Nuestra guerra sin nombre: Transformaciones del conflicto en Colombia*, edited by Gonzalo Sánchez and Francisco Gutiérrez, 267–311. Bogotá: IEPRI, Editorial Norma, 2006.

Gutiérrez, Francisco, and Ana Maria Jaramillo. "Crime, (Counter-) Insurgency and the Privatization of Security: The Case of Medellín (Colombia)." *Environment and Urbanization* 16, no. 2 (2004): 17–30.

Gutiérrez, Francisco, and Ana María Jaramillo. "Paradoxical Pacts" In *Democratizing Democracy: Beyond the Liberal Democratic Canon*, edited by Boaventura de Sousa Santos, 193–219. New York: Verso, 2005.

Gutiérrez, Francisco, and Gonzalo Sánchez. *Nuestra guerra sin nombre: Transformaciones del conflicto en Colombia* (Our War without a Name: Transformations of the Armed Conflict in Colombia). Bogotá: IEPRI, Editorial Norma, 2006.

Gutiérrez, Francisco, María Teresa Pinto, Juan Carlos Arenas, Tania Guzmán, and María Teresa Gutierrez. "Politics and Security in Three Colombian Cities." Crisis States Research Centre, Working Paper Series no. 2, Working Paper 44, London School of Economics, Development Studies Institute, 2009.

Guzmán, Alvaro. *Diagnóstico sobre la violencia homicida en Cali* (Diagnosis of Homicidal Violence in Cali). Cali: Desepaz, Cidse, 1993.

Guzmán, Alvaro, and Álvaro Camacho. *Colombia: Ciudad y Violencia* (Colombia: City and Violence). Bogotá: Ediciones Foro Nacional, 1990.

Guzmán, Alvaro, and Renata Moreno. "Autodefensas, narcotráfico, y comportamiento estatal en El Valle del Cauca, 1997–2005" (Self Defense Forces, Drug Trafficking and State Behavior in Valle del Cauca 1997-2005). In *La parapolítica. La ruta de la expansión paramilitar y los acuerdos politicos*, edited by Mauricio Romero, 165. Bogotá: Corporación Nuevo Arco Iris, 2007.

Hagedorn, John. *A World of Gangs: Armed Young Men and Gangsta Culture*. Minneapolis: University of Minnesota Press, 2008.

Hansen, Thomas Blom, and Finn Stepputat. *States of Imagination: Ethnographic Explorations of the Postcolonial State*. Durham, NC: Duke University Press, 2001.

Heinle, Kimberly, Cory Molzahn, and David Shirk. "Drug Violence in Mexico: Data and Analysis through 2014." Justice in Mexico Project, University of San Diego, 2015.

Heinle, Kimberly, Cory Molzahn, and David Shirk. "Drug Violence in Mexico: Data and Analysis through 2015." Justice in Mexico Project, University of San Diego, 2016.

Herman, Edward S., and Noam Chomsky. *Manufacturing Consent: The Political Economy of the Mass Media*. New York: Random House, 2010.

Hernández Navarro, Luis. "Peña Nieto's Victory in Mexico Is a Vote for the Old Regime." *Guardian*, July 2, 2012. http://www.guardian.co.uk/commentisfree/2012/jul/02/pena-nieto-mexico-old-regime

Hernández, Tania, and José Negrete. *La experiencia del PAN: Diez años de gobierno en Baja California* (The PAN's Experience: Ten Years of Government in Baja California). Tijuana: El Colegio de la Frontera Norte/Plaza y Valdés Editores, 2001.

Herrera, Luis Alfonso. *El desgobierno de la ciudad y la política de abandono: Miradas desde la frontera de México* (The Ungovernance of the City and the Policy of Abandonment). Ciudad Juárez: Universidad Autónoma de Ciudad Juárez. Universidad Complutense de Madrid, 2008.

Hervella, Jaime. *Ciudad Juárez: Residencial narcofosas* (Ciudad Juárez: A Condominium of Mass Graves). El Paso, TX: Jesus A. Blanco, 2006.

Hess, Karen. *Introduction to Law Enforcement and Criminal Issues*. 9th ed. Belmont, CA: Wadsworth Cengage Learning, 2009.

Hoffman, Bruce, and Gordon McCormick. "Terrorism, Signaling, and Suicide Attack." *Studies in Conflict and Terrorism* 27, no. 4 (2004): 243–281.

Hope, Alejandro, and Eduardo Clark. "Si los vecinos legalizan" (If Our Neighbors Legalize). Instituto Mexicano para la Competitividad IMCO, 2012. http://imco.org.mx/wp-content/uploads/2012/10/reporte_tecnico_legalizacion_marihuana.pdf.

Hoyos, Carlos Mauro. Intervención del Procurador General de la Nación ante el Congreso de la República (Procurator's Intervention Before the Senate). *Anales del Congreso de la República de Colombia*. Bogotá, August 30, 1983.

Human Rights Watch. *Los desaparecidos de México: El persistente costo de una crisis ignorada* (The Disappeared in Mexico: The Persistent Cost of a Crisis Ignored), Washington DC: Human Rights Watch, 2013. https://www.hrw.org/es/report/2013/02/20/los-desaparecidos-de-mexico/el-persistente-costo-de-una-crisis-ignorada.

Human Rights Watch. *Paramilitaries Heirs: The New Face of Violence in Colombia*. Washington, DC: Human Rights Watch, 2010. https://www.hrw.org/report/2010/02/03/paramilitaries-heirs/new-face-violence-colombia.

Idler, Annette. "Arrangements of Convenience: Violent Nonstate Actor Relationships and Citizen Security in the Shared Borderlands of Colombia, Ecuador, and Venezuela." PhD diss., University of Oxford, 2014.

Idler, Annette. "Exploring Agreements of Convenience Made among Violent Nonstate Actors." *Perspectives on Terrorism* 6, no. 4–5 (October 2012). http://www.terrorismanalysts.com/pt/index.php/pot/article/view/217/html.

Indepaz. *Séptimo reporte de la presencia de grupos paramilitares 2011* (Seventh Report on Presence of Paramilitary Groups 2011). Bogotá: Indepaz, 2012.

INEGI (Instituto Nacional de Estadística y Geografía de México). "Datos preliminares revelan que en 2014 se registraron 19 mil 669 homicidios" (Preliminary Data Reveals 19,669 Homicides in 2014). Press Release No. 276/15. July 20, 2015. http://www.inegi.org.mx/saladeprensa/boletines/2015/especiales/especiales2015_07_4.pdf.

Instituto Popular de Capacitación. "Desponjándose de los miedos . . . Emergen las víctimas: Informe de Derechos Humanos 2007" (When Fears Are Abandoned, the Victims Emerge). *Relecturas* 31. Medellín: Instituto Popular de Capacitación, 2007.

Instituto Popular de Capacitación. "En deuda con los derechos humanos y el DIH: Diversas miradas críticas en Medellín" (In Debt with Human Rights and International Humanitarian Law). *Relecturas* 27. Medellín: Instituto Popular de Capacitación, 2003.

Instituto Popular de Capacitación. "Entre la adversidad y la persistencia: Derechos humanos en Medellín" (Between Adversity and Persistence: Human Rights in Medellín). *Relecturas* 30. Medellín: Instituto Popular de Capacitación, 2006.

Instituto Popular de Capacitación. "El péndulo de la violencia: Rupturas y continuidades del conflicto en Antioquia" (The Pendulum of Violence: Ruptures and Continuities of Conflict in Medellín). *Relecturas* 33. Informe de Derechos Humanos 2009. Medellín: Instituto Popular de Capacitación, 2009.

Instituto Popular de Capacitación. "Un poco de luz en la oscuridad: Derechos humanos integrales" (Some Light in the Darkness: Integral Human Rights). *Relecturas*. Medellín: Instituto Popular de Capacitación, 2004.

Instituto Popular de Capacitación. "Selectividad y guerra: Avanza el círculo vicioso" (Selectivity and War: The Vicious Circle Advances). *Relecturas* 32. Informe de Derechos Humanos 2008. Medellín: Instituto Popular de Capacitación, 2008.

Instituto Popular de Capacitación. "Transporte público: Un botín en contextos de conflicto" (Public Transportation: A Booty during Conflict Times). Information bulletin no. 1, February 10, 2011.

Insuasty Mora, Raul. "Delitos sexuales en Colombia, 2008" (Sexual Crime in Colombia). *Revista Forensis*, 2008:153–188. http://www.medicinalegal.gov.co/documents/10180/34156/2.

Interamerican Commission on Human Rights (IACHR). *Human Rights Situation in Mexico.* Washington, DC: Organization of American States, 2015.

International Crisis Group. *Desmantelar los nuevos grupos armados ilegales en Colombia: Lecciones de un sometimiento* (Dismantling New Illegal Armed Groups in Colombia: Lessons of a Surrender). Bogotá/Brussels: Latin America Report, no. 48, June 8, 2012.

Jaramillo, Ana María. *Milicias populares en Medellín: Entre la guerra y la paz* (Popular Militias in Medellín: Between War and Peace). Medellín: Corporación Región, 1994.

Jaramillo, Ana María, Ramiro Ceballos, and Martha Villa. *En la encrucijada: Conflicto y cultura política en Medellín en los noventa* (At a Crossroads: Conflict and Political Culture in Medellín in the Nineties). Medellín: Corporación Región, 1998.

Jones, Nathan. "Explaining the Slight Uptick of Violence in Tijuana." James Baker III Institute for Public Policy of Rice University, Houston, TX, 2013.

Jones, Nathan. "The State Reaction: A Theory of Illicit Network Resilience." PhD diss., University of California, Irvine, 2011.

La Jornada. "Asesinaron en 10 años a 75 alcaldes, reporta la Anac" (In 10 years, 75 Mayors Have Been Murdered According to Anac). *Jornada*, May 15, 2016. http://www.jornada.unam.mx/ultimas/2016/05/15/asesinaron-en-10-anos-a-75-alcaldes-reporta-la-anac.

La Jornada. "Cuatro ejecutados en Chihuahua y Sinaloa: Uno era jefe policiaco de la primera entidad" (Four Dead in Chihuahua and Sinaloa: One Was a Police Chief in Chihuahua). *Jornada*. December 25, 2005. http://www.jornada.unam.mx/2005/12/23/index.php?section=politica&article=019n1pol.

La Jornada. "Hallan en Tijuana tres cadáveres en tambos con ácido" (Three Bodies Found within Barrels with Acid in Tijuana). *Jornada*, October 1, 2008. Article no longer available online.

La Jornada. "Operativos conjuntos detonaron homicidios en seis entidades" (Joint Operations Precipitated Homicides in Six States). *Jornada*, May 8, 2011, p. 9.

Juris, Jeffrey. "Violence Performed and Imagined: Militant Action, the Black Bloc, and the Mass Media in Genoa." *Critique of Anthropology* 25, no. 4 (2005): 413–432.

Jusidman, Clara, ed. *La realidad social de Ciudad Juárez, análisis social* (The Social Reality of Ciudad Juárez, Social Analysis). Vol. 1. Ciudad Juárez: Universidad Autónoma de Ciudad Juárez, 2008.

Kachin Women's Association Thailand. *Silent Offensive: How Burma Army Strategies Are Fuelling the Kachin Drug Crisis*. Thailand: Kachin Women's Association Thailand, 2015. http://womenof-burma.org/wp-content/uploads/2014/10/Silent-Offensive-Drug-Report_English.pdf.

Kaldor, Mary. *New and Old Wars: Organized Violence in a Global Era*. Stanford, CA: Stanford University Press, 2001.

Kalyvas, Stathis. *The Logic of Violence in Civil War*. Cambridge, UK: Cambridge University Press, 2006.

Kalyvas, Stathis. "Wanton and Senseless: The Logic of Massacres in Algeria." *Rationality and Society* 11, no. 3 (1999): 243–285.

Karlin, Mark. "Fueled by War on Drugs, Mexican Death Toll Could Exceed 120,000 as Calderon Ends Six-Year Reign," *Truthout*, November 28, 2012. http://www.truth-out.org/news/item/13001-calderon-reign-ends-with-six-year-mexican-death-toll-near-120000.

Kenney, Michael. *From Pablo to Osama: Trafficking and Terrorist Networks, Government Bureaucracies and Competitive Adaptation*. University Park: Pennsylvania State University Press, 2007.

Kenny, Paul, and Mónica Serrano. "Introduction: Security Failure vs. State Failure." In *Mexico's Security Failure: Collapse into Criminal Violence*, edited by Paul Kenny, Mónica Serrano, and Arturo Sotomayor, 1–54. New York: Routledge, 2012.

Kilmer, Beau, Jonathan Caulkins, Brittany Bond, and Peter Reuter. "Reducing Drug Trafficking Revenues and Violence in Mexico: Would Legalizing Marijuana in California Help?" Santa Monica, CA: RAND Corporation, 2010. https://www.rand.org/pubs/occasional_papers/OP325.readonline.html

Kleiman, Mark. "Surgical Strikes in the Drug Wars: Smarter Policies for Both Sides of the Border," *Foreign Policy* 90, no. 5 (September–December 2011): 89–101.

Kydd, Andrew, and Barbara Walter. "The Strategies of Terrorism." *International Security* 31, no. 1 (2006): 49–80.

Koonings, Kees, and Dirk Kruijt. *Societies of Fear: The Legacy of Civil War, Violence, and Terror in Latin America*. London: Zed Books, 1999.

Kramer, Tom. "The Current State of Counternarcotics Policy and Drug Reform Debate In Myanmar." Foreign policy paper, Brookings Institution, Washington, DC, 2015.

LaFranchi, Howard. "Mexico Declares War against Drug Traffickers." *Christian Science Monitor*, January 30, 2001. https://www.csmonitor.com/2001/0130/p7s1.html.

Lamb, Robert. "Microdynamics of Illegitimacy and Complex Urban Violence in Medellín, Colombia." PhD Diss., University of Maryland, 2010.

Lankina, Tomila. "Sisyphean Endeavor or Worthwhile Undertaking? Transcending within Nation, within Region Sub-National Democracy Analysis." *Comparative Democratization Newsletter, America Political Science Association* 10, no. 1 (2012): 2–14.

Latin American Commission on Drugs and Democracy (LACDD). *Drugs and Democracy: Toward a Paradigm Shift*. Report by the Latin American Commission on Drugs and Democracy. Geneva: Latin American Commission on Drugs and Democracy: 2012.

Lazcano y Ochoa, Manuel. "Una vida en la vida Sinaloense: Memorias de Manuel Lazcano y Ochoa" (One Life in the Sinaloan Life: Memoirs of Manuel Lazcano y Ochoa). Culiacán: Universidad de Occidente, 1992.

Lee, Rensselaer, and Francisco Thoumi. "The Political-Criminal Nexus in Colombia." *Trends in Organized Crime* 5, no. 2 (1999): 59–84.

Lessing, Benjamin. "The Logic of Violence in Criminal War: Cartel-State Conflict in Mexico, Colombia, and Brazil." PhD diss., University of California, 2012.

Lessing, Benjamin. "Logics of Violence in Criminal War." *Journal of Conflict Resolution* 59, no. 8 (2015): 1486–1516.

Lessing, Benjamin. "When Business Gets Bloody: State Policy and Drug Violence." In *Small Arms Survey 2012: Moving Targets*, 41–72. Cambridge: Cambridge University Press and Small Arms Survey, 2012.

Levitsky, Steven, and Lucan Way. "The Rise of Competitive Authoritarianism." *Journal of Democracy* 13, no. 2 (200): 51–65.

Ley, Sandra. "El desafío de contar a nuestros muertos" (The Challenge of Counting our Deceased). *Letras Libres*, September 12, 2012. Http://Www.Letraslibres.Com/Blogs/Polifonia/ El-Desafio-De-Contar-Nuestros-Muertos,

Lieberman, Evan. "Nested Analysis as a Mixed-Method Strategy for Comparative Research." *American Political Science Review* 99, no. 3 (2005): 435–452.

Llorente, María Victoria. "¿Desmilitarización en tiempos de guerra? La reforma policial en Colombia" (Demilitarization in Wartime: Police Reform in Colombia). In *Seguridad y reforma policial en las Americas: Tendencias y Desafíos*, edited by Lucia Dammert and John Bailey, 192–218. Mexico City: Siglo XXI, 2005.

Lohmuller, Michael. "No Solution in Sight for Mexico's Vigilante Problem." *InSight Crime*, November 13, 2015. http://www.insightcrime.com/news-analysis/no-solution-sight-mexico-michoacan-vigilante-problem.

Lomnitz, Claudio. *Death and the Idea of Mexico*. New York: Zone Books, 2005.

López, Andrés. "Narcotráfico, ilegalidad, y conflicto en Colombia" (Drug Trafficking, Illegality, and Conflict in Colombia). In *Nuestra Guerra sin Nombre: Transformaciones del Conflicto en Colombia*, edited by Gonzalo Sánchez and Francisco Gutiérrez, 405–440. Bogotá: IEPRI, Editorial Norma, 2006.

López López Andrés. *El cartel de los sapos. La historia secreta de una de las mafias más poderosas en el mundo: El cartel del Norte del Valle (The Snitches Cartel. The History of One of the World's Most Powerful Mafias: The Norte del Valle Cartel)*. Bogotá: Planeta, 2008.

López, Claudia, ed. *Y refundaron la patria: De cómo mafiosos y politicos reconfiguraron el estado colombiano* (And they Refounded the Motherland: How Mafiosi and Politicians Reconfigured the Colombian State). Barcelona: Random House Mondadori Debate, 2010.

Lozano, Juan José, and Hollman Morris. *Impunity*. 2011. Documentary.

Lupsha, Peter. "Drug Lords and Narco-Corruption: The Players Change but the Game Continues." *Crime, Law, and Social Change* 16 (1991): 41–58.

Lupsha, Peter, and Stanley Pimentel. "The Nexus between Crime and Politics: Mexico." *Trends in Organized Crime* 3, no. 1 (1997): 65–67.

Mafia&Co. "Polarization and Sustained Violence in Mexico's Cartel War" January 27, 2011. https://mafiaandco.wordpress.com/2012/01/27/polarization-and-sustained-violence-in-mexicos-cartel-war/. Originally published on Stratfor, January 24, 2011.

Magaloni, Beatriz. *Voting for Autocracy: Hegemonic Party Survival and Its Demise in Mexico*. New York: Cambridge University Press, 2008.

Malm, Aili and Gisela Bichler. "Networks of Collaborating Criminals: Assessing the Structural Vulnerability of Drug Markets." *Journal of Crime and Delinquency*, 48, no. 2 (2011): 271–297.

Malone, Mary. "The Verdict Is In: The Impact of Crime on Public Trust in Central American Justice Systems." *Journal of Politics in Latin America* 2, no. 3 (2010): 99–128.

Marenin, Otwin. "Review: Police Performance and State Rule: Control and Autonomy in the Exercise of Coercion." *Comparative Politics* 18, no. 1 (1985): 101–122.

Marosi, Richard. "Antidrug General Ousted." *LA Times*, August 9, 2008. http://articles.latimes.com/2008/aug/09/world/fg-general9.

Marten, Kimberly. *Warlords: Strong Arm Brokers in Weak States*. Ithaca, NY: Cornell University Press, 2012.

Martínez Canizales, Georgina, and Cheryl Howard. "Mortalidad por homicidio: Una revision comparativa en los municipios de Tijuana y Juárez, 1985–1997" (Homicide Mortality: A Comparative Review of the Municipalities of Tijuana and Juárez, 1985–1997). In *Entre las duras aristas de las armas: Violencia y victimización en Ciudad Juárez*, edited by Patricia Ravelo and Héctor Dominguez, 85–115. Ciudad Juárez: Publicaciones de La Casa Chata, 2006.

McCaffrey, Barry. "After Action Report—General Barry R McCaffrey USA (Ret). Memorandum for Colonel Michael Meese on Visit to Mexico 5–7 December 2008." Council on Hemispheric Affairs, January 19, 2009. http://www.coha.org/After-Action-Report%E2%80%94general-Barry-R-Mccaffrey-Usa-Ret/.

McCormick, Gordon, and Frank Giordano. "Things Come Together: Symbolic Violence and Guerrilla Mobilisation." *Third World Quarterly* 28, no. 2 (2007): 295–320. Special issue: *The Long War—Insurgency, Counterinsurgency, and Collapsing States*.

Medina Franco, Gilberto. *Historia sin fin ... Las milicias de Medellín en la década del noventa* (Never-Ending Story . . . Militias in Medellín during the Nineties). Medellín: Instituto Popular de Capacitación, 2006.

Mejía, Daniel. "Evaluating Plan Colombia." In *Innocent Bystanders: Developing Countries and the War on Drugs*, edited by Philip Keefer and Norman Loaiza, 135–164. Washington, DC: World Bank and Palgrave Macmillan, 2010.

Mejía, Daniel, Pascual Restrepo, and Sandra Rozo, "On the Effectiveness of Supply-Reduction Efforts in Drug-Producing Countries: Evidence from Colombia." Unpublished manuscript, Universidad de los Andes, 2013.

Mendoza, Enrique, and Rosario Mossa. "El presidente de las 83 mil ejecuciones" (The President of the 83,000 Executions). *Zeta*, November 26, 2012. http://zetatijuana.com/2012/11/el-presidente-de-las-83-mil-ejecuciones/.

México Evalúa. *Presentación índice de víctimas visibles e invisibles de delitos graves* (Index of Visible and Invisible Victims of Grave Crimes). September 11, 2011. http://mexico-evalua.org/portfolio-items/presentacion-indice-de-victimas-visibles-e-invisibles-de-delitos-graves/.

Merino, José. "Los operativos conjuntos y la tasa de homicidios: Una medición" (Joint Operations and Homicide Rates: A measurement Exercise). *Nexos*, June 1, 2011. Http://Www.Nexos.Com.Mx/?P=14319.

Meyer, Kathryn, and Terry Parssinen. *Webs of Smoke: Smugglers, Warlords, Spies, and the History of the International Drug Trade*. Lanham, MD: Rowman & Littlefield, 2002.

Misión de Apoyo al Proceso de Paz en Colombia, Organización de Estados Americanos (MAPP-OEA). *Séptimo informe trimestral del secretario general al consejo permanente sobre la misión de apoyo al proceso de paz en Colombia MAPP-OEA* (Seventh Quarterly Report of the Secretary General to the Permanent Council About the Mission to Support the Peace Process in Colombia). August 30, 2006.

Misse, Michel, and Joana Vargas. "Drug Use and Trafficking in Rio de Janeiro." *Vibrant-Virtual Brazilian Anthropology* 7, no. 2 (2010): 88–108.

Molano, Alfredo. "Buenaventura: Entre la pobreza y la violencia" (Buenaventura: Between Poverty and Violence). *Espectador*, February 23, 2013. http://www.elespectador.com/noticias/nacional/buenaventura-entre-pobreza-y-violencia-articulo-406499.

Molloy, Molly. "The Mexican Undead: Toward a New History of the 'Drug War' Killing Fields." Small Wars Journal, no. 12, August 21, 2013, p. 28.

Molzahn, Cory, Viridiana Rios, and David A. Shirk. "Drug Violence in Mexico: Data and Analysis through 2011." Trans-Border Institute, University of San Diego, San Diego, 2012.

Molzahn, Cory, Octavio Rodríguez, and David Shirk. "Drug Violence in Mexico: Data and Analysis through 2012." Transborder Institute, University of San Diego, 2013.

Monárrez Fragoso, Julia. *Trama de una injusticia: Feminicidio sexual sistémico en Ciudad Juárez* (Tale of Injustice: Systemic Sexual Feminicide in Ciudad Juárez). Tijuana: El Colegio de La Frontera Norte, Porrúa, 2009.

Moncada, Eduardo. *Cities, Business, and the Politics of Urban Violence in Latin America*. Stanford, CA: Stanford University Press, 2016.

Moncada, Eduardo. "Counting Bodies: Crime Mapping, Policing, and Race in Colombia." *Ethnic and Racial Studies* 33, no. 4 (2010): 696–716.

Moncada, Eduardo. "Toward Democratic Policing in Colombia? Institutional Accountability through Lateral Reform." *Comparative Politics* 41, no. 4 (2009): 431–449.

Moncada, Eduardo. "Politics, Business, and Violence: Urban Security in Colombia (1988–2008)." PhD diss., Brown University, 2011.

Moncada, Eduardo. "The Politics of Urban Violence: Challenges for Development in the Global South." *Studies in Comparative International Development* 48, no. 3 (2013): 217–239.

Moncada, Eduardo. "Urban Violence, Political Economy, and Territorial Control: Insights from Medellin." *Latin American Research Review*, 2016: 225–248.

Moncada, Eduardo, and Richard Snyder. "Subnational Comparative Research on Democracy: Taking Stock and Looking Forward." *Comparative Democratization Newsletter, America Political Science Association* 10, no. 1 (2012): 4–9.

Moodie, Ellen. *El Salvador in the Aftermath of Peace: Crime, Uncertainty, and the Transition to Democracy*. Philadelphia: University of Pennsylvania Press, 2010.

Moore, Gary. "The Legacy of Sinaloa Cartel Lieutenant El Flaco." *Insight Crime*, October 17, 2011. http://www.insightcrime.com/investigations/the-legacy-of-sinaloa-cartel-lieutenant-el-flaco

Moore, Molly. "Drug Traffickers Thrive amid Tijuana Terror." *Washington Post*, February 16, 1997, p. A1. https://www.washingtonpost.com/archive/politics/1997/02/16/drug-traffickers-thrive-amid-tijuana-terror/f25902f6-1b23-4bc8-8968-fb9600355f2d/

Moore, Molly. "Mexican Drug Lord Found Slain." *Washington Post*, September 12, 1998. https://www.washingtonpost.com/archive/politics/1998/09/12/mexican-drug-lord-found-slain/305609c0-f7a1-4f91-8257-666f7db058a0/.

Moser, Caroline. *Reducing Urban Violence in Developing Countries*. Brookings Institution: Washington, D.C, 2006.

Moser, Caroline, and Cathy McIlwaine. *Encounters with Violence in Latin America: Urban Poor Perceptions from Colombia and Guatemala*. New York: Routledge, 2004.

Moser, Caroline, and Dennis Rodgers. *Change, Violence, and Insecurity in Nonconflict Situations*. London: Overseas Development Institute, 2005.

El Mundo. "Confesiones de un alcalde de Ciudad Juárez: No hay colaboración entre gobiernos" (A Mayor's Confessions: There Is No Cooperation between Authorities). *Mundo*, October 13, 2010. http://www.elmundo.es/america/2010/10/12/mexico/1286839864.html.

Murillo, Maria Victoria, and Cecilia Martínez-Gallardo. "Political Competition and Policy Adoption." *American Journal of Political Science* 51, no. 1 (2007): 120–139.

Naím, Moisés. *Illicit: How Smugglers, Traffickers, and Copycats Are Hijacking the Global Economy*. New York: Anchor, 2006.

National Drug Intelligence Center. *National Drug Threat Assesment 2011*. Washington, DC: US Department of Justice, 2011.

Naylor, R. Thomas. "Mafias, Myths, and Markets: On the Theory and Practice of Enterprise Crime." *Transnational Organized Crime* 3, no. 3 (1997): 1–45.

El Noroeste. "Arroja hora violenta cuatro muertos en Culiacán" (Deadly Hour Leaves Four Deceased). *Noroeste*, May 1, 2008. http://www.noroeste.com.mx/pub/32187.

El Noroeste. "Más narcomantas" (More Narcobanners). *Noroeste*, May 5, 2008. http://www.noroeste.com.mx/pub/33967.

El Noroeste. "Son doce los detenidos por balacera en La Guadalupe" (Twelve Arrested After Shooting at Guadalupe). *Noroeste* May 1, 2008.

El Noroeste. "Vuelve el pasado: Regresa Alfredo Mejía Pérez a la PEP" (The Past Returns: Alfredo Mejía Pérez Is Back at the PEP). *Noroeste*, March 30, 2011. http://www.noroeste.com.mx/pub/332365.

North, Douglas. *Institutions, Institutional Change, and Economic Performance*. Cambridge, UK: Cambridge University Press, 1990.

North, Douglas, John Joseph Wallis, and Barry Weingast. *Violence and Social Orders: A Conceptual Framework for Interpreting Recorded Human History*. New York: Cambridge University Press, 2009.

Observatorio Social Alcaldía de Cali. *Homicidios y pandillas juveniles en Santiago de Cali 2005–2009* (Homicides and Youth Gangs in Cali). Cali: Alcaldía de Santiago de Cali, 2010.

Ochoa Reza, Enrique. "Multiple Arenas of Struggle: Federalism and Mexico's Transition to Democracy." In *Federalism and Democracy in Latin America*, edited by Edward Gibson, 255–297. Baltimore: Johns Hopkins University Press, 2004.

O'Donnell, Guillermo "Delegative Democracy." *Journal of Democracy* 5, no. 1 (1994): 55–69.

Office of the High Commissioner for Human Rights. *Informe de la Alta Comisionada de las Naciones Unidas para los Derechos Humanos sobre la situación de los derechos humanos en Colombia 2005* (Report of the High Commissioner about the Human Rights Situation in Colombia 2005). Bogotá: Office of the High Commissioner for Human Rights: 2006.

Office of the High Commissioner for Human Rights. "La oficina en Colombia del Alto Comisionado de Las Naciones Unidas para los Derechos Humanos reitera su posición sobre la 'Ley de Justicia y Paz' " (The Office of the High Commissioner for Human Rights Reiterates its Position About the Peace and Justice Law) Bogotá: Office of the High Commissioner for Human Rights: October 13, 2006.

Office of the High Commissioner for Human Rights. *Report of the United Nations High Commissioner for Human Rights on the Situation of Human Rights in Colombia*. Geneva, February 3, 2011.

Olson, Mancur. "Dictatorship, Democracy, and Development." *American Political Science Review* 87, no. 3 (1993): 567–576.

Organization of American States. *Pandillas delictivas*. Washington, DC: January 28, 2010. http://scm.oas.org/pdfs/2010/CP23778S.pdf.

Órtiz Pinchetti, Francisco. "El hombre más buscado del mundo" (The World's Most Wanted Man). *Proceso*, no. 650 (April 17, 1989). Reprint, special edition no. 32, February 2011, 18–20.

Osorio, Javier. "The Contagion of Drug Violence: Spatiotemporal Dynamics of the Mexican War on Drugs." *Journal of Conflict Resolution* 59, no. 8 (2015):1403–1432.

Osorio, Javier. "Hobbes on Drugs: Understanding Drug Violence in Mexico." PhD diss., University of Notre Dame, 2013.

Oude Breuil, Brenda Carina, and Ralph Rozema. "Fatal Imaginations: Death Squads in Davao City and Medellín Compared." *Crime Law and Social Change* 52, no. 4 (2009): 405–424.

El Pais. "El Ocaso de los Narcos" (The Narcos' Decline). *País*, January 15, 2007. Article no longer available online.

Padgett, Tim. "Guatemala's Kaibiles: A Notorious Commando Unit Wrapped Up in Central America's Drug War." *Time*, July 14, 2011. http://world.time.com/2011/07/14/guatemalas-kaibil-terror-from-dictators-to-drug-cartels/

Palacios, Marco, and Frank Safford. *Colombia: País fragmentado, sociedad dividida* (Colombia: Fragmented Country, Divided Nation). Bogotá: Editorial Norma, 2002.

Palacios, Marco, and Mónica Serrano. "Colombia y México: Las violencias del narcotráfico" (Colombia and Mexico: The Violence of Drug Trafficking). In *Seguridad nacional y seguridad interior*, edited by Arturo Alvarado and Mónica Serrano. Mexico City: El Colegio de México, 2010: 105–155.

Paley, Dawn. *Drug War Capitalism*. Chico, CA: Ak Press, 2014.

Pansters, Wil, ed. *Violence, Coercion, and State-Making in Twentieth-Century Mexico: The Other Half of the Centaur*. Stanford, CA: Stanford University Press, 2012.

Paoli, Letizia. "The Paradoxes of Organized Crime." *Crime, Law, and Social Change* 37 (2002): 51–97.

Pardo, Rafael. *De primera mano: Colombia 1986–1994, entre conflictos y esperanzas (A Firsthand Account: Colombia 1986–1994, between Conflict and Hope)*. Bogotá: Editorial Norma, 1996.

Payan, Tony. *The Three US-Mexico Border Wars: Drugs, Immigration, and Homeland Security*. Westport, CT: Praeger Security International, 2006.

Pérez-Espino, José, and Alejandro Paez. "Los Carrillo llegan a Chihuahua" (The Carrillos Arrive in Chihuahua). *Universal* April 3, 2009. http://archivo.eluniversal.com.mx/nacion/166844.html.

Personeria de Medellín. *Informe sobre la situación de derechos humanos* (Human Rights Report). Medellín: 2005.

Personeria de Medellín. *Informe sobre la situación de derechos humanos en Medellín* (Human Rights Report). Medellín: 2011.

Petrich, Blanche. "Librarse de la sombra de Hank Rhon, el mayor reto para el PRI, según EU" (To Free Itself from Hank Rhon's Shadow, the Greatest Challenge for the PRI, according to US). *Jornada*, June 6, 2012. http://www.jornada.unam.mx/2011/06/05/politica/006n1pol.

Pierson, Paul. "Increasing Returns, Path Dependence, and the Study of Politics." *American Political Science Review* 94, no. 2 (2000): 251–268.

Pineda Jaimes, Servando, and Luis Alfonso Herrera Robles. "Alternancia y violencia: La seguridad pública en Ciudad Juárez 1992–2004" (Alternation and Violence: Public Security in Ciudad Juárez). In *La seguridad pública local: Inseguridad, delincuencia, y participación ciudadana en Ciudad Juárez*, edited by Jose Alfredo Zavaleta Betancourt. Ciudad Juárez: Universidad Autónoma de Ciudad Juárez, Consejo Nacional de Ciencia y Tecnología, Presidencia Municipal de Juárez, Fondo Mixto de Fomento a la Investigación Científica y Tecnológica, 2007.

Pinheiro Gawryszewski, Antonio Sanhueza, Ramón Martínez-Piedra, José Antonio Escamilla, and Maria de Fátima Marinho de Souza. "Homicídios na região das Américas: Magnitude, distribuição, e tendências, 1999–2009 (Homicide in the Americas: Magnitude, Distribution, and Trends, 1999–2009)." *Ciência & Saúde Coletiva* 17, no. 12 (2012): 3171–3182.

Pinto, María Teresa. "La disputa política en torno a la Alcaldía de Santiago de Cali de 2007 (The Political Dispute Surrounding Cali's Mayor Election in 2007)." *Revista Sociedad y Economía* 14 (2008): 201–226.

Poire, Alejandro. "Los homicidios y la violencia del crimen organizado" (Homicides and Violence from Organized Crime)," *Nexos*, February 1, 2010. http://www.nexos.com.mx/?p=14126.

Poppa, Terrence. *Drug Lord: The Life and Death of a Mexican Kingpin*. El Paso, TX: Cinco Puntos Press, 1990.

Presidencia de la República de México. "Boletín de la puesta en marcha del Operativo México Seguro" (Press Release of the Launching of Mexico Seguro Operation). June 13, 2005.

Pressly, Linda. "The Dump That Holds the Secrets of the Disappeared." *BBC News Magazine*, December 30, 2014. http://www.bbc.com/news/magazine-30573931.

Priest, Dana. "US Role at a Crossroads in Mexico's Intelligence War on the Cartels." *Washington Post*, April 27, 2013. http://www.washingtonpost.com/investigations/us-role-at-a-crossroads-in-mexicos-intelligence-war-on-the-cartels/2013/04/27/b578b3ba-a3b3-11e2-be47-b44febada3a8_story_4.html

Procuraduría General de Justicia del Estado de Campeche. Dirección de Averiguaciones previas "A." Novena agencia investigadora del Ministerio Público. Averiguación previa número: aap-4474/9ª/2007. Declaración del C. Abar Alvarado Beauregard. (p.r). (Testimony of C. Abar Alvarado Beauregard before the Campeche state Attorney General's Office During Preliminary Inquiries). 2007.

Procuraduría General de la República (PGR). Declaración Ministerial MESA III AP/PGR/BC/TIJ/217/09-M-III (Testimony of Santiago Meza before the Attorney General's Office). Tijuana: January 25, 2009.

Programa de Naciones Unidas para el Desarrollo (PNUD). *Hacia un Valle del Cauca incluyente y pacífico: Informe regional de desarrollo humano 2008* (Toward an Inclusive and Peaceful Valle del Cauca). Cali: PNUD, 2008.

Przeworski, Adam. *Democracy and the Market: Political and Economic Reforms in Eastern Europe and Latin America*. Cambridge, UK: Cambridge University Press, 1991.

Przeworski Adam, and Henry Teune. *The Logic of Comparative Social Inquiry*. New York. Wiley, 1970.

Putnam, Robert. "Diplomacy and Domestic Politics: The Logic of Two-Level Games." *International Organization* 42, no. 3 (1988): 427–460.

Quinn, Tom. "A Day with the Chessplayer." *Time*, July 1, 1991. http://content.time.com/time/magazine/article/0,9171,973268,00.html.

Quintana, Victor. "Informe que presenta el Diputado Victor Manuel Quintana correspondiente al periodo de receso de los meses de Enero–Febrero de 2008" (Report by the Deputy Victor Manuel Quintana). Congreso del Estado de Chihuahua, 2008.

Ragin, Charles. *The Comparative Method: Moving beyond Qualitative and Quantitative Strategies*. Berkeley: University of California Press, 1987.

Ramírez, Iván Darío. "Medellín: Los niños invisibles del conflicto social y armado" (Medellín: The Invisible Children of Social and Armed Conflict). In *Ni la guerra ni Paz: Comparaciones internacionales de niños y jóvenes en violencia armada organizada*, edited by Luke Dowdney, 150–172. Rio de Janeiro: Editorial Viveiros De Castro, 2005.

Ramírez, María Clemencia. "Maintaining Democracy in Colombia through Political Exclusion, States of Exception, Counterinsurgency, and Dirty War." In *Violent Democracies in Latin America*, edited by Enrique Desmond Arias and Daniel Goldstein, 84–107. Durham, NC: Duke University Press, 2010.

Ramírez Sánchez, Miguel. "Inseguridad pública en Tijuana, Tecate, y Rosarito: La paradoja del miedo y los delitos violentos" (Public Insecurity in Tijuana, Tecate, and Rosarito: The Paradox of Fear and Violent Crime). In *Diagnóstico sobre la realidad social, económica y cultural de los entornos locales para el diseño de intervenciones en materia de prevención y erradicación de la violencia en la región Norte: El caso de Tijuana, Baja California Norte*, edited by Silvia López Estrada, 365–397. México: SEGOB, Comisión Nacional para Prevenir y Erradicar La Violencia Contra Las Mujeres, 2009.

Ravelo, Ricardo. "Los Carrillo, bajo protección militar" (The Carrillo Family, Protected by the Army). *Proceso*, no. 1732, January 10, 2010. Reprint, special edition no. 32, May 2011, 77–80.

Ravelo, Ricardo. "Estructura intocada" (Untouched Organization). *Proceso*, no. 1324, March 17, 2002. Reprint, special edition no. 32, May 2011, 49.

Ravelo, Ricardo. "Historias de familia" (Family Stories). *Proceso*, no. 1630 (January 27, 2004). Reprint, special edition no. 33, May 2011, ##.

Ravelo, Ricardo. "La hora del desquite" (The Time to Get Even). *Proceso*, no. 1455, September 2004. Reprint, special edition no. 32, May 2011, 72–74.

Reed, Susan. "Certifiable: Mexico's Corruption, Washington's Indifference" *New Republic*, 1997. http://www.pbs.org/wgbh/pages/frontline/shows/mexico/readings/newrepublic.html.

Reno, William. "Congo: From State Collapse to 'Absolutism,' to State Failure." *Third World Quarterly* 27, no. 1 (2006): 43–56.

Restrepo, Jorge, Michael Spagat, and Juan Fernando Vargas. "El conflicto en Colombia ¿Quién hizo qué a quién? Un Enfoque Cuantitativo" (The Conflict in Colombia: Who did What to Whom?). In *Nuestra guerra sin nombre: Transformaciones del conflicto en Colombia*, edited by Francisco Gutiérrez and Gonzalo Sánchez, 505–542. Bogotá: Editorial Norma, 2006.

Reuter, Peter. *Disorganized Crime: The Economics of the Visible Hand*. Cambridge, MA: MIT Press, 1983.

Reuter, Peter. "Systemic Violence in Drug Markets." *Crime, Law, and Social Change* 52, no. 3 (2009): 275–284.

Reuter, Peter, and John Haaga. "The Organization of High-Level Drug Markets: An Exploratory Study." A Rand Note. Santa Monica, CA: Rand Corporation, 1989.

Revista Cambio. "El hombre que maneja medio país desde la cárcel" (The Man Who Handles Half of the Country from Prison). *Revista Cambio*, September 17, 2011. http://www.semana.com/nacion/articulo/el-hombre-maneja-medio-pais-desde-carcel/246553-3.

Revista Semana. "Un año de masacre de Jamundí en la que Batallón del ejército aniquiló la mejor unidad antidrogas de la policía" (A Year since the Jamundí Massacre: Army Battalion Slaughtered Police Antinarcotics Unit). *Revista Semana*, May 21, 2007. http://www.semana.com/on-line/articulo/un-ano-masacre-jamundi-batallon-del-ejercito-aniquilo-mejor-unidad-antidrogas-policia/86105-3.

Revista Semana. "Corrupción hasta el tuétano" (Corruption to the Core). *Revista Semana*, August 11, 2007. http://www.semana.com/nacion/articulo/corrupcion-hasta-tuetano/87562-3.

Revista Semana. "Don Diego permanecerá en el bunker de la fiscalía antes de ir a Combita" (Don Diego Will Remain in the Attorney General's Building until He Is Transferred to Combita Prison). *Revista Semana*, September 10, 2007. http://www.semana.com/on-line/articulo/don-diego-permanecera-bunker-fiscalia-antes-ir-combita/88166-3.

Revista Semana. "La entrega de Don Berna" (Don Berna's Surrender). *Revista Semana*, No. 1204 May 30, 2005. http://www.verdadabierta.com/victimarios/los-jefes/304-la-entrega.

Revista Semana."El fin del terror de Don Berna" (The End of Don Berna's Terror). *Revista Semana*, No. 1206 June 13, 2005. http://www.verdadabierta.com/victimarios/los-jefes/305-contra-la-oficina-del-terror.

Revista Semana. "¿Fracasó la extradición de narcotraficantes?" (Failure to Extradite Drug Dealers?) *Revista Semana*, April 14, 2012. http://www.semana.com/nacion/articulo/fracaso-extradicion-narcotraficantes/256408-3.

Revista Semana. "La jugada de Macaco" (Macaco's Plot). *Revista Semana*, November 22, 2005. http://www.semana.com/nacion/articulo/la-jugada-macaco/75271-3.

Revista Semana. "Los secretos de Don Berna" (Don Berna's Secrets). *Revista Semana*, July 14, 2007. http://www.semana.com/nacion/articulo/los-secretos-don-berna/87046-3.

Revista Semana. "La vida útil de los capos" (The Drug Lords' Life Span). *Revista Semana*, April 21, 2009. http://www.semana.com/nacion/narcotrafico/articulo/la-vida-util-capos/102283-3.

Riaño, Pilar. *Dwellers of Memory: Youth and Violence in Medellín.* New York: Transaction Publishers, 2006.

Rico, Daniel. "Las dimensiones internacionales del crimen organizado en Colombia: Las Bacrim, sus rutas, y refugios" (The International Dimensions of Organized Crime in Colombia). In *La diáspora criminal: La difusión trasnacional del crimen organizado y cómo contener su expansión, edited by* Juan Carlos Garzón and Eric Olson, 27–58. Washington, DC: Woodrow Wilson International Center for Scholars, 2013.

Rio Doce. "El otro frente: Copan al General Hidalgo Eddy y se le vence el plazo" (The Other Front: General Hidalgo Eddy Is Threatened and Faces an Ultimatum). *Rio Doce*, June 11, 2007. Article no longer available online.

Rios, Viridiana. "How Government Structure Encourages Criminal Violence: The Causes of Mexico's Drug War." PhD diss., Harvard University, 2012.

Rios, Viridiana. "Why Did Mexico Become So Violent? A Self-Reinforcing Violent Equilibrium Caused by Competition and Enforcement." *Trends in Organized Crime* 16, no. 2 (2013): 138–155.

Rios, Viridiana, and David Shirk. "Drug Violence in Mexico: Data and Analysis through 2010." Transborder Institute, University of San Diego, 2011.

Rodgers Denis, and Gareth Jones. *Youth Violence in Latin America: Gangs and Juvenile Justice in Perspective.* New York: Palgrave Macmillan, 2009.

Rodríguez, Armando. "La Iniciativa Mérida y la guerra contra las drogas: Pasado y presente" (The Merida Initiative and the War on Drugs). In *Crimen organizado e Iniciativa Mérida en las relaciones México–Estados Unidos,* edited by Raúl Benítez Manaut, 31–68. Mexico City: Colectivo de Análisis de la Seguridad con Democracia, 2010.

Rodríguez, Sandra. "Truncaron sus estudios de secundaria—y se volvieron el 'terror' de 3 colonias" (They Did Not Finish High School—and Became the Source of "Terror" in Three Neighborhoods). *Diario*, December 26, 2011. Article no longer available online.

Rodríguez, Victoria, and Peter Ward. "Policymaking, Politics, and Urban Governance in Chihuahua: The Experience of Recent Panista Governments." US-Mexican Policy Report no. 3, Lyndon B. Johnson School of Public Affairs, University of Texas at Austin, 1992.

Rodríguez, Victoria, and Peter Ward. "Political Change in Baja California: Democracy in the Making?" Vol. 40, Monograph Series. San Diego, CA: Center for US-Mexican Studies, University of California San Diego: 1994.

Rodríguez Orejuela, Gilberto, and Miguel Rodríguez Orejuela. *Las confesiones secretas de Miguel y Gilberto Rodriguez Orejuela: Documentos desclasificados* (The Confessions of Miguel and Gilberto Rodriguez). Bogotá: Quintero, 2005.

Roldán, Mary. "Wounded Medellín: Narcotics Traffic against a Background of Industrial Decline." In *Wounded Cities: Destruction and Reconstruction in a Globalized World,* edited by Jane Schneider and Ida Susser, 129–148. Oxford: Berg, 2003.

Romero, Mauricio. *Paramilitares y autodefensas 1982–2003.* Bogotá: Instituto de Estudios Políticos y Relaciones Internacionales Universidad Nacional de Colombia, 2003.

Romero, Mauricio, ed. *Parapolitica: La ruta de la expansión paramilitar y los acuerdos políti- cos* (Parapolitica: The Paramilitary Expansion Route and Political Agreeements). Bogotá: Corporación Nuevo Arco Iris, 2007.

Rosi, Gianfranco. *El Sicario, Room 164.* Film Forum, 2011. Documentary.

Ross, Michael. "What Do We Know about Natural Resources and Civil War?" *Journal of Peace Research* 41, no. 3 (2004): 337–356.

Sáenz Rovner, Eduardo. *La conexión cubana: Narcotráfico, contrabando, y juego en Cuba entre los años 20 y comienzos de la revolución* (The Cuban Connection: Drug Trafficking, Smuggling, and Gambling in Cuba between the Twenties and the Beginning of the Revolution). Bogotá: Centro de Estudios Sociales, Universidad Nacional de Colombia, 2005.

Sáenz Rovner, Eduardo. "Las redes de cubanos, norteamericanos, y colombianos en el narco- tráfico en Miami durante los años sesenta" (The Networks of Cubans, Northamericans, and Colombians in Drug Trafficking in Miami during the Seventies). *Innovar* 18, no. 32 (2008): 111–126.

Safford, Frank. "Foreign and National Enterprise in Nineteenth-Century Colombia." *Business History Review* 39, no. 4(1965): 503–526.

Salazar, Alonso. *No nacimos pa'semilla: La cultura de las bandas juveniles en Medellín* (Born to Die: The Culture of Youth Gangs in Medellín). Bogotá: CINEP, 1990.

Salazar, Alonso. *La parábola de Pablo: Auge y caída de un gran capo del narcotráfico* (Pablo's Parable: Rise and Fall of a Drug Lord). Bogotá: Editorial Planeta, 2001.

Salazar, Alonso, and Ana María Jaramillo. *Medellín: Las subculturas del narcotráfico.* (Medellín: The Drug Trafficking Subcultures). Bogotá: CINEP, 1992.

Samper, José. "Urban Resilience in Situations of Chronic Violence: Case Study of Medellín, Colombia." Document Prepared for MIT's Center for International Studies for the Urban Resilience in Chronic Violence Project. Cambridge, MA: Massachusetts Institute of Technology, 2012. https://www.researchgate.net/profile/Jota_Jota_Samper/publication/ 279821839_Urban_Resilience_in_Situations_of_Chronic_Violence_Case_Study_of_ Medellin_Colombia/links/58ab38fda6fdcc0e079bb770/Urban-Resilience-in-Situations- of-Chronic-Violence-Case-Study-of-Medellin-Colombia.pdf.

Sartori, Giovanni. "Concept Misformation in Comparative Politics." *American Political Science Review* 64, no. 4 (1970): 1033–1053.

Schatz, Sara, Hugo Concha, and Ana Laura Magaloni. "The Mexican Judicial System: Continuity and Change in a Period of Democratic Consolidation." In *Reforming the Administration of Justice in Mexico*, edited by David Shirk and Wayne Cornelius, 197–224. South Bend, IN: University of Notre Dame Press, 2007.

Schelling, Thomas C. *The Strategy of Conflict.* Cambridge, MA: Harvard University Press, 1980.

Seguridad, Justicia, y Paz, Consejo Ciudadano para la Seguridad Pública y Justicia Penal. "La impunidad en México" (Impunity in Mexico). Mexico City: Seguridad, Justicia y Paz: January 10, 2013. http://www.seguridadjusticiaypaz.org.mx/biblioteca/analisis-estadistico/send/ 5-analisis-estadistico/161-la-impunidad-en-mexico-2013.

Seguridad, Justicia, y Paz: Consejo Ciudadano para la Seguridad Pública y Justicia Penal. "Metodología del ranking 2012 de las ciudades más violentas del mundo" (Methodology of the Ranking of the World's Most Violent Cities). Mexico City: Seguridad, Justicia y Paz, February 6, 2013. http://www.seguridadjusticiaypaz.org.mx/biblioteca/download/6- prensa/163-san-pedro-sula-otra-vez-primer-lugar-mundial-acapulco-el-segundo.

Serrano, Alfredo. *La multinacional del crimen: La tenebrosa Oficina de Envigado* (The Multinational of Crime: The Sinister Envigado Office). Debate, 2010

Serrano, Mónica. "Narcotráfico y gobernabilidad en México." *Pensamiento Iberoamericano* 1 (2007): 251–278.

Shapiro, Jacob. *The Terrorist's Dilemma: Managing Violent Covert Organizations.* Princeton, NJ: Princeton University Press, 2013.

Shirk, David. "Drug Violence in Mexico: Data and Analysis from 2001–2009." Transborder Institute, University of San Diego, 2010.

Shirk, David. "The Drug War in Mexico: Confronting a Threat." Council Special Report no. 60, New York: Council on Foreign Relations, 2011.

Shirk, David, and Joel Wallman. "Understanding Mexico's Drug Violence." *Journal of Conflict Resolution* 59, no. 8 (2015): 1348–1376.

El Siglo de Torreón. "Operan en Ciudad Juárez 250 bandas dedicadas al secuestro" (In Ciudad Juárez There Are 250 Gangs Kidnapping People). *Excelsior*, November 16, 2010. https://www.elsiglodetorreon.com.mx/noticia/575862.operan-en-juarez-250-bandas-dedicadas-a-secue.html.

Skaperdas, Stergios. "The Political Economy of Organized Crime: Providing Protection When the State Does Not." *Economics of Governance* 2 (2001): 173–202.

Skaperdas, Stergios, and Kai Konrad. "The Market for Protection and the Origin of the State." *Economic Theory* 50, no. 2 (2010): 417–443.

Skocpol, Theda. "Bringing the State Back In: Strategies of Analysis in Current Research." In *Bringing the State Back In*, edited by Peter Evans, Theda Skocpol, and Dietrich Rueschemeyer, 3–38. Cambridge: Cambridge University Press, 1985.

Slone, Michelle. "Responses to Media Coverage of Terrorism." *Journal of Conflict Resolution* 44, no. 4 (2001): 508–522.

Smith, Peter. "Drug Trafficking in Mexico." In *Coming Together: Mexico-US Relations*, edited by Barry Bosworth, Susan Collins, and Nora Lustig, 125–147. Washington, DC: Brookings Institution, 1997.

Snyder, Jack. *From Voting to Violence: Democratization and Nationalist Conflict*. New York: Norton, 2000.

Snyder, Richard. "Scaling Down: The Subnational Comparative Method." *Studies in Comparative International Development* 36, no. 1 (2001): 93–110.

Snyder, Richard, and Angélica Durán-Martínez. "Does Illegality Breed Violence?: Drug Trafficking and State-Sponsored Protection Rackets." *Crime, Law, and Social Change* 52, no. 3 (2009): 253–273.

Snyder, Richard, and Angélica Durán-Martínez. "Drugs, Violence, and State-Sponsored Protection Rackets in Mexico and Colombia." *Colombia Internacional* 70 (July–December 2009): 61–91.

Soares, Rodrigo, and Joana Naritomi. "Understanding High Crime Rates in Latin America: The Role of Social and Policy Factors." In *The Economics of Crime: Lessons for and from Latin America*, edited by Rafael Di Tella, Sebastian Edwards, and Ernesto Schargrodsky. Chicago: University of Chicago Press, 2010. http://www.nber.org/chapters/c11831.pdf.

Staniland, Paul. "Cities on Fire: Social Mobilization, State Policy, and Urban Insurgency." *Comparative Political Studies* 43, no. 12 (2010): 1623–1649.

Staniland, Paul. *Networks of Rebellion: Explaining Insurgent Cohesion and Collapse*. Ithaca, NY: Cornell University Press, 2014.

Staniland, Paul. "Militias, Ideology, and the State." *Journal of Conflict Resolution* 59, no. 5 (2015): 770–793.

Staniland, Paul. "States, Insurgents, and Wartime Political Orders." *Perspectives on Politics* 10, no.2 (2012): 243–264.

Stannow, Lovisa. "Social Cleansing in Colombia." MA thesis, Simon Fraser University, 1996.

Steele, Abbey. "Electing Displacement: Political Cleansing in Apartado, Colombia." *Journal of Conflict Resolution*, 55, no. 3 (2011): 423–445.

Steller, Tim. "Years of Killing Hard to Add Up in Mexico." *Arizona Daily Star*, November 27, 2012. http://tucson.com/news/local/years-of-killing-hard-to-add-up-in-mexico/article_482c219b-0587-5629-9e50-22fb244dacd8.html.

Stone, Hannah. "Under Calderón 80% of Organized Crime Detainees Went Free." *Insight Crime*, November 4, 2012. http://www.insightcrime.org/news-briefs/calderon-80-organized-crime-detainees-free.

Sullivan, John, and Samuel Logan. "La Línea: Network, Gang, and Mercenary Army." *Free Republic*, August 4, 2011. http://www.freerepublic.com/focus/f-news/2762765/posts.

Swanger, Joanna. "Feminist Community Building in Ciudad Juárez: A Local Cultural Alternative to the Estructural Violence of Globalization." *Latin American Perspectives* 34, no. 2 (2007), *Globalizing Resistance: The New Politics of Social Movements in Latin America*: 108–123.

Tanner, Murray Scot. "Will the State Bring You Back In? Policing and Democratization." *Comparative Politics* 33, no. 1 (2000): 101–124.

Tarrow, Sidney. *Power in Movement: Social Movements, Collective Action, and Politics*. Cambridge, UK: Cambridge University Press, 1994.

Tate, Winifred. *Drugs, Thugs, and Diplomats: US Policymaking in Colombia*. Stanford, CA: Stanford University Press, 2015.

Thelen, Katherine, and Wolfgang Streeck. *Beyond Continuity: Institutional Change in Advanced Political Economies*. Oxford: Oxford University Press, 2006.

Thomas, Kedron, Kevin O'Neill, and Thomas Offit. "Securing the City: An Introduction." In *Securing the City: Neoliberalism, Space, and Insecurity in Postwar Guatemala*, edited by Kevin O'Neill and Kedron Thomas, 1–21. Durham, NC: Duke University Press, 2011.

Thoumi, Francisco. "Illegal Drugs in Colombia: From Illegal Economic Boom to Social Crisis." *Annals of the American Academy of Political and Social Science* 582, no. 1 (2002): 102–116.

Thoumi, Francisco. *Political Economy and Illegal Drugs in Colombia*. Boulder, CO: Lynne Rienner, 1995.

Tickner, Arlene. "Colombia and the United States: From Counternarcotics to Counterterrorism." *Current History* 102, no. 661 (February 2003): 77–85.

Tickner, Arlene, Diego García, and Catalina Arreaza. "Actores violentos no estatales y narcotráfico en Colombia" (Nonstate Violent Actors and Drug Trafficking in Colombia). In *Politica antidrogas en Colombia: Exitos, fracasos, y extravios*, edited by Daniel Mejía and Alejandro Gaviria, 413–445. Bogotá: Ediciones Uniandes, 2011.

Tilly, Charles. *Regimes and Repertoires*. Chicago: University of Chicago Press, 2010.

Tilly, Charles. "War Making and State Making as Organized Crime." In *Bringing the State Back In*, edited by Peter Evans, Theda Sckocpol, and Dietrich Rueschemeyer, 169–186. Cambridge, UK: Cambridge University Press, 1985.

El Tiempo. "Ante violencia urbana, Cali promueve el desarme" (Facing Urban Violence, Cali Promotes Disarmament). *Tiempo*, August 31, 2010. http://www.eltiempo.com/archivo/documento/MAM-4120796.

El Tiempo. "Asesinada Lorena Henao Montoya, viuda del narco Iván Urdinola Grajales" (Lorena Henao Montoya, Narco Iván Urdinola Grajales' Widow Murdered). *Tiempo*, December 27, 2012. http://www.eltiempo.com/archivo/documento/CMS-12479635 http://www.elespectador.com/noticias/judicial/quien-era-lorena-henao-montoya-viuda-de-mafia-articulo-394298.

El Tiempo. "Bajo la presión de EU asume comandante de policía de Cali" (Under U.S Pressure Cali's Police Commander Swears In). *Tiempo*, March 9, 1995. http://www.eltiempo.com/archivo/documento/MAM-272840.

El Tiempo. "Detenido el Senador Gustavo Espinosa" (Senator Gustavo Espinosa Was Captured)." *Tiempo*, February 15, 1996. http://www.eltiempo.com/archivo/documento/MAM-360107.

El Tiempo. "En libertad siete agentes del DSC" (Seven Agents of DSC Are Free). *Tiempo*, September 22, 1991. http://www.eltiempo.com/archivo/documento/MAM-158733.

El Tiempo. "Extraditables: Fin del Terror" (The Extraditable Ones: The End of Terror). *Tiempo*, July 4, 1991. http://www.eltiempo.com/archivo/documento/MAM-114707.

El Tiempo. "Senador Juan Carlos Martínez se enreda por presuntos vínculos con narcotraficantes" (Senator Juan Carlos Martinez in Trouble Due to His Presumed Links to Narcotraffickers). *Tiempo*, November 2, 2008. http://www.eltiempo.com/archivo/documento/CMS-4380024.

El Tiempo. "Son 903 los desplazados por bandas en el litoral del San Juan, Chocó" (There Are 903 People Displaced by Gangs in San Juan). *Tiempo*, January 17, 2013. http://www.eltiempo.com/archivo/documento/CMS-12525771.

Tokatlián, Juan Gabriel. "The War on Drugs and the Role of SOUTHCOM." In *Drug Trafficking, Organized Crime, and Violence in the Americas Today*, edited by Bruce Bagley and Jonathan Rosen. Gainesville: University Press of Florida, 2015.

Transform Drug Policy Foundation. *The Alternative World Drug Report: Counting the Costs of the War on Drugs*, 2012. www.countthecosts.org.

Trejo, Guillermo, and Sandra Ley. "Federalismo, drogas, y violencia" (Drugs, Federalism, and Violence). *Política y Gobierno* 23, no. 1 (2016): 11–56.

Trejo, Guillermo, and Sandra Ley. "High-Profile Criminal Violence in Mexico: Why Drug Cartels Murder Subnational Authorities and Party Candidates in Mexico." Paper presented at the Workshop on Subnational Violence, Centro de Investigación y Docencia Económica Mexico City, September 2016.

Tuckman, Joe. "Life after El Chapo: A Year on from Drug Kingpin's Capture, Business Is Booming." *Guardian*, February 20, 2015. http://www.theguardian.com/world/2015/feb/20/mexico-drugs-trade-el-chapo-arrest-joaquin-guzman-sinaloa-cartel.

UN Committee on the Elimination of Discrimination against Women CEDAW. Report on Mexico produced by the committee on the elimination of discrimination against women under article 8 of the optional protocol to the convention, and reply from the Government of Mexico, Thirty Second Session 10–28 January 2005. New York: CEDAW, 2005.

UN Office for Drug Control and Crime Prevention (UNODCCP). 1999. Global Illicit Drug Trends 1999. New York: UNODCCP, 1999.

UN Office on Drugs and Crime (UNODC). *Colombia Coca Cultivation Survey 2011*. Bogotá: UNODC, 2012.

UN Office on Drugs and Crime (UNODC). *World Drug Report 2008*. Vienna: UNODC, 2008.

UN Office on Drugs and Crime (UNODC). *World Drug Report 2011*. Vienna: UNODC, 2012.

UN Office on Drugs and Crime (UNODC). *World Drug Report 2012*. Vienna: UNODC, 2012.

UN Office on Drugs and Crime (UNODC). *World Drug Report 2016*. Vienna: UNODC, 2016.

El Universal. "Balean a activista en Ciudad Juárez" (Activist Shot in Ciudad Juárez). *Universal*, December 2, 2011. http://archivo.eluniversal.com.mx/notas/813478.html.

El Universal. "Desertan 1,382 militares de elite" (Desertion of 1,382 Elite Soldiers). *Universal*, March 28, 2004. http://archivo.eluniversal.com.mx/nacion/109186.html.

Universidad del Valle, Instituto de Altos Estudios Juridicos Politicos y Relaciones Internacionales. *Construir la paz: Elementos de diagnóstico para el diseño de un modelo estratégico hacia el desarrollo, la seguridad y la Paz en Cali* (Building Peace: Elements to Build a Development Model for Cali). Cali: Universidad Del Valle, 1998.

Uprimny, Rodrigo, and María Paula Saffon. "La ley de 'justicia y paz': ¿Una garantía de justicia y paz y de no repetición de las atrocidades?" (The Law of Peace and Justice: A Warranty for Justice, Peace, and No Repetition of Atrocities?). In *Justicia transicional sin transición: Verdad, justicia y reparación para Colombia*, edited by Rodrigo Uprimny, Catalina Botero, Esteban Restrepo and Maria Paula Saffon, 173–197. Bogotá: Dejusticia, Anthropos, 2006.

Uribe, María Victoria. "Dismembering and Expelling: Semantics of Political Terror in Colombia." *Public Culture* 16, no. 1 (2004): 79–95.

Uribe, María Victoria. *Matar, rematar, y contramatar: Las masacres de la violencia en El Tolima, 1948–1964*. Serie Controversia 159–160. Bogotá: CINEP, 1990.

Uribe, María Victoria, and Teófilo Medina. *Enterrar y callar: Las masacres en Colombia 1980–1993*. Bogotá: CINEP, 1995.

US District Court for the Western District of Texas El Paso Division. Indictment of Joaquín Guzmán Loera et al., Criminal No. EP-12-CR, April 11, 2012.

Vanguardia. "En Juárez ejército se dedicó a ver pugna entre carteles: Consulado EU" (In Juárez Army Just Witnessed the Turf Fight among Cartels). *Vanguardia*, March 16, 2010. http://www.vanguardia.com.mx/enjuarezelejercitosededicoaverpugnaentrecartelesconsuladoeu-675388.html.

Vanguardia. "Violencia en Juárez por falta de coordinación: Comisión Nacional de Derechos Humanos" (Violence in Juárez Results from Lack of Coordination: National Commission for Human Rights). *Vanguardia*, February 21, 2011. http://www.vanguardia.com.mx/violenciaenjuarezporfaltadecoordinacion-468655.html.

Valencia, León. "Los caminos de la alianza entre paramilitares y politicos" (The Paths of the Alliance between Paramilitaries and Politicians). In *La parapolítica: La ruta de la expansión paramilitar y los acuerdos politicos*, edited by Mauricio Romero, 11–58. Bogotá: Corporación Nuevo Arco Iris, 2007.

Valenzuela, José Manuel. *El futuro ya fue: Socioantropología de los jóvenes en la modernidad* (The Future Is Gone: Social Anthropology of Youth in the Modernity). Mexico City: El Colegio de la Frontera Norte, Juan Pablo Editores, 2009.

Valenzuela, José Manuel. *Impecable y diamantina: P.S. Democracia adulterada y proyecto nacional* (Spotless and Shiny: P.S. False Democracy and National Project). Mexico City: El Colegio de la Frontera Norte, Juan Pablos Editores, 2009.

Vanegas, Gildardo. *Cali tras el rostro oculto de las violencias: Estudios etnográficos sobre la cotidianidad, los conflictos y las violencias en las barriadas populares* (Cali under the Hidden Faces of Violence). Cali: Instituto Cisalva, 1998.

Vargas, Mauricio, Jorge Lesmes, and Edgar Tellez. *El presidente que se iba a caer: Diario secreto de tres periodistas sobre el 8000* (The President Who Was Going to Fall). Bogotá: Planeta, 1996.

Vélez, Juan Carlos. "Conflicto y guerra: La lucha por el orden en Medellín" (Conflict and War: The Struggle for Order in Medellín). *Revista de Estudios Politicos* 18 (2001): 61–89 http://aprendeenlinea.udea.edu.co/revistas/index.php/estudiospoliticos/article/view/17428/15033.

Venkatesh, Suddhir, and Brenda Coughlin. "The Urban Street Gang after 1970." *Annual Review of Sociology* 29 (2003): 41–64.

Venkatesh, Sudhir Alladi. "The Social Organization of Street Gang Activity in an Urban Ghetto." *American Journal of Sociology* 103, no. 1 (1997): 82–111.

Verdad Abierta. "Cinco años de parapolítica" (Five Years of Parapolitica). *Verdad Abierta*, June 12, 2012. http://www.verdadabierta.com/politica-ilegal/el-estado-y-los-paras/4050-especial-cinco-anos-de-parapolitica-ique-tan-lejos-esta-el-fin.

Vicepresidencia de la República de Colombia, Observatorio del Programa de Derechos Humanos y Derecho Internacional Humanitario. *Dinámica reciente de la violencia en Cali* (Recent Trends of Violence in Cali). Bogotá: Vicepresidencia de la República, Teck Color Editores, 2006.

Vicepresidencia de la República de Colombia. *Caracterización del homicidio en Colombia 1995–2006* (Characterization of Homicide in Colombia). Bogotá: Observatorio del Programa Presidencial de Derechos Humanos y DIH, Vicepresidencia de la República de Colombia, Editorial Scripto, 2009.

Villagran, Lauren. "The Victims' Movement in Mexico." In *Building Resilient Communities in Mexico*, edited by David Shirk, Duncan Wood, and Eric Olson. San Diego: Woodrow Wilson International Center for Scholars, University of San Diego Justice in Mexico Project, 2013.

Vivanco, José Miguel. "Discurso de José Miguel Vivanco ante el Consejo Permanente de la OEA" (Jose Miguel Vivanco's Speech before the OAS Permanent Council)." Washington, DC, February 6, 2004.

Walton, John. *Elites and Economic Development: Comparative Studies on the Political Economy of Latin American Cities*. Austin: Institute of Latin American Studies, University of Texas at Austin, 1977.

Washington Valdez, Diana. *The Killing Fields: Harvest of Women: The Truth about Mexico's Bloody Border Legacy*. Burbank, CA: Peace at the Border, 2006.

Weinstein, Jeremy. *Inside Rebellion: The Politics of Insurgent Violence*. New York: Cambridge University Press, 2006.

Weinstein, Lisa. "Mumbai's Development Mafias: Organized Crime, Land Development, and Globalization." *International Journal of Urban and Regional Research* 32, no. 1 (2008): 22–39.

Weisel, Deborah. "The Evolution of Street Gangs: An Examination of Form and Variation." In *Responding to Gangs: Evaluation and Research*, edited by Winifred Reed and Scott Decker, 25–66. Washington, DC: National Institute of Justice, 2002.

White House Office of the National Drug Control Policy. "Survey Shows Significant Drop in Cocaine Production in Colombia." Press Release July 30 2012.

Williams, Phil. "Cooperation among Criminal Organizations." In *Transnational Organized Crime and International Security: Business As Usual?* Edited by Mats Berdal and Mónica Serrano, 67–80. Boulder, CO: Lynne Rienner, 2002.

Williams, Phil. "The Terrorism Debate over Mexican Drug-Trafficking Violence." *Terrorism and Political Violence* 24, no. 2 (2012): 259–278.

Wilkinson, Steven. *Votes and Violence: Electoral Competition and Ethnic Riots in India.* New York: Cambridge University Press, 2006.

Windle, James. "Drugs and Drug Policy in Thailand." Foreign policy brief, Brookings Institution, Washington, DC, 2015. https://www.brookings.edu/wp-content/uploads/2016/07/WindleThailand-final.pdf.

Windle, James. "A Slow March from Social Evil to Harm Reduction: Drugs and Drug Policy in Vietnam." Foreign policy brief, Brookings Institution, Washington, DC, 2015. https://www.brookings.edu/wp-content/uploads/2016/07/WindleVietnam-final.pdf

WOLA: Advocacy for Human Rights in the Americas. "UN and US Estimates for Cocaine Contradict Each Other." July 31, 2012. http://www.wola.org/commentary/un_and_us_estimates_for_cocaine_production_contradict_each_other.

Wood, Elisabeth. "Variation in Sexual Violence during War." *Politics and Society* 34, no. 3 (2006): 307–342.

Yongming, Zhou. *Anti-Drug Crusades in Twentieth-Century China.* Lanham, MD: Rowman & Littlefield, 1999.

Youngers, Coletta, and Eileen Rosen, eds. *Drugs and Democracy in Latin America: The Impact of US Policy.* Boulder, CO: Lynne Rienner, 2005.

Zavaleta Betancourt, José Alfredo, ed. *La seguridad pública local: Inseguridad, delincuencia, y participación ciudadana en Ciudad Juárez.* Ciudad Juárez: Universidad Autónoma de Ciudad Juárez, Consejo Nacional de Ciencia y Tecnología, Presidencia Municipal de Juárez, Fondo Mixto de Fomento a la Investigación Científica y Tecnológica, 2007.

Zavaleta Betancourt, José Alfredo, R. Chavira, and Carlos Sánchez. "El consenso de la inseguridad y las tasas delictivas" (The Consensus on Insecurity and Crime Rates). In *La Seguridad Pública Local: Inseguridad, delincuencia, y participación ciudadana en Ciudad Juárez,* edited by Jose Alfredo Zavaleta Betancourt, chapter 1. Ciudad Juárez: Universidad Autónoma de Ciudad Juárez, Consejo Nacional de Ciencia y Tecnología, Presidencia Municipal de Juárez, Fondo Mixto de Fomento a la Investigación Científica y Tecnológica, 2007.

Zepeda Bustos, Carmen. "Violencia y política electoral en Chihuahua." *El Cotidiano,* 164 (2010): 11–18.

Zeta. "Pandillas: Una amenaza en Tijuana" (Gangs: A Threat for Tijuana). *Zeta,* December 29, 2006–January 4, 2007. Article no longer available online.

INDEX

CPSIA information can be obtained
at www.ICGtesting.com
Printed in the USA
BVHW080222231119
564540BV00002B/11/P

9 780190 695965